WILLIAM ALWYN
THE ART OF FILM MUSIC

William Alwyn, August 1960; study by Wolfgang Suschitzky. Suschitzky and Alwyn were cameraman and composer on several documentaries, finishing on Paul Rotha's feature *No Resting Place* in 1951.

These Children Are Safe (1940) was Alwyn's first war-propaganda film. Produced by Strand towards the end of 1939, at a time when the Blitz was only a threat, the film seeks to reassure the public that children evacuated from the cities are happier, safer, and actually better off. They are depicted as enjoying the delights of the countryside, watched over by caring surrogate parents and conscientious teachers. Alwyn was again working with Alexander Shaw, and, like *The Future's in the Air*, the film is cleverly structured around its music track, utilising the jaunty folk song "Billy Boy" as a reference. It is first heard under the opening titles as a repeated phrase in a minor key, and later it returns in beautifully orchestrated passages for a small chamber orchestra and solo clarinet and solo piano. When the commentary ceases, the visuals and music are given their own space to accompany the children at play and in a lullaby rhythm as they settle for the night. Ultimately school-children pick up the song, joined again by piano and clarinet, all touchingly overlaid with the voices of boys and girls reading letters home against scenes of their daily round.

The conclusion is an exemplar of propagandist structure using voice track, silence, actuality, and studio music. Light-hearted music accompanies a eulogistic commentary encouraging everybody concerned with the evacuation (except the children; the film is not for them), until it arrives at its summation, when music ceases altogether and words alone give weight to the message: "Our towns have become too big, too crowded. For years sensible people have said it: it may be that in getting together to master this vast wartime problem we've taken a bigger step than we know towards happier living when we are again at peace." The emotional sting follows: actuality of children's games, followed by more singing (the traditional "My Old School") overlaid with teacher and pupils in the healthy outdoors and close-ups of healthy children. A short rising orchestral scale from Alwyn concludes. Without a single reservation about the social and psychological consequences of wrenching children from their homes, director, writer, and composer assume equal weight in their expression of the propaganda message.[5]

Alwyn's credit appeared on two more Strand shorts in 1940, released in the middle of the October Blitz on London. Both *Big City* and *The New Britain* were produced by Alexander Shaw, but their agendas were very different. Directed by Ralph Bond, the *Big City* is supposedly about London's transport systems but soon loses its way as it attempts to illustrate "workaday London". In Bond's London, prattling on about perfume factories and gramophone records,

---

[5] Compare the crude propaganda of Thorold Dickinson's treatment of the subject in *Westward Ho!* (1940). British evacuation scenes, sweetened by light-hearted Viennese waltzes, are darkly contrasted with dire warnings from the continent of what happens to non-evacuated children.

the war not only seems a long way off but also is not even alluded to. Alwyn's score sparks imaginatively where it can. In one scene, flute trills against plucked cellos and basses bring life to bubbling laboratory jars, while the music merges delightfully into a lively waltz theme on a cut to the perfume factory. Alwyn would remember those bubbling jars years later when he came to score a laboratory montage in the feature film *The October Man*. By and large, however, the score is suppressed behind the commentary, and its routine newsreel style evidently offered little challenge to the composer.

Big City's patronising commentary is by Reg Groves, a staff scriptwriter with Strand and at one time editor of Grierson's prestigious magazine *World Film News*. Groves also wrote the scenario for Ralph Keene's *The New Britain*, although the running commentary is attributed to Graham Greene.[6] The initial propagandist intention seems to have been to show off Britain's economic and social achievements between the wars. By the time the film was tracked the draft script[7] was significantly changed. Nearly every alteration hardens up the text to explicitly condemn the Germans as despoilers. Thus, to the line of the original, "There were infant welfare centres and day nurseries where the children were taught nothing but how to be happy", is added the phrase "not drilled in brown shirts for war". Later, film propaganda would be subtler. The additions are not only of interest to scholars of Greene and of propaganda: they are relevant to the structure of the soundtrack. At the end of sequences extolling British architecture, dams and bridges, electricity, and medicine, Greene has added the sentence, or one similar: "We forgot Germany." It is a compelling punctuation point that gives verbal rhythm to the scenario, and it is sustainable because, at just over ten minutes, the film is brief. Hand in hand with the commentary is a musical score that shapes the sequences and matches the unquenchable propagandist script with an inspirationally patriotic message.

The score is constructed around a vaulting ceremonial subject:

The titles open to a rapid military drum-beat, soon joined by a motif based upon the first four notes of the theme, which develops into a short canon, first on brass and followed by strings ascending to a resolute spirit, tutti. It quickens in rhythm and declines in pitch, increasing in menace as the visuals change to library shots of the 1914–1918 war, and battle effects supplant the music. Germany was beaten then, declares the commentary, but amongst the demobi-

---

[6] Frances Thorpe and Nicholas Pronay, *British Official Films in the Second World War: A Descriptive Catalogue* (Oxford and Santa Barbara: Clio Press, 1980), 64; David Parkinson (ed.), *Mornings in the Dark: The Graham Greene Film Reader* (Harmondsworth: Penguin, 1995), 504–7. Greene's name is not on the credits.

lised was a corporal named Hitler. This brief historical prelude establishes the threat that will dramatically underlie, and punctuate, the film's positive picture of British achievement, to which it now quickly turns: "Over our one million dead we raised this colossal monument . . .". At these words the music expands to the full theme, introduced first on horns, joined by strings, and then horns and strings answer each other in an intricate fugato, cascading and ascending, joining and separating, as the commentary outlines triumphs of architecture, construction, highways, and transport. At one stage the horns gallop across the countryside with a speeding express train. But the fugato continually holds back, augmenting emotional excitement and expectation until finally climaxing, tutti, with a piccolo trill as a seaplane rises into the air ("Above the seven seas we showed our wings across the world in peace"). Twice the commentary sounds the warning "We forgot Germany", to which Alwyn makes no gesture: by shunning the refrain musically it becomes a worrying, irritating, negative undercurrent to the impassioned music and pictures. The Germans are not merely a threat, but a nuisance for spoiling the British achievement.

But, as Alwyn has taught us, music loses its power unless it is balanced by silence. Similarly, to sustain at length the emotional heights would be to dull their power too. So now, apart from some minor cues, natural sound-effects predominate until Alwyn's major theme insinuates itself as the final minutes approach. Violins trill and cymbals crash as swimmers dive into a pool to conduct us into a sequence of the British at play, swimming, tennis, pub, library, and outdoors, ending on a shot of a sleeping child, mainly accompanied by strings. Almost unobtrusively, on the words "we will not let Germany ruin their future", the major musical subject enters and soars triumphantly again: thus commentator and composer have cleverly combined the emotional needs of contentment and a safe family life, with the determination to retain them. At the same time they neatly seal the film by returning to its opening thought, "the spirit of the men who broke the German army in 1918", and the director illustrates it with shots of marching forces and new recruits. At the end, scenic views match the commentary's boast of "the spirit bred behind the long coastline and among quiet fields, simple, unboastful and unbreakable", leaving the final impression to the score as it rises with dignity and resolution.

Watching this film it comes as little surprise that, along with several other documentary makers, Alwyn was placed on Hitler's "blacklist". He was proud of this in later years, but he remembered how, while "it meant little enough to me during those first months of waiting before the German offensive in the spring of 1940 . . . it took a more ominous aspect when our allies were swept aside by the Nazi blitzkrieg and Britain faced the imminent prospect of invasion".[8]

---

[7] Parkinson, *Mornings in the Dark*, pp. xxxvi, 507.

[8] Alwyn, *Winged Chariot*, 9–10.

The "musical advisor" to *Big City* and *The New Britain* was Muir Mathieson, who had recently taken up a contract with Strand Films. Without question, through their professional relationship Alwyn not only acquired a musical rapport but cemented a real friendship. James Muir Mathieson, born in 1911 in Stirling, was another of those stunningly brilliant musicians snapped up by the film industry. In his powers of organisation, assertiveness, and industriousness he was something of a prodigy. At only thirteen years of age he had set up the Stirling Boys Orchestra, appointing himself both conductor and pianist, and secured several broadcasts from the Glasgow studios of the then British Broadcasting Company. Later he studied at the Royal College of Music and followed that with a short spell conducting for the ballet in Toronto and Montreal. Still only twenty, he joined Korda's London Film Productions in 1932 as assistant to the music director Kurt Schroeder.

In 1933, on the completion of *The Private Life of Henry VIII*, Schroeder rather mysteriously disappeared, presumably following a disagreement with Korda. Mathieson thereupon assumed the role of music director, a power-base upon which he built a lifetime's career. Mathieson was scathing about Korda's musical sense. "He only knew it was 'God Save the Queen'", he remarked sarcastically, "because the crowd stood up, other than that he hadn't got a clue."[9] But Korda's fellow Hungarian Miklós Rózsa called the story "a malicious invention" and was certain that Korda knew about music.[10]

Whatever Korda's musical perception, his financial astuteness resulted in Mathieson's influence in the studios for the next 30 years. Director Guy Hamilton has explained:

> Until the late sixties all recording and subsequent dubbing was done on optical film. Consequently, any error necessitates junking reels and reels of exposed film, reloading and starting again. An expensive and time consuming process, particularly with a symphony orchestra on a three-hour session, sitting around. This is where Muir Mathieson stepped in. His experience in conducting film scores was second to none and he was much trusted by classical composers who relied on his profound knowledge of film and the recording process. To see Muir get two or three seconds behind on a long musical section and watch him drive the orchestra back into sync for the vital, climatic high points, was a sight to behold.[11]

By the late 1930s nearly all London Films' departmental chiefs came from

---

[9] Kulik, *Alexander Korda*, 313 n.
[10] Miklós Rózsa, *Double Life* (London: Midas Books; New York: Hippocrene Books, 1982), 89.
[11] John Williams, "Guy Hamilton: Spitfires in the Night", *Music from the Movies*, 8 (Spring 1995), 52–3.

America or the continent — the exceptions were Mathieson and the heads of the sound recording and costume departments. Mathieson's policy was three-pronged: to establish as perfect an orchestra as possible; to work closely with A. W. Watkins in the recording department; and to open up film music to the best composers. He employed more Britons than any other department, with Mischa Spolianski and Miklós Rózsa the exceptions. He persuaded Arthur Benjamin, under whom he had studied at the RCM, to compose for him; Sir Arthur Bliss wrote the score for *Things to Come* (1936); and Mathieson drew in and collaborated with John Greenwood, Geoffrey Toye, and Richard Addinsell.

After Korda lost control of Denham shortly before the outbreak of war, Mathieson worked for the other companies that continued to use the studios, and subsequently for Rank. His influence was felt not only in features but also in factual films. By 1940, he was contracted to Strand, and in the following year he joined Film Centre as producer and supervisor of Documentary and Propaganda Films. An inevitable step in 1942 was to become music director and adviser to the MoI, where he had full–time responsibility for Crown, the service film units, and some of the other units. He was the most powerful person in British film music. Mathieson maintained his policy of nominating the best composers for shorts throughout the war. Alwyn thought it a "brilliant idea of recruiting the experience of the great ones of music",[12] but it was no different from what Mathieson was doing for features at Denham. He introduced new and younger talent too — documentary was ideal for training and experiment.

Supported by the Mathieson alchemy, Alwyn never really looked back. Documentary scores flowed; his first feature film came in 1941 and his first BBC commission not long afterwards. By the beginning of the period, Alwyn's reputation for documentary and propaganda had already grown rapidly. An advertisement placed by Donald Taylor in the *Documentary News Letter* for February 1941 announces that "STRAND FILMS BRING DISTINGUISHED NAMES TO THE MAKING OF PROPAGANDA FILMS"; the distinguished musicians listed are three: Mathieson, Alwyn, and Richard Addinsell.[13]

[12] Alwyn, *Sight and Sound*, 177.
[13] *DNL* 2:2 (Feb. 1941), 40.

4

Intoxicating Documentary Days; First Feature

DOCUMENTARY films had small budgets and tiny orchestras, and they paid poorly, but — compared with the composer's solitary toil at piano and manuscript — the milieu was exciting. Alwyn's passionate belief that the art of film lies in its "co-ordination of a team, director, producer, designer, cameraman, musician and actor, all working together and interlocking"[1] had its seed in his intoxicating documentary days. This can be sensed in *SOS* (1941), produced and directed in the earlier part of 1940 by the young John Eldridge, who at the age of 23 had set up his own company after working as an assistant editor for Herbert Wilcox. Eldridge's well-balanced, well-edited documentary depicts the lifeboat service in Mousehole, Cornwall, but, perhaps because the pictures are less exciting than he had hoped, he depends on Alwyn's instrumental colours to paint the moods. Thus, tremolo strings, surging horns and trumpets, and ominous timpani create a sensation of gales and high waves as the film opens on a long shot of a ship riding for the shore. Subsequently, too, pictures and score are sustained for long passages without the "distraction" of a commentary. Far from palling, the continuous music track adds dramatic tension and camouflages a deficiency of sound-effects — rather in the manner of an accompanied silent narrative film. So, when fine weather finds the girls making camouflage nets and the fishermen about their business, *giocoso* woodwind have a little game to accompany the work,

---

[1] Alwyn, "Film Music: Sound or Silence", 5.

until the theme is thrown to a playful string section. Elsewhere, cymbal clashes mark a lifeboat launch, and choppy violins match flashlight signals and the puffing of a train. The film culminates in a sea rescue with a stirring timpani and brass and woodwind fanfare and fast strings mixed with wind and sea. After the completion of *SOS*, Eldridge joined Donald Taylor at Strand. Here his history of architecture, *Architects of England* (1941), called for a pastiche of musical styles reminiscent of, but less exuberant than, Taylor's earlier *Of All the Gay Places.* "Apologies to Mozart!" scribbled Alwyn on a section of his score.

Alwyn's belief in the co-ordination of the team could result in his placidly taking the bottom of a pecking-order of picture, commentary, and music. In the twelve-minute *It Comes from Coal* (1940), for example, the music is continuous but suppressed behind the spoken commentary. It is not what might be called "wallpaper" music, scored by the yard, because Alwyn's score continually enlightens the pictures. It is ceremonial when the commentary stresses coal's national importance, mechanically repetitive to illustrate the manufacture of by-products, pastoral over agricultural scenes, marches against the construction of warplanes, excited when they take off, and so on. But after a while it becomes irritating, at least to modern ears, and breaks one of Alwyn's first rules of film composition, that to make its impact music needs the contrast of silence. Nevertheless, even a film like *It Comes from Coal* could be a valuable vehicle for experiment: a musical climax against an ambulance halting abruptly, adding excitement where there is none, is quoted later in *Fires Were Started.*

The joy of these shorts, however, was that they were a mixed bag. In complete contrast to *It Comes from Coal*, which smothered the composition, was the musical freedom of *Queen Cotton* (1941). This eight-minute short directed by Cecil Musk claimed to be an account of the Lancashire cotton industry but was really an excuse to experiment with Technicolor. Photographed by Jimmy Rogers, with Jack Cardiff as the Technicolor advisor, the film is structured around three major musical entertainments with Alwyn himself conducting the LSO. After a brief introduction the commentary moves quickly to the first: "Now let the looms of Lancashire tell their own story as they weave their Symphony in Cotton for the people of the world". A fast, dazzling $\frac{2}{2}$ march follows, its phrases matching film editor Charles Beaumont's quick cuts of darting shuttles, jerking machinery, and extruded cloth with a rhythm in brass, the music as colourful and crisp as the pictures. A second sequence as "the machines capture the colours of the rainbow and fix them on to a roll of cotton" is accompanied by a swirling $\frac{12}{8}$ and $\frac{4}{4}$ contrapuntal composition, in the lower registers breathlessly capturing the speed and rhythm of the inky rollers as they impress their bright dyes on to the fabrics, while in the upper registers violins, violas, and cellos in more romantic mood offer imaginative vistas to match the saturated patterns. Suddenly, a short fanfare sweeps in the third sequence: a pleasant Viennese-style waltz to accompany a fashion parade. Then, in case cinemagoers got the idea this was too exotically remote from the war effort and their clothing ration, the film blurs class distinctions. In a curious sequence, the parade, its music, and the fashion audience depart, and are usurped by the sound-effects of marching feet and men whistling and singing the "Glory, glory, hallelujah" refrain from "John Brown's Body" (1861). Through a door the camera glimpses passing troops — a reminder that there is a war on. The sound of the march is sustained over a shot of mill girls entering the factory gates, followed by a smoking chimney with the lecture that "in peace or war Britain delivers the goods." The orchestra re-enters with a short recapitulation of the waltz, and the film concludes. The contrast of *Queen Cotton*'s previous cheeriness with the astringency of the unreal march plainly enacted in the film studio, contrasting again with the Dickensian shot of the mill girls, all photographed in bright saturated colours, clothes the last moments of this perhaps unique war-time short film with a veneer of Surrealism.

Reviewing the film some years later, Hubert Clifford, while especially praising Alwyn's rhythmic fast sequences, asked, "why must there always be a waltz for dress parade shots? The pre-talkie musical director always put out *The Skaters* [Emil Waldteufel, *Les Patineurs,* 1882] for such things. If one must have 3-4 waltz-time music, then surely the thing to do is have bigger and better Skaters rather than dim-hearted parodies."[2]

Listening today to Alwyn's rhythmic and memorably tuneful waltz the criticism seems unkind. *Queen Cotton*'s score fits the light-music category, a genre that has been defined as hovering between the popular and the symphonic, with melody all-important.[3] The definition should be refined by adding that, while listeners often need to work at more seriously-intentioned pieces to reveal their treasures, light music's appeal is immediate. Immediate appeal is also required of film music, and even in the 1940s some music tracks were popular, independent of their cinema origins. The trend accelerated into the 1950s. Richard Addinsell's "Warsaw Concerto" from *Dangerous Moonlight* (1941) is the classic early example, but Alwyn was also successful with his "March" from *Desert Victory*, and later the "Calypso" from *The Rake's Progress* (1945) and the "Theme" from *The Cure for Love* (1949). Light music's main strength resided in radio, whence it was eased in the late 1960s, when it was found to fit none of the new BBC programme genres, though it has recently returned.

Light music, however, was not only to be heard on the wireless, and not only in the major feature films with their catchy tunes and potential sheet music and record sales. It was also a component of short films like *Queen Cotton*. Clifford's criticism can be put into perspective. Alwyn did not need to aim at

[2] Hubert Clifford, "Music from the Films", *Tempo* 11 (June 1945), 13.
[3] Ernest Tomlinson, Foreword to Philip L Scowcroft, *British Light Music* (London: Thames Publishing, 1997), 5–17.

something "bigger and better than the Skaters". His waltz is enjoyable for its own merits as a light-hearted, balanced component of a short film.

Alwyn composed another light and appealing piece for Ralph Keene's *Green Girdle* (1941), which depicted in colour Londoners' leisure activities in the countryside and woods surrounding their city. Spoken commentary is min-imal, and a leisurely composition, in which a pleasing pastoral main theme predominates, accompanies the film throughout its eleven minutes, which the *Documentary News Letter* critic considered a "rare balance" between "visuals, music and commentary".[4] Richard Addinsell was credited as composer, but Al-wyn's autograph score dated 2 June 1941 is still extant and corresponds to the final track.[5] Since a few early sketches by Addinsell for *Green Belt* (the working title) are also extant, it would seem that Alwyn took over the score.[6]

Although we cannot be certain of the exact number of Alwyn's films, as not all his short films were credited, it would seem that in 1941 he composed at least twelve shorts and one feature, while in 1942 at least fifteen shorts and two features can be identified. Such a large output demanded quick inspira-tion, and often he found it in folk or nursery tunes. Thus for *Steel Goes to Sea* (1941), the sea shanty "Shenandoah" is the inspiration for the titles, and shanty rhythms are hinted at elsewhere. *Steel Goes to Sea* is an almost perfect short film, made largely by the same Merton Park crew that put together *Queen Cot-ton*, with Cecil Musk producing, John Lewis directing on this occasion, and Alwyn again conducting the LSO. Just as Alwyn sometimes drew inspiration from well-known songs, so he relied on the similitudes of some of his own rhythms and harmonies. Thus a busy construction sequence from *Steel Goes to Sea* is echoed in a firemen's exercise sequence in *Fires Were Started*, composed only months later, and there is a close propaganda resemblance between the closing marches of both films, as ships set sail in the national interest.

Familiar melodies can be picked out in other films, too. *Living with Stran-gers* (1941), a Realist Film directed by Frank Sainsbury, was concerned to reas-sure both evacuees and the country people they were billeted upon. The film is without a composer credit, possibly because it relies throughout upon Alwyn's gentle arrangement for flute and piano of Handel's Air and Variations in E ma-jor for harpsichord, "The Harmonious Blacksmith" (1720). The score, which is not continuous, makes its impact by its economy; it is entirely reasonable to suppose that the flautist is William Alwyn himself.

Traditional tunes associated with children are a rich source of inspiration, and as an expression of the national identity they served a propaganda purpose

---

[4] *DNL* 2:6 (June 1941), 108.
[5] Alwyn Archive.
[6] Philip Lane, the composer and arranger, holds copies of the Addinsell sketches. I am grateful for his confirmation of the attribution.

too. Alwyn had already employed "Billy Boy" for *These Children Are Safe*; now for *Playtime* he taps into variations of "Boys and Girls Come Out to Play" and "Oranges and Lemons", as well as original melodies of his own. This fresh and charming film, based on children's games, was filmed for his small Raylton Pictures company by S. Raymond Elton, who made his living as a lighting cameraman for Verity. Originality shines out from the start, a top shot of children dancing around straw laid out in the shape of the title, "Playtime". The film is short, just over nine minutes, and, although the music is continuous, because of its light-hearted gaiety it never palls. Amidst several characteristic touches are an appealing lullaby as two small girls play at nurses and a brief string ostinato passage where two boys fish, later recalled in the opening scenes of *Fires Were Started*. Of particular interest is a fanciful sequence, which has an affinity with a scene in Alwyn's later *I See a Dark Stranger* (1946), where an aspiring Eileen Joyce picking out the scale of C on the piano allows her daydream to take flight in an "Emperor Concerto".[7] The film's wartime sting comes in its tail, as against a low angle shot of a group of children the commentary gazes into a war-free future ("who can doubt . . . that it will be a better one than ours today?"), but Alwyn resists the temptation of a ponderous score and concludes gaily with the "Oranges and Lemons" theme as the children again dance around the straw, which now spells "The End".

In the meantime Sydney Box's Verity Films, soon to become the largest of the short-film independents and insistent on squeezing entertainment from even its instructional shorts, was finding work for filmmakers from every craft. Amongst Alwyn's first compositions for the company was a score for the first documentary by Box's wife Muriel Baker, *The English Inn* (1941). Another was for Henry Cass's first documentary, *HMS Minelayer* (1941). This film is notable for stressing the quiet, secretive night activities of the ship, but its eight minutes contain only a tense 25-second title theme. The score was also minimal for Harold Cooper's *Jane Brown Changes Her Job* (1941), an ingredient in the intensive propaganda campaign to entice women into industry. Jane Brown (Anne Firth) gives up an office job to train in a factory making Spitfires. Musically the film consists of a short introduction constructed around a four-note trumpet fanfare, some skilfully-matched dance music over mute footage of an RAF band, and an imposing conclusion as a Spitfire that Jane Brown "helped to build" takes to the air.

The labour shortage not only affected the factories. On the land the shortage in 1940 amounted to 100,000, and the government was desperate to lure labour from anywhere: the Women's Land Army, prisoners of war, soldiers on leave, children, businessmen at the weekend. Cinema was a powerful propaganda tool, and of the several films with farming themes scored by Alwyn, *Salute*

---

[7] Beethoven's Piano Concerto no. 5 in E-flat major, Op. 73 (1809).

to Farmers (1941) was the first, a paean to farm workers. Directed by Montgomery Tully, the film mixes farming sequences with short stilted dialogue scenes and ultimately teeters into the boring. Nevertheless, especially in the opening sequences, Alwyn seizes the opportunity to draw on his own melodic resources and to enhance them with a hint of the colour and harmony that find more copious expression in later productions. The film commences with a fanfare on trumpet and two horns, soon discovered to be the commencement of a short fugal sequence answered by strings and counterpointed by brass. Once the titles are finished, it merges into a tranquil pastoral "English" theme on plaintive strings and oboe, clarinet, and flute in turn. Before long the film introduces us to the "giant Giro-Tiller" a truly huge machine with rotating claws to break up difficult soils. It could have sprung from science fantasy, and Alwyn's sturdy rhythmic march with inspirational string and brass in the upper registers against a throbbing percussion ground was a more than adequate substitute for actuality sound-effects. For much of the film the score is hardly more than a light pastoral "background" against a variety of farmers' voice-overs. It ends full circle with a ceremonial arrangement of the opening theme as horses plough steadfastly, but picturesquely, towards the camera.

Least demanding of their audiences were the dramatised fiction propaganda shorts. Strand's *Night Watch* (1941), a "five-minute film" produced and directed by Donald Taylor, started life with the less reassuring and non-paternalistic working title of *Footsteps in the Night*. In less than eight minutes, the film narrates the tale of Bill (Cyril Chamberlain) — who is due to return to armed duty that night — and Sally (Anne Firth), looking for a "nice quiet spot" but repeatedly disturbed by air-raid wardens. Bill's frustration is eased when he learns about the debt owed to the ARP workers, and the film ends with his demanding to know whether a warden safely patrols Sally's street. The theme allows Alwyn scope for a slow foxtrot tempo (Alwyn calls it "Blues") played by a dance-band combination of instruments. These include a guitar and a prominent solo trumpet,

This is later almost imperceptibly replaced by sweetly sorrowful strings as parting time approaches. A trumpet call to action ends the film. This tiny film

was unknowingly several years in advance of its own time, when it was almost unthinkable to underscore for jazz or dance bands. That innovation had to wait for the 1950s, when it became at first fashionable and finally commonplace.

By now Alwyn was more than ready to tackle a feature film. *Penn of Pennsylvania* (1941) was produced by Lady Annie Yule's British National Films, whose director John Baxter was giving several filmmakers their first chance. It was a first also for both producer Richard Vernon and director Lance Comfort, an up-and-coming talent of the 1940s who somehow slipped into "B"-film direction during the 1950s. Alwyn probably owed his contract to Mathieson, who was music director. More commissions from Comfort would follow.

   Penn of Pennsylvania is propaganda in an historical setting and finds company with *The Prime Minister* (1941), *The Young Mr Pitt* (1942), and *The Great Mr Handel* (1942). But with Anatole de Grunwald's screenplay aimed specifically at an isolationist United States of America, Penn is also linked with two films with a contemporary setting, Michael Powell's *49th Parallel* (1941) and the Boultings' allegorical *Thunder Rock* (1942).

   Historical productions had not matured since Korda's pre-war biopics. The comic-strip feel about this tracing of Penn's career as the Quaker founding father of Pennsylvania derives not only from the shallow depiction of its hero (Clifford Evans) as a condescending paragon, but also from implausible scenes like that of his miraculous conversion of eight kitchen staff to Quakerism in two minutes. However, if the script leaves much to be desired, the same cannot be said for the score. Having served a four-year apprenticeship in short films, Alwyn now approached his first feature with a maturity revealed in a stylish opening. The title credits introduce the main theme, based on developments of a four-note motif, which moves quickly into a pleasantly lyrical arrangement. Then, after the credit lettering clears, the motif emblazons a depiction of Penn treading a cloudy heaven with a piercing trumpet fanfare against high long-bowed strings:

As the plot unfolds, this simple theme assumes diverse melodic and harmonic hues, from the romantic to the sombre, from the menacing to the ceremonial. In the simple clarity of the fanfare it represents both Penn and Penn's ideal — as leitmotif, the Wagnerian device, common in film composition, of a recurring melodic theme to represent characters, places, emotions, or ideas.

   The fanfare is immediately echoed in a minor key as the scene changes to "London, 1667". There follows murky, atmospheric, descending light strings and woodwind, with brass ***pp*** and *con sordini*, counterpointed by a solemn church bell. A complicated camera movement pans across a model of smoky city rooftops and, aided by a camouflaged edit, sinks into a shadowy studio street where a lamplighter is at work. "God save the —" cries the night watchman, and the music and effects skilfully anticipate a cut to a group of courtiers raising their glasses and concluding: "— king", as the main theme passes to a bright Baroque pastiche in the style of Scarlatti:

Retention of the harmonies masks an almost imperceptible change as the scene moves to an anteroom where, to playful mickey-mousing[8] and pizzicato strings, Charles II (Dennis Arundell) makes a merry failure of seducing his mistress. The king's entry to the public banqueting hall is signalled by a reprise of the ceremonial Baroque, to continue until the camera rejoins the grim alleyways outside where the night watchman is still crying "God save the king". A sudden cessation of the orchestra points the contrast with the sumptuous glitter of the court. In these opening four minutes the musical composition has achieved a great deal. It has swept us to the heart of the drama, set both scene and mood, articulated the character of a key player, and knitted two dissimilar locations whilst underlining the contrast.

The changes rung on the leitmotif are instructional. It is next encountered as underscore when Penn proposes to his future wife Guli (Gulielma Springett, played by Deborah Kerr). The "libretto" could have been lifted from an opera, or perhaps a Mills and Boon novel. Alwyn's motif swells from the wistful (as he suggests his love and regret at departing), to the high romantic (as he declares, "But I can come back . . . tell me do you think she'll wait for me?"), and back again to the wistful (as Guli affirms, "For ever"). The manuscript score is carefully marked with dialogue extracts to ensure the orchestral patterns closely match the spoken dialogue, an art allied to theatrical melodrama. Leitmotif stresses Penn's domination of the film in a variety of musical styles. At Penn's audience with the king, it is *nobilmente*; as Guli enflames Penn to found a new society in the New World, its style is quietly measured horns; as the ship sets sail, the leitmotif heaves ocean-like with high ostinato strings, brass, and harp arpeggios; on Guli's death, delirious clarinet and long bowed strings symbolise Penn's derangement as the camera rises up to the shadow of a cross — when the leitmotif trembles, Penn is wobbling too:

---

[8] To closely co-ordinate film music to the action on the screen. See Glossary.

To the modern ear the sugary religious spirituality of the high octave strings as Penn calms a sailor's fears of the smallpox,

implies sanctity, probably because of their strong resonance with the harmonies of the scene of Christ's offering of water in Rósza's much later *Ben-Hur* (1959). There are other reverberations. The "Bridal Chorus" from Wagner's *Tannhäuser* (1845) is recalled when the ship beaches at Pennsylvania, the leitmotif here achieving a powerful feeling of resolution as it mixes with welcoming cheers and repeatedly-descending strings representing bells. A montage of colonial development, hammering, tree-felling, sowing, ploughing, harvesting, and so on, woven around the Penn motif, is comparable with the sequences of military preparations in Alwyn's own *Desert Victory*.

There are several composer characteristics in this early feature. The ethereal, dreamy music for which Alwyn was soon to become renowned enters briefly after Guli's death. A classic example of the style also underscores a camera pan over a dark, shadowy lake to the sound of croaking frogs. Repeated chords on celesta and harp are soon joined by the flute as against slow tremolo strings as Penn lifts a pipe of peace with Red Indians.

Irish traditional music is of significance in Alwyn's film music. In *Penn of Pennsylvania*, an Irish jig rhythm enlivens a crowded market scene. *Vivace* in $\frac{6}{8}$ time with piccolo, it is in a variation of the motif, brazenly close to the court Baroque. The jig offers important information to the picturegoer, for in the previous sequence Penn announced his return to London, and not even a subtitle hints that instead he has somehow crossed the Irish Sea. In the manuscript score the Irish scene occurs earlier, and was probably moved in the final cut: an example of how examination of the film score may provide valuable clues to the film historian.

Alwyn's instinctive understanding of the value of silence is already apparent, too. As Penn prays for the safe delivery of his child, the midwife announces "It's a boy." Penn rushes to the bedroom to a musical climax followed by silence in which audience anticipation rises, as he tiptoes apprehensively to the bedside. The break also permits the introduction of a tender leitmotif theme as Penn lifts the baby. Not for long: a stone crashes through the window with the message "Death to the Quakers". The montage sequence that follows, depicting torture against hysterically descending strings, is a striking musical figure that Alwyn recalled later in *Great Day* (1945) and *I See a Dark Stranger*.

Silence also adds solemn emphasis to speech. One trick is to underscore speech, and then stop the music against the significant passage. In audience with King Charles, Penn requests a site to establish a settlement in America: the orchestra plays on until the King reaches an important propagandist message. Against musical silence, and raising his eyes to some point above and to the right of the camera, Charles prophetically, nonsensically, and anachronistically asserts, "Who knows? One day across the sea, which shall be our defence, this undeveloped colony of which you speak may become the champion of the truth, and the freedom of all men."

The reality was 1941, not 1667, and Alwyn's contribution to the British propaganda effort had four more years to run.

5
An Art of Persuasion

B Y the end of 1941 America had entered the war, and in 1942 Strand's *Bat-tle for Freedom* could use the term "United Nations" and depict a global theatre of war. This film's attempt to précis every war front overloads its fifteen minutes, which was perhaps the propagandist intention — by inducing mental indigestion and awe at the scale of the allies' deployment and organisation. The script by Dylan Thomas is over-literate and over-packed ("liberty against butchery, against the German locust and the mechanised plague of Japanese annihilation"). With a proliferation of shots struggling to follow the words, music is very much a third partner. Only occasionally does the commentary breathe for as long as two or three seconds to allow music or effects to shine through. While Alwyn attempts to reflect words and pictures, his most suc-cessful achievement is the introduction of a perky patriotic march as the film rises to its conclusion ("And in England now . . ."), which ends with a triumphal brass and cymbal fanfare.

Alwyn liked to associate with literary intellectuals like Thomas, especially after 1942 when new opportunities arose as a composer of incidental music for BBC feature programmes. Now classified as of "national importance", the BBC had invested heavily in new resources, and its listening figures exploded as the working class tuned in to what had been formerly a middle-class preserve.

Alwyn's initiation was a rush job for the first of a series called *Britain to America* (Plate 3), on which Mathieson, fingers in many pies, was music di-rector. The programme was a prestigious one, produced by D. G. Bridson of the Features and Drama Department in answer to an appeal by the National Broadcasting Company (NBC) for a series presenting a taste of British war-time life for American listeners. Since the programme was set up at only ten days' notice,[1] Alwyn had even less time than usual. Reliably, however, he met his deadline with a "Moorland Theme" for timpani, percussion, harp, and strings lasting one and a half minutes and "Music for Lovers" for percussion, harp, and strings lasting a minute. Mathieson conducted the LSO and the Alexandra Choir with Clive Wilson as soloist. The programme was transmit-ted in North America at the end of July, and repeated on the Home Service in August.

Between film directors and radio producers there was virtually no cross-

---

[1] *BBC Year Book* (1943), 47.

3 *Britain to America*, August 1942. Alwyn's first radio feature. Left to right: Alwyn, Muir Mathieson (who conducted the London Symphony Orchestra), Leslie Howard (narrator), John Glyn-Jones (producer), and Denis Noble (singer).

fertilisation. Laurence Gilliam, who as Head of Features had more power than most to change things, wrote of his sorrow at the few examples of

> intermingling of talents between documentary film and radio. In the main the two have followed parallel lines without meeting. This, I think, has been mainly due to the exigencies of the job, and, more recently, to the inhuman pressures of the war, rather than to any deep-rooted differences. I don't know how many documentary film people listen seriously to radio features. I do know that radio producers are, as a body, avid filmgoers. I remember, some years ago, with the aid of Basil Wright, trying to arrange a regular get-together of film and radio documentary people, but it soon fizzled out.[2]

Gilliam's viewpoint was focused on his staff radio producers. He forgot his writers — Dylan Thomas was one — and he forgot the "voices" who spoke the film commentaries and belonged to familiar wireless names. He forgot, too, the musicians: Richard Addinsell, Benjamin Britten, Hubert Clifford, Walter

---

[2] Laurence Gilliam, "Documentary Radio", *DNL* 6:55 (Jan.–Feb. 1947), 72.

Goehr, John Greenwood, Victor Hely-Hutchinson, Gordon Jacob, Leighton Lucas, Alan Rawsthorne, Guy Warrack, Charles Williams, and others, who contributed to both the airwaves and the film track. William Alwyn found his niche fairly early, and, since radio feature work appealed both to his cross-cultural talents and to his fascination with sound, he subsequently became associated with some of radio's most important broadcasters and broadcasts. Amongst producers, Louis MacNeice, Laurence Gilliam, Alan Burgess, Leonard Cottrell, and Denis Johnston worked with Alwyn. From 1945 until 1952 he composed the important *Christmas Features*, which accompanied the royal broadcasts on Christmas Day. Perhaps his most prestigious radio composition was *Long Live the Queen* (1953), "a radio pageant linked by the narration of Robert Donat and William Alwyn",[3] which joined Home Service and Light Programmes on the evening of Coronation Day to bring greetings from all over the world and culminated in an introduction by Winston Churchill to Elizabeth's first broadcast as Queen. It is worth remembering, when considering Alwyn's large output of film music, that he was sought after in other fields too.

In 1942, however, his sole contribution to radio was tiny compared with film work. Early that year he joined the technicians and artists at Denham who were giving their talents free in a co-operative gesture to the war effort organised by the three film trades unions.[4] The aim was a thirteen-and-a-half-minute short called *Our Film* (1942), scripted by the Austrian writer John Hanau, who contrasted the co-operation between workers in a Soviet factory with the divisions among their British counterparts. In the face of the Nazi threat, says Hanau's script, management and workers must pull together.

At the studio, raffles and fund-raising schemes had collected nearly £600, and enthusiasm for the project ran high. Alwyn became involved because he happened to be at Denham working on RKO's quota feature *Squadron Leader X* (1942) with Mathieson and the LSO, who donated £15.[5] Alwyn donated four cues, which though short are imaginative and meticulous. Visually the film opens with library shots of the Russian prairie, the wheat moving in slow motion with the wind and reminiscent of many a Sovfilm production. It is followed by a shot of a thresher, huge but dominated by the landscape. Against these two shots, Alwyn starts ponderously with horns, answered by trumpets. Soon ominous strings representing the wind join in, as a third shot alerts us to tragedy as trees stir restlessly against ominous clouds. The music all this while has had a Russian feel, largely from the development of themes based on the start of the Soviet anthem, the "Internationale".[6] As the score develops, the

[3] *Radio Times* (29 May 1953), 9.
[4] ACT, NATKE, and the ETU.
[5] Roy Fowler, "Their Film", *The Veteran*, 87 (Winter 1999), 16.
[6] The following year Nicholas Brodszky wove the melody into the title sequence of *The Demi-Paradise* (1943), but his score lacks Alwyn's verve and imaginative textures.

"Internationale" theme gains prominence, a plaintive clarinet starts to dominate, and the feeling of threat partially disappears (although the viewer is left uneasy) when the scene mixes to a peaceful Russian family at their meal. A sudden crash of glass and a whip-pan to the window reveals a grinning German soldier. He machine-guns the family. The shock is the greater because the noise cuts across the musical theme without warning from the composer. Two years later Alwyn remembered the technique in *The Way Ahead*.

There follows a quick mix to a British working-class household, also at its meal. Alwyn introduces a pleasant rural English theme, not readily identifiable, with a plaintive clarinet and oboe, darting flute and violin. Again a noise, again a pan to the window, but this time it is a family friend tapping the glass. The music now finishes, having set the mood and articulated the similarities and the contrasts between the two sequences, especially in national identification.

Alwyn's other cues are equally short but equally vital, until a final ponderous pomp-and-circumstance theme, starting low on double-bass and cellos and rising in pitch and emotional intensity as other instruments join in, signals a change of heart between British management and workers. The theme draws the film to a triumphant conclusion over an artist's impression of Denham and Pinewood studios.

The notion of linking the urgency for British industrial co-operation with the desperate situation in the USSR was clever propaganda. Nevertheless it was only with difficulty that the production committee secured the film's release.[7] One reason was *Our Film*'s length. By 1942 it was already felt that the weekly "five-minute films" were too short to get their messages across. Worse, some cinemas cut them out entirely owing to programming difficulties. The result was their replacement with a series of monthly titles of between ten to fifteen minutes. The first was *Lift your Head, Comrade* (1942) a documentary about the Pioneer Corps, written by Arthur Koestler, then a refugee, showing how anti-Fascist Germans and Austrians were fighting alongside the British. Its music track was by Alwyn, but in truth there was little to score: the film consists almost entirely of a piece to camera by a colonel and interviews with the soldiers, anticipating more recent television news techniques. Musically all that was called for were two short pieces for the opening titles and closing shots, and some music for a training episode, which was recorded at such a low volume as to be almost indiscernible.

Filmmakers of utilitarian information and instructional films in 1942 may have felt that if they restricted the music content their messages would be taken more seriously. Even Rotha's information films were restrained, although being Rotha he could not resist brief moments of musical release. *Rat Destruction*

---

[7] Sidney Cole, "Our Film", *Film and Television Technician* (July 1990), 26–7.

(1942) follows a rodent officer as he tracks down and destroys infestations. It gives Alwyn the opportunity for a brief moto-perpetuo scurrying on woodwind — piccolo, flute, oboe, and clarinet — over the opening and closing titles, and during a 20-second sequence as grain is unloaded from the ships and welcomed by the rats in the stores, preening themselves on top of the sacks.

etc

In their perky musical livery the rats seem more attractive than the plodding rodent officer in his trilby and raincoat. Similarly, the most entertaining sequence in Rotha's *Life Begins Again* (1942), an account of the rehabilitation of the injured, is a lively minute-and-a-half fugal passage in Baroque style that matches to perfection a montage of invalids exercising their legs and backs.

More substantial is Alwyn's contribution to Louise Birt's *WVS* (1942), a twenty-minute film about the work of the Women's Voluntary Service. With themes reminiscent of *These Children are Safe* and *Playtime* it enters serenely, gently adding enchantment to scenes of evacuated under-fives. To conclude, a lifeboat crashes into the waves to resounding side drum and cymbal, and "our story ends with the sea". Although Birt probably hoped that the subsequent sequence of a lifeboat rescue would be suspenseful, her pictures let her down. "Somewhere out there a trawler has been bombed and sunk", runs the commentary, but with the camera stuck on a bleak beachside road, the tension is kindled mainly by the composer. It is for Alwyn to uncover the aching anxiety of wives and sweethearts, to find pity through brass instruments counterpointed by steady ostinato strings, strings that rise triumphantly as the lifeboat returns home and the rescued fishermen are taken off by the waiting cars, vans, and ambulances. The film ends with a uniformed WVS member gazing out to sea, against an inspirational fanfare. The story of the work of the WVS is told, not so much by its pictures, and not at all by its sound-effects, but by the commentary and the musical score.

WVS was one of several female-orientated films. Although it was no part of the patriotic ethos to stress the importance of one gender over another, nevertheless the female recruitment drive after 1941 targeted the cinema's mainly female audiences. The screens flickered with scenes of women at work in factories (as in *Jane Brown Changes her Job*), in former jobs-for-the-men like the buses, and especially in the uniformed services.[8]

Of the latter genre was Alwyn's second feature film *They Flew Alone* (1942), a biopic of the popular flying heroine Amy Johnson (Anna Neagle), her often troubled relationship with her husband and fellow flyer Jim Mollison (Robert Newton), and her final days in the Air Transport Auxiliary (ATA). Since Johnson had been killed in service little more than a year before the film's release in March 1942, it had an immediacy that its producer and director Herbert Wilcox probably hoped would be reflected at the box office. Moreover, Johnson's story was a perfect vehicle for a subtext empowering women to abandon their traditional roles for the "glamour" of the auxiliary services. The propagandist message is encoded with subtlety, not least in the musical subtext.

The film (in the manner of news-stories) commences with the most recent event, news that Amy has gone missing in the air, followed by a suggestion of her last moments as she is shown desperately jumping from the plane.[9] Alwyn cleverly builds tension through menacing tremolo bass strings followed by descending scale figures in string, brass, and woodwind; cymbal clash and strident orchestral chord mark the cut to her parachute floating limply and tragically on the sea. Having seized the audience's attention, the filmmakers now validate the film's authenticity and assert the fullness of Amy's short life — as a role model for the female picturegoer. They achieve this with a montage of scenes from her life in reverse chronological order, picture mixes and music speeding up to whirling ostinato strings and brass chords until reaching back to Amy's school days.

Whatever its detractors may argue, well-done mickey-mousing is effective film-music technique. Alwyn deploys it for the ensuing school sequence to sweeten the underlying propagandist message. Since that message is established here, and only at the conclusion stated more transparently, the sequence is clearly of utmost importance. On the first day at her new school, Amy and

[8] Antonia Lant, *Blackout: Reinventing Women for Wartime British Cinema* (Princeton: Princeton University Press, 1991): 63–5.

[9] The true manner of her death is disputed.

her parents face a grim head teacher (Martita Hunt). "Above all," she pontifi-
cates, ". . . a woman's place is in the home. And always to be like the others . . ."
The new pupil is made to try on the school straw hat, which she obviously dislikes. Outside a piano strikes up the perky school marching song:

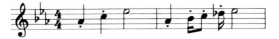

Through a window behind the head teacher can be seen a procession of straw-
hatted girls entering the cloakroom, the uniformity of the regular beat of the
march mirroring their conformity, the little rhythmic hiccup in bar two their
youthful comicality. The theme will soon be recognised as the motif for Amy's
pre-flying career. Amy is sent out of the room to join them, and the orchestra
in turn picks up the melody and rhythm. When Amy is seen making a political speech to her new friends, who cheer and hang their hated hats on their
pegs, the agenda is suggested in mime and especially by haranguing oboe and
ostinato and descending strings. The school song re-enters in its primary form,
and the scene changes to a general view of Amy's house, past which a chick-like
row of girls march, still in time to the music. Amy drops out, enters, and gazes
in the hall mirror as the school song slows thoughtfully; a clarinet holds a single note as Amy takes courage, then mimics with a quickly descending arpeggio her movement as she swings the hat over the floor. There is a brief pause as
Amy drops it, until it lands with a timpani thump. The camera holds the shot of
Amy's feet and the threatened hat as the orchestra trembles and pauses in time
with Amy's hesitations, until finally she summons up courage and jumps on the
crown to timpani accompaniment.

As Amy returns next day in a stylish but forbidden new hat, a nervous oboe
sounds a fanfare on the school motif (thus unifying the sequence). The orchestra, speeding up as she passes the headmistress, reflects her haste. So far Amy's
campaign has been told solely by movement and music; now dialogue re-enters
as the head seizes Amy and melancholic strings and harp take up the motif:
"How often have I told you, you must be like the others." She follows Amy's
eyes and sees the other girls throwing new hats on the pegs in time to triumphant fanfares, still based on the school motif. Nothing daunted, she pursues
the argument: "How can you hope to succeed in anything if you flout conven-
tion", belied by the succeeding Elgarian pomp and circumstance (continuing
the motif) as Amy receives her degree. The motif continues, with variations,
through successive stages of Amy's career. The sequence is amusing and light-
hearted, but a message is being conveyed to female audiences, and its delivery
is in the musical score.

Despite its questioning of the conventional female role, the film never undermines the family — an unthinkable concept. Amy's parents are always there
for her, solely for her it seems: her (evidently wealthy) father purchases her first

Tiger Moth. Her mother's role is to play, on the piano, a harmonically evocative nocturne:

It is heard first when Amy explains that her ambition lies in flying. As her mother listens she (rather improbably) plays the nocturne; and as the pictures mix to gulls swooping and rising in the sky, the orchestra takes up the theme over a sequence showing Amy in the freedom of the pilot's seat, all harp arpeggios, amidst the clouds. Flight is an almost perfect symbol for freedom, and the nocturne now becomes a motif in three particular ways. It is motif for Amy and for her pioneering successes: as such it is repeated, for example, at the climax to her solo flight arrival to Darwin, and on her arrival at Buckingham Palace to receive a CBE. It is also motif for Amy's close relationship with her parents, whether as piano nocturne or quiet orchestral background. Thus, it underscores her mother's prayer as Amy passes through bad weather on her flight to Australia, or when she talks over with her parents the problems of fame. Most importantly, however, it is a motif for woman's freedom. The screenplay (by Miles Malleson) takes pains to show that Amy is not a spoilt rich woman, but a role model for the average cinemagoer. As Amy's life becomes increasingly complicated by her husband, and by her own success and competitiveness, to sustain her freedom becomes increasingly difficult too, until war work offers release.

To authenticate its message, period authenticity is important in turn. Like the piano nocturne, much of the musical tension is sustained by diegetic music, especially by the use of well-known period dance tunes. Moreover they validate Johnson as the role model for the modern woman. In particular, the love motif between Johnson and Mollison is Robert Katscher's waltz "When Day is Done" (1927). The tune is introduced and imbued with a particular poignancy as Mollison's promised, but missed, dance when first he meets Amy. Naturally the song is also playing in the restaurant when Amy accepts Mollison's proposal of marriage, to be echoed by Alwyn (with wedding bells) for the mix to the marriage scene and sustained during the post-honeymoon sequence that immediately follows. The real irony of the libretto of "When Day is Done" comes with the couple's final break-up. With the melody playing diegetically on the radiogram, the couple discuss their way of life. Amy has "had enough" of the extravagant "social whirl" in which they find themselves. "You know, Amy," says Jim, "you've got a regular mind and you live in the future. I've got irregular habits and I live in the present. There's no contact." At this point the music forgets it is diegetic (as the viewer already has) and moves to increasingly gloomy themes to match the voice rhythms of the protagonists. The phone rings, and as Amy leaves the room she overhears Jim's greeting, "Oh, hello darling!" Cut to newspaper placard: "AMY DIVORCES JIM".

Another contemporary song, "All the King's Horses" (1930), is twice played in conjunction with "When Day is Done". Since the first occasion precedes Jim's proposal in a restaurant, the audience anticipates another happy outcome on the second occasion, also in a restaurant. But the scene shifts to Amy alone, anxiously awaiting a long-distance phone call from Jim, and reflecting on their life together in flashback with "When Day is Done" as background. When the call comes, Jim is surrounded by girls in a noisy nightclub and through Amy's reedy earpiece the sound of his voice is drowned by Dixieland. Disillusioned, she replaces the receiver. But the noise of the jazz band stays (impossibly) with a close-up of Amy, until the scene fades to black a few seconds later: thus emphasising her feeling of rejection. For Alwyn discordantly ugly actuality jazz is always an ominous emotional signal.[10]

Despite the film's publicity as the story of both Amy Johnson and Jim Mollison, its propagandist purpose biases it towards Amy's story, a woman's story. The score reflects the same prejudice. Amy's arrival in Australia is matched by triumphant ceremonial music; Mollison's successful first solo flight to England is recognised with a noticeably brief score; his flight to Cape Town has no music at all. Both flyers find fulfilment in time of war, but the emphasis is on Amy, and soon after joining the ATA she gives what amounts to a short voice-over commercial extolling the merits of her service.

The film moves swiftly to her death, a résumé of the opening parachuting and drowning sequence acting as a structural frame, and supported by a shortened version of the same music score. Afterwards it is time to reflect on Amy's life relative to the film's propagandist message, so now her motif — also representing woman's freedom, and the pride and love of her parents — is reintroduced. The audience's emotions need to be worked at this stage, and there is no surer way than by sharing the grief of her devoted parents who are joined as the mother, again, plays the nocturne. As the telephone call comes she breaks off playing, and the silence is all the more poignant.

The film ends with a message from Amy, preaching ghost-like from the sea, and including a prolonged montage of newsreel shots of the women's services parading to a rousing march based on the melody of the nocturne-motif — already symbolically equated with female freedom. Slowly and deliberately, the

[10] Over actual newsreel footage of Buckingham Palace showing all the king's men changing from fur to tin hats on 3 September 1939, music is shunned for a chilling mix of Big Ben's chimes and an air-raid siren.

motif in orchestral unison punches home the propaganda message against end-titles dedicating the film to "all the Amy Johnsons of today". Thus the film does not pursue the logic of its school sequence that donning a uniform, marching, and "being like the others", is a conformist action. But when domestic and family relationships were collapsing under the pressure of war, logic was not of paramount importance.

The unchallenged acceptance that the crews of the Royal Navy shared their loyalty unequally between their ships (and country) and their families was a major theme of *In Which We Serve* (1942). Told largely in flashback through the memories of the surviving crew of HMS *Torrin* after it is crippled in battle, the film was the most expensive British production up to that time. It was scripted by Noel Coward and directed by Coward and David Lean. The music was, and always has been, credited to Coward. Yet in the Alwyn Archive lies a four-page pencilled piano sketch, in Alwyn's hand, of the major themes of the film, including a draft of the opening titles and the last twenty seconds of the end titles. The dominant theme is sketched on the manuscript in waltz form and developed into a stirring march reminiscent of *Desert Victory*. On the screen this theme is given its first major hearing in an important sequence showing *Torrin*'s return from her first sortie, and frequently recurs in linking passages.

However, no other documentation has been discovered concerning Alwyn's involvement with *In Which We Serve*. In early June 1942 the film trade papers reported that Coward was "well ahead with the music he is composing for *In Which We Serve*", and towards the end of the month he was said to be "devoting as much time as possible" to the score.[11] By the beginning of July, *In Which We Serve* must have been more or less wrapped up, for by now Coward was reported to be working with Lean and Ronald Neame on the shooting script of *This Happy Breed* (1944) which was expected to go on the floor in early October.[12] The question of Alwyn's association with the film's music is therefore open to interpretation and guesswork. The Alwyn style seems noticeably apparent in the finished film. Perhaps Alwyn was asked (via Mathieson) to creatively arrange and orchestrate tunes supplied by Coward. Collaboration in some form seems certain.[13]

[11] *The Cinema*, 58:4731 (3 June 1942), 5, 33; *Kinematograph Weekly*, 304:1836 (25 June 1942), 24.
[12] *Kinematograph Weekly*, 304:1837 (2 July 1942), 30.
[13] I am indebted to Richard Andrewes, Head of Music, Cambridge University Library, for drawing my attention to this sketch.

6

"Pulling Together"

L ong after they had left their film careers behind them, Rotha wrote to
Alwyn proposing an LP record called "Music for Documentary".[1] One of
his suggested tracks was from *World of Plenty* (1943), with its score now ar-
chived, said Rotha, at the University of California. Alwyn was not opposed to
re-shaping film music for the concert hall or for recordings,[2] but the visual,
musical, and sound components of *World of Plenty* are so interconnected that
Rotha could hardly have suggested a less suitable score.

When the MoI commissioned Rotha for this survey of "the problems of
world food, its production, its distribution, and its eating"[3] he had eight other
titles in production. Since, however, he could not turn down a major contract,
he experimented and cut corners. He collaborated with Eric Knight — the title
was suggested by Alwyn himself — on a script that illustrated its thesis through
a discussion between the voice-overs of a narrator and questioning sceptics.
All the visuals were rummaged together from film libraries, apart from the
graphics and interviews. Like many of Rotha's titles, the result is instructional
film as entertainment, brims with innovation and imagination, and balances
music and sound-effects equally with the pictures. Alwyn's composition is
mainly instrumental punctuation, enlivening the pictures with a type of simple
mickey-mousing. In the first graphics sequence, for example, each item in a list
of foods is musically ticked off in turn by a plucked d' string: "Cereal (d'), veg-
etables (d'), wheat and dairy produce (d')," and so on. More graphics sequences
follow, which Alwyn tickles with rising and falling glissandi, xylophones, drum
rolls, drum beats, a vibrating cymbal, and other fancies, including at one point
a backwards drum roll.

There are few even moderately long music cues. Early on a march enlivens
a succession of worldwide farming and factory processing shots; but after an
initially stirring timpani beat, the score becomes relatively bland, perhaps to
avoid distracting from the argument. These filmmakers knew what they were
about, and it is interesting to contrast this march with another depicting the effort against the threat of the swastika (which, to harp glissando, zooms alarm-
ingly out of the sky, Rotha-style). Here, all is determination. A sharp, energetic,

[1]   29 May 1973, Alwyn Archive.
[2]   William Alwyn, "An Introduction to Film Music", *RAM Magazine*, 154 (January 1953), 33–4.
[3]   Rotha, *Documentary Diary*, 137.

articulation of ostinato marching strings gradually climbs the scale, counter-pointed with terse and aggressive outbursts on higher chords and interspersed by trumpet fanfares. It crescendoes against scenes of British farm-workers and a commentary lauding the achievement of growing "probably more food than ever before in our islands' history — this in the middle of the greatest war of all time". It ends as the shadow of a plane crosses the fields. Its musical climax is contrasted immediately by a startling silence on a sign: "No eggs today" to commence a sequence on food shortages.

Alwyn was composing *World of Plenty* around the same time as *Desert Victory*, which resonates with his score for the short battle sequence in *World of Plenty*. But lengthy musical cues are not a part of its agenda, and as *World of Plenty* progresses, filmed interviews and an increasing authoritativeness of argument force the music out. The film ends by showing a plane flying over fertile fields, looking forward to a world without starvation, and Alwyn holds out for that hope with a succession of calmly dignified brass fanfares against ostinato strings, to conclude with a triumphant orchestra tutti.

The Minister of Agriculture considered *World of Plenty*'s scenario as "danger-ous".[4] "Year after year," says a farmer in the film, "what I got back was barely enough to keep flesh and blood together." It was a theme that had been extensively treated in *The Harvest Shall Come* (1942), an important document that interweaves the broad history of the political neglect and social decay of British agriculture with the story of an individual farm labourer, Tom Grimwood. Grimwood starts as a youngster of twelve in 1900 for half a crown a week and keep, and doggedly sticks to the land despite a wage barely above subsistence. By the end, he is middle-aged and doing his utmost for the war effort at three pounds a week and a cottage.

Documentary News Letter elected the film as "Documentary of the Month", claiming it as "the first genuine story film made with the documentary purpose and by documentary method".[5] It was directed for Realist by Max Anderson, who shot it entirely on location — even to the interiors. Many another documentary found such luxury technically impossible or too expensive, particularly with synchronous sound — the film's Imperial Chemical Industries (ICI) sponsorship must have helped. Actors filled the main parts, but the dialogue by H. W. Freeman is realistic, and the roles of both actors and local Suffolk people blend seamlessly. John Slater in particular seems entirely authentic as Tom.

Alwyn's score is all the more telling because it is sparing. For in a film in which dialogue is more important than commentary, music has not only to

---

[4] Clive Coultass, "The Ministry of Information and Documentary Film, 1939–45", *Imperial War Museum Review*, 4 (1989), 110.

[5] "Documentary of Month: *The Harvest Shall Come*", unsigned, *DNL* 3:5 (May 1942), 68.

fulfil its primary role of evoking mood, but must also direct attention to the
message. A part of that message is to instruct the uneducated in the realities of
agricultural life, in which lyrical pastoralism has no part. Alwyn warns us from
the start with a series of fanfares, although a lyrical harp attempts to convince
us otherwise.

The music then becomes deceptively bucolic as the young boy, box in hand,
tramps across the fields to start his new life, his steps matched by tripping flute
and strings (opposite). But the photography is grey, and those warning triads,
echoes of the fanfares, continually undermine, mock, and finally suppress the
pastoral. A trilling flute, representing birdsong and freedom, emerges briefly
and is crushed.

The commentary now predominates ("farm labourers were treated little better than the cattle in the fields"), and Tom is shown learning his trade. At 21
he strikes a deal with a new employer and gets a "full man's wages" and a cottage for himself and his intended wife Lil (Eileen Beldon). Here the adult Tom

is introduced, together with an extension of the message: that Tom deserves respect as a loyal fellow countryman in a land vitally dependent on his labour. His humanity is exposed by his love for his fiancée, and our response is aided by Alwyn's touching love theme on solo oboe as, at dusk, they take a first look at their future home, the tied cottage:

Alwyn labelled this part of his score "Love in a Cottage", but threatening descending string chords comment on the interior slum, the rats, the wrecked ceiling, and the damp. The plaintive oboe of the love theme returns, however, as soon as the couple step outside: "It might be worse — we can't do much better around here", says Lil, thus recalling the film's other theme: stoic poverty. They decide to put up the marriage banns . . . fade to black, and to the next scene six years and three children later.

Alwyn's restrained score structures without ostentation. The most blatant punctuation points are military trumpet calls signalling 1914 and 1939; other cues are short and discreet. In the First World War, reports the commentary, farmworkers "became our front line of defence", and rhythm and harmonies metamorphose from a military march melody to a slow pastoral setting of the same melody to flute and harp. The plaintive and reedy characteristic of the oboe, too, is drawn on extensively to depict national neglect, derelict farms, and — when Tom's son leaves for the city — the departure of labour for the rewards of industry.

The final propagandist thrust rests almost entirely on Alwyn's nostalgic "Love in a Cottage" motif. At first it is recalled briefly: there is a structural need to remind the audience of it, and it primes the emotions of love, security, and loyalty. Tom comes home at day's end, late because — dependable — he stayed on to finish a job. He has Home Guard duty tonight, and changes into uniform. As he dresses the radio extols the importance of the farmworkers: "Never again must we neglect our land and the men and women who live by it." "That means you and me, girl", says Tom; "I reckon that's right." "They said all that in the last war", Lil replies cynically. "Ah well," murmurs Tom, "this time it's gotta be different." With these words the story concludes, Tom sets off on Home Guard duty, and the music rises to the "Love in a Cottage" motif. Tom's naïvety is no match for Lil's insight, and without musical guidance the audience would be suspended in a state of ambiguity. The addition of the sentimental motif, however, kindles affection for Tom, inducing an anxiety — a determination, even — to improve the lot of the loyal labourer who provides the nation's bread and meat.[6] So strong is the concluding musical propaganda that at the sponsor's preview several ICI directors were outraged at what they regarded as the film's communist message.[7]

The Harvest Shall Come ran counter to a prevailing national sentiment. The *Documentary News Letter*'s anonymous reviewer commented:

> The film has deliberately eschewed the lyrical approach to the countryside so beloved of the romantic impressionists of documentary.

---

[6] The following year the theme was borrowed for the titles of a farming instructional film, *Potato Blight* (1944).

[7] Imperial War Museum, Sound Archive No. 7259. Interview with John Taylor.

Here there are no fine billowing clouds and rich meadowland looming through the filters. It is not forgotten that behind the beauty of the rambler roses and the thatched roof is the squalor of rural housing . . .[8]

The "lyrical approach" that earns this faint contempt is what Jeffrey Richards in a study of national attitudes in the Second World War calls the "rural myth",[9] an idealised pastoral nostalgia, perpetuated from the late-19th century. The fiction that the countryside in some way belongs to every individual, that it is worth fighting for to the death, was a *sine qua non* of 1940s propaganda. Nevertheless, although a powerful propagandist tool, it seems genuinely to have sensed something in the national psyche, or at least in the middle-class psyche. Perhaps it exposed a national trauma. It was amplified in magazines and books, poster propaganda, radio, and the cinema. Feature films embodied the myth, notably *This England* (1941), *Cottage to Let* (1941), *Went the Day Well?* (1942), *The Demi-Paradise* (1943), *Tawney Pippet* (1944), *A Canterbury Tale* (1944), and *The Way to the Stars* (1945). In others the theme was implicit: of Alwyn's few wartime features, for example, in *Medal for the General* (1944) and *Great Day*. In *The Way Ahead* the soldiers isolated in a seedy bar in North Africa become homesick when their radio picks up a programme about the country harvest.

The pastoral myth found a perfect medium in documentary film. It was insinuated in *These Children are Safe* and *Playtime*, was explicitly designed to recruit in *Salute to Farmers*. In *Green Girdle* London's countryside is implicitly a playground for tired factory workers and bombed city-dwellers.

The textural incorporation of the rural myth into ostensibly objective instructional films about land utilisation can be unpicked from a series directed by Ralph Keene for Greenpark and the Ministry of Agriculture (Plate 4). Each looks at a single season of the country year in a different locality: *Winter on the Farm* (1942) in Dorset, *Spring on the Farm* (1943) in Ross-on-Wye, *Summer on the Farm* (1943) in South Lancashire, and *Crown of the Year* (1943) in East Norfolk. Of their educational value there is no question, but their use as a vehicle for the myth is disclosed partially in their photography and script, but most importantly through the musical textures and rhythms of Alwyn's score, conducted by himself with nine players from the LSO.[10]

All four titles state the myth from the first note and frame. *Crown of the Year* has the richest composition, the thickest musical textures, with brass fanfare symbolically sounding the triumph of the farming year over pictures of fields

[8] "Documentary of Month: *The Harvest Shall Come*", 68.
[9] Jeffrey Richards, "National Identity in British Wartime Films", in Philip MacNeice Taylor (ed.), *Britain and the Cinema in the Second World War* (London: Macmillan, 1988), 44.
[10] BFI Special Collection, *The Technique of Film Music*.

of ripened grain. But *Winter on the Farm*, for instance, is subtler, commencing with a picturesque skyline photographed in first light and accompanied by dreamy harp and woodwind in a pastoral idiom. Following the titles, scenes

Spring on the Farm

Summer on the Farm

Winter on the Farm

Crown of the Year

THE FARMER'S YEAR

A cycle of four films illustrates the work of British farmers throughout the year. They show farms of various types and acreage all directed to one end — the maximum production of food for the British people and the thousands of members of the United Nations who live in wartime Britain.

These four films were made to show the invaluable contribution that the workers on the land are making to the war effort, and also to help city people now living in the country to understand their new surroundings.

17

4 Propaganda. Music was important in incorporating the "rural myth" into ostensibly objective instructional films. A page from a British Information Services sales brochure *Films of Britain at War* (undated, *c.*1943/4), published in New York to promote short films for the US market. Alwyn composed for all four films.

and commentary are interlaced in variations from the factual to the almost po-etic as in the commentary to *Spring on the Farm*, "The silver green of the young corn alternates with the lush green of the meadow pastures": this accompanied by tranquil flutes and strings. Nevertheless, the music composition is not tied to the words, but is free to illustrate without commentary or to accompany the most factual of scripting. In *Spring on the Farm* a didactic — to some ears horrific — commentary, "When the trees are in pink-bud stage, just before the blossom opens, they are sprayed with a solution of lead arsenic to kill the cat-erpillars", is followed by an evocative harp and string melody accompanying a sequence depicting the apple blossom at its most beautiful. It is not that the music and script are pulling in different directions. Rather, the music is roman-tically dressing often naked facts. The MoI could claim, "we are telling you how it is", but the pictures and particularly the music undercut the raw truths with delicious half-truths.

The government's desperation to attract extra hands of whatever capability to help on the land was important to the agenda of these films. Most appealing are *Summer on the Farm*'s Lancashire Land Clubs, cycling out of an evening and at the weekends. They are met first through the tinkle of their bicycle bells, a refreshing contrast with the immediately preceding strings and fanfare, and there is an infectious excitement about the trilling woodwind and strings as they bike off "to do their extra bit for the service of the country". In this film particularly, matching music to the action, while not obvious mickey-mousing, adds a frisson as the mower ripples the hay, or makes attractive what in reality must be the backbreaking tedium of scything or feeding the hayloader.

The rural myth feeds on nostalgia, which is also served by scenes of the so-cial life. Christmas comes to *Winter on the Farm* with an impressionistic mon-tage of crackers, presents, children, cake, and dancing; it is accompanied by a hint of "The First Noel" (traditional) and a little jig, but the timbre (flute, oboe, viola, and cello) is nostalgic. Alwyn is so intent on this effect he does not even attempt to match the rhythm of the dance. A harp arpeggio wafts us to the New Year and the similarly nostalgic chimes of wartime Big Ben on the radio and "Auld Lang Syne" (1783?). In *Crown of the Year* the Lammas Festival brings the community to church with a hymn of Thanksgiving. This long sequence with its intercut shots of the congregation, including young land-girls far from home, is elegantly prefaced by Alwyn's orchestral introduction. By pre-echoing the sung hymn with brass Alwyn resonates a small-town band. The apparent simplicity of this short passage is deceptive, however, for, by introducing and counterpointing the brass with fervent strings rising to greet the hymn, Alwyn creates a feeling of exquisite nostalgia, which cannot be sustained to such an intensity by the actuality of the hymn that follows.

The contribution of ordinary people to the war, their courage, their "pulling together" in teamwork, their loyalty towards and consideration of each other, is evoked in *Fires Were Started*, to which Alwyn's contribution is outstanding. Later he would write of the "excitement of working on *Fires Were Started* with [director] Humphrey Jennings and [producer] Ian Dalrymple — to spend one's nights as an air raid warden in the London Blitz and see it recaptured by day with humanity, pathos and truth in one of the most moving films of all time".[11]

Fires Were Started is the only full-length feature film of the documentarist Humphrey Jennings. A Cambridge intellectual, poet and literary critic, painter with an interest in Surrealism, and expert on the Industrial Revolution, Jennings was steeped in nostalgic community-centred English culture. Whether they knew it or not, Jennings and Alwyn had an affinity in their common love for art, poetry, Romanticism, and the cinema. There was something more: both endeavoured to understand the inner workings of filmic construction, especially in the use of the soundtrack. Working with his editor on the small Moviola editing screen, Jennings dissected his material at one remove from real life. He experimented with mood, romanticism, surrealism, and poetry even, by the juxtaposition of images with each other and with sound. Controlled manipulation of picture and sound can make for persuasive cinema. It also makes for good propaganda.

Unlike much of Jennings's other work, *Fires Were Started* explores character: a tribute to the fire service, it is as much a study of the fire-fighters as of the fire. It has a dramatic structure, too: the narrative is limited to time (24 hours) and place (the Auxiliary Fire Service [AFS] in the dockside area of London's East End). Nevertheless, several of Jennings's analytical traits may still be discerned. There is distancing. Jennings distanced himself historically: his first treatment was drafted during the 1941 Blitz. By the time the film was finished in July 1942[12] the AFS had been reorganised as the National Fire Service (NFS), the "difference between sail and steam" comments Daniel Millar in *Sight and Sound*.[13] There is also an outsider, fireman Barrett (William Sansom), who becomes the insider by the end, and seems to represent Jennings the observer, especially in the early routine scenes set in the fire station. Millar also remarks that "the fire is abstract and almost symbolic",[14] and thereby draws attention to another of Jennings's characteristics. The men, too, are symbols of ordinary men at their patriotic duty — the death of Jacko is a "symbol of the British patriotic spirit", wrote Philip Strick in *Films and Filming*, "the willing involvement of the individual in the social act".[15]

[11] Alwyn, *Sight and Sound*, 177.
[12] It did not open until March 1943. The commercial release, entitled *Fires Were Started*, was a shortened version of the original, *I Was a Fireman*, which is considered here.
[13] Daniel Millar, "Fires Were Started", *Sight and Sound*, 38:2 (Spring 1969), 103.
[14] Ibid., 102.
[15] Philip Strick, "Fires Were Started", *Films and Filming*, 7:8 (May 1961), 15.

Jennings wrote his own script and divided the film into three simple, obvious acts: before the fire, the fire, after the fire. Within each act, Jennings devises scenes that frequently rely upon cross-cutting, even montage. As a consequence Alwyn's music had to knit together each cross-cut sequence and also to establish, reflect, and emphasise the overall structure. His music, as will be seen, served the film's propagandist purpose, too.[16]

There is not a great deal of music. Certainly, there is not a single unnecessary note, a reflection of Alwyn's beliefs in the value of the absence of music and in teamwork. Sound is important, and that includes the choreography of literary quotations, diegetic music (a tin whistle, the men singing and playing the piano), non-diegetic music, the intelligent use of silence, of natural effects, the sound of planes and bombs, burning buildings, the whole apparatus of fires and fire-fighting. Team effort between the writer and director, working with his sound unit and composer, is evident from the start.

A bas-relief of firemen hosing flames illustrates most of the title sequence, at the beginning of which Alwyn introduces a few bars of menace, enough for the viewer to feel uneasy and alerted to the frightening drama about to unfold. It is the familiar horror-film technique of imparting menace to the otherwise neutral shot of the old dark house. A series of heroic fanfares quickly follow and Alwyn introduces a plaintive string melody not encountered again until the tragic denouement of the plot. A pedal point is introduced here with a resultant creation of tension. More fanfares follow, still against pedal points and sustained high strings, followed by alternating heroic and fearful themes. At this stage, too, the captions alert us to a tale about "the bitter days of Winter and Spring 1940/41" and the visual image is of a pan across a smoking oil fire. After more hints of menace, this opening theme changes again, to a ceremonial and heroic measure discovered again at the conclusion. By the alternation of its heroic and threatening themes the score fulfils an illustrative function: the fireman's battle against flame and conflagration, his triumphs and setbacks.

Act One commences with a fire pump's journey to sub-station 14Y. From Jennings's several pre-shooting treatments[17] it is apparent that he intended this sequence to be an attention-grabber, for example starting on a close-up of a wheel, and later depicting scared pigeons and a dog as the pump hurtles round a corner. However, good intentions are easier in the imagination than on the road, for in this sequence camerawork and editing are unexciting, the urgency imposed entirely by the music. One might compare it with the often-cited tension of Bernard Herrmann's score for Hitchcock's *Psycho* (1960), which paints a similar emotion over otherwise neutral pictures of Janet Leigh's drive

---

[16] Apart from a very few fragments of sketches, the score no longer survives.

[17] Preserved in the Special Collection at the BFI, and partially reproduced in Kevin Jackson (ed.), *The Humphrey Jennings Film Reader* (London: Carcenet, 1993).

through the rain near its start. In *Fires Were Started*, as the van pulls through the fire-station gates, its bell clanging from time to time, the music slows and calms, and stops on a loud abrupt minor chord which coincides with the slam of the van door — visually it is a gesture of casualness, yet the chord raises a startling sense of dramatic anticipation. Now the action continues without music, but so far (despite some visual images and information captions that have hinted at the emotional guidelines), the tone and the structure have been established predominantly by the strong musical score.

After a short sequence at the fire station the scene changes to the docks, and the audience is alerted once more by menacing notes over a shot of the doomed warehouse. However, these notes are held back for two or three seconds: their late introduction over what the viewer at first assumes is simply a general view insinuates an uncomfortable feeling that this building is linked with misfortune — even tragedy. The musical mood quickly changes, however, to a theme which develops into a long passage of descending strings sequencing in a high key against lower strings in a staccato rhythm. Descending patterns of music often express negative feelings, but these high strings are fast and quickly repeat from the top of the scale. The mood is one of a constant effort at cheerfulness, which is dragged downwards to an unsettled, restless — perhaps slightly threatening — emotion.

However, there is more to this sequence. Again, comparison with the original scripts is illuminating: in the early drafts it was intended that a prototype Jacko and Johnny meet on the way to work.[18] In the finished film, however, Jennings, the Surrealist artist and experimentalist, paints the scene with bold impressionistic brush strokes. Spreading across a broad canvas, he flings down a variety of camera set-ups, elaborates on details within the frame, and contains everything within well-paced editing and the musical score. His collaborators are his editor Stewart McAllister and William Alwyn the composer with an acutely tuned visual sensitivity. The pictures are of fire-fighters as they leave their homes for the start of their shift, ordinary people doing ordinary things on a fresh sunny morning. Johnny Daniels (Fred Griffiths) finishes a game with his son; Jacko (Johnny Houghton) bids "cheerio" to his wife and cycles off from his newsagent's shop; "Sub" (George Gravett) walks smartly past the "Cat and Cucumber" dining rooms; B. A. Brown (T. P. Smith) sniffs at some kippers on a barrow. These and other casual street scenes are cross-cut with the armaments ship loading at the docks. Snatches of conversation half-heard and of no consequence are drowned out by the music. The viewer is persuaded that he is making his own connections.

At the same time, the propagandist subtext is at work. These firemen, it says, are ordinary people, a microcosm of their nation: the similarly ordinary war-

[18] BFI Special Collection. Rough treatment, 22 Nov. 1941.

time audience is invited to identify with them. Later, when the firemen are shown reacting to the danger to their homeland, members of the audience will be able to empathise. Moreover, by cross-cutting, Jennings clinches the affinity between firemen and the munitions ship their heroism will save. In the original draft, the dock sequence was planned as quite separate, with a consequently much weaker linkage.[19] The unifying musical score in the finished version embraces both Jennings's impressionistic vision and the patriotic message, and informs the whole with an anticipatory tension.

The sequence moves towards its conclusion. The symbolic importance of the ammunition ship, impossible to impart by pictures alone, is now emphasised by a brass fanfare as the music continues to structure. Descending strings again follow, but the tempo suddenly slows to not only match the visual (Johnny walking along the road pauses to pick something up and throw it away again), but to key with the succeeding actuality sound — a tin-whistle tune played by a down-and-out standing by the fire-station as the men arrive.[20] The tune has a strong affinity to the preceding string music, and is in fact its "echo", thus unifying the two scenes and continuing to structure the film. But because he is diegetic, rather than a "background orchestra", the tin whistle player normalises the scene. The director's impressionistic cross-cutting is abandoned, and the viewer is about to touch the people previously only observed.

Barrett arrives and gains acceptance by his newfound fellow crewmembers of Heavy Unit One. There is a reassuring English — East-End cockney — ambience, and Barrett is put in the hands of the cheery and willing Johnny Daniels to be shown around. Jennings loiters while the men clean the fire engine, their song knitting the small sequences together in a similar way to a normal "composed" score, yet humanising them as no orchestral score could manage. Johnny's solo performance of "I Do Like To Be Beside the Seaside" (1909) as he finishes polishing the van ends with a "diddly-um-pom-pom". Alwyn promptly picks up, echoes, the "pom-pom" with an orchestral one of his own and jumps in with a busy, cheerful string sequence that glues together a series of instructional scenes of the daily duties at the fire stations. It is both good documentary instruction and good propaganda: a demonstration of fire-station routines through good-humoured, efficient teamwork, clearly labelled by the dialogue ("Right, now ladder drill . . ."), and easily digested through its pleasant musical accompaniment. The audience is invited to place its trust in these safe, ordinary, "English" hands.

The orchestral range for this sequence compares as a whole with the men's voice-register from which it takes over; thus, even though the audience remains

---

[19] Ibid.

[20] "An old man who comes in and plays the flute superbly well on Fridays". Jennings to Cicily Jennings, 12 April 1942, quoted in Jackson, *The Humphrey Jennings Film Reader*, 57.

observer, Alwyn helps it to empathise with the work in hand. To understand this, compare this score with the disassociative, impressionistic effect of the predominantly high strings that accompanied the earlier scenes of the men leaving for work. The demonstration of the fireman's working morning ends on cymbal-crash and fanfare as cook cries, "Come and get it!": lunchtime. The punctuation is hard and sharply defined, and it is time to proceed to a new paragraph.

After lunch, Johnny sets off with Barrett to show him around the docks area, important because later it will be seen only in darkness and under threat. Johnny points out the main features of the docks and riverside with pride. Alwyn accompanies them with a lyrical, nostalgic music sequence.[21] The strings predominate. Of all orchestral instruments, strings most closely resemble the human voice; they express the most heart-rending, most personal moments. Humphrey Jennings — and Alwyn picks this up — is taking a lovingly nostalgic look at a part of his England, a part of his London — a part that the enemy is set upon destroying. Their presence at the docks integrates the two firemen with the dockers and the seamen, and by implication with the nation. It is an interdependence suggested by intercutting and gentle music. A sailing barge sweeps past on the Thames, but this long, beautiful shot and Alwyn's restful score lulls into complacency, for each of the following casually-introduced scenes nevertheless has a terrible relevance to the action to follow that night. "That's, er, Trinidad Street down there, Bill", says Johnny, as an aside before passing to Alderman's Wharf, where the wharf manager is ordering the chief stevedore to load guns and cases of cartridges into the ship's hold; the next scene is the sunken barge ("That holds about 10,000 gallons . . ."). Nevertheless, the music gives warning hints — although always gentle: it crescendoes and pauses to mark Johnny's pride as he shows us the ship ("Ain't she a smasher, cock, eh?"), there is a hint of menace over a shot of cases of cartridges, alarm at the sight of the sunken barge. Jennings takes a final look at the scene in daylight, and the music fades as a passing barge transports a barrage balloon hovering warningly above the river as it catches the light of the late afternoon sun. Nevertheless, in dramatic terms, Alwyn's earlier musical forewarnings have been allowed to largely die away: a classic scheme of anti-climax before the climax.

Evening comes, and the men draw on their fire-fighting gear while Barrett plays the piano. Jennings, or perhaps his editor McAllister, overlays Barrett's notes with gloomy, ominous shots of Trinidad Street and the docks, empty at dusk. Alwyn's orchestral music is never required where authentic diegetic music already exists. Barrett, encouraged by Johnny, moves on to play "One Man Went to Mow" (traditional), adapting the style of the verses to match

---

[21] A close relative in melodic and harmonic shape was written during the same period to illustrate sheaves being loaded on to a cart in *Crown of the Year*.

each crewmember's personality. It is a device that could have seemed strained and unlikely (each character appears singly on cue), and succeeds because it is handled with such natural good humour and charm.

Act Two. Tension mounts as the increasingly busy scenes in the control room intercut with the men of Heavy Unit One having a singsong (ominously "Please Don't Talk About Me When I'm Gone", 1931). Suddenly it's their turn, and the fire appliance sets off to the burning warehouse in Trinidad Street: the tensions begin of a night in which one man, Jacko, is killed. The very little music in this act is appropriate and enhances the drama. Tension is enhanced by natural sound — the hum of the pumps, the hiss of the hoses, the drone of planes, and the explosion of bombs.

Music flows in naturally and probably un-noticed by most viewers, in a single prolonged music sequence that serves as an adhesive between two high-action scenes. Soon after arrival of the Heavy Unit, a bomb hits the water main, and the water dries up. More fire units arrive, but they are forced to obtain their supply from the old barge, some distance away. As the fireboat plunges its hoses into the water of the old barge, music commences. Pipes are connected, and suspense builds up as we await the water flow, a strange emotional effect of the linear (hosepipes stretching along the streets) combined with the temporal. The strings jab at repeated minor chords, contrasting with a low pedal point, which, increasing in intensity, encourages an emotion of impatience and frustration. The mood terminates in orgasmic release on a rising theme with triumphant cymbals as the water spurts through. It was not the last time that Alwyn was to use this musical device. Most famously it is heard in *Desert Victory*, which he composed not long after *Fires Were Started*.

One short phrase of music in this Act is horrifying and tragic. As Jacko falls to his death through the flaming building, descending chords end on cymbal crashes over a wide shot of the burning docks; thus the drama of the moment and of the individual is subsumed into a wider social tragedy and significance.

More reinforcements arrive. "You people seem to have a regular pasting down here tonight", says one relief fireman to a controller. "Yes", she replies, "Our boys at the docks." We cut back to the fire, and chilling rolls on the timpani followed by menacing brass create a powerful emotional impact. But the mood of foreboding lifts surprisingly quickly as Act Two continues with a triumphal ceremonial march, over more impressionistic montage cutting that follows the (fairly quickly-disposed-of) victory over the fire. However, it has been the score, and the score alone, that has informed us that the fire is being conquered, and it is the score that encapsulates the film's important patriotic message: London can take it.

Act Two is divided from Act Three by a short but effective punctuation. A cut to the Control Room. The room is quiet. A controller repeats out loud a telephone message, "Fire at 150 degrees appears to be under control." "Thank goodness for that", comes the comment. The scene is followed immediately by Act Three. Daylight is greeted by a fanfare against a silhouette of St Paul's, a symbol of England to both Jennings and his audience. The music is brief and ends by merging with an "all clear" siren. The feeling of relief clearly signals and structures the start of a new mood.

The firemen are served tea from a mobile canteen before they start to clear up, pulling away the hoses. Slow woodwinds and low strings reflect their weariness. Barrett wanders off and searches amongst the rubble, while the music becomes anticipatory. To a short burst of strings and a five-note trumpet fanfare ending on an interrupted cadence, he discovers Jacko's helmet. The feeling of discovery, enlightenment even, is mixed with dismay as after a pause the strings echo the final feminine beat of the fanfare. But as our attention is drawn to the undamaged ship the music again enters, triumphantly ceremonial and patriotic: "A sight for sore eyes", proclaims Johnny. The day starts, people arrive to move around the smouldering ruins, and the firemen leave. Soon, the busy, light, impressionistic string music we heard in Act One returns, thus providing a frame and structure for the film as the docks spring into action again — in propaganda terms, patriotism is again alerted, the justification for both firefighters and the loss of life.

But back at the fire station there is gloom as the crew mourn the death of Jacko. Then Brown shouts out, "Come on chums. Snap out of it!" A psychotherapist would despair, but in a propaganda movie it works. A bright chord strikes up over streaming, sparkling river water, followed by what at first appears to be a bugle fanfare over the parting ship. Soon we realise that the fanfare is "The Last Post" (18th century), as we cross-cut backwards and forwards between Jacko's funeral, attended by his wife and colleagues, and the saved ship, the "sight for sore eyes". There is not a wet eye in the house: the film ends with the stiffest of lips, for Jacko — the "ordinary man" — having sacrificed himself for his country, has become a symbol of the integration of the individual into the good of the community. The message is powerfully augmented by Alwyn's inspirational symphonic music. The ship sails away to a heartfelt theme on strings, which merge to triumphal military brass: for the war has yet to be won.

Evelyn Russell, noting the film's release in *Sight and Sound*, was perceptive enough to appreciate the music's contribution, which, she commented, "is so closely knit with the shape of the film that one would be incomplete without the other".[22] She was one of the few, then or since, to give the underscore its due, although the diegetic music — the penny whistle, and especially the "One Man Went to Mow" sequence — has been often commented upon and praised.

In the 1940s filmgoers frequently found fiction less compelling than documentaries, where they could identify with real characters and events. "Never

---

[22] Evelyn Russell, "The Quarter's Films", *Sight and Sound*, 12:45 (Summer 1943), 16.

have ordinary people been more convincingly done", commented a report for Mass Observation (MO)[23] of *Fires Were Started*, which was consistently placed high in MO lists of most-liked films. In contrast, Alwyn's single fiction feature of 1943, *Escape to Danger* for Lance Comfort, received not a single mention, and has eluded film archives. Romantic tributes to resistance fighters in Nazi-invaded countries were fashionable, a trend started perhaps by *Dangerous Moonlight*, with its improbable yarn about an amnesiac Polish airman. The film owed much of its popularity to Addinsell's "Warsaw Concerto", which saturates the film to the point of tedium, inspired several imitations, and has remained a concert piece. *Escape to Danger* found heroism among Danish patriots, with Ann Dvorak and Eric Portman starring as British agents. Alwyn's piano solo for a sequence entitled "Eric escapes by car" prompted his pencilled inscription, "the worser concerto".[24]

[23] Jeffrey Richards and Dorothy Sheridan (eds.), *Mass Observation at the Movies* (London and New York: Routledge & Kegan Paul, 1987), 225.
[24] Annotation on list of film titles, Alwyn Archive.

7
The People's War
▐▐▐▐▐▐▐▐▐▐▐▐▐▐▐▐▐▐▐▐▐▐▐▐▐▐▐▐▐▐▐▐▐

DOCUMENTARIES about the battle front came under the aegis of the forces film units. In charge of the Army Film and Photographic Unit (AFPU) was David Macdonald, a director of bad-to-middling features and a 25-minute documentary, *Men of the Lightship* (1940), which arguably owed its artistic success to its editor Stewart McAllister.[1] At the AFPU, Macdonald set in motion a series of feature-length compilation documentaries: *Desert Victory* (1943), *Tunisian Victory* (1944), and *Burma Victory* (1945). Alwyn wrote the score for *Desert Victory*, "co-wrote" with Dmitri Tiomkin for *Tunisian Victory*, and scored a similar AFPU compilation feature *The True Glory* for Carol Reed in 1945.

Of the three, the first was the greatest box-office success, and it still stands as a model of documentary and propagandist filmmaking. *Desert Victory* tells the story of the Eighth Army's advance across Libya and is edited from combat footage, stock footage, newsreels, interviews, animated graphics, and reconstructions filmed at Pinewood and in the desert. The combat material was filmed by some twenty army cameramen, of whom three were killed and two seriously injured.

It was generally released on 15 March 1943, shortly before *Fires Were Started*, and it similarly betrayed the "documentary" mood pervading the media of the period: journalism, photography, social commentary, and cinema. That mood was encouraged by the propaganda machine, which fostered the notion of a "people's war". But it could not have taken hold without the willing participation of "the people", who were flattered by their own participation in the message.

Annette Kuhn makes a distinction, well-known to filmmakers, between two types of factual films: the "observational" where the image is pre-eminent and offers itself as evidence of the "reality" of what has happened, and the "voice-over" in which the commentary dominates and the pictures serve as illustration. The second type, she rightly suggests, "tends to limit the range of readings available from the image; it directs, in other words, the reading of the film".[2]

"At first sight," she continues, "*Desert Victory* seems to be exemplary of this

[1] Dai Vaughan, *Portrait of an Invisible Man: The Working Life of Stewart McAllister, Film Editor* (London: BFI Publishing, 1983), 46–53.
[2] Annette Kuhn, "*Desert Victory* and the People's War", *Screen* 22:2 (Summer 1981), 45–68.

classic documentary form. Nonetheless, there are moments of the film when
the fixity of the image/voice-over relationship is somewhat shifted." A National
Film Theatre programme note elucidates Kuhn's observation: "this shifting relationship is to move the spectator from being simply witness to the events on
North Africa to being a participant".[3] In other words, there are sequences in
Desert Victory in which pictures predominate over script, and the commentary
ceases. At these times the viewer becomes participant. The result is superb
propaganda: audiences are encouraged to own what they are seeing, to believe
that this is their war. Music, with its important filmic purpose of shaping the
propaganda by swaying emotion and viewpoint, usually takes a pre-eminent
role. Thus, for the opening titles Alwyn composed a quick march, setting
a confident mood suggestive of a happy ending, no matter what follows:

Its urgency also suggests that "we" should "get on" with the war. Alwyn refrains
from re-using this victory motif until the end of the film, where the emotion
is repeated, "Where next? Let's get on with it." In this way the composition
frames the film. The businesslike opening titles give way to a panning shot
across the sand, military vehicles, and personnel, a view of distant sand ridges
and dust storms. The pictures are neutral. The unexpected contrast, a sense
of wastelands and brooding suspended mobility, is created by J. L. Hodson's
sparse commentary — "The Western Desert is a place fit only for war . . ." — and
masterly musical tone-painting. The cinemagoer hovers between the emotions
of witnessing and participation.

There is another form of the march, another victory motif: it is the ceremonial trio, or middle section, of an orchestral march. Like Elgar, Walton, Bliss,
and others, Alwyn was at home with this English form. In *Desert Victory* it
not only symbolises victory and patriotic pride but strengthens the association
between patriotism and Winston Churchill, a paternalistic reassurance that all
is well:

³ Anonymous NFT programme note; *Desert Victory* microjacket at BFI.

Churchill, says the commentary, "had brought good news . . .": Generals Alexander and Montgomery were to lead the battle. A letter from Churchill is shown outlining Montgomery's instructions, and the audience feels "part of", an insider to, the high-level decisions. Later the same theme injects a short burst of pride during a sea victory, and later still (amidst a musical passage of menace and determination) it tinges a foretaste of coming victory as Montgomery's "final preparations begin". Towards the end of the film the motif again links Churchill with victory, until in the final minutes it moves into the fast march that frames the film. Both march themes enliven shots of parades and the Union flag.

However, audience identification and the perception of victory are encouraged not only by the musical composition. The film is an elegant balance of teamwork, which leads us through the campaign, insisting upon the people's trust in the military planning and its inevitably victorious working-out. The voice-over is dryly factual, measured, scientific: it allows no possibility of failure. Similarly, the animated graphics impart the atmosphere of the lecture room — even to the use of a pointer in one shot. The viewer soon becomes linked with the common soldier too: "General Montgomery", runs the track, "saw to it that the plan of battle was known to everybody from general to private soldier." This information, relayed over shots of Montgomery at his tent, covers an otherwise silent track, the absence of music and effects reinforcing the seriousness and "genuineness" of the moment.

Patchworked with the didactic are moments when the classroom is escaped for active practical work — the excitement of trees being felled, planes taking off, supplies being loaded. Picture sequences take pre-eminence, and the music takes on the role of commentary, informing our emotions. The audience's emotion is that of getting on with the job. Recalling Kuhn's analysis, these are the sequences where the audience member becomes the participant, as opposed to the viewer.

The team together has settled the film's music spotting, when to introduce music and when to leave it out and allow sound-effects to speak for themselves. It is worth bearing in mind — especially later when *The True Glory* is considered with its almost continuous musical soundtrack — that since Macdonald's cameramen were for the most part using mute clockwork cameras, most of the effects were on wild track, which had to be laboriously laid: the sound editor Bob Carrick, was a key member of the production team. Soldiers dig in to the sound of shovels, we hear the drills and trucks. There is the sound of distant gun rattle. In battle, tanks and guns and missiles explode in quick cuts. Often Alwyn's cues end with an interrupted cadence or otherwise unresolved. It is as if the composer is making a gesture — look, he is saying, watch what comes next. The audience is conducted into these sequences and then allowed to feel the moment for itself, without any encouragement from music or commentary.

Just one example: Alwyn's score of airborne planes gives way on a rising note to the sound of the planes themselves and the dropping of bombs. This is adroit propagandist technique of a very high standard indeed.

The most famous sequence, both in the film and musically, is the scene leading up to and including the battle of El Alamein. The sequence commences in quietly reflective mood, over the setting of the sun . . . the final moments . . . a haircut, a rest, a swim in the sea, washing clothes, cooking the evening meal, the writing of letters . . . The audience participates, identifies with the troops. Then dawn. The orchestra takes up a quiet theme against a constant string inverted pedal point on *e'*. A lone piper plays "Highland Laddie" (traditional), the men lounge back and listen, the pipes fade to silence. Tension mounts. Alwyn's score re-enters restrainedly against the sound of tanks taking up position. A short comment by Bernard Miles, quietly spoken . . . Now Alwyn uses a device he was to re-employ again and again, but under different guises so that it seems always fresh. It is a form of sequencing, the creation of tension by the continual raising in pitch of a musical idea. He was particularly proud of its use in *Desert Victory*. He quoted it in his lectures on film music and once told Roger Manvell he thought it the "best individual piece of scoring he had ever achieved".[4] Manvell recounted the technique in his works:

> Music building up or reflecting dramatic tension has its primitive origins in the old musical effects of the silent film days. Tension deliberately

[4] Roger Manvell, *The Film and the Public* (Harmondsworth: Penguin Books, 1955), 67.

plays on the nerves of the audience when some climax of violence or threat is anticipated, but the moment of its release is unsure. Music can introduce the feeling of tension into a situation while the images on the screen retain their calm.

A remarkable example of this is the musical device used by William Alwyn in his score for the official wartime documentary, *Desert Victory*; it is a case of music adding an entirely new dimension to what is being done. Before zero-hour for the great night assault on Rommel's defences, the tension of silent waiting is expressed through close-ups of the men's faces and shots of military equipment standing poised in readiness, while the eyes of the officers are concentrated on their synchronised watches. Alwyn uses a single persistent note which rises octave by octave until it feels like the stretched nerves of the waiting men and snaps when the barrage breaks loose in the wild crescendo of a great storm.[5]

The note is E, and its association with the pedal point on *e'* chosen for the earlier day sequence unites the scenes and supplies an important dramatic structure.

Desert Victory was a deserved smash hit, the most financially successful of all the official films. Released only four months after the events it portrayed, it packed the cinemas with audiences anxious to see a big story of the war, events in which they may even have participated. Alwyn's "March" became popular, was published as sheet music, and, unusually for film scores of the time, was marketed as a gramophone record.

But within the industry, and politically, *Desert Victory* was producing rows and disagreements. At Crown, Ian Dalrymple moaned that his unit had received no credit despite providing the services of its art and construction departments, the music director, the commentator, and library footage. Only the scriptwriter and composer were acknowledged: "I don't feel very comfortable", wrote the writer J. L. Hodson in his diary, "that the only names given a screen credit are William Alwyn's and mine".[6] In the end, the tussle was a factor in Dalrymple's resignation from Crown.

Worse, the film was a source of bitter feelings between the British and American allies. *Desert Victory* was making box offices sing across the United States, and critical acclaim from the American press culminated in an Oscar for "the most distinctive documentary achievement of 1943". But the film never allowed its audience to forget that this was a British "people's war". Americans were looking askance: where were the pictures of their troops? And the film com-

---

[5] Manvell and Huntley, *The Technique of Film-Music*, 135. Much of the text is taken over verbatim from Manvell, *The Film and the Public*, 67.

[6] James Lansdale Hodson, *Home Front* (London: Gollancz, 1944), 307.

panies were wondering why they couldn't get a bite of that sort of commercial cherry.

Meanwhile the British were pressing ahead with a sequel called *Africa Freed* (1943), depicting the conquest of Tunisia and made for the AFPU by Major Hugh St Clair Stewart, who had come back to England to direct the film in Pinewood. Captain Roy Boulting was its supervising editor. A rough cut was privately screened in late July 1943, but we know the Alwyn score had not been added at that stage, as the film was projected mute with the commentary read against the pictures.[7] It was finally finished by August, but by this time the Americans had made representations at the highest level, and *Africa Freed* was grudgingly shelved.

Whatever the rights and wrongs of the political decisions, the copy preserved in the Imperial War Museum reveals that from an artistic point of view *Africa Freed* was perhaps the greatest of the wartime feature documentaries with which Boulting was associated. The critical success of *Desert Victory* seems to have instilled in the filmmakers a real sense of confidence, a self-assurance to give the head to techniques that were merely essayed in *Desert Victory*. The narrative line, again scripted by Hodson, is clean and intelligible. The newsreel style of narrative has been largely shunned, and the filmmakers have instead concentrated on a series of sequences depicting a limited time and space, often at considerable length. During these sequences it is not unusual for the commentary to lie dormant while pictures, effects, and music take up the story — a perfect illustration of Kuhn's analysis of documentary's involvement of the viewer. The result is that this feels very much like a "people's film": pervaded by a socialist mood (in keeping with the wider national feeling), as opposed to a lecturing commentary. In sustaining this mood the photography, even in the war situation, sometimes achieves a breath-taking beauty. The editing has pace, tension, and an overall structure, to which Alwyn's music is not only a perfect foil but contributes a further dimension.

The narrative is framed by the jubilation at the conquest of Tunisia and reflects a history dating back to 1942. Again like *Desert Victory*, the film attempts to suggest the audience possesses inside knowledge. For example, once the background to the campaign has been outlined near the start, we are "let into" (through a closing door) scenes of the chiefs of staff at work. The scene is cut against the loading of ships, as the commentary, detailing the inventory, almost demands we gasp in astonishment at the organisation and quantity of supplies needed. All is movement and bustle. Then with a proud exclamation, "And every ship sailed on time . . .", a six-note brass fanfare from Alwyn heralds the embarkation and introduces the score in a beautifully calm and poignant

---

[7] Clive Coultass, "*Tunisian Victory*: A Film Too Late?", *Imperial War Museum Review*, 1 (1986), 64.

passage. Thus, the tension is released — the alternate imposition and relaxation of tension is a facet in the structuring of this part of the film — and the full orchestra takes up the same six-note theme of the fanfare, mixed with the cries of seagulls, and the horns and whistles of the navy, as the ship sails out of harbour. All is relaxation, held together by the score, against shots of men, some in close-up watching the departing shore, others writing letters, gazing through binoculars, or signalling. In three successive general views, the scene grows misty, dusk sets in, night falls. The viewer — his emotions alerted by the stoical sonority of the music — associates himself with all the mixed feelings of departure, of homesickness and anticipation.

The pictures demand of the music a variety of moods. Often Alwyn utilises techniques surviving from *Desert Victory*. Appropriately for what was in effect a sequel, both the fast and ceremonial marches are reworked for similar ends. The fast purposeful march lends support to the troops getting down to the "business" of war; at one moment accompanying the posting of "Important News" as the camera zooms to a notice: "Africa Korps in full retreat." The ceremonial march marks victorious occasions or respect for heads of states, but Alwyn also finds another purpose: to dignify what must in reality have been like Hell. "Life had now become bogged down with mud", runs Hodson's commentary; "weapons were coated with it, dugouts foul with it, and clothing made heavy as lead. Roads turned into quagmires, and lorries and jeeps sank to the axles." Alwyn's quiet pomp and circumstance not only ameliorates the shots of drudgery and degradation that accompany Hodson's honest narration, but invests them with a noble grandeur that is purely propagandist.

Elsewhere Alwyn's tone-painting draws on experience and technique: the slow drip of strings while waiting for battle to commence; the distraction of an enchanting waltz as aircrews rest in the mountains; and when we are told that "Spring comes early to North Africa", the enhancement by mellifluous strings and flute of the paradox of flowers even in the midst of war. In other places, graphic expositions are punctuated and invigorated by ominous timpani rolls or menacingly tinged by barely perceptible pedal points. Shots of Hitler with his generals are given sinister overtones by a martellato rhythm of the side drums accompanied by slanted commentary, "Hitler, whose newly acquired silence is more eloquent than his ravings of the past . . .", immediately contrasted by a ceremonial march and patriotic commentary, "As the shadows deepen round the Führer, King George brings to his armies the thanks of the British Commonwealth . . .".

We notice, too, musical traits to which Alwyn will return in later films. Fast orchestra tutti with sequenced strings and stabbing brass depict a speed in the battle of the bridgehead, recalled not long afterwards in *The Way Ahead*.[8]

---

[8] Where military vehicles are cast overboard in the carrier ship.

In another sequence, falling bombs are accompanied by fast strings similar to orchestrations that are uncovered again in *Odd Man Out*.[9]

Mindful that perfection is often indebted to omission, Alwyn's score is restrained, giving priority to sound-effects and their rhythms, especially in the long battle scenes. One scene, however, of a mere 30 seconds, stays in the memory after others have faded. Bombers raid Italian cities. Shots of the half-lit crew in the darkness of the cockpit intercut with flashes of explosion flickering across the land thousands of feet below. We have seen similar scenes in other films, perhaps to the accompaniment of the drone of the engines, or to the screaming of bombs, or to dull thuds representing the bomb blasts (though they could not possibly be heard in the plane). Alwyn treats the sequence in a highly original manner. He introduces a rapidly repeated descending phrase of very high strings, against a lower pedal point and low and short woodwind interruptions. A mood is induced, the strongest I can recall in a film, of the drowsy half-awake, half-asleep unreality of the night flight, a dream-like — almost hallucinatory — sensation. Before long Alwyn would gain a reputation for his handling of dream, hallucination, and flashback sequences.

For all its brilliance, effort, and cost, *Africa Freed* has been seen by few. In 1943, amidst seemingly interminable arguments, a substitute production to be called *Tunisian Victory* was agreed upon jointly with the American Service Film Unit. The unit had also been making a film on the same subject under the direction of Frank Capra, who arrived in London at the end of August, although his footage was noticeably inferior to the British. In the end a co-production was decided upon, with credits to Stewart and Boulting for the UK, and Capra for the US. In November Capra departed for America, taking a version of *Tunisian Victory* with him, to be completed in the US with the excuse that his negatives were there. Stewart joined him to represent British interests. Much of the British footage, together with sections of the commentary, was transferred from *Africa Freed*. Alwyn's tracks were also carted off, and the whole finished by Dmitri Tiomkin who is credited with the composition alongside Alwyn. At this time Tiomkin was employed by his "lifelong" friend Capra,[10] at the Army Film Center in Hollywood churning out scores for hundreds of propaganda and training films. In *Africa Freed* Alwyn's score is controlled, working to a purpose, and with a structure. It is difficult to find either purpose or structure in the co-scored *Tunisian Victory*. Although praised by several contemporary reviewers, it is, to put it bluntly, a mess.

The film bears scarce resemblance to *Africa Freed*. One or two sequences and some shots are recognisably lifted from that production, but they have

---

[9] Johnny's run to the bombsite after falling from the car, and Dennis's dash from the shelter.

[10] Frank Capra, *The Name Above the Title* (New York: Macmillan, 1971; London: W. H. Allen, 1972), 152.

been rescripted and reassembled to baser ends. *Tunisian Victory* starts with the usual jaunty Alwyn march, but within 35 seconds heads off into a theme from Rachmaninoff's second Piano Concerto (1900–1901). The concerto makes so many subsequent entries that one questions why Rachmaninoff is uncredited, and whether David Lean was watching.[11] At about this time Tiomkin was assembling a score from the works of great Russian composers for a documentary, *The Battle of Russia* (1943). The use of obvious and unsubtle themes appealing to a low popular response also has a distinctly Tiomkin ring: "Yankee Doodle" (18th century) accompanies the US troops, "La Marselleise" (1792) symbolises the French, and "Jingle Bells" (1859) and "Roll Out the Barrel" (1939) accompany scenes of Christmas at home in America and Britain. Some shreds of Alwyn still remain: the use of interrupted cadences or inconclusive passages to lead off into sound-effects of the action can be attributed to his composition. Some hard, even abrupt, music cuts suggest either incisions in the finished film, or perhaps joins of separately edited and assembled sequences. At the very end a victory scene is crudely hacked on, complete with Alwyn's victory march. Over shots of jubilant crowds the commentary follows: "Africa is freed and Europe that much nearer freedom . . .".

Tunisian Victory was previewed in London on 17th February 1944, and largely because it depicted events which had taken place nearly a year earlier, it flopped in both Britain and America.

Away from the army documentary battlefront, Anglo-American understanding was in better shape. A guide to the British way of life for visiting GIs was the aim of *Welcome to Britain* (1943), a prestigious production for the MoI by Strand, which had been bought out by Lady Yule the previous year. It was directed by Anthony Asquith with Burgess Meredith, who also co-wrote it and had a starring role. A selection of local customs are illustrated in a chronology extending from the day of disembarkation on British soil, and ending with Meredith himself being hassled off to the battlefront. The pill of the serious is sugared by the humorous, and even Bob Hope and Beatrice Lillie creep in on the act.

Meredith is the structural glue, smoothly linking sequences and ideas together in a good-humoured, sometimes funny way. Another structural linkage is the occasional appearance of an attractive girl on a bicycle, her arrival signalled by Meredith's roving eye and a pleasant waltz in the same key as the sporadic tinkling of her bicycle bell (actually the triangle). Each of her appearances points Meredith towards a new sequence, although the device does seem to give GIs a nod and a wink to chase the local girls.

---

[11] In the following year Lean borrowed Rachmaninoff's second Piano Concerto as underscore for *Brief Encounter*.

The variety of situations calls for a variety of moods, which Alwyn paints with considerable ingenuity. A purely musical sentimental motif to illustrate the "people of England" is accompaniment to Meredith as he pokes around the privacies of a British home and to illustrate library shots of workers on the home front. Melancholia is evoked by woodwind and string with a military bugle simulation, suggestive of Vaughan Williams's use of the natural trumpet in *A Pastoral Symphony* (1921), to illustrate bombed buildings ("old Charlie, the greengrocer, he got it too . . ."). Vaughan Williams is recalled again by slow strings in simple tonal combinations, counterpointed by woodwind . . . a suggestion of hymn music in a bombed church open to the sky. A frugal family dinner is joined by a foxtrot rhythm (on the score: "trombone close to mike" and wire brush) to suggest a tea dance, and one can almost feel the rain as Meredith turns up his coat collar against a track of descending plucked strings accompanied by oboe. When an American soldier empties British rainwater from his boot, with a couple of tuneless bars from "Home Sweet Home" (1823), Alwyn humorously echoes the theme and counterpoints it with brief snatches of "Over There" (1918), which recall a lively performance by a military band at the opening. He also introduces appropriate pastoral, military, dance music, and a first cousin to the training music in *Fires Were Started* (as well as a dentistry scene in *A Letter from Ulster*, 1943), as a gruff sergeant marches, exercises, and goads Meredith — protesting that he hasn't yet finished his film — towards the front. From here both film and score speed up, the music becomes increasingly tense and military (trumpet calls and the beat of timpani reflecting both march and heart rhythms), until all concludes with explosions and bullets followed by a hopeful ceremonial fanfare as Meredith scampers across the beach to do battle.

A Letter from Ulster, directed by Brian Desmond Hurst for Crown, was also aimed principally at American servicemen, and similarly assembles an unconnected series of scenes. On this occasion they are held together by the loose framework of two GI brothers writing home; perhaps "Postcards from Ulster" would have been a more suitable title. The story climaxes with brief tours of three cities. Alwyn's contribution is uncredited, and his opportunity is overall limited to the provision of mood music rather than to structure. Nevertheless, by the use of rubato and complex harmonic changes he could not resist developing one melody as structural device, which, stated first as an amusing little repetitive country-dance theme, receives its an ultimate variation in a fast and often menacing passage accompanying an assault training course, which also — surprisingly — quotes from "Jupiter" in Holst's suite *The Planets*.

A Letter from Ulster could have been an opportunity to exploit Alwyn's familiarity with the Irish folk idiom. However, apart from the traditional "Londonderry Air" to accompany a visit to that city, it has not been possible to identify any other melodies, although one or two undeveloped phrases hint

at the familiar. The score at the conclusion is arranged to allow for the introduction of a wordless tenor and harp, a kind of keening, which against the
evocative sound and pictures of a departing train creates a feeling of nostalgia,
especially when it is taken up by Alwyn's strings as coda. Presumably it is a
director's whim. It is structurally deficient; unreferenced and too late, it would
have worked better if it reflected an earlier mood or scene.

Strand's *Wales: Green Mountain, Black Mountain* (1943) creates a lyrical
mood akin to the conclusion of *A Letter from Ulster* by starting and ending in
a similar way — with tenor accompanied by harp and flute. Directed by John
Eldridge, and scripted and produced by Dylan Thomas, the film is ostensibly
a depiction of the contrast between the green farming fields and the black min-
ing villages. With Thomas's script and bleak library shots of dole queues and
worn faces, it became a passionate protest against unemployment and poverty:
the script was initially rejected by the MoI censors as unsuitable for foreign audiences.[12] Nevertheless, while its pictures and a hauntingly poetic script never
fail to move, to modern viewers the soundtrack sounds woefully inadequate.
With mobile sound recording still in a cumbrous infancy, many non-fiction
films of the 1940s were deficient in sound-effects — often they had none at all
— and neither critics nor general public passed comment. Yet *Wales: Green
Mountain, Black Mountain* cries out for effects, especially over script-lines like
"the singing in the chapels is never grim or grey". Sadly, apart from the opening and closing sequences already mentioned, the film owns only one short
passage of effects — a dubbed-on choir — and one sequence of original music track. This underscore lasts no longer than a minute, and beautiful it is.
"Wales is a mountain of strength", declaims the commentary, and it is Alwyn's
opportunity for a simple lyrical flute solo accompanied by harp over views of
the countryside, joined after some 40 seconds by Thomas's euphonious script:
"And in the north the farmer drives his sheep over the wind-blown heights."
Script, pictures, and music should have fused into a memorable sequence.
Alas! insensitive dubbing-down of the music track and the irritatingly harsh
voice of the reader steal the poetry. Poetry would have to wait a year, until
Thomas, Eldridge, and Alwyn collaborated in one of the great documentaries
of the war, *Our Country* (1945).

[12] John Ackerman (ed.), *Dylan Thomas: The Filmscripts* (London: Dent, 1995), pp. xiv, 25–7.

8
Ordinary People
▆▆▆▆▆▆▆▆▆▆▆▆▆▆▆▆▆▆▆▆▆▆▆▆▆▆▆▆

(O)UR *Country* is a documentary masterpiece, and one curiously neglected: an alchemy of moving poetic commentary by Dylan Thomas, captivating photography by Jo Jago, and painstakingly apt, lyrical musical composition by Alwyn. Its celebration of landscape and countryside, of industry and labour, and of the spirit of the people is a model of inspirational propaganda. "*Our Country*", writes John Ackerman, "has a pastoralism that is both refuge and touchstone of innocence and joy, in contrast to war's constant present and threat."[1] Alwyn put it more simply: "*Our Country* — most lovely of wartime documentaries."[2] Directed by the talented John Eldridge, originally for distribution within the USSR and the USA, it was one of the last of Donald Taylor's productions for Strand and the fulfilment of his ideal. It was, he said, to enable people "to see on the screen the fine part their native land is playing in helping to win the war" and to "make people all over the world . . . appreciate for what we are fighting".[3]

It was widely released in the United Kingdom, with premieres at two London West End cinemas,[4] and it aroused fierce opinions. While some saw the film as "boldly experimental . . . exciting and provocative",[5] others regarded Thomas's poetry as a "monotonous . . . barrier between spectator and screen".[6] Whatever one's view of the film's achievement, it was unique to its medium — the co-operative creative product of artists from diverse fields.

A documentary in the genuine Grierson tradition of ennobling the ordinary lives of working men and women, *Our Country* narrates an impressionistic journey across wartime Britain taken by a merchant seaman on leave after an absence of two years and seeing as if through the eyes of a foreigner. The actors were non-professional. David Sime, the merchant seaman, returned to active service after making the film. His girlfriend was played with conviction by seventeen-year-old Molly Staniland after Eldridge spotted her in a Sheffield

---

[1] Ackerman, *Dylan Thomas: The Filmscripts*, 67.

[2] Alwyn, "Ariel to Miranda", 55.

[3] Ackerman, *Dylan Thomas: The Filmscripts*, 63. His reference to *Kinematograph Weekly*, 281:1736 (25 July 1940), 21 is incorrect.

[4] The British premier was in June 1945, but the film was classified by the British Board of Film Censors in October 1944.

[5] Edgar Anstey, in *The Spectator* (19 June 1945), 594.

[6] *The Times*, undated clipping in BFI Microjacket.

street. An ordinary chap, and an ordinary girl, with whom audiences could easily identify.

The actors did not speak, however, for in place of dialogue was what Alwyn called "the verbal rattle and poetic fervour" of Thomas's commentary. "'But who is to speak it?' 'Dylan, himself!'" suggested Alwyn, "'He has the loveliest voice I know.'"[7] In the end it was left to professionals. After the irritatingly dry voices of *Wales: Green Mountain, Black Mountain*, Stephen Murray's reading of the main commentary was a positive choice. The girl's voice-over was read movingly by Terry Randal, best remembered for a minor role in *Millions like Us* (1943).

Our Country has an appearance of transparency and simplicity. This it achieves by the clarity of its structure, and importantly by Thomas's non-didactic verse commentary and Alwyn's musical commentary. Recalling the distinction between "observational" and "participatory" films drawn in the discussion of *Desert Victory*, *Our Country* is a "participatory" film. But although participatory, it makes subtle comment through a complex artifice of both text and texture. One may make an analogy with a tapestry: the parts, shot by shot, sequence by sequence, music, effects, and words, are composed into a beautifully proportioned whole, so that in retrospect it is the overall shape one remembers rather than the detail. Alwyn was adamant that in his film music his sole consideration was the place of the underscore within the structure of the film, the music not to be prised from a finely crafted work of art. Similarly, Thomas allowed his verse to be cut for *Our Country*'s artistic end, and thereby destroyed its continuity as pure verse.

Alwyn's music connects, enhances, and comments, is full of contrasts and dramatic strokes. Yet because to Alwyn the artistic fusing of image and sound is pre-eminent, and because of the variety of moods and images in this film, musical themes are developed and neglected, forgotten, recalled later in passing . . . Hubert Clifford, as composer, understood this. After praising the "wonderfully plastic score", he doubted

> whether any of this music of William Alwyn would make coherent sense if performed apart from the film, but this is probably an index of its proper excellence. The motivation of the music comes from the film and not, as in the case of absolute music, from within itself. Heard with the film, it always seems natural, unforced and fluent — a model of accurate timing, combining appropriate character with musical flexibility.[8]

There is a natural movement in *Our Country*'s shape. From its introduction it progresses to London and Dover as heritage and defence of the nation, and

---

[7] Alwyn, "Ariel to Miranda", 55.
[8] Hubert Clifford, "Music from the Films", *Tempo* 13 (Dec. 1945), 11.

passes through Britain's agricultural base to her industrial base. Its climax is shown in human terms, the sailor seeking out his girlfriend who recounts her suffering on the home front. Finally, in anti-climax, the action gently moves back among working men, to the sea.

As the film ends with the sea, so it begins: a natural framing device for the adventures of a seaman on leave, perhaps, but also emphasising the self-containment of the island nation. The film's introduction by actor Burgess Meredith to the American audience is retained in the home edition, no doubt to induce a sense of pride in showing off "our country" to the American allies. Even before Meredith finishes setting the scene, the pictures cut away with dark strings and fanfare to a rough sea, suggesting danger from the enemy, danger faced by our sailor. The presence of war is constant background, insinuating a peace-loving nation determined to fight for what it loves.[9] It is reinforced by another sub-text, the theme of "the beckoning sea", as if the sailor is observer only, impatient to return to ship. In these early sea shots swirling water is suggested by harp *arpeggio*s, but moving up the Clyde to Glasgow's docks, shot by shot, pictures and music gradually resolve and calm, the harp ebbing to a pleasing ripple, until, with strings in unison, we gently dock — safe harbour. Hand in hand, editor Jack Ellitt and composer Alwyn draw the audience into the narrative. Throughout this calming navigation into port the waters are busy with ships; what these home waters mean to the nation at war must never be forgotten. In the middle of the sequence sudden trumpets proudly announce a battleship sailing into sight. The music calms as the shot changes to a frigate moving across the frame, but momentarily sparks again, excitedly, as the same or another battleship is revealed behind the frigate. This is meticulous scoring, pointing up and informing its audience's precise emotional reaction to images within the frame.

The sailor disembarks, and the score, timpani and basses and cellos, soon joined by the bassoon, clarinets, horns, and trumpets, mocks in friendly semi-humorous vein the regular pace of sea-legs on dry land as he makes his way to the seamen's club. Inside, Meredith in voice-over shouts "Hey sailor! Show the folks around will you?" The sailor looks up and nods into the camera lens. It is one of the film's mistakes. Where the viewer should be eavesdropper, Meredith's intrusive demand breaks the mood and draws attention to the camera. Fortunately, Meredith's "Good luck!" is his last comment until the final reel.

Freed from the introduction, the sound narrative becomes sewn into the complex tapestry. Often the stitches are Alwyn's, less often the sound-effects of the recordist Harold King, and sometimes snatches of Thomas's imagination pierce the cloth. Each comments in its manner, not didactically but interpretively, seducing the audience with the mood. It is truly participatory cinema.

[9] Ackerman, *Dylan Thomas: The Filmscripts*, 63.

Consider the ensuing sequence. The sailor catches a tram into the city centre, accompanied at first solely by Alwyn's music, initially cascading strings
contrasting with purposeful ascending strings, which finally dominate. A lively
flute joins in, this bright morning; the sailor seats himself, the sunlight flashes
through the tram window, and Alwyn's composition is chirpy and bright, suggesting the pleasure, after two years at sea, of the tram-ride through the Glasgow streets. Thomas's script commences: "To begin with / a city / a fair grey
day / a day as lively and noisy as a close gossip of sparrows", and Alwyn's flute
does service for the unseen sparrows. But, says Thomas, these sparrows are "as
terribly impersonal as a sea cavern full of machines": thus while the composer
maintains the "lively and noisy" surface texture, at a deeper level the poet is
probing the sailor's emotions. Verse and music are not in contradiction, however, but in complement. For Thomas, morning "is driving down from the roofs
of buildings into stone labyrinths and traffic webs", yet it is important that this
darker mood is counterpointed by the "lively" freshness of the start to both day
and adventure, which only the music can suggest.

Quite quickly — a mix, a train, and a wipe held together by Thomas's script —
and the sailor is on Westminster Bridge gazing into the Thames, as the chimes
of Big Ben usurp the harmonies of Alwyn. Thomas continues the story, "the
sound itself of smoke and sailing dust", for which only the dry sound of motor engines will do, while the camera accompanies the sailor along the London pavements. At St Paul's (Plate 5) the verse rests, and a pan down the huge
dome of the cathedral, centre of the nation's spirit "miraculously" saved from
the Blitz, is joined by the grandeur of horns, trombone, and trumpet; the sailor
enters and a gentle solo string quartet, perhaps a nuance too saccharine, accompanies the seaman along the aisle. Half-a-dozen words catch the mood:
"There is peace under one roof". Then the seaman is outside, hurrying down
the cathedral steps and disturbing a flight of pigeons, pointed up by Alwyn's
tremolo flute and harp arpeggios and taken up by Thomas's lines: "and then
birds flying / suddenly easily as though from another country".

Our sailor makes his way to Dover where at the white cliffs Alwyn's inspirational main theme enters, at first accompanied by trilling flute to remind us of
birdsong, then crescendoing:

This sweeping English ceremonial, certainly not used to excess by Alwyn (only
main titles, this sequence, and end titles), is entirely appropriate to the emotive

5 Propaganda and the national spirit. *Our Country* (1945), described by Alwyn as "most lovely of wartime documentaries", achieved a unique unison of image and sound through the direction of John Eldridge, the photography of Jo Jago, the words of Dylan Thomas, and the music of William Alwyn.

Dover cliffs. Just as Thomas seized on the flying pigeons at St Paul's to remind us of England's frail vulnerability to invasion, so here "the shape of another country lies so near / the wind on Dover cliffs could touch it with its finger". But while Thomas continues the imagery of the white cliffs, the pictures change to the seaman playing with dogs on the beach and distract from the meaning of the verse. Here Alwyn subtly merges the dichroism of pictures and words, dimming the ceremonial to a lesser theme, which catches up with the verse as the sailor strides inland. A strange, almost surreal sequence follows, as the sailor walks across the Kentish Weald accompanied by tanks ("the armoured floods"), and past aircraft standing ready. The mood hovers between an in-nocent country stroll, suggested by light strings and woodwind, and the raw ostinato phrases resonant of the motion of the trundling tanks or a low-flying plane. It is music's turn, now, to suggest the threat from beyond the Channel.

The pastoral scenes that follow utilise the imagery and sound of the ru-ral myth — musical themes, for example, drawing upon the rhythms of the country-dance. Sometimes these musical sequences adopt a ternary form, albeit with the freedom of the film medium. Travelling inland through the Weald of Kent, the seaman joins sunshine-dappled apple-picking in the company of a pretty girl and a graceful slow-measured country-dance. Taking up the three-movement form, the orchestra commences with full strings, developed and varied with woodwind and harp, until, as airmen arrive to chat, the music changes to an uneasy second section. As the dance begins to recapitulate in a third movement, the roar of overhead engines distracts the pickers and silences the music altogether. Again, the images of war have intruded to recall that what is loved must be protected . . . It is time to move on, however, and a Pied-Piper-like flute solo leads to the hop-pickers and a country-dance tune almost worthy of Percy Grainger:

Again a ternary form: a brief first movement of the dance calms to a second movement as the sailor wearily sits against a wall, and a hop-picker takes pity and darns the heel of his sock. A long third movement, the recapitulation, follows as the revived sailor joins in the gathering of the hop flowers.

The next sequence also suggests the three-movement form, commencing with a lively trotting theme as a fenland farmer gives the sailor a lift on his pony and trap. But a following fast dance, accompanying hay loading, lacks any development of the form. Here, the music of "the rejoicing land" gives way to dark chords and the music falls silent as a plane drops to a death in the fields. Innocence, war, and innocence . . . the film relentlessly pursues the mixture: for, as the sailor joins the harvesters at table, variations on "Sir Roger de Coverly" (traditional) strike up — how Alwyn rings the changes! The sailor entertains, too, in his own way, on his mouth organ, and a genuine, diegetic country-dance follows.

The joy and freedom of birdsong are frequently suggested in the musical harmonies of these pastoral sequences, usually by the flute, and, as at dawn a lorry carries the sailor through sleepy villages, Alwyn recalls the birdsong in the Glasgow tram. This is impressionistic music, without strong melody, but the harmonies and rhythms suggestive of the movement of the lorry and, subsequently, a busy market day in a country town. Appropriately a harp accompanies us to the sweeping hills of Wales, accompanied at first by solo horn and flute, then by violin, and the nation's children are discovered in a Welsh classroom.

References to industrial Britain thicken the scenario and the texture of the film. As the camera pans across the rooftops of rows of tiny terraced houses in the Rhondda Valley, a gentle, sentimental violin theme introduces the second major theme of the film, which will be recognised later as the love motif of the seaman's girlfriend. Here it unites the gloomy Welsh streets with the grey terrace where the girl lives, overlooking the factories of Sheffield. Alwyn's fellow composer Hubert Clifford recognised his "attempt at thematic co-ordination, but", added Clifford,

> I feel sure that he intends this as a nucleus or a scaffolding around which the musical invention takes place — a stylistic discipline in fact — rather than for its effect upon the audience. The impact upon the cinema-goer of the schematic use of a musical subject is negligible unless the subject is "plugged" under conditions which allow the primary attention of the audience to be focused upon the music.[10]

But Alwyn knew what Clifford did not — the cinema audience's unconscious absorption of musical themes.

After Wales, another impressionistic journey by coach to Sheffield. Here "the clamorous galleries and metalscapes of mechanical night" are emphasised by ponderous ostinato strings, counterpointed by gongs and cymbals matching fearsome showers of sparks and timpani the beats of monstrous hammers. At this armaments works (another reminder of Britain at war), and to the roar of the machinery, the sailor visits his girl at her workbench, "who is there because she is your girl or mine (and therefore in this film, the sailor's . . .)".[11] After clocking off, the girl joins him outside the factory (a delightful long shot, body movement saying everything as the girl takes the sailor's arm), and the light violin theme, heard previously at the Rhondda, returns.

They visit the Regal cinema, where in a clever sound mix (and no doubt with prior arrangement between director, composer, and organist) the Wurlitzer picks up and diegeticises Alwyn's love theme.

Afterwards over tea and a high, thin, sentimental violin, the girl talks about the air raids, which the film now illustrates in a sophisticated exponential flashback ("Night after night, night after night . . ."). The sequence is notable for something else. Dylan Thomas's text for the male voice-over has been of the observer, speaking in the third person, "a man". It is shocking, now, to hear the female voice-over as participant, in the first person: "This is the end of the world I would say to myself."

Only natural sound-effects could be appropriate to the scene of the girl running home to the sound of an air raid warning, and the camera's observation

---

[10] Clifford, "Music from the Films", 24. Clifford's italics.
[11] "Two Views on *Our Country*", unsigned, *DNL* 5:4 (1944): 46.

of the minutiae of her sheltering with her parents. Outside the sounds of guns and bombs, inside the fear of death in the dark: "This is the end of the world". But with the light of the morning the love theme returns on a poignant solo violin, with passing references to the main theme and a military bugle suggesting an unconquerable spirit, and the girl rejoices in being alive and in love . . . The scene returns to the present meeting with her sailor friend, and, after a visit to the local palais, the plaintive melody is heard in full during a walk home in the dark (no raids tonight!) beneath the pylons and bill-hoardings, and a farewell kiss at the gate.

That farewell is a climax, like the climax of a fiction feature film. Not long ago the sailor had his arm round the girl in their cinema seats — there, perhaps, they saw a romantic scene not unlike the one they are now acting out. But like an image multiplied in two facing mirrors, they themselves are being watched in a real cinema by a real audience — encouraged to identify with this screen couple by their ordinariness in ordinary locations ("your girl or mine"). Importantly, the emotions of this real audience are informed by the screen music which conveys a deep yearning, a high romanticism. It is the romantic love music of the "big feature" — almost a pastiche — and it elevates to the big feature the loves and wartime separations of the ordinary picturegoing man and woman: they themselves become the "stars". Consequently the sequence, served vitally by its music in its blurring of reality and illusion, is a fascinating web of patriotic cinema, propagandist cinema, and social cinema.

Moreover, music not only informs the emotions of this boy–girl sequence but also supplies a structure. In the concert hall one might look for a structure such as, for example, a sonata. In the cinema we can discover four movements too, and although beyond that the comparison more or less ceases, the sense of artistic form is as satisfying. The scene of the boy and girl sharing a visit to the pictures represents a statement (A). The flashback including its sound-effects and morning-after-the-raid music represents a contrasting second movement (B), while the diegetic dance-hall scene, which adds substance and universality to the sequence, is a third movement (C). The farewell scene is a recapitulation of the first (A). The girl is left behind, and a rail journey to Scotland follows, a sequence of signals, tracks, passing views, and rushing trains. It is cut confusingly across the continuity of the visual movement, but that does not seem to matter because of its loving choreography in sound, to the extent that another sense is implicated, and one can almost smell the soot. After the climactic love scene, this sequence serves to release sexual tension, gradually calming to anticlimax as the sailor enters the Scottish mountains and joins a lumber camp.

Here Alwyn does not match the cut of the axe, for the sequence is impressionistic — not only of the romanticism of the forest, lyrical woodwinds and harp, but in anticipation of a return to the sea, a feeling of tired resolution imparted by the slowing, fading notes of a horn:

There is an exception: just once image, words, and music join on the fall of a tree, to remind the sailor of the "end of the journey / commanding your coming back / behind each fated tree".

Amongst the tree fellers a jazz band has fun, a reminder of the importance to this film of home-made music. The audience has watched a harvest dance, joined a pub singer and a Welsh choir, been taken to the cinema and the dance floor. Now it taps its feet to jazz. The seaman's mouth organ, too, has been a symbol of community, and as he leaves the forest on a log trailer he plays again. In home-front films, both documentaries and features, communal leisure activities are common, valued as "images of national cohesion among citizens whose loves and lives run close to those of the audience".[12] Moreover, they have been invaluable both as punctuation and as a way of imparting reality to a film that otherwise would have portrayed life at a step distant by underscore and non-synch effects.

The film draws to its end. A triumph of British achievement, the Forth Bridge is introduced by a stately fanfare, followed by ascending and descending brass and harp, suggesting the flow of water. Then "to end with a quayside / a fair grey day", and later, "to end with / the faces of fishermen", flute and woodwind with dancing ostinato strings, joined by a fleeting reminder of the hop-pickers' dance, as the fishermen spin a yarn, drink, smoke, and laugh. A cadenza recollects some of the themes of the film, then all calms as we cut to the coastline and ships, and a memory of the love theme climaxes swiftly to trumpet cry and a crescendo of strings as a seagull skims from the heaving waves into the sky. The music grows terse, aggressive, and triumphant as a caption "June 6th 1944" over a flotilla recalls the valiant seamen of D-Day. A triumphant coda based on the main theme concludes as a seaman climbs the rigging, porpoises plunge through surging waves, and, in salt-sprayed close-up, our sailor looks out to sea . . .

Alwyn and Thomas made no further films together. But in 1955 Alwyn recalled their friendship:

> I can see him with his jaunty walk, a cloth cap pulled to one side of his fresh round face — a pop-eyed baby with cherubic lips. He burbled happily; strings of lovely phrases rolling glibly off his tongue, phrases with a salty relish, bawdy and beautiful and rich with impromptu witticisms — he could no more resist words than Mr Polly. The village came alive and each lace-curtained cottage window concealed a new identity — a Milk Wood populated by a living caste [*sic*].[13]

---

[12] Lant, *Blackout*, 43.

[13] Alwyn, "Ariel to Miranda", 55.

At about this time, Alwyn set to work on a new film for Frank Sainsbury, with whom he had previously worked on *New Worlds for Old* and *Living with Strangers*. Now, with *Atlantic Trawler* (1944) he discovered a subject with an affinity to *Our Country*, both in its treatment in the documentary tradition, and in its subject of the life of seamen on shore. However, his musical treatment was very different.

Films about fishing boats were no rarity in the documentary movement, but this affectionate depiction of a crew on both active service and shore leave had unusual elements. One was the jokiness of the crew, which Alwyn reflected in a joky score. In search of fish, the ship moves south, "South" giving Alwyn the opportunity for a jest of a slow syncopated calypso-style theme, marked *allegretto semplice* and played on the vibraphone and with wood sticks on muffled timpani. It anticipates his "Calypso" for *The Rake's Progress*. Later, a seaman puts small pieces of coal into the skipper's boot, to which the clarinet and oboe are accomplices in a short scherzando figure. The captain's subsequent wobbly lurch at an angle along the deck is in lovely rhythm to the returned calypso. Later still, a good catch leads to a witty and ingeniously scored sequence of contrasting piccolo, xylophone, triangle, and staccato and tremolo strings, as the fish are sorted and gutted.

Home is never long forgotten, and a plaintive oboe accompanies pictures of the trawlermen's wives collecting the pay, shopping, and pushing prams. But neither is humour long absent, and *spiccato* strings usher us back to sea in a sea-shanty fiddle theme as the men mend their nets. As shore leave approaches the men are increasingly cheerful. A crew member sings "I've Got a Lovely Bunch of Coconuts" (1944) — the latest popular song, so new that he gets the words wrong — and Alwyn wittily picks up the theme on clarinet and develops it for the final preparations.

"Two weeks at sea, two days ashore . . ." The *Documentary News Letter* called this "the first true picture of the trawlermen ashore; this sequence is one of the nicest jobs seen in a short documentary for some time".[14] It is structured largely by the musical device of alternation between a "jaunty" and a slow nostalgic theme. The syncopated "jaunty" tune is of the same family as a Scottish march in *On Approval*, written about this time; its use of coconuts in a "clip-clop" rhythm make it suitable for a horse and carriage, though none appears. The slow sentimental theme was heard earlier behind scenes of Grimsby town. The contrast is both amusing and poignant: a crewman with his wife and son sit contented in their own company on a park bench (slow theme); a crewman with bottle in pocket exits a pub to greet his colleagues (jaunty theme); a wife inveigles her husband into a cinema and a couple at the seafront gaze at a passing trawler (slow theme); a short visit to the snooker hall (jaunty theme)

---

[14] Unsigned in *DNL* 3 (1944): 29.

is followed by a scene of the skipper at home playing cards with his family, and moves to the lighthouse and seashore at dusk (slow theme). The calypso-like theme returns to show the skipper leaving for sea next morning. It is an optimistic "all in a day's work" ending, which is rendered the more poignant by the closing titles: "The steam trawler HONDO on which this film was made went back to sea with a different crew. She was lost with all hands. THE END."

While the fate of British servicemen had to be accepted, their contribution was not to be undervalued. Few British wartime films portray more convincingly the sense of confinement and the dogged endurance of both servicemen and civilians than *There's a Future in It* (1944). Some of its authenticity derives from its obviously rationed budget and a terse supporting length of 43 minutes. Scripted by H. E. Bates from his own short story, it was produced and directed towards the end of 1943 for the MoI and Strand by Leslie Fenton, a British-born director of American B-movies.

This simple tribute to men of the Bomber Command tells of Kitty (Ann Dvorak) anxiously awaiting the return of her boyfriend pilot Johnny O'Connor (Barry Morse) from a raid. Kitty's father (John Turnbull), an armchair critic of the Air Force, rebukes her for spending the previous evening with Johnny at the pub, but nevertheless she goes back and finds him returned after a near-fatal trip. There, too, she meets other airmen, real RAF non-professional actors, and a spirit of camaraderie. They have a singsong. Afterwards, alone with Kitty, Johnny confesses his hatred of the war, but justifies his role in it by his greater hatred for the enemy. She returns home to more of her father's criticisms, but looking through her tears to the searchlight-streaked sky from her bedroom window she voices her thoughts, "There's no future except through you. And because of you and those like you . . . The future: God help us to be worthy of it when it comes."

Never mind the technician's head bobbing on the edge of frame in that last shot; never mind Barry Morse's uninvolved playing as Johnny; never mind the cut-price, set-bound, look about this film. Strand's minor quota romance of a pilot and the woman who loves him invites direct comparison with the mighty Two Cities' *The Way to the Stars* (1945). Unquestionably the greater emotional authenticity is to be discovered in *There's a Future in It*. Bates's characters are identifiably "ordinary" people: Kitty living with her mother and father in a suburban street is more likely to be sitting next to you in the cinema than Rattigan's heroines in *The Way to the Stars* — Toddy the hotel owner (Rosamund John) who befriends an American pilot and Iris (Renée Asherson) the mouse-like companion to her caricatured "gorgon" aunt (Joyce Carey). Restricting its action to hours rather than to years helps *There's a Future in It* to explore emotions more thoroughly. Johnny O'Connor's declared hatred for his work is more telling than the inarticulate and stunted emotions of John Mills's Peter

Penrose of *The Way to the Stars*. Ann Dvorak, the American actress, shows
Kitty as confused and frightened and shedding real tears compared with the
dry eyes and concrete upper-lips of the heroines of *The Way to the Stars*.

The broad, emotional *The Way to the Stars* musical theme became popular after the film's release, and even today it has a sentimental edge related to
1940s nostalgia. It is attributed to Nicholas Brodszky, a songwriter who was
unable to score for films and reputedly relied on collaborators to develop his
minuscule sketches — in this case Charles Williams, who receives a conductor's
credit onscreen.[15] It is hardly surprising, therefore, that musically *The Way to
the Stars* should appear unsubtle. Its structure amounts to no more than a couple of appropriate American Army themes, and a predominance of the main
theme applied without modulation to every climactic situation. There is no
suggestion of balancing the relative emotional climate between scenes, leitmotif, action-matching, the dramatic counterpointing of music with silence and
sound-effects, phrasing the drama, enhancing the psychology, rhythmically
structuring the dialogue, the subtleties of orchestration, or any of the other
tools of the skilled film composer.

Each drama gets the musical score it deserves. What *There's a Future in It*
lacks in a memorable melodic theme, it compensates for by painstaking sensitivity to the requirements of the scenario. A few examples must serve. The
musical prologue accompanying the titles conveys the confused emotions of
the players and of the times. It is turbulent and passionate, descending strings
caught up at the end of their cascade by woodwinds and brass, then contrasted
by ascending brass, to descend finally in terse introduction of the first pictures,
planes returning from a mission, where light descending strings and woodwind
mirror the descent of the aircraft. Alwyn takes trouble too, to underpin the dialogue rhythmically. In the crucial conversation between Johnny and Kitty, the
background music reflects and keeps in step with the dialogue, moving from
poignancy to fanfares as Johnny's resolution strengthens.

Scenes of Kitty gazing from her bedroom window are important. Antonia
Lant has focused attention on the concept that the sky in British wartime films
is a "masculine sphere", reinforced by "another, complementary iconography,
this time of home front women looking towards the sky from the land".[16] Kitty's
retreats to her bedroom emphasise not only her apartness from her mother
and father, but her affinity with the sky and the pilot. After her first argument
with her parents she rushes to the bedroom accompanied by a passionate out-

[15] It is rumoured that Brodszky composed only the first four notes of *The Way to the Stars*,
      Williams the rest. See David Ades and Alexander Gleason, case notes to *British Film Music
      from the 1940s and 1950s* (EMI CDGO 2059, 1994). For an insight into Brodszky's technique,
      see Anthony Hopkins, *Beating Time* (London: Michael Joseph, 1982), 132–4.
[16] Lant, *Blackout*, 53. *They Flew Alone*, about a female pilot, is an exception to the rule.

burst on brass and timpani and rising strings, an expression of both the anger and her ascent. The music assumes an ethereal feeling akin to the sky and fly-ing, changing to a compassionate oboe as she opens the curtains and looks at the sky. Later, when Kitty leaves for the pub, her descent on the stairs from the bedroom is emphasised by plucked strings. Her final quarrel with her parents is made all the more shocking by the implication of her response to her moth-er's question, "Is he married, dear?" "Does it matter?" shouts Kitty,[17] fleeing the room to climaxing brass and ascending the staircase in a rush sharply deline-ated by strings — emphasising now, at the final, her closeness to the sky.

In her passionate delivery Kitty sheds real tears, looking up to the night sky where her pilot will be. Compare the end of *The Way to the Stars*, where Toddy stares at the sky too, dry-eyed, accompanied by Brodzsky's main theme and a voice-over recitation of John Pudney's poem "For Johnny" (1941). The emo-tion is a mixture of the nobility of achievement, certainty of the cause, grati-tude to the pilots, the value of the tragedy of sacrifice. In *There's a Future in It* Alwyn's music dims and takes second place to Kitty's thoughts, but after her soliloquy it rises to blend with the sound of an air-raid warning and ends inconclusively, in confusion and uncertainty. The difference reflects the dates. *The Way to the Stars* was filming during the certainty of victory as V-E Day was declared; *There's a Future in It* appeared in the dark winter of 1943–4.

As the war progressed, the number of films depicting "ordinary" people in-creased. It was not unusual for wartime productions to cross the thin lines be-tween documentary, dramatised documentary, and fiction. By mixing a group of non-professionals with real "stars" in a studio setting, *There's a Future in It* is more honest than *Our Country*. There, the sailor is real enough, but the girl is an office-worker pretending to be a factory-worker, a fictional romance is contrived between two "real" people, and the King's English of the professional voice-overs effaces regional dialects.

The Way Ahead, one of the biggest critical and box-office successes of the war, represents the final stage of evolution to fictionalised documentary — scripts acted out entirely by Equity members, but portraying "common" people in "common" situations. "Few films had brought the audience so close to the peo-ple on the screen", wrote C. A. Lejeune,[18] and its veneer of authenticity (for its period) led to its classification as "semi-documentary", although to the picture-goer it looks like a normal feature.

---

[17] We should have expected this. The libretti of songs in wartime films reflect the drama. Thus, Jean Simmons singing "Let Him Go, Let Him Tarry" (1945) in *The Way to the Stars* suggests the relationship between Peter and Iris at a key moment. In *There's a Future in It*, the second of the two pub songs, "I've Got Sixpence" (1941), suggests Johnny had a wife and did not care much for her.

[18] C. A. Lejeune, in *The Observer* (11 June 1944).

It came about in a curious way. In 1943 Carol Reed had been assigned by the Army Kinematograph Service (AKS) to make a film that would help raise morale among new recruits. The result was *The New Lot* (1943), a 42-minute short, made under the supervision of military psychiatrists, about the conversion of a group of raw recruits into a fighting team. But it was for the indoctrination of Army personnel only; the psychiatrists wanted the public at large to see civilians being trained, and Brendan Bracken, the Minister of Information, agreed. Eric Ambler and Peter Ustinov set to work on the script for a longer version, *The Way Ahead*, which opened on D-Day in June 1944. Their carefully packaged propagandist message has layers of meaning. On one level this tenacious little battalion, fighting against the odds, stands for every British battalion of the war. On a deeper level it represents the nation itself. Hence Reed's closing caption "The Beginning?"

The New Lot had been lightly and often amusingly scored by Richard Addinsell; his use of Wagner's "The Ride of the Valkyries" (1870)[19] for an alarming confrontation between the new recruits and a "welcoming" corporal is particularly witty. For *The Way Ahead*, however, Reed turned to William Alwyn.

Two action scenes illustrate both the principle of teamwork and Alwyn's belief in the role of music in the cinema: "sensed and not predominant; predominant but only sensed". Reed decided that these scenes should have the feeling of a newsreel, that its propagandist value would be increased if it looked as realistic as his team could make it. The result is the perfect conception, construction, and integration of music and sound-effects. The sound editor was Harry Miller, with whom Alwyn was to have subsequent happy working relationships.

The first action sequence portrays the battalion setting sail for North Africa. It is night. An atmosphere of anxious calm is carefully built up, starting with the captain on the ship's bridge: "Jerry's around again . . ." A cut to below decks: here too, all is quiet. A long tracking shot shows the men in their hammocks, some sleeping, most staring thoughtfully about them or at the ceiling; we feel their anxiety. Brewer (Stanley Holloway), a stoker in civilian life, is in the engine room silently watching, with professional interest, the ship's stokers. Quietly he rejoins his colleagues, exchanges a few quiet words to Lieutenant Perry (David Niven) as he leaves ("Good evening, sir"), and turns to speak to a colleague: "I've been down —". An explosion rocks the ship, and the score bursts in simultaneously and shockingly, for the audience has been lulled by the preceding calm. The underscore continues excitedly as the panicked men grab rifles and lifebelts. Perry re-enters and gives the order: "Stand still!" The music ceases, and in the sudden silence calm is restored as the men stand to attention. "Now," resumes Perry, "walk to your boat stations . . ." The sentiment here — stressed

<hr/>

[19] From *The Valkyrie* (*Die Walküre*), the second of Wagner's *Ring* cycle (*Der Ring des Nibelungen*).

by an absence of music — is of control, authority, and trustworthiness, in which (by extension) the British military command itself participates.

As the platoon makes its way to the decks, an alarm bell adds an edge of tension. On deck the scene is what looks like confusion — carried initially by the sound-effects: a jumble of sirens, hose sounds, scrambling, the fire, bells, shouting, whistles, and loud-hailer commands. It is more gripping than *Fires Were Started*. A cargo of Bren carriers and trucks is shifting, and the crew needs help. Perry turns to his men: "Leave your rifles here! Follow me!" and, as the men race along the decks, Alwyn's score surges in. A midshipman (Trevor Howard) gives precise orders: "Lose as much weight as possible from this side of the ship. Start with this transport . . ." While he speaks, the orchestra rumbles ominously beneath the effects. I doubt if it is consciously audible to one person in a million, but it turns the stomach, a portent: sensed and not predominant; predominant but only sensed.

The troops heave the blazing vehicles over the ship's side to splash one by one into the sea. The music, largely violins and trilling flutes, is perfectly balanced beneath the effects and shouted orders, both stressing the menace of the situation and providing a constant gluing-together of the changing shots. Soon, repeated again and again as the vehicles are cast into the sea, there emerges a repetitive "pomp and circumstance" theme. The score encompasses the moods of both local heroism and the greater national glory.

The excitement never lets up, continually shifts the centre of action. Now the call comes: ". . . Can't hold it much longer . . ." to a lengthy string pedal point, a version of the sequencing in *Desert Victory*. Then the call: "The fire's out of control . . .", and the strings sustain the tension on the pedal point. Finally: "Abandon ship!" and the tension snaps precisely on a shot change and a simultaneous klaxon and the crash of music. The dramatic tension owes a huge debt to the musical composition.

Tension stays to the end of the fire sequence. The action changes to crosscutting between troops abandoning ship by clambering up nets on the side of a rescuing destroyer, and the lower hold where Perry and Private Luke (John Laurie) struggle to save Sergeant Fletcher (William Hartnell) whose leg is trapped beneath a hatch cover. Above decks, the dizzying height of the nets linking the ships is emphasised by sharp cymbal clashes against quick cuts as waves crash in the gap between. Below decks Alwyn re-introduces the ceremonial phrase until — as the two men struggle with a pulley to raise the hatch cover and free Fletcher's leg — the arrival again of a stretch of tremolo strings. As they heave on the tackle their muscle tension is reflected by a timpani roll, sustained against rising orchestral chords. Then, a pause which fits precisely to a cut above decks and megaphone instruction: "How many more are there? Time we were leaving", and intensifies the tension. The chords rise again, and "Right!" — both leg and tension are released, and the men escape to a triumphal crescendo of brass and strings. Evoking the Dunkirk spirit, a defeat becomes a national triumph.

The newsreel style of authenticity Reed aimed for is as evident in the second action scene: the battle in the desert. Here tension is built by an alternating rhythm of climax and anticlimax, incorporating a complex pattern of sound and music. The action opens at night, the troops gazing anxiously across the sands, listening to the distant sounds of battle. Their comments are hushed. There is no music, and shortly afterwards even the battle clamour ceases. The ensuing quiet sets up a real tension, just as in the below decks sequence preceding the ship's fire. Perry's reassuring leadership is again felt. "All right here?" he murmurs as he enters the trench. (Compare his walk among the hammocks in the ship). "Yes, sir", come the replies. There follows a series of close-ups of the men staring at the silent, dark, desert.

Perry fires a flare, and the second movement commences. The flare exposes advancing German troops. With a percussion-like rhythm the British open fire, and the enemy retreats. "I say, corporal", murmurs somebody. "Quiet, Vic", comes the reply.

The third movement. The troops continue on guard, and Alwyn gently introduces a light wistful score, which smoothes an optical mix to daylight. Tension is partially relaxed as tired soldiers share a drink and a cigarette. A shell whistles close by and is followed by a cacophony of bursting shells swamping the music beneath — cymbals, brass, full orchestra. The shelling ceases, the enemy sets a smoke screen, and the score ends on a trill that ceases unresolved and precisely on the cry: "Watch your front! Watch your front!" It is perfect punctuation — maintaining pace even as the track quietens — until the creak of caterpillar tracks signals enemy tanks approaching under cover of the smoke. The order comes: "Fire!" The orchestra rushes in beneath the roar of the guns, and the enemy retreats.

In these two examples is the perfect expression of Alwyn's analogy of the circus ring's musical drama,[20] the careful punctuation of music with effects and silence — even to the timpani roll (compare with the circus drum roll) as Fletcher's leg is freed in the ship's hold.

Alwyn would have been proud of C. A. Lejeune's notice: "A glorious film score by William Alwyn has been worked into the final phase of the picture as a part of the integral pattern. I cannot remember, since *The River* [Pare Lorentz, 1937], experiencing sound and image on the screen more highly wedded."[21] It recognised his ideal: the integration of image, effects, and music, the creative achievement of team co-operation.

---

[20] Quoted in the Introduction.
[21] Lejeune, in *The Observer* (11 June 1944).

9
The Success of the Season

A ROUND the time he was working on *The Way Ahead* Alwyn was also composing for *On Approval*, an adaptation of Frederick Lonsdale's 1920s drawing-room classic. The two films could not have been more different in mood.

On Approval was set up by the actor Clive Brook and produced by Sydney Box, for whose thriving documentary company, Verity Films, Alwyn had contributed several scores. It was Box's first feature and its production was cluttered with mishaps[1] culminating in the front office shelving it, convinced it was unshowable. A few months later Brook retrieved it from the shelf, spent three weeks reshooting at his own expense, cut it around, and added a prologue. The result was the success of the season.

On Approval was one of a series of escapist entertainments, a reflection of the public's war weariness. It is a tale about a near penniless gentleman Richard (Roland Culver) and an American heiress Maria (Beatrice Lillie) who settle for a month's trial marriage in a Scottish castle, joined by their colleagues Helen (Googie Withers) and George, the Duke of Bristol (Clive Brook). Lonsdale's original drama had been set in 1927, but Brook, scripting with Terence Young, moved the action back to the "Naughty Nineties". Whatever the mood of Lonsdale's original play, Brook's considerably revised film version was a mixture of cynical romance, humour, and faintly Wildean wit. It is a mood well served by Alwyn's flexible score. Mood is set at the very start of the titles with a staccato four-note horn fanfare:

It sounds like the chimes of a church clock or Big Ben. The rhythm is right, but the proper note sequence is *C g' a' e'*. The little melody is therefore humorously flattened off-key and prepares the audience for farce. Continuing *vivace*, the score leaps into a short and breathlessly vigorous polka. Further evocation of period and mood is introduced with a change of pace to a leisurely Viennese waltz. Its immediate repetition increasingly relaxes its audience, confirming its anticipation of escape from an anxious present into the comfort of a golden age.

[1] Entertainingly documented in William MacQuitty, *A Life to Remember* (London: Quartet, 1991), 277–86.

The shock is the greater, therefore, of a sudden cut to contemporary news-reel war shots of aircraft guns rattling, explosions, ships' guns, bombs, and general battle mayhem. For the audience of 1944, the pictures must have been depressing. The music starts loudly — newsreel battle style, second nature to Alwyn after his documentary work — but barely distinguishable, after a couple of seconds, beneath the roar of explosions and gunfire. Suddenly all turns to laughter as E. V. H. Emmett, a familiar Gaumont British News voice of the period, sighs: "Oh dear, is this another war picture? . . ." Brook evidently decided, rightly, that if his original ballroom scene were too slow an opening, this exciting prologue would most certainly grab his audience's attention.

"Let's go back to the quiet and peaceful time before this war . . .", adds Emmett. There follows an interesting curtain-raiser compiled from short sequences of stock, newsreel, and studio-shots knitted together with natural sound and music, and a droll commentary, characteristic of its time, in the style of ministry propaganda shorts and the facetious photo-captions in the popular *Lilliput* magazine.

A study of the four-minute sequence reveals a subtlety in the sound track reflecting decisions that were certainly not random or light, and would have involved close co-operation between director, music director, composer, and sound editor. The ringing of so many changes within such a short time span is an event that — with the blessing of a commentary — offers the good fortune to examine them in chart form (see opposite).

This is the feature film soundtrack in miniature, and is representative of the tracks of the 1940s: a time-consuming, almost loving concern with detail. The makers of cheap factual films would have been tempted to wash the whole sequence with a bland music track. But for these feature craftsmen, every foot of track served a purpose. Note, for example, scenes 5 and 11–12, where the absence of music emphasised its use in the neighbouring scenes, a device upon which Alwyn often laid emphasis.

The film as a whole is an amalgam of musical devices, often humorous and foreshadowing Alwyn's later films. Unusually, it lacks any overall leitmotif: indeed Alwyn makes only one concession to the device, a waltz associated with the romance between George and Helen. As Helen lingers at night by a fountain in the Duke's garden, she hums the melody in the hope of attracting George to marriage. Later, as piano music drifts through an open window in a similar setting, she turns him down and asks: "Do you remember this music?" His reply, "I've heard it so many times before . . .", reveals his thoughtlessness. Its third use is non-diegetic, as Helen sitting at the foot of a wide staircase makes her final refusal of George. There is a visual prompting here as she walks away up the staircase leaving him dejectedly behind. In all three scenes the romance fails, and the music is a mocking counterpoint to the dialogue rather than an emotional reinforcement.

	Commentary	Shots	Music/effects	Suggested motive for music or effects used
1	Oh dear, is this another war picture? Let's go back to the quiet and peaceful time before this war . . .	Battle pictures: in the air, at sea, on land (the three services).	Newsreel style action music mixed with, and after first 2–3 seconds dominated by, loud battle effects	1. Shock of battle scenes in contrast to preceding period waltz. 2. Set-up for humorous comment, and to point-up peaceful pre-war scenes.
2	So this is peace. So these are the tranquil days of 1939. Yes, for this is the age of speed and noise so much like war you'd hardly notice the difference.	Sports activities: motor-cycle racing, car racing, water-skiing, dirt-track racing: all concluding in accident.	(Loud effects). Engines roar. Crowd cheering.	Compares with loud battle effects. Excuse to move later to more detached, "peaceful", dignified – and even earlier – historic period.
	This is the day of athletic sports of all kinds	Men in night-shirts in comic "kitten and bed" race.		
3	This is the day of devotion to the graceful art of dancing . . .	Bebop dancers.	Loud bebop music.	Ditto – lack of calm.
4	This is the day of the worship of the beautiful wide-open spaces.	The countryside and open road. Track into large buttocks of walkers in shorts. Littered field.	Bebop continues.	Ditto – lack of calm.

	Commentary	Shots	Music/effects	Suggested motive for music or effects used
	And for giving thanks for all the blessings of the green and lovely countryside. This is 1939.			
5	No, this isn't what we want either . . . . . . although it's very pleasant.	Couple on motor-cycle, wind blows back woman's skirt to reveal . . . . . . shapely leg in stockings with suspenders. Frame freezes.	Roar of motor-cycle, quick fade to . . . . . . mute on freeze.	1. Ditto. 2. Silence emphasises the freeze (like a still picture) and points up the "humorous" lasciviousness of the commentary. Viewer allowed time to ruminate on shot of leg (sound forgotten for brief moment!). 3. A break between noisy scenes 1–4 and scene 6, allowing a smooth transition to the calm period music. Scene 5 breaks the argument of the commentary and appears to have been inserted mainly for this purpose.
6	Let's go back further still to grandmama's day. Don't you think it was so much nicer, so much more stately and dignified? Lazy days and gentle evenings undisturbed by any . . .	Grandmother's day: boating scene, croquet scene.	Barcarole: period "Palm Court" music.	Calm

	Commentary	Visuals	Sound	Notes
7	. . . harsh note of reality.	Baritone singing to piano accompaniment: as he reaches low note vase of flowers breaks, picture falls off wall.	Actuality of singing: "Beware!"[a]	Broad humour: raises another laugh. Suggestion that grandmother's day is old-fashioned — and silly.
8	Yes, these were the days. Grandmama knew that her place was in the home although grandpapa could go in for a stern life of dangerous sport. Women were women and they didn't forget it. And when they had finished their embroidery and needed a fill of excitement they could always unpick it and start again. While their menfolk roved abroad. Aweel! Aweel! And you needn't think that they never had their moments. A young man was more or less expected to sow his wild oats . . .	Shot of mother embroidering intercut with various poses (as in photographic studio) of man at his "work": cricket, football, cycling. Woman stands on table while young man drinks from her slipper.	Barcarole.	Wistful nostalgia.

[a] The refrain from Henry W. Petre's "Asleep in the Deep" (1897), where the baritone descends to a very low note as he repeats the word "Beware!"

	Commentary	Shots	Music/effects	Suggested motive for music or effects used
	. . . always provided there was no harvest.	Photographic studio picture of man with two babies.	Horns *cuivré* at "harvest" in commentary.	Mockingly points up humour.
9	But a young lady knew nothing of that. She lived in a world apart in a day of true romance.	Woman and man romantically posed on park bench.	("Palm court" music continues).	
	A never to be forgotten moment in a young girl's life.		Woman hiccups.	Natural sound — humour.
10	So different from modern times. Before the times of petrol rationing young moderns looked on the motor car as a most useful invention.	Modern times: kissing in open sports cars at secluded country spot.	Jazz: loud saxophone.	Sexy, steamy.
11	It's hard to believe that the biggest thrill a Victorian girl got out of a carriage was this . . .	Passing of carriage in park. Man at side of road raises hat. Chaperoned maiden in carriage gives light, guilty, acknowledgement.	Hooves and carriage springs. (Not even a hint of birdsong).	Cold feeling in contrast to sexy jazz of 10. Even the palm court music would have bestowed too much romanticism on this scene.
	You can't get into much trouble doing that.	Carriage trots away and into distance.		

12	Very little remains undiscovered about the modern girl. You can see she is beautiful. You know she is no fool. But there used to be a song, "Be good sweet maid and let who will be clever".	Modern girls in bathing suit competition at poolside.	Applause effects.	1. Voyeurism under guise of reasoned comment and observation. FX are objective and neutral (music would have imposed emotion) 2. Another buffer before returning to period music.
13	But she was clever enough to be good. And the result, you must admit, was elegant and charming. If she seemed a little shy, it was because as far as the dashing stronger sex were concerned she had to be so modest. She is gowned for the theatre . . .	Maid dresses Victorian woman for the theatre.	"Palm court" music.	Calm elegant period feel.
14	and I wonder what it will be like, that play she was going to see. Would it be dull and stuffy, or would she hide her blushes in the programme? Hm, hm . . . Perhaps we're going to find out just why they were called the "Naughty Nineties". . .	Close-up of programme for *On Approval* and woman's gloved hands on edge of theatre box.	Effects of theatre orchestra tuning. Out of vision woman whispers: "They say it's very modern and terribly daring."	Cheap way of moving action to the theatre (no major theatre set required). We approach the substance of the film (a film adaptation of a theatrical production).

Compared with the stage version, Brook's film is replete with movement, and music is an important component. After the prologue the scene opens on a ball, where the characters weave about in an atmosphere of waltz and polka. Even this diegetic music, seemingly random, is structured, carefully arranged to match interactions between the major characters. Other short musical pieces and links illustrate Alwyn's point about film music, made in his 1958 lectures:

> One of the first lessons a composer learns is that music can do most things, but it cannot describe — except by verbal or visual implication. It is the constant association of visual ideas with music which unhesitatingly makes us think of these when, say, Mendelssohn's *Fingal's Cave* [1830–32] is played. This piece could quite as easily have been associated with "Forest Murmurs": again — Debussy's piano piece *Gardens in the Rain* [*Jardins Sous le Pluie*, 1903] would still function as music if he had called it, less poetically but equally appropriately, "Hail on a Hot Tin Roof"!
>
> I, myself, had the amusing experience of hearing some music of mine, aptly, I thought, composed to accompany a film about "Butterflies", just as aptly, some years after, fitted to a film about "Elephants"! (Without my permission of course).[2] The points I hope I have made are that film music performs an entirely specialised function, distinct from any other musical function, and that — far from being descriptive music, this is the one thing that it is worst fitted for, and for which it is most rarely used in a film. (I am of course speaking of good films, intelligently produced).[3]

Thus in *On Approval* music accompanies, amongst others, a hansom cab, a drunk, "the morning after" (with a hint of "for he's a jolly good fellow"), a fast train, rowing over the water (a waltz), dripping rain, waiting, and a wedding march. How many of these illustrate solely by description, rather than by association? Perhaps only the hint of the unmistakable "clip-clop" (played on wood blocks) of the horse's hooves in the hansom — but even that could represent, say, the drip of water in a bucket.

Two sequences depend upon Alwyn's talent for combining the comic with plot structure. In the first, the unmarried party of four arrives at Maria's Scottish establishment and are met by the dour domestic staff. A Scottish march reflects their disapproval of the arrangements, matters worsen and climax to

---

[2] Anne Surfling draws attention to a passage in Alwyn's score for *Fingers and Thumbs* (1938) marked "butterflies". A ten-minute amateur film of wildlife in Assam, *Butterflies and Elephants*, was filmed by G. Mackrell in 1948 (NFA catalogue entry 4383 and BFI: Summary of Information on Film and Television (SIFT) database).

[3] Alwyn, "Film Music: Sound or Silence", 2.

their filing off to more marching, the whole sequence built to a sprightly climax through the intelligent deployment of music.

In another comic sequence, the arrogant George needs a slice of bread for breakfast, and Helen rushes to fetch one in a flurry of busy strings. She returns, the music ceases. But George needs butter. More busy strings, she returns, the music ceases. George needs . . . and so on. The scheme of exaggerated intervals contrasting with bursts of music is reminiscent of the music hall or theatre: something Alwyn learned in his hard-up days of theatre session playing.

The often commented-upon comic dream sequence was choreographed by Box's wife Muriel who considered it "in a sense a ballet".[4] Critics like it, although it is embarrassingly unsuccessful and only partially salvaged by Alwyn's score. It starts promisingly with the customary shot of the dreamer's face (Helen's as she murmurs George's name in bed), mixes to a misty sea, and then to a startling close-up of Helen in Greek costume. Alwyn's score, marked "very slow", employs glissando harp and trilling strings, contrasted with short woodwind phrases. It was a combination he would use again — we hear it next in *I See a Dark Stranger*. Helen in close-up turns to the camera and winks, which Alwyn amusingly points with a squeaky piccolo. So far the sequence has worked perfectly, but two main faults mar the remainder: a paucity of ideas and a lack of pace.

The classical scene develops into a shot of George and Maria casting petals and falling over at first in slow motion, later in normal speed: at odds both textually and with the late-Victorian setting. A similar criticism applies to a sequence showing Maria entering a railway carriage and thumping George on the head with a sledgehammer. (Why a railway carriage? Why a sledgehammer? — perhaps both prop and set just happened to be available at Merton Park Studios on the day of filming.) These sequences are cross-cut with George's attempts to strangle Maria as she sings at the piano and his astonishment when she literally disappears in his hands. The notion is unfunny, the shots overlong, and the dream-like flow of the sequence is disrupted.

The sequence continues with Richard's dream of Maria and George in several passionate embraces, himself embarrassed by various kinds of Freudian undress: kilt, nightgown, and so on. On each occasion they turn to him and shout "Ho!" — again unfunny. The dream cuts back to the Greek scene in frenetic fast motion as Maria chases George around the statue of Helen who finally crashes them on the head with her orb, which Alwyn appropriately matches with a reverberating gong. It concludes with another attempt by George to strangle Maria, who this time turns into Helen. At which point both dreamers awake screaming.

The rhythm of a sequence depends upon a feel for the medium. Here the

---

[4] Muriel Box, *Odd Woman Out* (London: Leslie Frewin, 1974), 165.

touch is lacking, despite some intellectual attempt at imposing a pattern; as a result Alwyn's task was difficult. He had not only to infuse a dreamy musical atmosphere, but was called upon to accent, often create, humour. If he could help with the structure, too, so much the better. So he strove hard at something poorly assembled, and probably viewed by him no earlier than the rough-cut stage: the score is peppered with Mathieson's heavy blue wax-pencil timings, suggesting the conductor's difficulty in following the action. In creating the ethereal harmonies and rhythms Alwyn does well, considering the disjointedness of the scenes. Especially commendable are the slow beat to the slow-motion scene, which crescendoes and climaxes on a mix of screams and orchestra tutti. To the dream sequence as a whole Alwyn undoubtedly adds wit — for example, the scene of Maria carrying her sledge-hammer into the train would be pointless and unfunny but for his matching coconuts (Alwyn calls them "cokernuts") to her footsteps. In the strangling scenes, too, if anything makes George's empty handedness funny it is Alwyn's "wa-wa" mutes. As for the structure — probably nothing could have put that right.

10
War's End

THE elegance and sophistication acquired by the British propaganda machine after some five years of war is suggested by Frances Thorpe and Nicholas Pronay:

> A film apparently designed to provide straightforward "instruction" on how to approach a government agency for relief might in fact be effective propaganda designed to show how comprehensively the government cared for those suffering from needs resulting from the war.[1]

Moreover,

> a series of beautifully made "educational" documentaries about the history of various medical discoveries with apparently no "propaganda" purpose . . . were in fact part of a propaganda campaign designed to bring home to the public how many of the wounded in the present war were being saved by lavish medical attention, how many of the maimed and disfigured were at this very time being successfully rehabilitated, and how strongly and effectively the present government cared for the wounded soldiers and civilians . . . The makers of these films might themselves have been quite innocent of the real propaganda purpose which gave them their commissions, and which gave them subjects and scripts quite free from any overt "propaganda". . .[2]

Nevertheless, no matter how "innocent" of propagandist intent an instructional film appears, its music score often contains a message "unheard" by the average viewer. Caution is advised: such messages could be conveyed by the composer's unconscious mind-set, rather than from a conscious propagandist intent. Moreover, one must beware of "finding" something that is not there. Alwyn's thesis that music is non-representational, illustrating whatever the listener imagines it to illustrate, is a reminder and a warning.

Despite the caveats, however, listening to the "hidden message" of the music track is revealing. From the very start of the war Alwyn's contribution to propaganda films was enthusiastic and industrious, and covert propagandist content can be detected in many of the titles already considered here. Throughout

---

[1] Thorpe and Pronay, *British Official Films*, 49.
[2] Ibid., 49–50.

1944 and 1945 Alwyn was called upon to score some twenty official propaganda films, including contributions to Rotha's *Worker and Warfront* magazine series and the RAF newsreel *The Gen*.

Realist's *A Start in Life* (1944), directed by Brian Smith for the MoI and Board of Health, was originally for the Latin-American market, but its value at home was plain. As propaganda, documentaries about the care of children have much to offer — for who else's sake was the war being fought? — and this one makes plain that the British child is being given not only a start, but the very best start. Alwyn nearly always launches his films with a fanfare, but here he starts quietly with something that could be a lullaby, for under titles a tiny baby is bathed in a bowl of contentment. In the midst of this soothing scene, two faint bugle calls hints at war. Hint becomes fact on a change to the watch room of a fire station. In a smooth camera pan a woman enters, pulls two switches (two heavier chords in the score), and speaks into a microphone (another musical punctuation). The pan continues past her to show through a glass door firemen pulling on their gear (a prolonged bugle call and climax). Even as the portentous jabs of the chords stirred apprehension, the bugle calls summon to important work, war work. The commentary commences: "Nothing less than war could have transformed a ladies' hairdresser into a member of the National Fire Service. Her husband, once a librarian, into an air gunner." So shots and musical score juxtapose a baby in safe hands, leaving its parents free for vital national work.

Safe trusty hands, from pre-birth to senior school, are what this film is about. Over pictures of bombed houses the commentary runs, "expectant mothers, living in danger areas as badly hit as this, cannot have their children at home as easily as Mrs —", while Alwyn's bugle call again supplies the sound of war; a calm lullaby follows pictures of a safe haven for mothers and their babies — a government-requisitioned stately home. In this way state cotton-woolling, depicted through commentary, music, and pictures, follow the progress of the British child all the way to senior school.

As a piece of filmmaking *A Start in Life* is a model, the first of five well-crafted documentaries Alwyn and director Brian Smith worked on together over the next few years. They were souls in sympathy. Smith had a background in commercial art and had recently joined Realist after four years as director-cameraman with the AFPU. He believed an audience should "participate in a film, instead of remaining outside the window that is the screen",[3] and he often lightens his film by ignoring the boundaries between spoken and musical commentary. This may be meticulously close: for example, a teacher's nod is followed by an almost unobtrusive harp glissando as the other pupils turn to look at the girl who actually responds. In close affinity to such high-class

---

[3] Letter to *Film Sponsor*, 1:3 (June 1948), 95.

mickey-mousings is the breaking of boundaries between the diegetic and non-diegetic. In one example, a little rising melodic string sequence (in the musical sense) expressing both motion and anticipation as the camera tracks a small boy pushing a wheelbarrow cuts to a close-up piano glissando and a diegetic music scene of dancing children. Elsewhere a violin plays "Pop Goes the Weasel" (traditional) (played without vibrato for authenticity) to accompany dancing children, and a children's circus is illustrated non-diegetically, although one would hardly notice. Most memorable is the pause in the score as a boy turns in close-up to shout "Yippee" before diving into a pool.

A Start in Life was released non-theatrically in September 1944. Within a year the war had ended and Labour surged to victory at the general election. In its rosy determination to stress the state's devoted care for child and family, *A Start in Life* encompasses the optimism that led to that electoral victory. Suggestions that not every child is so fortunate would have to wait until after the war, in films like *Home and School* (1947) with its grim, factory-like school, detritus of the mid-Victorian period.

Covert musical propaganda can also be discovered in formal instructional films. *Accident Service* (1944), a training film for showing only to medical and nursing audiences, was one of Alwyn's few scores for Gaumont British Instructional (GBI). The film examines the work of the hospital accident service and its attempt to both heal and rehabilitate an injured miner. Alwyn scored about fifteen of the film's 42 minutes, but only the title sequence and closing cues were used. Perhaps the orchestral costs were uneconomic for an instructional film, perhaps it was felt that music added too much emotion to the film's deadpan objectivity. The titles start with ceremonial themes, rising brass answering brass, even a cymbal clash. This is indeed inspirational music, no doubt in honour of the accident service, but suggestive also of the bright achievement of British hospitals in general. Over shots of factories and a steel mill, the music calms and trumpets imitate military bugles, until the rattle of a snare drum leads to a marching theme. The film is not concerned (overtly) with military casualties, its commentary listing only home-front injuries. Nevertheless, the musical allusion to military themes – bugles, *martellato* drums, and march rhythm – imply the war effort and the vital need to keep home-front workers (the choice of a miner as subject is significant) fit and at work.

Penicillin (1945), which was important enough to receive a West End showing, was directed for Realist by Alwyn's old colleague Alexander Shaw on the Continent, and in Britain by Kay Mander. It gives an account of the drug's discovery, but couples that achievement with intercut sequences of the effort to save the leg of a wounded infantryman. In this way the propagandist message of the government's care for its fighting men (Thorpe and Pronay's analysis) is introduced. The film is closely scored by Alwyn, who adds moods not inherent in the visuals. This is particularly obvious in Shaw's opening sequence of the rescue from behind the lines in the Netherlands, which he attempts to enliven with racing strings, cymbal clashes, plucked strings, and trills not justified by the dull picture coverage. The first sighting of the wounded soldier merits the "Last Post", a time to rest. The "lavish medical attention"[4] then devoted to the man as he is moved by stages further behind the lines could excuse a belief that he is the war's sole casualty. When he is far enough removed to the safety of a hospital, Alwyn dispenses a peaceful "pastoral" theme. The wounded man's injection with penicillin is matched by ethereal violins, which suggest the mysterious, even miraculous, workings of the drug, while another hint of the "Last Post" suggests bravery as fragments of metal are removed from his wound. Finally back in hospital in Britain, visits by both military "brass" and orchestral brass and strings bring the film to its resolution and (as the script lauds the value of penicillin) suggest "how strongly and effectively the present government cared for the wounded soldiers and civilians".[5]

Of course, much propaganda was not covert, and often converged with the national sentiment. In 1944 director Alexander Shaw and photographer A. E. Jeakins had been on location in Europe filming the Dutch sequences for Realist's *Penicillin* and *French Town: September 1944* (1945). In *French Town* they examine Pont-à-Mousson on the Moselle[6] shortly after its liberation from the Germans. Much of the town is in ruins, but the allied troops and French civilians are shown setting about restoring normality.

Its pictures are objective, and the spoken commentary by actor Cedric Hardwicke is level and superficially calm and factual, too. Yet his measured delivery is undercut by an inflection of repressed anger and sadness, which, together with a bitterly anti-German script by Lester Cooper, reflects the British national sentiment of the time. It is a mood that Alwyn's score both mirrors and enhances. Importantly, however, because the mood is commentary-led, the score reflects commentary rather than pictures. Mournfully slow strings (*con sordini*) and military trumpet calls accompanying the opening shot of a damaged shrine to Joan of Arc. Because the commentary has not yet commenced the viewer is ignorant of what the shot represents, and music and picture seem to comment on a sad result of war. Once the commentary explains the shrine was used by the Germans as an observation post our understanding of both picture and accompanying music changes to one of condemnation of the German Army. (The script does not remind us that the shrine was destroyed by Allied guns). The bugles, we learn from the commentary, represent the continued fighting in the hills overlooked by the shrine. But the view of the countryside shows nothing of that: the music is reflecting only the evidence of the words.

---

[4] Thorpe and Pronay, *British Official Films*, 50.

[5] Ibid.

[6] The town is unnamed in the film.

Commentary and mournful strings continue over scenes of empty streets, damaged steelworks, and a deserted railway station. Then the mood lightens, and the strings become *spicatto*, buoyant — almost playful — over pictures of boys exploring a burnt-out Jesuit seminary, pictorially a solemn scene that could have been represented by solemn chords. But the score reflects not the depicted scene but the commentary's satisfaction at the return of the towns-people to their hometown.

The pictures in this film have become almost a third partner to script and score, mere illustration of the message. Presumably the crew shot at random around the town and depended on scripting to shape their footage. Something not dis-similar occurred with another of Alexander Shaw's location efforts of the year, *Soldier–Sailor* (1945). It was scripted by Frank Launder, who recalled that the crew "had filmed a great deal of material. Unfortunately nothing had happened as envisaged, which is customary in war, with the result that the footage they returned with tended to be repetitive, and lacked any true thread to hold it to-gether." Launder was "called in to write a screenplay using as much as possible of the material already shot. . ."[7] He managed to concoct a story, set in 1943, of two gunner members of the Defensively Equipped Merchant Ships (DEMS) who are picked up off North Africa after being torpedoed. With a second engi-neer (David Sime, who had played the merchant seaman in *Our Country*), they are posted to a troopship carrying New Zealand troops. Various shipboard ad-ventures are recounted, there are nostalgic flashbacks to shore romances, and a moderately exciting climax of an attack by German E-boats.

Since the film was a "salvage job", the composer's role was important both to structure the plot and to maintain viewer interest. An attempt to grab atten-tion is made from the start, with overblown opening titles showing individual portraits of the three main characters, in advance of the main titles. Alwyn responds with a vigorous and varied score, with an early hint at the sustaining motif. Over the succeeding titles proper a few bars of the *Desert Victory* theme and a burst of unsettling fugal activity propel us into the motif, reintroduced in a serious style by triumphant rising horns and strings.

A fanfare conducts us to the torpedoed sailors on a deserted beach at dusk, its remoteness evoked by high strings succeeded by plucked double-bass and low cellos and a plaintive Arabic-sounding flute, skilfully evoking a sense of the exotic. Daylight finds an aeroplane flying overhead, the noise of its engines

---

[7] Geoff Brown, *Launder and Gilliat* (London: BFI, 1977), 114.

juxtaposed with music score, but the men's hopes are disappointed as it flies away, evoked by tailing off the music. When the plane turns, however, it is to cheers and a triumphant fanfare based on the main motif. After this build-up, it is disappointing that the coverage was inadequate to show the actual rescue.

Having initiated interest, Alwyn sustains it by musical punctuation and enlivenment, and by emotional responses to the drama. Arabic-sounding music to accompany a belly dancer does not call for imagination, but music in the style of a dance from an Italian opera — as the crew tour an Italian dock town — vitalises dull pictures. As usual, too, Alwyn knows when to keep quiet: in the battle sequence the score offers only occasional punctuation to predominating guns and explosions.

Apart from the main theme, there is a motif. Against the diegetic music of a radio playing Joyce Grenfell's signature tune, Richard Addinsell's "I'm going to see you today / All's well with my world . . ." (1942), the film mixes to flashbacks as the homesick men think about home and loved ones. Later the men discuss their own romantic lives, again to flashbacks to short dramatised sequences. Here Alwyn picks up Addinsell's tune as non-diegetic motif, and finally as brief commencement to the end titles and a reminder of home.

The film is not a success; lacking overall dramatic development, it becomes a succession of loosely related situations. Nevertheless, Alwyn's score does impose some unity, and polishes the less graceful sequences.

Launder chose to set *Soldier–Sailor* in 1943, but the *Kinematograph Weekly* critic viewing it a month before V-E Day not unnaturally found it "hopelessly belated".[8] In contrast, a fortnight later, the trade paper was thoroughly approving of Lance Comfort's *Great Day*, described as a "sunny topical and, at times, moving domestic comedy drama, set in a charming English village".[9] The "charming English village" was a cosy concept of the national rural mythology as self-contained community and symbol of peace — in wartime a nostalgic reminder and a hope for the future. It was a myth that persisted into the 1950s, especially in the Ealing comedies, and was firmly grounded in shorts and documentaries, too. *Country Town* (1945), a short film about a Lincolnshire market town, opens with a delicate sound picture of cathedral bells against scenes of a horse passing into a field, a train (we hear its whistle), rooftops and the cathedral itself. As the camera pans down the old street, the chimes finish and Alwyn's delicately pastoral strings and oboe are introduced, mixed with the mooing of cows in the market. The working title was *Our Town*,[10] the perfect expression of a close community.

---

[8] *Kinematograph Weekly*, 338:1981 (5 April 1945), 20. The theatrical release in June was even more belated.

[9] Ibid., 338:1983 (19 April 1945), 20.

[10] Presumably changed to avoid confusion with Sam Wood's *Our Town* (1940).

A similar air of community feeling, a sunny freedom from war worries, together with a dash of indulgent amusement, sets up the start of *Great Day*. A pre-credit sequence shows Norah Mumford (Marjorie Rhodes) cycling along the village street to a few bars of a brass arrangement of Parry's "Jerusalem" (1916): the brass is portentous, but exaggeratedly so — suggestive of the self-importance of a small piece of England. By way of a gentle gong and harp arpeggio Parry yields to a cathedral-like clock chime on flutes (in the manner of Big Ben's eight opening notes and *On Approval*'s shorter opening fanfare) — symbolising, like *Country Town*'s cathedral chimes, the English country town or village. In quickly rising succession there follows a pleasant contrast of tone-colour, bassoon, clarinet, and flute, which make friendly mockery of the bicycle ride while imitating its motion.

In seconds Alwyn has conveyed rural myth, community, affectionate humour, weight, and urgency. Mrs Mumford pauses to summon a neighbour to the village hall for a matter of "national importance" — "secret!" Now titles and credits sweep in as the camera tracks through the village street, and after another hint of "Jerusalem", strings in unison offer up an elated romantic response to the glorious "sunny English village". It is Alwyn's leitmotif for the enchantment of the pastoral scene, and to which he will return.

To this, his last score for Lance Comfort, Alwyn brought a wonderfully fresh vision, enlivened, dynamic. One senses relief and pleasure beyond the demands of the scenario. Perhaps it was a response to the rural setting. Perhaps it was the contrast from the pressure, even drudgery, of the other film scores. Comfort was an exception in a hard industry: a gentle, friendly personality. Brian McFarlane suggests he was "uniformly liked as a director who respected his actors sufficiently to give them room to breathe in shaping their characterisations".[11] One supposes Comfort allowed the same interpretative freedom to his composer.

McFarlane sees Comfort as a genre director in the melodramatic mode, especially in his depiction of the obsessed individual. It is not surprising, therefore, that although *Great Day*'s opening sequence seems to support *Kinematograph Weekly*'s promise of a "sunny" village, before long, darker undertones, rivalries, and bickerings surface as at the Women's Institute the members prepare for a "surprise" visit of Mrs Roosevelt. Even darker, however, is the *Angst* of the First-World-War veteran Captain John Ellis (Eric Portman). His problem had already been essayed in Maurice Elvey's *Medal for the General*, also graced by an Alwyn score, in which a Blimpish World-War-1 general (Godfrey Tearle) becomes reclusive and suicidal on being turned down for active service or even the Home Guard. His salvation is the billeting of half a dozen evacuees on his home. For Ellis in *Great Day*, however, there is no chance deliverance.

[11] Brian McFarlane, *An Autobiography of British Cinema* (London: Methuen, 1997), 140.

His embitterment at being too old for service has led to drink and an obsession with the regimental "old days". He has a romantic love of the countryside and the "freedom" symbolised by the flight of birds.

Ellis's favourite spot is the Long Barrow, and his escape there offers Alwyn the chance of fine rhapsodical pastoral music, variations on the title music.

Alwyn responded sensitively to long pastoral passages, as we have already observed in *Green Girdle*. Here, the strings take the dominant theme, counterpointed by harp arpeggios, and every cut to a kestrel flying free in the sky finds joyful exhilaration in trilling flutes. Mixed in is the dog's happy barking. When Ellis is joined by his daughter Meg (Sheila Sim), Alwyn retains the feeling of pastoral freedom but closely matches both action and dialogue. First the score pauses to include the intrusive "parp-parp" of her lorry, but repeating a phrase as if catching up with the broken mood,

the music dawdles as she runs over to him and they greet each other. She follows his gaze, "What is it?" "A windhover". The music repeats, then surges to match the movement. As father and daughter talk, harp, elated violin, and occasional airy flute trills continue to recall the freedom of the bird, whilst closely matching the peaks and shallows of the dialogue: "No cages for him — that's the only thing that matters, freedom." Warning minor chords reflect Ellis's warning to his daughter "Don't you get trapped. Keep out of the cage, ducky", echoed by a flurry of feathers. Then rapturous horns seize the melody against winging woodwind and strings as Ellis quotes Siegfried Sassoon's "Everyone Sang" (1919): "Everyone burst out singing; / And I was filled with such delight / As prison birds must find in freedom . . ." The mood declines as Meg mundanely reminds him "I've got some work to do." When she has left, a solo violin resumes and rises ever higher as Ellis repeats the line "as prison birds must find in freedom . . . on — on — and out of sight".

Alwyn's variants of the hawk's flight by flute, harp, and violin, conclude in recollection of the soaring violin of Vaughan Williams's *The Lark Ascending* (1914, rev. 1920).

By degrees Ellis descends into his inferno. Later on, returning to the Long Barrow, his tranquillity (a brief recapitulation of the motif) is disturbed by a shotgun. Sustained strings held on a single crescendoing chord mirror his shock until, suffused with anger, they explode in a chaos of orchestra tutti resolving into ascending brass as he descends on the farmer — Meg's elderly fiancé. A break no longer than an intake of breath impacts Ellis's enraged "You bloody murderer, what do you think you're doing?" Ominous rumblings on low strings and timpani underpin the ensuing row (*sempre agitato*), until Ellis's rage rises again propelling more rising chords, joined by the bassoons and brass, until he clutches at his heart and apologises. The farmer leaves, tossing aside the dead pheasant, to poignant oboe and dark and foreboding strings while Ellis remains staring at the ground.

Nemesis arrives when Ellis is arrested for stealing a ten-shilling note from a woman's handbag at the pub. The scene is without music. As Ellis sidles to the open handbag, the camera tracks his movement at a low angle from behind the bar and through a distorting glass jar. There is a secretive, guilty, fascination about the sequence which renders music unnecessary; the trivial prattle of the woman (Kathleen Harrison), and Ellis's tuneless humming (an attempt to appear natural) are adequate. A light orchestral cue follows the seizure of Ellis, and as, in close-up, he represses his tears, ends with a mock military "bugle" to point up the disgrace of an ex-Army captain.

Having been charged, Ellis returns home where he confesses to his wife Elizabeth (Flora Robson) to being one of life's failures and refers not to the "charming English village" of pastoral mythology and *Kinematograph Weekly* — but the "stinking village" where there will be gossip, "talk behind our backs". Again, this scene is played in musical silence, the tension upheld by the dramatic interplay of the characters and by Erwin Hillier's lighting and camera angles: Elizabeth is seated at her sewing machine for most of the scene, a symbol of stability, while Ellis restlessly changes position about the room. At one stage Comfort has the room's single ceiling lamp lowered between shots in order to darken Ellis's eyes behind the shade. In fact, Comfort uses camera and lighting to match voice rhythms in much the same way that directors often depend upon Alwyn's music to underpin the drama.

Now, the sudden chord as Elizabeth shuts the door after her husband has left (perhaps, as the audience believes, to kill himself) makes an emotional impact as it contrasts with the musical silence of the previous scene. The music continues as Ellis wanders across the wild dark countryside towards the Long Barrow, and Elizabeth weeps at her sewing machine — high passionate violins contrasting with violas brooding in their lower registers, joined by a melancholic solo oboe in themes distantly cousin to the earlier pastoral Long Barrow scenes. Meg returns home and, fearing for her father, runs after him.

Less than a year after composing *Great Day* Alwyn worked for Carol Reed on *Odd Man Out*, one of his great scores. The film ends with the dying IRA man, Johnny, staggering through inhospitable snow-covered city streets sought by his girl. Like Ellis, Johnny is a tortured personality, spurned by society. Composing that final sequence for *Odd Man Out*, Alwyn must have been struck by similarities between Johnny's final march through the snow and Ellis's "suicide" march through the dark inhospitable countryside pursued by his loving daughter. For both sequences Alwyn adopts a broadly similar compulsive funeral march rhythm with a fitful melody:

The sequence incorporates another style which was part of Alwyn's musical temper at this time. This is the use of rapidly cascading strings:

etc

Similar scale rhythms characterised the torture scene of *Penn of Pennsylvania*, and the pattern is repeated in the pre-credit sequence of *I See a Dark Stranger* (1946). On all three occasions they represent confusion. In *I See a Dark Stranger*, where they illustrate mysterious French signposts on the Isle of Man, and equally mysterious gunshots, they compound the cinema audience's confusion. In *Penn of Pennsylvania*, they represent the mental confusion of a tortured man. In *Great Day*, they represent Ellis's tortured mental state, and especially the confusion and anxiety of Meg as she pursues him across country.

Now, as Meg learns from her mother that her father has left for the Long Barrow, the steady march rhythm, Ellis's "suicide" motif, is introduced. Then it is forgotten — for the moment — as she rushes across the village street and the cascading strings enter while pictures cross cut between father and daughter. For a few moments another tense theme interrupts, but the cascades come to predominate and grow increasingly wild and frantic, until slowing to the solemn "suicide" motif. This slow march with its driven inevitability is appropriate for the intended death of a military man. Suddenly, lit by moonlight through the gloom of the trees, Ellis sights the pond. A plucked chord shimmers against a low pedal point. It is now that the cascading strings and "suicide" theme join in vivid contrast: hysterical confusion and grim resolution. Determination finally usurps the cascading strings, and the Long Barrow theme climaxes in four descending chords.

The shock is considerable, therefore, as Meg's voice cuts through the mood: "Daddy!" And all is silence. The expected climax, the suicide, is aborted. Another climax — the climax of silence — is introduced as Alwyn once again turns to the trick of the circus drum roll.[12]

In the scenes that follow Ellis finds enough self-respect to see through the crisis. The film shows, and hints at, other underlying problems in the village, but — like life — none are resolved apart from Meg's rejection of her elderly fiancé for a dashing young officer. Nevertheless, Alwyn serves his subject well, ending as he began with Parry's "Jerusalem" while the camera passes across proud patriotic faces at the welcome ceremony for Eleanor Roosevelt. A final caption dedicates the film to the work of the Women's Institute. The darker side to village life is concealed behind the pastoral myth, fortified by Alwyn's score, of "England's green and pleasant land".

Nor would it have seemed appropriate to dispel the myth in April 1945 when the film was released, and shops were already filled with bunting in anticipation of the peace. In the euphoria following the formal announcement of 8 May, Norman Walker at Denham produced a short film possibly entitled *Peace Thanksgiving* (1945), to which Alwyn supplied nine minutes of score for orchestra and chorus.

There was hardly a breathing space before Alwyn found himself at work on the score for *The True Glory*. The D-Day landings were of immediate public interest. A film of the final campaign on the Western Front had been conceived as early as 1943, the producer being Eisenhower himself, who had insisted on another Anglo-American Army Film Units co-production after the propaganda success of *Tunisian Victory*. It was planned that David Macdonald, now returned from the continent, should be the British producer, while the Americans were to be represented by director George Stevens.

Preparations for the campaign were surveyed in *Eve of Battle* (1944). This seventeen-minute short has an imaginative opening: no music, simply the growing roar of planes passing overhead. Alwyn was responsible for the composition,

---

[12] See Introduction.

again incorporating a passage from the *Desert Victory* march, now becoming almost a tiny leitmotif for the major operations documentaries of the war. For the most part, however, the score was held down beneath the commentary. *Eve of Battle* was finished in June 1944, but work started almost immediately afterwards on the feature-length compilation of the campaign which was to become *The True Glory*. Macdonald dropped out early on, and for the second time Alwyn found himself working with Carol Reed. Reed's American counter-part was Garson Kanin.

Alwyn, who had not been assigned to the film originally, was called in when the American composer, Marc Blitzstein, fell ill. Alwyn had to start from scratch, and time was short. The task was eased by a decision to rework some of the material from *Eve of Battle*. Even more helpful was the release for six weeks of the composer Alan Rawsthorne from his normal duties as an Army sergeant; together the two of them scored from Alwyn's sketches (Plate 6).[13] Afterwards Rawsthorne went on to compose the impressive score for Boulting's final compilation war documentary, *Burma Victory*.

The True Glory was intended as a tribute both to the fighting men of all the Allied service units, and to Western democratic ideals. It received high praise at the time (and since) and was awarded an Academy Award as best documentary, although it is less satisfactory than *Desert Victory*. Chastened by their experience of *Tunisian Victory*, the Americans had gone for blanket coverage, and their operation comprised a huge number of 400 cameramen, compared with the much smaller British units, which were also beset by technical problems with their new Vinten cameras and a shortage of filmstock. As in the previous productions, the filmmakers boasted about the number of cameramen as well as the number of casualties: a total of no less than 700 cameramen from the United States, Canada, France, Poland, Belgium, the Netherlands, Czechoslovakia, Norway, and the United Kingdom; 32 were killed, 101 were wounded, and sixteen reported missing in action.

"Boast" is the right word — it ran that the film was compiled from 6,500,000 feet of film. As an off-mic introduction by General Eisenhower states: "to tell the whole story would take a year". But this was the root problem: there was simply too much material for a documentary edited down to 8,000 feet and lasting under one-and-a-half-hours. Few shots last longer than three seconds; most are two seconds or less. The result is a lack of pacing within sequences, the film resembling a long newsreel assembly rather than a considered documentary.

A second result is an over-reliance on Alwyn's score to carry sequences and to create emotion, so that there is too much music — 50 minutes out of the film's duration of 87 minutes. The sound-effects are genuine, recorded on location by

---

[13] Private interview with Mary Alwyn.

6 Sergeant Alan Rawsthorne, Muir Mathieson, and Alwyn recording *The True Glory* at the Scala Theatre, London, in 1945. Rawsthorne was given special leave to help Alwyn meet a deadline.

a small unit commanded by Captain D. P. Field, but they risked their lives for virtually nothing. Although the normal practice was to lay effects against mute visuals, effects are so noticeably absent that one queries whether normal practice was followed. Music may have been felt an easy option to assemble the film with speed. In the short pauses between the music, only general sound-effects are common, with at best an occasional spotted gun shot, explosion, and so on. The overall final impression is of "wall-to-wall" dialogue and music. Such overreliance on the music saps the score of impact and often significance, and illustrates perfectly Alwyn's maxim that "music depends for its maximum effect on the absence of music".[14]

Nevertheless, the film has virtues. While individual shots are too short, the overall structure has tempo and a cumulative impressiveness. Partly this is due to the almost continuous multi-voiced commentary — taking turns between the narrator and 130 soundbites of American and British regional voices, often compassionate, ironic, wry, or heartfelt. Another success is that, paradoxically, because of the sheer accumulation of quick-cut shots, the film really does capture the mood and speed of the whole operation, the embarkation from

[14] Alwyn, "Film Music: Sound or Silence", 2.

England, the landings, the fighting, the liberated townspeople and peasants, problems of supply, the set-backs of snow, the Bulge.

Alwyn successfully resists the temptation to score everything. A sequence of snowbound troops is successful because only the lightest chill wind touches its silence. Neither are there music or effects over the scenes of the release of Belsen. Perhaps the filmmakers could think of nothing appropriate, but the very absence of sound adds a chill. It is a pity that immediately following this shocking sequence Alwyn strikes up a jaunty tune — the change of gear is too swift, inappropriate. It reflects the view of the film's planning committee that Belsen was merely an "incident along the way".

Roger Manvell thought Alwyn's music "dramatically impressive, up-pointing the excitement and feeling of the action".[15] It certainly does that, and in the process Alwyn draws on styles evoking tension, fast-paced excitement, and newsreel techniques, as well as jazz, music-hall, and Russian-sounding idioms. He also intrudes (yet again) hints of the *Desert Victory* march, as well as the ceremonial, especially over shots of the meeting between Stalin and Churchill.

Despite *The True Glory*'s scenario, its final message is anti-war, or more precisely, "no more war". The cumulative effect of the long campaign, the fast cutting, the long stretches of music, and the unrelenting voice-overs, sate the viewer. Only in its closing minutes does the mood change to one of reflection and dignity, as the editing pace slows to allow subdued ceremonial brass over shots of graves, the capitulation of German military, and the dead and rubble of fallen Berlin.

The True Glory was premiered simultaneously in London and Paris on 2 August. The year was 1945. A week later the war came to its conclusion with Hiroshima and Nagasaki. The film accurately reflected the public mood of war exhaustion.

---

[15] Roger Manvell, *Films and the Second World War* (South Brunswick and New York: A. S. Barnes; London: Dent, 1974), 157.

11
Reconstruction

R OTHA'S companies Paul Rotha Productions and Films of Fact had not been short of work. Between 1942 and 1945 Rotha produced eighteen issues of his newsreel *Worker and Warfront* for screening to war-industry workers, pushing out five final issues in 1945. To these Alwyn contributed title music, breaks, and end titles. The company was also occupied with documentaries. Alwyn wrote the scores for two, and although release was delayed until the following year they reflect the national mood of early 1945.

Rotha's intention in *Total War in Britain* (1946) was to show that central planning was as important to winning the peace as it was the war. At times its stridency verges on the hysterical. It commences with a depiction of the front pages of European newspapers circling around the screen, against which the titles appear word by word: "Total — War — in — Britain", a chord beating against each word and ascending in scale. The musical composition then adopts a deferential grandiose tone as a caption acknowledges a government source for the statistics of D-Day mobilisation. The titles set the technical style, which is mainly a sophisticated variant of what Rotha essayed in *World of Plenty*, with its origins dating back a further seven years to *New Worlds for Old*: that is to say, compilation pictures and graphics choreographed with music and sound-effects of all kinds. Alwyn obviously enjoys Rotha's challenge, his score moving from pathos to the ceremonial, with many short cues, drum rolls, drumbeats, explosions, tambourines, recorded cymbals played backwards, and so on. The film ends as hysterically as it begins, with the commentator John Mills uttering "Fulfilment!" against shots of the D-Day landings, and Alwyn's Elgarian theme climaxing over British newspaper headlines such as "This Their Final Hour". Although today its contrived style is out of fashion, the film's meticulous balance of music, effects, and pictures holds a fascination, and even perhaps a few technical lessons.

The second of Rotha's 1946 releases to which Alwyn contributed, *Land of Promise*, received high praise. RM of the *Monthly Film Bulletin* called it "an important film in the development of British Documentary",[1] although time has tempered that judgement. It preaches a compelling Socialist sermon on the need to plan for decent housing and dramatises much of the argument,

---

[1] *Monthly Film Bulletin* [*MFB*] 13:149 (31 May 1946), 59–60. RM was almost certainly Roger Manvell.

especially through the offscreen and onscreen debate between three buffers, Mr Know-All (Miles Malleson), Hansard (Henry Hallat), and History (Herbert Lomas). They are reproved by the voice of an unseen young Socialist soldier (John Mills), who claims to represent the views of the audience, and, in a kind of diegesis towards the end of the film, appears to climb out of the stalls into the screen. The on-screen appearance of these and others is interspersed with a repeat of Rotha's proven successful assembly of library footage and graphics against bursts of harp, timpani, cymbals, celesta, triangles, xylophone, glockenspiel, side drum, a bell, a backwards flute, and other instruments. Alwyn's hints are often faint, perhaps a suggestion of the Big Ben chord or a barely heard drum rattle or an ethereal celesta chord, but always sufficient to lubricate the pictures. No doubt making it was fun.

In its more developed passages, the music bolsters the film's powerful demagogic message, from the opening bucolic shot of a family strolling down a country lane against a pastoral oboe as Mills suggests: "A home of your own, that's what most of us want . . .", to a stirring march an hour later, which leads to the end titles following Mills's impassioned declaration: "no power on earth can stop us once we've the will to win".

Land of Promise: the very title reflects the propaganda of 1945. Inadequate housing was just one of the problems facing the country as the war drew to a close. Britain was saddled with massive overseas debts, a shortage of jobs, an intensification of food and clothing rationing, disrupted personal relationships. At the same time, a wide social revolution had engendered a mood for reconstruction — soon to be reflected politically. To sustain morale, the documentary film units at first slipped into a natural continuation of their wartime role. It was not immediately apparent that their day was passing, signalled by the replacement of the MoI by the bland Central Office of Information (COI). Within a few years the movement had withered, and Rotha's vision of documentary leading the march to Socialism was seen to be flawed.[2]

Of immediate concern was demobilisation, and a series to guide service personnel back to "civvy street" was initiated even before the war ended. The AKS's *What's the Next Job?*, the second in the series, was approved for exhibition in March 1945, a few weeks before V-E Day. There are no screen credits, but Alwyn as composer seems to have co-operated in some way with Rawsthorne, who is acknowledged as "music supervisor".[3]

Roy Baker directed an entertaining and well-paced twenty-minute dramatised instructional in which four service personnel meet at the significantly named Doves pub at Christmas (that is, next Christmas, the Christmas of peace) and express their concerns about finding ex-service jobs. They agree to

---

[2] Paul Maris (ed.), *BFI Dossier No 16: Paul Rotha* (London: BFI, 1982), 78–82.
[3] SIFT, credit list "compiled from secondary sources".

meet up again a year later to see how well each has succeeded. The film charts
their progress, and, needless to say, all do well. These few months at the close of
the war were a moment for optimism, and many must also have warmed to the
final Christmas greetings, and especially Lesley Brook's (of the Women's Royal
Naval Service [WRNS; familiarly "Wrens"]) carefully stressed "And a happy
New Year". Faithful to the film's sanguinity, Alwyn composed a series of short
and unfussy cues, the longest a 56-second busy $\frac{2}{4}$ alternation of the masculine
roles of car maintenance, joining, and accounting with a waltz as the ex-Wren
pins hems in a dress shop. However, it is the opening sequence, with its lively
waltz under titles leading to diegetic Christmas bells and "Once in Royal David's City" against the snow-covered Doves pub, that is memorable for its emotional evocation in sound of the land at peace.

The Labour landslide victory in July 1945 mirrored widespread expectations
of a welfare state, the protection of the vulnerable from cradle to grave. The
cornerstone of the programme was public health, culminating in the creation
of the National Health Service (NHS) in 1946. To foster support for its birth
and to nurture its infant years, the government called upon the still malleable
propaganda machine. The BBC sustained interest in health matters by Charles
Hill's Radio Doctor's homely dispensations, its equivalent in film being a series
of critically acclaimed medical documentaries for which Alwyn composed the
scores: *Your Children's Ears* (1945), *Your Children's Eyes* (1945), *Your Children's
Teeth* (1945), and *Your Children and You* (1946). Produced initially by John Taylor and Alexander Shaw for Realist, they have an educational value even today.
Later there were other titles for which other composers were commissioned,
and by 1947 Alwyn had time for only one more, *Your Children's Sleep* (1948).
Here only *Your Children and You* and *Your Children's Sleep* need detain us, for
the musical contribution to *Ears*, *Eyes*, and *Teeth* amounts to an identical opening and closing composition of twenty seconds or less.

For *Your Children and You* Alwyn again worked with Brian Smith, whose
brief was to advise parents on the psychological care of young children. The
result was a witty, common-sense script by Smith, which shows concern for
parents' difficulties while never failing to empathise with the child. "His point
of view is very different from yours", runs the commentary, and frequently
Smith shows precisely that. Thus the camera is taken for a ride in a pram, is
barked at by an angry dog, or sits under a table with meddlesome fingers pulling a tablecloth and unseeable objects on its head. To Smith's sensitive and imaginative direction Alwyn responds with one of his lightest and most delicate
documentary scores. Instrumentation is important in sustaining the mood, so
that to his little orchestra of flute, clarinet, two violins, viola, and cello Alwyn
adds a vibraphone and a glockenspiel — and having done so makes sure they
pay for themselves. The fanfares common to Alwyn's openings are shunned,

and the film commences gently with light shimmering climbing chords by vibraphone and tremolo violins on a *d'''* octave. Soon, flute and clarinet join to harmonise in a simple lullaby theme:

Alwyn's judgement never falters: matching pictures or commentary rhythms with short motives or longer themes, never obtrusive, frequently self-effacing. He is witty, too. From baby's point of view (POV) we gaze at a dangling woolly ball in the pram, and the score plays a few notes from the Gershwins's "I Got Plenty o' Nuttin'" (1935) — and returns later (to structure the scenario) as the one-year-old rattles on his drum. Elsewhere, the camera gazes skywards from baby's pram POV at a flag fluttering temptingly to a military fanfare, not brass but the gentlest of strings. Later, Red Indian drumbeats mimic a child's make-believe.

The underscore is particularly revealing during its depiction of night terrors. So far Alwyn had had few opportunities to illustrate fear. One early, brief experiment was in *Royal Mile, Edinburgh* (1943), a densely-composed 14-minute documentary for Merton Park. Here a visit to Canongate Graveyard finds menacing, shimmering strings suddenly interrupted by a feline clarinet as something creeps from the shadows:

In *Your Children and You* the camera stares around a dimly-lit bedroom from a child's POV, who, the commentary discloses, in its "lonely ordeal" finds fear in "formless shapeless horrors of the cupboard and the stair": light shining across a soft toy and clock on the mantelpiece, shadows cast from the landing on to the ceiling, formless shapes in black corners. Alwyn's score is economical but telling: echoing celesta chords, a wailing flute, repetitive woodwind.

Two years later Alwyn had another chance to tackle the disturbing coalescence of fear and the child, in *The Fallen Idol* (1948). Here, in a darkened house, a boy crawls beneath a long table in a game of hide-and-seek as the vibraphone's rarely used sustaining pedal shimmers evocatively in harmony with tremolo strings, with stabbing punctuations from the clarinet. But on this occasion the child is having fun — it is the audience, knowing more than the child, that feels the terror. In *Your Children and You*, on the other hand, camera and orchestra co-operate not just to communicate a child's fear but to create a mood of empathy with that fear.

In 1947 Smith and Alwyn co-operated once more on the *Your Children* series with the title *Your Children's Sleep*. Again the relationship between parents and children is explored, the emphasis this time on the psychological origin of children's sleeping problems. Although the film was directed by Jane Massy, Smith produced it, and it is covered with his imaginative fingerprints, including subjective POV camerawork;[4] the editing is both brilliant and daring and is credited to Gwen Baillie. Alwyn, who loved the freedom and flexibility of working with the smaller chamber orchestra, composed a fresh and spontaneous score in perfect proportion to pictures, commentary, and dialogue. Adroit technique is evident from the opening shot of rooftops at night, accompanied by slow and sleepy strings, punctuated at first by flute and clarinet in unison to suggest the melodic chime of a clock, followed by the darker resonance of a bassoon for the strokes. More importantly, his music is suggestive of psychological states. These can be simple, so that when "worry . . . like a great dark shape" looms like a huge jelly on to the screen it is accompanied by tremolando strings; and fearful dreams are represented by vague surreal textures surrounded by barbed wire, punctuated by spiky clarinet and flute in dissonance. Or, when the camera becomes a footballer recollecting his superb ball control leading to a brilliant goal in front of the Spurs talent scout, a perky clarinet and flutes in racing dialogue not only speed the action but recall the joy and ease of the moment. More subtly, a little boy is shown real firemen training in the street: the shot is mute POV, suggesting the absorption of the child's attention. The next scene bursts into a lively musical dream (again, child's POV) of his tiny toy fire-engine speeding across the sitting-room carpet, little bell ringing and clarinet and violin vying to catch up, until the leaden toy firemen bravely extinguish the hearth fire. The tension of *Fires Were Started* this is not, but a child's safe view of grown-up things. When another child scared of a darkly severe adult looks up the stairs in her home, a *spiccato* violin bounces fearfully up the treads with her POV, to climax in dissonant clarinet and flute to abrupt silence as she imagines the (bogey) man standing there. Such opportunities to experiment with the depiction of mental states were invaluable to Alwyn and would pay rich rewards in the feature films that were soon to come his way.

Crown's *Home and School*, produced by Alexander Shaw and directed by Gerry Bryant for the Ministry of Education and the COI, also dealt with the subject of parental understanding of their children's psychological needs. This time it dramatised the single issue of a parent's responsibility to share discipline equally with the school. The production is well constructed and never dull, helped not a little by Maurice Denham's leading role as the father and by the beguiling performances Bryant encourages from David Mercer (aged

---

[4] At this time POV interested documentary filmmakers. Max Munden and Dennis Shand's *One Man's Story* (1948), sketching the story of Dr McGonigle, the reforming medical officer of health for Stockton on Tees in the 1930s, utilises POV for both narrator and McGonigle. In the final mix Alwyn's underscore is kept at such a low level that he was mainly wasting his time, although faint violins do give a nostalgic aura to some of the scenes. The mix is so bad that on one of two occasions when the music needs to be heard, the sound mixer misses the first notes, thus initially rendering unintelligible an arrangement of "O Come All Ye Faithful".

ten) and Marion Strauss (aged six). The track called for less subtlety than *Your Children's Sleep*, but Alwyn's score is never less than sensitive. Of particular note is a long sequence of over two minutes in which the music mickey-mouses the boy's creeping and escape from the house with his friend to the woods. The orchestra stealthily follows with beats in the lower strings, plucked descending treble strings, and a slowly descending clarinet and flute theme, suddenly to speed like a racing pulse as a "Trespassers Will Be Prosecuted" sign is passed. The boys' misbehaviour is intercut with the little sister at home quietly and deliberately snipping a cushion to shreds, to a contrasting slowing of the rhythm.

Elsewhere, in a lovely moment, the girl sets out on an errand, endlessly repeating the rhythm of the memorised shopping list and reflected by light flutes and clarinet and happy strings with a short bowing — until the inevitably awful moment when she forgets the "tin of cocoa". Heavy gloom sets in with strings taking contrasting longer strokes in a lower, sombre, register. Fortunately, memory happily unblocks to a flighty flute arpeggio.

In one of its few real documentary sequences, *Home and School* depicts a school resembling more a Victorian prison than a place of education and suggesting much work for the new Socialist government. In London the devastation of vast areas by enemy bombings was seen as the opportunity to initiate utopian rebuilding schemes. *The Proud City* (1945), a Greenpark Production directed by Ralph Keene for the MoI, was an important film in which the visionary Greater London Plan was explained by the authority on town planning, Sir Patrick Abercrombie, and the LCC's Chief Architect, J. H. Forshaw.

In a largely explanatory film, Alwyn illustrated where he could. The film opens with inspirational fanfares of horns and trumpets alternating with flute, oboes, and a clarinet, while lofty strings grow rapt over traditional Thameside landmarks — St Paul's, the Houses of Parliament, the Tower of London, and so on — and harp arpeggios suggest the flowing river. Later the brass return to suggest the majesty of the Thames, and one is reminded of Alwyn's later score for the Festival of Britain's three-dimensional journey down the *Royal River*. Elsewhere, fast strings suggest a busy draftsman's office, all plans unrolling and bustle, while Georgian squares are illustrated appropriately by a minuet. Alwyn's task was to suggest the vision, and his music sustains the inspirational to the end. Nevertheless, the composer had little room to manoeuvre in this wordy film, and Alwyn did not deserve the stricture of the *Monthly Film Bulletin*: "The background music belies its name by being obtrusive and trying"

It is likely, although his credit cannot be confirmed, that Alwyn also composed the music for *The Plan and the People* (1945), directed by Frank Sainsbury

---

[5] RM in *MFB* 13:149 (31 May 1946), 72.

for Realist, described as presenting "the human angle on the LCC plan for London".[6]

When the corporation of Britain's second city, Manchester, felt it too deserved a film, Paul Rotha was approached. The result was *A City Speaks* (1947); a film so weighted with civic consciousness that it misses the ponderous by a milligram. To retain interest Rotha called to his aid some of the punctuation tricks of his earlier films, such as a dispute between two voice-overs, dramatised action, and graphics and charts, but shunned the short musical chords and sound-effects. They were unnecessary, for he had a prestigious source of music — nothing less than Manchester's Hallé Orchestra and its conductor John Barbirolli. Their presence adds glitter and suggests a desire to impress, a mood established beneath the titles by a ponderous roll of timpani and majestic horns.

Alwyn recalled, "At the first recording session Barbirolli was very much aloof, and cold in his attitude to me. He quite obviously regarded me as yet another hack film composer and unworthy of his attention." But by the end of the week the conductor had warmed considerably, so much so that he promised to give Alwyn's First Symphony its first performance at the following year's Cheltenham Festival. It was followed by a performance at the Royal Festival Hall in London. "Thus began a fruitful association," concluded Alwyn, "for John commissioned my *2nd Symphony* for a world premiere with the Hallé, and followed it by the first performance of my Symphonic Prelude *The Magic Island*. Later, John's wife, Evelyn Rothwell, introduced my *Oboe Concerto* to London at the Proms." [7]

It was unsurprising that Barbirolli modified his presumed conception of Alwyn as "yet another hack film composer" — for Alwyn's contribution was not a "hack" film score. Instead of drawing on his customary techniques as a film composer, he contributed five concert pieces,[8] against which Rotha cut his pictures in a cousin to the musical film or stage-show technique of freezing plot development while players and orchestra burst into song. For Alwyn, who in *Queen Cotton* set the colourful shots of spinning and weaving to music, the idea was not new. For Rotha, the attraction was in displaying Barbirolli and the Hallé, the stars of his film, without the necessity of tiresome commentary writing. Thus the opening titles are succeeded by a repeat of the opening motive *moderato* over an aerial journey across Greater Manchester. Elsewhere the industrial scene is illustrated by flutes and strings in a rhythmically propulsive march, plucked strings gallop in contrapuntal cascades over scenes of the peo-

---

[6] *DNL* 6:51 (1946), 8.

[7] Alwyn, *Winged Chariot*, 13–14.

[8] Performed in concert by Barbirolli and the Hallé Orchestra in November 1947 as the *Manchester* suite (1947).

ple at play, while a harp arpeggio conducts us to the hillsides and a brief flute tremolo (Alwyn's rising lark) and a plaintively beautiful violin solo.

When, well before the end of his 69 minutes, Rotha has said all he has to say, he introduces his *tour de force*, a special Hallé performance — not of Alwyn's music but — of that film editor's friend: Wagner's "Ride of the Valkyries", whirling to scenes of the city at leisure. It says nothing about Manchester that could not be said of many another city, and the relief is tangible when the reel finishes with moody contrasty shots of wet cobblestones against the sound of the last tram. Simple pictures and simple sound-effects are all that are needed to evoke the mood of the real city.

For the finale a musical texture is woven to attest civic pride, the main theme now pierced with horn fanfares and drumrolls as achievements are declaimed; now hushed — perhaps with a harp arpeggio — as commentary becomes thoughtful, until quite suddenly Rotha's Socialist conscience ushers in pictures of children in slum conditions, accompanied by a plaintive musical mood. Up to and including this point, Alwyn has been marking time with harmonic patterns but little melody: musical soup to obscure turgid babble. Now another horn fanfare ushers in a repetition of the strong opening music while aerial views glide backwards from the city hall, as commentary and music join in empty bombast, "From the very centre of our city let us resolve that the lessons of yesterday shall not be forgotten in our plans for tomorrow . . ."

A City Speaks commences with a motto: "What is the city but the people?" But a city can be a lonely place, and some turn to their trades union to find community feeling. To that extent, and in its opening, *Each for All* (1946), Verity Films' short introduction to the trades union movement, written by Reg Groves and directed by Montgomery Tully, is not dissimilar to Rotha's film. The full force of prominent timpani, brass fanfare, and cymbal clash introduce the film, leading to a ceremonial theme bestowing a weighty dignity to shots of speakers at the Trades Union Congress. Without a pause tremolo violins swirl the music from $\frac{4}{4}$ into a rushing $\frac{3}{4}$ theme as we mix to newspapers stacking off the presses of the *Daily Herald* and meet John Slater who in the guise of a print worker reads the headline hot off the press: "Trades Union Congress Debate Britain's Future". This short film effortlessly crams information into its eleven minutes, and although there are only three cues Alwyn obviously spent time on each. Its middle cue carefully matches the depiction of a variety of trades (a hint of $\frac{3}{4}$ "valse tempo" for the garment workers, pastoral for the agricultural workers) while the third and closing cue skilfully bolsters and enhances Slater's delivery of Reg Groves's script. Thus, a ceremonial march accompanies the words "our aim is not only to improve conditions for our own members but to build a nobler and better world for all men . . ." In the split second between that and the next sentence Alwyn squeezes in a cymbal clash and commences a fanfare, which continues under the voice-over and repeats itself in a framework of rising motives, ". . . so that all who work for the common weal, who build the boats to bridge the world [variation of fanfare], who weave the cloth to clothe the world [variation of fanfare], who build the homes to house the world, who harvest the fruits of land and sea [cymbal clash and rising variation of fanfare motive] to feed the world [cymbal clash; fanfare rises even higher], shall have voice in the world's government, and shall share in the good things their labour produces". Appropriate library pictures accompany words and music, until at the final words the music continues briefly to illustrate the "good things" with stirring fanfares and cymbal clashes over shots of Slater and a child amongst sunny apple blossom, followed by a country garden, a cricket match, and finally, the TUC emblem.

How vividly these documentaries recall the Socialist vision of those early post-war days.

12
Launder and Gilliat: Soundtrack as Art Form

W ITH confident financing — by Korda, Del Giudice, and especially Rank — British feature technicians had emerged at the end of the war possessed of a bravura the equal of Hollywood. Alwyn shared in the blossoming, his name joined on the credits with Boulting, Launder and Gilliat, Neame, Roy Baker, Asquith, Pélissier, Lean, Frend, Negulesco, Mackendrick, Hamer, Dearden . . . and others, including Carol Reed.

Quite possibly it was the association with Reed that brought Alwyn his first contract with Launder and Gilliat. Frank Launder and Sidney Gilliat had made their name as the directors of *Millions Like Us* (1943), but they had worked with Reed as scriptwriters and knew him well. More recently, Alwyn had worked on Shaw's *Soldier–Sailor*, which Launder scripted. After the war they joined Independent Producers, a loose confederation under the Rank umbrella, and called themselves Individual Pictures. Their first production was *The Rake's Progress*, which they wrote jointly, Launder produced, Gilliat directed, and Alwyn composed.

Alwyn's most remembered contribution is his "Calypso", written to scent the studio-bound coffee plantation scenes with an aroma of local atmosphere. Strictly speaking the piece is both calypso and rumba, commencing and ending on a languid calypso rhythm, with a lively rumba in the middle section to accompany a montage. Two record companies pressed it at the time of the film's release, and it has been popular since. But the film has more interesting discoveries than this pastiche.[1]

The Rake's Progress narrates the unhappy life of Vivian Kenway (Rex Harrison), a spoilt playboy sent down from Oxford in 1931. Sacked by a South American coffee company, he becomes a successful racing driver and marries a half-Jewish German girl Rikki (Lilli Palmer) to help her evade Nazi persecution. He treats her so badly that she attempts suicide, and he kills his father through drunken driving. After a series of degrading jobs, he finds fulfilment in the Army and dies heroically on a reconnaissance mission. Critics saw him as a true portrait of a pre-war type of personality, and today one can enjoy the film for its sly humour and bittersweetness, even though it never quite reaches the heart of real human tragedy.

The titles start with an engraving from Hogarth's "A Rake's Progress" (1735)

---

[1] Analysed in Manvell and Huntley, *The Technique of Film-Music*, 113–14.

7 In the Autumn of 1946 Paul Rotha and his second wife Margot accompanied Alwyn to Prague for the British Film Festival. The Festival concluded with a Concert of British Film Music, conducted by Muir Mathieson, and included the calypso music from Alwyn's *The Rake's Progress* (1945).

and continue with a series of sketches by Feliks Topolski illustrating scenes from our own rake's misspent life. Curiously, this good idea is marred by the credit lettering, which obscures the sketches, a mistake that could easily have been avoided by briefly delaying the superimposition over each illustration. As a result, the titles depend for their effectiveness on Alwyn's score, which takes the form of an "overture" illustrating not the chapters of Kenway's life but his lifestyle. This Alwyn achieves by alternating fast, syncopated rhythms with slow, languorous ones. The composition commences with full orchestra, tutti, playing the simple stressed five-note rake's leitmotif:

This is in elaborated developments in which the piano and a mellow, sexy saxophone take solo turns. In one passage the saxophone is counterpointed by the jaunty main theme staccato on the piano. The whole sequence is punctuated by fidgety rising and falling string passages, mood swinging from the languorous to the buoyant: a disconcerting effect that prepares for the main text about a restless wastrel. The crescendo on a rising gesture, concluding with predominant brass, anticipates the heroism of the opening scene to which the titles mix. Whether by coincidence or by design, the words "An Individual Picture" also float on to the screen at this point, so that the music is also a paean to Launder and Gilliat's new commercial arrangement.

Gilliat later acknowledged the work's unevenness,[2] and he seems to have tried to use the underscore to iron it out. The film is framed as flashback, its first scene depicting Kenway in an armoured vehicle as he approaches a mined bridge, its last scene returning to the warfront and confirming his death. To have mirrored the film's framing device could have proved an opportunity for Alwyn, but, to end, Gilliat chose a solitary bugle over a shot of Kenway's "lucky" talisman, a cap badge — implying that Kenway finally found purpose in his life by laying it down for his country.

The composer is also complicit with the film's jokes. In an early scene Kenway invites a roommate's girlfriend to a theatrical performance of Shakespeare's *Anthony and Cleopatra*. The evening's entertainment commences with a shot of two torn-up theatre tickets floating on the river, followed by a pastiche of 1940s and 1950s cinema conception of the Tudor setting (Olivier's and Walton's *Henry V* was released the previous year) in which harp and muted unison strings, like the viol, create a courtly air. The joke is completed by a well-chosen verse, "The barge she sat in, like a burnish'd throne / Burn'd on the water: the poop was beaten gold", together with an optical mix to a pair of vacant theatre seats, and a mix back to the water which discovers Kenway making love to the girl in a punt. A sexy saxophone and the leitmotif on a dissonant piano underline the descent from Shakespearean romanticism to Kenway's shabby bathos:

---

[2] Geoff Brown, *Launder and Gilliat*, 115.

The close working relationship of director and composer may be discerned in another scene. The narrator Jennifer, who cares deeply for Kenway, having accepted his proposal of marriage, leaves by train to purchase a wedding dress. He follows, and from the carriage window she watches his car diminish amongst the countryside. Margaret Johnston's voice-over as Jennifer — "I can still see his car winding away from me down that country lane, getting smaller and smaller . . ." — is accompanied by memorably poignant strings tensioned against a fast harp rhythm suggesting the irreversible momentum of the train:

It is his final appearance in her life. The blend of voice-over and musical composition is a reminder of Alwyn's experience in the purely auditory skills of radio.

Despite Gilliat's overall control of both script and direction, *The Rake's Progress* is unbalanced. Some of the scenes are too hurried, too episodic — Kenway's racing career is skipped over with a few library shots and some back-projection — whilst others are too long, even theatrical. Plot dominates character motivation, rather than character development determining plot — Lilli Palmer is given no chance to really explore the despair that leads to Rikki's attempted suicide. Against these comic-strip weaknesses, Alwyn tries to formulate the structure that Gilliat misses — his leitmotifs for both Kenway and Rikki are important in establishing a consistent theme. Faced, however, with a fundamental structural imbalance, there is sometimes little the composer can do except patch and repair.

That could not be said for *I See a Dark Stranger*, a well-structured comedy-thriller scripted by Launder, Gilliat, and Wolfgang Wilhelm and directed by Launder. Its many Hitchcockian touches are a reminder of Launder and Gilliat's co-operation on the scripting of *The Lady Vanishes* (1938) and Gilliat's work on *Jamaica Inn* (1939). It is nothing less than a delight. Aided by a charming voice-over and full of delectable touches, *I See a Dark Stranger* concerns the naïve but spirited Irish girl Bridie (Deborah Kerr), her head crammed with nationalist fervour, who sets off for Dublin on her 21st birthday to join the IRA. When that endeavour fails, she settles in an English village, where she attempts to aid the escape of the Nazi spy Miller (Raymond Huntley). Plunging into waters of increasing depth, her adventures take her on to Liverpool, the Isle of Man, and the Irish border, pursued by the British army officer David Baynes (Trevor Howard).

I See a Dark Stranger demanded a constant reminder of the Irish background. The Irish flavour is established in full lyrical mood by what Alwyn called "Bridie's Tune"[3] under the opening titles, superimposed over a pan across an Irish mountain scene. The theme suggests an arrangement of an Irish idiom, although it has not been identified. Owing to Bridie's extremism and naïvety, the film's treatment of Irish nationalism is humorous rather than romantic, established early on in a scene depicting her indoctrination as a young girl. Hiding behind the bar door, she overhears her father blarneying to a group of eager cronies about his heroism in the 1916 uprising. The sequence ends with a rousing rendering (synched near-disastrously) of "Kelly the Boy from Killane", a song by P. J. McCall extolling the gallantry of a leader of the Wexford Rising of 1798.[4] Later the action moves to an English village, where a statue of Cromwell is doused with paint. The locals gaze mystified as to culprit or motive, but when Bridie appears all innocence pushing a wheelchair down the street, Alwyn's jaunty tongue-in-cheek underscore arrangement of McCall's song is a witty hint.

As illustration of the imaginative integration of music, effects and visuals, two scenes in *I See a Dark Stranger* demand extensive comment.

In the first the combination of camerawork, dialogue, editing, sound mixing, and musical composition suggests comparisons with the evocation of the fear of discovery in Carol Reed's *Odd Man Out*, for which Alwyn was composing during this same period. A hotel sign, swinging and creaking on a wild night, sets the scene. Inside, the pub is crowded, and Grandfather (James Harcourt) calls for Bridie to take him for his regular evening outing in his wheelchair. The mistress of the house tells him to be quiet. The bustle is then contrasted by a strangely angled shot of a ticking clock in the quiet hallway and up the stairs towards Bridie's room, where Miller, the German spy, has died. Bridie must dispose of the body. Ethereal music (strings succeeded by rapid scales on the clarinet) alerts the appearance of her shadow descending with the wheelchair, in which Miller's body is propped. Suspense intensifies as Alwyn introduces a dark menacing theme (strikingly similar to the opening phrase of his First Symphony, 1950) centred on a tritone (the *diabolus in musica*) with dark ostinato cellos and double basses prominent in the bass:[5]

etc.

---

[3] On what appears to be his earliest draft of the score.

[4] Alwyn has already introduced the main phrase of the song as a short jaunty woodwind pre-echo in the pre-title sequence. In this way he strengthens the structural unity of the film's opening.

[5] Only the piano draft of *I See a Dark Stranger* survives.

Bridie reaches the hotel door, and is stopped by the British officer Baynes. The low, ominous, music is interrupted, and once Bridie angrily rids herself of Baynes the ethereal clarinet recommences. But it is joined by the cellos and basses, which are sustained throughout as the camera tracks Bridie along the dark rainswept street. Bridie's anxious voice-over is pitched high against the underscore: "I'll never do it, I know I won't . . ."

Then, quite unexpectedly, normality enters the sequence: the strains of the national anthem, sounding odd against the emotional tension of Alwyn's chromatic theme. Suddenly, still tracking with Bridie, the camera mingles with a crowd leaving the cinema early to avoid standing for the anthem. The effect, counterpointed against the unsettling score, increases tension (will somebody notice Bridie's odd wheel-chair passenger?), and contrasts with Bridie's sinister behaviour — normal people, normal conversation ("Did you put Tiger out, Mum?"). Moreover, both national anthem and crowd throw an ironic cast across the action, eliciting guilty feelings around our concern for an IRA spy for Germany pushing a dead German spy along the street, and adding a propagandist point to boot (these are ordinary people like you and me). Music, dialogue, and imagery force the scene to an almost unbearable intensity; it must have felt really odd to the audiences of 1946, ordinary people like those on the screen, who later on would themselves be leaving the cinema. Something needs to happen.

Instead, the suspense intensifies: a man approaches Bridie and makes a sexual advance, ignoring her rebuttals ("I don't want your company"). When the village bobby rescues Bridie, he chats for a while, his conversation unconsciously ironic ("Between you and me 'e's been looking a bit seedy lately. I don't think 'e'll be with us much longer. Taking 'im down to the cliff row for a bit of sea air?") while the cellos and basses stretch the tension (will the policeman look too closely at the body?) on a sustained single note that — thankfully — releases as the conversation closes and the policeman sees Bridie safely across the road. This little scene with the policeman, particularly, in its mixture of music and dialogue — even to the use of short rapid chords on the clarinet contrasted against the dark sound of the strings — is strongly redolent of scenes in *Odd Man Out*.

The sequence concludes as it began at The George Hotel. Bridie's return with an empty wheel-chair is reflected in a mirror, watched by Baynes who saw her leave the hotel with "grandfather", and we hear again the ethereal strings and vibraphone (but not the clarinet on this occasion) and the sound of the ticking clock.

Attention is deliberately drawn to the clock, although it is not even shown in this scene. "Sounds," said Alwyn, "like music, must be used with imagination and discretion. Just as the factory din tends to disappear with familiarity, so a clock on the wall, though apparent to the eye through a whole scene in the film would not claim the whole attention of the ear by incessant ticking — as we all know if we have lived in a room with a grandfather clock."[6] Alwyn notes the "clock ticking" as early as the piano draft of his score. That the clock is an element in the diegesis of the film underlines its importance: not only to link the sequences, but to draw attention to the importance of "time" in two scenes that immediately follow. Firstly, "time" reveals to us the full extent of Bridie's duplicity: she will shortly confront Granddad and assert against his denials that she has taken him for his "airing"; then Baynes will confront her — against the background sound of the ticking clock in the hallway again — to insist he saw her in the mirror with an empty wheelchair, and she will tear herself away and run to her room.

There is a more subtle way, however, in which the emphasis on time becomes important. There follows a strange sequence in which, after hiding the dead Miller's hat up the chimney, Bridie stares at a picture of a bride hanging on the wall, underscored by her own motif, which suggests a romantic inclination towards Baynes. The film now discloses the manner of her disposal of Miller's body by means of a then-fashionable dream sequence. The wheelchair sequence had opened and closed with the sound of clocks, a regular beat. Now, the film picks up that rhythm by the regular creaking of the inn sign outside Bridie's window. In turn the beat is taken up by a metronome, a flashback to Bridie as a young girl practising piano scales. This curious image relates narratively to nothing else in the film.[7] The sequence then moves on (against an ascending and descending scale of C picked up orchestrally from the piano and counterpointed against the rhythm of the inn-sign and metronome) through close-ups of Bridie's face, shots of the dark cliff, the picture of the bride, and an indistinct picture, perhaps of an angel pointing to Hell as the wages of sin. Finally, frighteningly angled shots show Bridie tipping Miller's body over the clifftop, and the sequence ends as she sits up in bed scared stiff, to a fall of soot and hat down the chimney, while the regular rhythm of the creaking rusty inn sign continues. The whole sequence is a quick way of revealing not only how the body has been disposed, of but also Bridie's guilt-ridden, fearful state of mind. The time motif looks backwards to a strictly reared childhood and

---

[6] Alwyn, "Film Music: Sound or Silence", 12.

[7] Compton Bennett's melodramatic *The Seventh Veil* (1945), which was released nine months earlier than *I See a Dark Stranger*, was a talking-point at the time of the latter's production. *The Seventh Veil* concerns a concert pianist, Francesca (Ann Todd), who attempts suicide after her hands are burned in a car accident. Through hypnosis, a psychiatrist (Herbert Lom) discovers she had been forced into her career by her sadistic guardian Nicholas (James Mason). The scenes of Francesca's enforced practice at the piano (at one time Mason thrashes his walking stick on her fingers) are particularly vivid. I would suggest that just as Francesca's personality has been crippled by her tormentor at the piano scales, so Launder and Gilliat are implying that Bridie's personality has also been damaged by a similar process, and that they inserted this scene in the expectation that most of their contemporary audience would make the connection.

affords a glimpse of the present and future: her romantic leanings towards marriage and, by extension, towards Baynes. But how sophisticated to use the soundtrack as the means by which Bridie's fear-ridden journey in the rainswept street is connected with the dream, by recalling the rhythm of the clock by the swaying inn sign, the metronome, and so on! And we remember that it was to the tick of the clock that Baynes watched Bridie's reflection in the mirror. But a mirror image is not real — it too is an image, like a dream.

An advanced management of music and sound-effects distinguishes the best of Alwyn's work, but nowhere else does it reach such sophistication as in these related sequences of *I See a Dark Stranger*. It is usual for the composer to view a rough-cut before constructing his score, but there is no possibility that these sequences could have gone before the camera without prior planning of track and music. We detect here director, composer, and sound editor together constructing a minutely detailed scenario, adding layer upon layer to its meaning, and all unconsciously raising the soundtrack to an art form.

The fear portrayed in both the wheelchair and nightmare scenes is of the guilty fear of discovery of a crime, a sin. Another sequence, Hitchcockian in feeling, and very dependent on the interreaction of sound and music, explores the panic and fear of guilty isolation in a public place. Bridie's hurdle is to join the non-smoking first-class compartment of a train, make contact by means of passwords, and pass on a message to an unknown Nazi sympathiser in the carriage. As she enters the compartment, voice-over inner dialogue assesses the situation ("This is it, girl") accompanied by a hint of her leitmotif, light ethereal music, mainly strings, and encouraging an emotional association with her predicament. She manages to squeeze into the last seat, next to a kindly old lady (Katie Johnson) who offers her a sandwich. Almost immediately the train rushes into a tunnel, an effect that concentrates our attention on the sound of wheels and the chatter of two women sitting opposite. Seated next to them another woman rolls her eyes in an alarming fashion. There is a feeling of fearful urgency, dependant entirely upon the rhythm of the diegetic sounds, the train wheels and the conversation. The train leaves the tunnel. Bridie begins to convey the password, which is to ask for the window to be lowered, when a gentleman sitting in the corner lowers it first. As she breaks off her sentence the conversation of the two women stops and everybody gazes at her. Interior monologue recommences: "Now how can I ask to have the window half-way down, like Mr Miller said, if it's half-way up already?" This thought is accompanied by a few witty bars of woodwind with an Irish lilt. Foiled, she has no alternative but to ask him to raise it again: the conversation of the two women stops and everybody gazes at her. The sudden ceasing of their conversation stresses the action. After an appropriate pause she asks for the window to be lowered yet again: again the conversation of the two women stops and everybody gazes at her again.

A light solo violin is re-introduced — and more voice-over ("Oh, what am I going to do?"): to a sudden bass chord, the train again passes into a tunnel. The effect, on a visual cut, is startling and creates a mix of excitement, threat and unease. The rhythm of the wheels is loud and matches fairly quick cuts from each passenger matched by vibraphone "dongs" on each cut as the subjective camera looks at the fellow passengers from nightmarish angles, concluding on the woman with the wobbling eyes which shows that she is simply studying a book of eye exercises: Alwyn embellishes this shot wittily with trumpets *cuivré*. The train emerges rapidly from the tunnel into the station and shortly afterwards the other German spy is revealed: the old lady sitting next to Bridie, who is arrested.

The balance of diegetic sound-effects, music, and editing is judged to a nicety. Voice-over is vital, too, not only to contribute to the humour and tension of the scene, but to enlarge our appreciation of Bridie's character. In sound feature films, voice-over — that is to say, interior monologue — derives both from the soliloquy in drama and from the novel. In the novel the use of the first person is an early device, dating back at least to Richardson's epistolary *Clarissa* (1747–8) and brought to full flowering in Charlotte Brontë's *Jane Eyre* (1847). In *Bleak House* (1852–3), Charles Dickens alternated chapters supposedly written in the first person by the female lead character, with chapters in a detached third-person narrative. Dickens's technique is a forerunner of the cinema's voice-over, which affords the viewer the luxury of understanding character motivation from within while at the same time observing from the outside: attached and detached, as it were. The technique became fashionable in the cinema of the 1940s after Hitchcock lifted Daphne du Maurier's celebrated opening interior monologue from *Rebecca* (1938, filmed in 1940): "Last night I dreamt I went to Manderley again . . ." And from around that time character voice-over became something of a vogue, its adoption closely allied to the fashion for dream sequences, hallucinatory scenes, and flashbacks.

   Launder and Gilliat use voice-over to good effect in both *The Rake's Progress* and *I See a Dark Stranger*. In neither production does voice-over initiate the plot, *Rebecca*-style, but the plot is allowed to develop until a critical point enables its natural introduction. In *The Rake's Progress* an opening sequence shows Kenway's tank approaching and driving over a bridge to test for mines. The scene changes to a chance discovery by Jennifer that he is "missing". She takes up the narration in voice-over, and serves as both an objective commentator on his life and also an important character in the plot. Her voice-over commences as she stands in a crowded bus and begins to reflect on the life of her lover. Similarly in *I See a Dark Stranger*, a pre-title tease (with another, unidentified, quasi-documentary male voice-over), the titles, and a sequence detailing Bridie's background and departure to Dublin pass before she, too, begins the muse.

Public transport is a useful location for a voice-over — several of Bridie's voice-over thoughts take place on buses or trains, an opportunity for the character to be alone with her thoughts without slowing the action. David Lean had set an example with *Brief Encounter* (1945), introducing his heroine's lonely voice-over on a train at precisely the same point in the plot.

Alwyn's approach to the musical accompaniment of voice-overs is revealing. It would have been easy to use a similar musical device for each situation. Never lazy and ever the experimentalist, however, he approached each assignment with a fresh view. "A composer", he wrote, "does not get worse or stale by continual writing providing he sets a high value on his art; he is like an athlete who keeps his muscles flexible by constant exercise." [8]

In *The Rake's Progress* the sequence is removed from reality by shunning interior bus effects (they fade immediately the voice commences). The interior monologue continues against a long tracking shot into a close-up of Jennifer's face — "Vivian — can't believe it. He'll turn up again, just as he always used to when you least expected it, like a bad penny . . ." — and the dynamic of the music track is held down against the voice. Its etherealness is stressed by Alwyn's use of light strings and vibraphone. Faint brass is heard, a trumpet, and when the monologue finishes the sound recordist brings up this — military — effect loudly to introduce the next scene: a flash back to Trafalgar Square on Armistice Night, 1918. The overall effect is one of wistful, sad nostalgia.

It is instructional to judge the effectiveness of the score at any one point by testing the alternatives. The three elements are voice, effects, and music. Here, the voice track with its beautiful delivery is most effective. The second element, the sound-effects, is quickly disposed of: to retain the bus effects would have proved too much of an intrusion of the exterior world into the interior feelings of Jennifer, and they are wisely faded away. A consideration of the musical element, however, is not so easy: one option would have been to retain the voice track alone, against silence and without music. This would have been effective, and a solution that Alwyn may have approved of — he was much opposed to an unnecessary use of the score. However, as this way was not adopted we must ask what his score adds. First, its strange psychological feeling, contrasted with the everyday shot of the bus, signals that we are listening to interior monologue. Alwyn was rapidly making his reputation for the musical creation of ethereal effects in hallucinatory and dream scenes, and in time he would create masterpieces of the style in films such as *Odd Man Out* and *The Rocking Horse Winner*. This is the first use of voice-over in *The Rake's Progress*, and the filmmakers may have wished to emphasise the point. But there is more: the script concludes: "Truth is, people are what they are and there's nothing very much you can do about it. We are made mostly by what we inherit, and the

[8] Alwyn, "An Introduction to Film Music", 33.

circumstances around us from the cradle onwards. That's how it was with Vivian." The monologue therefore ends on a resolute note as Jennifer attempts to come to terms with her grief and to justify Kenway's behaviour. Alwyn subtly reinforces the emotion of the scene, stressing the "optimistic" element: brass is introduced, and as Jennifer's thoughts finish, the trumpet sounds loudly and confidently. Yet the music also points to the next scene depicting Kenway's boyhood adventure on Armistice Night. It is like the parting of a stage curtain: the prologue is over; the following acts will trace the story of Kenway's life.

In *I See a Dark Stranger* the voice-over has an authentic brogue, no doubt attributable to Liam Redmond's "additional dialogue". It is introduced at about the same point in the plot as in *The Rake's Progress*, but its purpose is different. It also starts on public transport, where the outside world counterpoints the character's inner musings. Bridie scrambles into a moving train carriage and sits opposite a man later revealed as the German spy Miller. Miller is introduced by his reflection in the carriage window as he slams it shut. Immediately the score alerts us: sinister, mysterious violins, to be shortly joined by the flute and ostinato cellos as the mood turns more menacing. Bridie considers her sole companion, her naïvety revealed by her racing thoughts and nuances of facial expression. The camera tracks in to full close-up, and a light solo violin accompanies her thoughts as she weighs up Miller's romantic appeal ("hasn't he the lovely nails . . ."). As in *The Rake's Progress*, the violin reinforces the monologue, but the emotional effect is different: while Jennifer's emotion is of grief, here the instrument emphasises Bridie's immaturity and simple romanticism.[9]

As Bridie spots Miller's name on his case, a vibraphone sounds a few notes, almost imperceptibly: "He's English!"

As the penny drops the music becomes nervously intense, reflecting Bridie's irritation: "Will you look at the cruel set of his jaw. You could take him for Cromwell." Bridie abandons her fleeting romantic monologue, and with it the musical underscore disappears too: the remainder of the scene is carried diegetically by the dry sound of wheels on track.

Launder, like Gilliat in *The Rake's Progress*, uses voice-over sparingly. In *I See a Dark Stranger* interior monologue is a necessity — perhaps a protection for the filmmakers — to show the essential innocence and gullibility of Bridie, who after all was a Nazi spy in a film released immediately after the war. The frequency of the interior monologue increases as her doubts about her role

---

[9] The other instruments are viola and harp; the harp suggests Bridie's Irishness.

increase, and ceases once she acknowledges her mistake. Her final voice-over carries itself without music. Anxiously she takes the hotel lift to her to burn a vital diary, unknowingly accompanied by a German spy: ". . . Hurry lift, oh hurry! I've the troubles of the world on my shoulders!" The hum of the lift takes on a menacing note. Natural effects — again — are enough to carry the scene.

The meticulous balance of sound-effects and musical score, the dependence on effects rather than music for emotional timbre, and an at times close correspondence between the scores, relate this film closely to Carol Reed's *Odd Man Out*, another film with an Irish setting, composed during the same period.[10]

---

[10] Music recording for *I See a Dark Stranger* finished in mid April 1946. Alwyn had sketched Johnny's theme some time before filming on *Odd Man Out* started on 27 March 1946

13
A "Big Score"

ALWYN was instilling a good deal of Irish atmosphere at this time. Amongst a busy schedule in 1945, scoring perhaps eleven short documentaries, *The True Glory*, *Great Day*, *The Rake's Progress*, and seven compositions for radio, he still had time in November 1945 to set off for Belfast with his friend the poet Louis MacNeice. Ostensibly the purpose was to oversee the music for MacNeice's local radio production about the city of Armagh, *City Set on a Hill*, but the trip was as much an excuse to visit Dublin for a rugby match, a passion of MacNeice's. After the recording they adjourned to the Georgian house of W. R. Rodgers, who had written the script. There was plenty to drink, and the party ended into the night with MacNeice and Rodgers dancing to Alwyn's flute and drumming on an empty box.[1]

Shortly after Alwyn's return to England he received a significant proposal:

> The first thing I knew about *Odd Man Out* was the arrival of the book by post with a note from Carol Reed to say that he thought this was the subject he was looking for — what did I think? I had worked with Carol before on the two war pictures, *The Way Ahead* and *The True Glory* and we had often talked of the ideal picture we should like to make with music playing an essential part in the story. Well, here it was — I read it — the novel was magnificent — and the scope for music obvious. By a strange chance only two days before, I had returned from a visit to Belfast — the wet — wintry November Belfast of the story — the very city and the very month in which the tale was set.[2]

At this time Reed's reputation was greater than David Lean's. With *The Way Ahead* and *The True Glory* behind him, he could find backing for a subject of

---

[1] Barbara Coulton, *Louis MacNeice in the BBC* (London: Faber, 1980), 78–9; Alwyn, "Ariel to Miranda", 71; William Alwyn, *The World in My Mind* (Southwold: Southwold Press, 1975), unnumbered introductory page.

[2] In *Film-Music Notes*, 7:2 (Nov.–Dec. 1947), unnumbered page; Muir Mathieson, "The Time Factor in Film Music", *Film Industry*, 4:23 (May 1948), 7. Some years later Alwyn gave a radio interview, "Writing Music for Films", William Alwyn interviewed by Ken Emrys Roberts, BBC Third Programme (25 February 1964), in which he related a slightly different version: "It was the oddest and most curious thing. I was in Belfast at the time. I was examining in music out there. I got a letter from Carol enclosing the book and saying, 'I'd like you to have a look at this, are you interested?' Well, it was November and it was snowing in Belfast. And this book was about Ireland and it took place in the snow and it took place in November."

his own picking, even to a sympathetic study of an IRA member. The finance came readily from an enthusiastic Del Giudice and his Two Cities Films, for whom Reed had worked on *The Way Ahead*.

Odd Man Out is a British film noir, one of a cycle of "man on the run" films of the period, the story of the final eight hours in the life of Johnny MacQueen, an IRA leader played with austere vulnerability by James Mason. Seriously wounded after accidentally killing a clerk during a raid on a linen mill, Johnny is separated from his companions when he falls from the getaway car. What follows is an allegorical, almost impressionistic tale of Johnny's delirious journey through the dark shadowy streets of Belfast, at first shiny and wet, then snowy, owing much to photographer Robert Krasker's experience of lighting in the German cinema of the 1930s, the visual counterpart of Alwyn's music. On his journey, the people Johnny meets — children, an IRA colleague, two middle-class English women, soldiers, a cabman, a publican, a failed doctor and an artist, and a crafty caged-bird seller as empty as his name Shell (F. J. McCormick) — shun him or use him for their own ends. Even Kathleen (Kathleen Ryan), the woman who loves him to desperation and searches for him, is not unselfish: she would rather kill Johnny and herself than see him executed and live long years without him. By doing so she robs him of moral choice.[3]

The film climaxes with Johnny, mauled and dying, hunted through the snow by police, Kathleen, Shell, and the meek-mannered but shrewd and determined priest Father Tom (W. G. Fay). Finally Kathleen, who has arranged Johnny's escape on a midnight sailing, finds him (Plate 8). But it is too late, and as the police close in she fires two shots, the police reply, and two bodies lie in the snow. The police examine the bodies; Fr Tom leads Shell away; the ship's siren sounds, and the clock strikes an ironic twelve o'clock.

The wartime tradition of teamwork was still alive in the studios, and Reed was of Alwyn's opinion concerning the artistic value of craft co-operation. He depended especially upon his composers: when they were weak his films showed their seams and joints. *Odd Man Out* is a masterpiece because of its structural indebtedness to Alwyn.

Music was considered so important to the mood of the film that Alwyn wanted to set it "from the very first flicker on the screen":

> Let me explain, just before a film begins, you are shown the censor's certificate. The cinema organist usually accompanies this. Then there's a lot more bits and pieces to do with the renting organisation and so on, including two big bangs on a gong for J. Arthur Rank Presents. I was very anxious that the right atmosphere of the picture should be estab-

---

[3] A point made by Andrew Sarris, "First of the Realists, Part 1", *Films and Filming*, 3:12 (Sept. 1957), 32; repr. from *Film Culture*, 4 (1956).

8 Carol Reed's *Odd Man Out* (1947). The music raises the emotional temperature as
Kathleen (Kathleen Ryan) finds the dying Johnny (James Mason) struggling hopelessly towards the docks and freedom.

lished at the earliest possible moment, and at the suggestion of Muir
Mathieson (who so brilliantly directed the music), we took the unusual
course of starting the music on the censor's certificate and even made
the two gong beats take their rightful place in the score.[4]

Today it is rare to see the film screened with the original censor's certificate,
but when it is, as during screenings at the National Film Theatre, the audience
observably shivers with excitement during the censor's certificate, as Alwyn
had hoped. When the music quickly reaches the two strikes on the Rank gong,
achieved by cymbal clashes, the effect is surprisingly thrilling.

However, it was not the first time Alwyn had backlaid the title music. As
early as 1940, *The New Britain* had commenced with a drumbeat followed by
trumpet fanfare over the Columbia Pictures title, and in *SOS* a year later the
music covers the end of the censor's certificate and the following distributor's

---

[4] Alwyn, in *Film-Music Notes*, 7:2 (Nov.–Dec. 1947); Mathieson, "The Time Factor in Film Music", 7.

card. Alwyn repeated the idea three months after *Odd Man Out* in *Take My Life* (1947) and on several later films, but to less powerful effect. Other composers copied the idea, and a year later Mathieson was writing as if it were standard practice.[5]

A film in which the music was composed first was unusual. By permitting Alwyn to consider the thematic material from the start, Reed entrusted him with the considerable role of determining the film's concept — the idea behind the drama. This is not to undermine Reed's overriding responsibility for the film's statement and artistic integrity, but it is suggestive of his debt to his artistic and technical collaborators. The importance of Alwyn's contribution to the dramatic-thematic structure of *Odd Man Out* cannot be overemphasised: his score knits together and defines the separate elements of the film, achieved largely through the use of motto and leitmotif; Johnny, Kathleen, and Shell are each bestowed with an individual theme.

The most memorable is Johnny's theme, appropriately also the film's main dramatic theme. Johnny is no glorious hero, and Alwyn's concept is slow, sonorous, and dark, punctuated in the film's opening movement and in the finale by low timpani beats. This is a funeral march, and it determines the shape of the film: Johnny's slow traipse around the darkened streets of Belfast, compared by some to the Via Dolorosa. Sketching this leitmotif was Alwyn's first task:

> We worked out the very pace of the music with the aid of a piano while I improvised and Carol limped up and down the room in the person of the wounded gangster, Johnny. Most of the scenes were shot to pre-recordings and transformed and orchestrated afterwards.[6]

A lesser composer could have saturated the entire film with this powerful theme, but Alwyn is sparing: he saves it to structure and for the climax. It also commences the film — following a funereal drumbeat, sombre fanfare, and tormented strings — with full orchestra over aerial shots of Belfast,

etc

and establishes, as Alwyn had hoped, the atmosphere, as well as a motto that the audience will recognise later.[7]

It is hinted with the lightest of touches as the wounded Johnny, having fallen from the getaway car into the road, rises to his feet to muted fanfare

---

[5] Muir Mathieson, "Contemporary Trends in Film-music", in *Winchester's Screen Encyclopaedia* (London: Winchester Publications, 1948), 326.

[6] Alwyn, "Film Music: Sound or Silence", 13.

[7] Sir Malcolm Arnold suggests Alwyn found his inspiration in Jerome Kern's song "Old Man River" from the musical *Showboat* (1927). Interview with writer, 25 Feb. 2000.

and staggers down a side street and across a bombed site. But the critical use of Johnny's leitmotif is to give form to the film's loose construction by cueing each occasion when Johnny leaves a temporary refuge to resume his journey. Therefore, in developed form it is held in reserve until Johnny, who has been hiding in a disused air-raid shelter, commences his trudge through the streets in an attempt to find refuge at Kathleen's house. This juncture of the film is seen by analysts as its turning-point. Until now the mood has been rooted in reality, but from this moment, as James Agee wrote, "the film, like the novel, tries for a broader and broader allegory and phantasmagoria".[8] Thus, major recapitulations of Johnny's theme recur, first when he leaves the refuge of Maudie and Rosie (Fay Compton and Beryl Measor), the two middle-class English women who dress his wound, and second when he leaves the refuge of a scrap-yard, the bandage now streaming from his arm in the falling snow.

Finally, and memorably, he leaves the refuge of the artist's studio in an attempt to reach Fr Tom's presbytery and Kathleen. This is the film's nine-minute climax, and the score is continuous, a rhapsody integrating Johnny's theme (now fully developed), Kathleen's theme, and moments of dramatic force. Alwyn's music knits together, and balances the tension of, the number of short scenes composing this ultimate climax. Thus, after leaving the artist's studio, Shell encourages Johnny to keep moving, and Johnny limps haltingly in close-up through the falling snow. The music climaxes suddenly on a sharp visual cut as Shell fears detection from passers-by, and the scene has changed to a wide-angle of an arched alleyway and shops.

The chord, added to the hard picture edit, shocks, and the wailing clarinets induce anxiety. A little later the scene mixes to Kathleen waiting outside Fr Tom's presbytery, but her theme is introduced late and continues over a mix to Johnny trudging alone through the snow. The cue for the arrival of a police car soon afterwards is also late, matching a close-up cutaway shot as Shell spots it, although the car has been shown already in the previous shot. Probably these late cues reflect a timing inaccuracy during recording, but perhaps Alwyn intended it that way. They work because the sliding of Kathleen's theme over Johnny's following shot links Kathleen and Johnny romantically, and the police car cue over Shell's reaction offers the audience a subjective rapport. The delay in the cues also seems important in linking and holding the separate short sequences together.

---

[8] James Agee, *"Odd Man Out"*, *The Nation* (19 July 1947), 79–81, quoted in James de Felice, *Filmguide to "Odd Man Out"* (Bloomington and London: Indiana University Press, 1975), 68.

The film moves to its resolution. The main theme swells as Johnny writhes in pain against iron railings. A fanfare raises hopeful expectations and a cut shows Kathleen running past and skidding on the snow as she suddenly sees him. The fanfare climaxes and there is a briefest of silences — a heartbeat — before Kathleen cries "Johnny!"

That hiatus, short as it is, coming after the extended sequence of music lasting many minutes, is lacerating.

"Kathleen!" cries Johnny, who has seen many visions. "Is it really you?" Kathleen's theme is quietly re-introduced, but, instead of running to him as we expect, she holds back: "Come to me and see!"[9] "I can't," replies Johnny. "If you are real, stretch out your hand to mine." Behind the dialogue, the score crescendos, and, as Johnny reaches out his hands and Kathleen runs to embrace him, cymbals and an orchestral surge hold out exquisite longings and a hope that Johnny will be saved.

[9] It was not apparent to me until I read the shooting script (BFI Special Collection) that the two
    characters are at cross purposes: "Behind Agnes [Kathleen] we see a distant view of the docks.

It is a moment of high romanticism, and Kathleen's theme is sustained quietly for a few seconds beneath more dialogue, until the sound of the ship's siren reinforces hope of salvation. But even as the siren sounds, a subdued menacing fanfare introduces Johnny's theme with its regular muted drumbeat, which leads to the film's tragic conclusion. Dai Vaughan's comment is worth quoting:

> We track sideways along the railings with Kathleen and Johnny, and an almost casual glance over her shoulder cues a cut to a line of police and police-cars advancing upon us, dimly seen, their torches and headlights glimmering through the snow. The music simply continues its steady tread; and the fact that there is no extraneous emphasis placed upon this cut gives it a quality of the inevitable. I know no other film which conveys such utter despair.[10]

Much of the film's poignancy is centred around the women, who must be ready to give up their men and their lives for the cause. When Johnny leaves Kathleen's house for the ill-fated robbery, Kathleen's wistful — and desperate — farewell introduces her leitmotif. Alwyn avoided sentimentality; instead its gentle mood of quiet parting is reminiscent of Walton's pastorale "Touch Her Soft Lips and Part" for the film *Henry v*. In another moving sequence, Granny advises Kathleen not to search the streets for Johnny, recalling that when she was young she too loved "a rebel on the run", but married another to great happiness and "grand times". Granny points to her wedding photograph, and Kathleen catches sight of her own reflection in a mirror and weighs her choice. Granny dozes off, Kathleen makes her decision, and "as she bends over to take the revolver, Alwyn's music, which quietly has used winds and strings to underscore Granny's meaningful nostalgia, suddenly becomes threatening and urgent".[11]

Musical "silence", which Alwyn valued highly,[12] is deployed in a variety of

---

She wants to take him in that direction." The original dialogue, "Come Johnny, and see", makes the exchange clearer.

    F. L. Green took a year, in collaboration with R. C. Sherriff, adapting his novel *Odd Man Out* for the screen. During that time and during shooting, Carol Reed shifted Green's blend of religious (perhaps quasi-religious) allegory and politics towards an emphasis on the allegorical. An obvious example at this moment in the film is the strong image of Johnny stretched out on the railings like Christ on the cross. The expression, "Come and see" could similarly be regarded as a reinforcement of scriptural allusion. A quotation from St John's Gospel (1:39), it is Christ's invitation to two of his disciples to join him. However, on a wider, theological, level, it is seen as meaning that we will gain nothing through finding Christ unless we are disposed to submit ourselves to him.

[10] Dai Vaughan, *Odd Man Out* (London: BFI, 1995), 63. Vaughan's only acknowledgement to the considerable achievement of the composer is his name in the credit list.

[11] De Felice, *Filmguide to Odd Man Out*, 48.

[12] See Introduction.

ways. Two examples must suffice. The robbery at the mill and the subsequent
killing of the guard and escape by car is without music. Underscore breaks
in only as Johnny falls from the car, mixed with the sound of the car engine,
an alarm bell, a screech of brakes, the men's excited voices: the heightened
sound accentuates our confusion and panic. In his classic study *The Technique
of Film Editing*, Karel Reisz described the significance of the introduction of
music here:

> With this shot . . . the situation is posed and the long tragic search be-
> gins. Johnny's fall, therefore, has significance beyond that of the cul-
> mination of an isolated exciting sequence: it is the motivating point of
> the whole film and as such its dramatic significance is conveyed by the
> sudden artificial entry of the music. Because the music has been used
> sparingly up to this point, its sudden entry makes a more precise and
> definite point than would have been possible with a continuous back-
> ground score.[13]

A second example, chosen at random: Johnny's IRA colleague Dennis (Robert Beatty) discovers him in the air-raid shelter. Their conversation is without
music. They hear the sound of police cars arriving. In a tense moment Dennis tells Johnny he will lead away the police. But Johnny asks, "Dennis — did
I kill that fellow?" Dennis does not reply, and the music strikes in suddenly as
Dennis runs off. The abrupt entry of the music, contrasting with the previous
quietness of the scene, heightens the action but also stresses the unanswered
question.

There is an opposite of silence. There is a sequence where a plainclothes policeman follows Kathleen. To shake him off, she enters a dancehall. An abrupt
cut to a sign, "No jitterbugging", is followed by a pan to jitterbugging couples.
Kathleen passes them by and leaves by an exit at the back of the hall. Originally
Reed had planned a more complicated sequence:

> A young man is standing at the edge of the floor. She joins him and they
> start dancing together — taking him across the floor to the opposite wall.
> The brass instruments of the band shriek and wail. The whole scene tilts
> and revolves and the slither and stamp of feet becomes louder and the
> grinning contorted faces of the musicians gloat over the scene. Agnes
> [Kathleen's name on the original screenplay] steers her partner towards
> a door marked Exit and suddenly breaks away from him. . .[14]

In adopting the simpler action, Reed's instinct was right. Much of the film's
subtext and poignancy depend upon Kathleen's ascetic/romantic image, which

---

[13] Karel Reisz, *The Technique of Film Editing* (London: Focal Press, 1953), 267.
[14] Shooting script, BFI Special Collection.

would have been destroyed had she joined the dance. Moreover, it would have been unnecessary, for the almost obscene feeling Reed wanted to suggest is conveyed by the dance music, scored by Alwyn as a rasping, blaring trumpet phrase continuously repeated. It is ugly and disturbing. Nevertheless, as it stands the scene illuminates the nature of the film: like a smack of real life, it reveals by contrast that the world of Kathleen is swathed in romanticism. If the cinema drugs us into a dreamlike state, then this sequence breaks into those dreams, and we are happy to leave the dance hall to return with Kathleen to the dreamworld of the Belfast streets. The trumpet also forecasts the later, and crucial, use of the Biblical expression "sounding brass", meaning pompously empty and meaningless.

It is evident that Alwyn did not pay mere lip-service to his claim to work as a team:

> film music should be written as music designed for, and to be placed on, film together with the dialogue and the effects of the sound track. It is one component of a complex intermarriage of sound related to visuals. Music has a special function to perform — primarily an emotional one (using the word in its broadest sense); natural sound-effects have also their special function, and the two should not be confused unless a deliberate musical effect is planned . . .[15]

For *Odd Man Out*, Alwyn worked closely with the sound editor, Harry Miller. "We knew what we were doing individually with sound-effects and music," wrote Alwyn, "and the final result was a complete integration of sound and visuals — a sound film in the real meaning of the word, where music had been allowed to speak in terms of the Film as a Fine Art."[16] In *Odd Man Out*, sound-effects are vital to the overall mood and craft of the film. The entire sequence of the mill robbery, played against "natural effects" — for example, the sound of the throbbing mill machinery in enhancing the tension of the robbery — has been carefully analysed in Reisz's *The Technique of Film Editing*.[17]

Other sounds are reiterated as motifs throughout the film and were carefully co-ordinated with the music in the planning stages: gunshots, the ship's hooter, and the clock chimes come together in the film's final moments. Between effects and music there is no competition: in some scenes the music predominates, in others it is subordinated to become nearly impossible to distinguish an individual rhythm, as in the getaway sequence from the mill.

There is a link between film and dream. Watching stories in a darkened cinema is akin to dreaming. The history of the dream or hallucinatory sequence

---

[15] Alwyn, "How Not to Write Film Music", 8.
[16] Alwyn, "Film Music: Sound or Silence", 13.
[17] Reisz, *The Technique of Film Editing*, 266–7

can be traced back to the medium's beginnings — Méliès springs to mind — and earlier, to the lantern-slide show. In the cinema of the 1940s, the filmically related "psychological" state of the dream, the hallucinatory sequence, the interior monologue, and the flashback became fashionable. Probably this was inevitable in Hollywood ("the dream factory"), where Freudian psychiatry was a fad, but such devices were popular in Britain too. It may be that in wartime the loss of both stability and loved ones creates the need for nostalgia and remembrances.

By now Alwyn was fully adept at hallucinatory scenes. In *Odd Man Out* there are four separately scored sequences where it would have been easy to repeat a single cue. However, although the "melody" necessarily remains broadly the same to maintain the film's homogeneity, each individual sequence reflects the needs of the scenario at that point, with variations in rhythm and orchestration. In the first, the drive to the mill, the score is the final of three changes of tempo in a continuous composition that commences with Kathleen's poignant farewell to Johnny at the house. It quickens as the members of the gang join the drive to the linen mill,[18] with effects held down behind the music, including a ship's siren at the docks — how this film's symbols are subtly infiltrated! Once Johnny joins the car, giddy tremolo strings and brass fanfares underscore a series of subjective hallucinatory shots, commencing with close-up tracking along tramlines, and a series of unsteady, hand-held, angled shots of street views to show Johnny's light-headed unfitness to take part in the robbery. The scene ends with a skewed shot of the approaching factory chimneys and a squeal of brakes the car pulls to a halt, followed by the clock chimes. The music, with its violin tremolo, descending scales, and strident trumpets and horns, matches perfectly the giddy sensation portrayed by the images and is faster than in the later hallucinatory sequences.

The second hallucinatory sequence is treated in exactly the opposite way. A ball bounces along the streets, and a girl chases it. The child is significant; later Dennis questions her in his search for Johnny, and she too, separated from the other children and wearing a single skate (which compares with Johnny's wounded arm), represents an "odd one out". The wounded Johnny, hiding in the air-raid shelter, sees the ball bounce through the door, and a harp glissando begins precisely on a cut to his close-up. Cutting away to a misty subjective shot, we see a prison warder unlocking a cell door and picking up the ball. Johnny speaks to him, and the music stops. At one stage Reed had planned "wild track shouts of children" against this shot, but wisely that decision, which would have intruded the real world and distracted, was abandoned.[19] Johnny, hallu-

---

[18] Variations are used for the chase sequence of three of Johnny's IRA colleagues, and for Dennis's attempt to lead off the police from the shelter. Here it smoothes out some slightly odd montage editing between location and studio.

[19] Reed's notation to *Odd Man Out* shooting script, BFI Special Collection.

cinating, believes he is still in prison and tells the warder about his dream. It is a monologue without music or effects. He is amused by this dream of a raid on a mill . . . he shot a man . . . he was wounded in his left arm . . . he fell from the getaway car . . . he was afraid he had killed a man . . . and he came to an air-raid shelter. The warder stares at him impassively. The sequence, musically silent, induces an intense feeling of dry horror because Johnny is unaware he has not been dreaming. He stops, and on another close-up the music returns. The image of the warder mixes to that of the child, who flees, and as Johnny touches his wound and realises that his "dream" is not a dream a heavy string passage ensues. Again musical silence is used creatively: emphasising the emotion of the monologue, increasing the impact of the music. It is with this sequence that Johnny's fevered state of mind begins to be woven into the fabric of the film.

Later, after Johnny has been mauled by his trudge around the streets of Belfast, he seeks refuge in a bar, is secured inside a "crib" by the publican, and endures a third hallucination. He knocks over a glass of beer, and in the separate bubbles of spilt froth sees some of the people he has encountered: the shot cashier, Maudie and Rosie, the cabman, and the soldier who helped him inside the cab. Their voices — accusing, mocking, comforting — intermingle with pub atmosphere and orchestra in a kind of counterpoint. Harp glissando and flutes are important to the score, which is almost lost beneath the babble but accentuates the mood of feverishness. A final cut to a wide shot shows all the faces in the bubbles, all speaking at once — plus two more: Rosie's husband and Kathleen. Kathleen's words are indistinct, but "I want you Johnny, I need you, I'm waiting for you" can just about be distinguished. Johnny screams with despair, and outside the crib the astonished drinkers fall silent.

As an illustration of the practical use of silence, one wonders how much the editing and soundtrack here owe to Alwyn. Normally, it would be foolish to attribute such influence to the composer, but *Odd Man Out* was different: we know Reed was listening to Alwyn. We also know that that a sudden and shocking silence was a favourite device of Alwyn's, and that the scene was changed significantly from the shooting script:

> The echoes of the voices [in the beer bubbles] subside. The faces dissolve after filling Johnny's vision. The voices merge into the general uproar of the pub. Johnny has brought up his left hand before his eyes. In doing so he has scraped the wounded back of it against the edge of the ledge. He groans loudly.
>
> A sudden silence and everyone looks to the crib at the sound of the groan . . .[20]

Johnny's last hallucination is the most significant. In the studio of the artist

[20] Shooting script, BFI Special Collection.

Lukey (Robert Newton), the failed medical student Tober (Elwyn Brook-Jones) dresses Johnny's wounds and is anxious to get him into hospital. But Lukey insists on capturing in oils the "truth of life and death", which he hopes to see in Johnny's eyes. Shell, anxious to take Johnny to Father Tom, joins the discussion. They fall into heated argument, and their voices become jumbled. Music enters as the camera tracks in to Johnny's face: strings, vibraphone, celesta and harp glissando, fluttering flutes, and brass are important. The camera makes rocking movements, and there is a cut to a subjective shot of Johnny's view of the studio (which is not real, but also a painting). Then, over talk about the police and trials, the pictures in the studio slide away from the walls and line up, deformed, frightening, and impersonal and reminiscent of the work of Edvard Munch[21] — like the faces in the beer froth, so many strangers staring at Johnny but not helping him.

There has been discussion about the underlying allegory of *Odd Man Out*. Some commentators have compared Johnny with Christ, but the analogy was denied by Reed,[22] and although Johnny may be a sacrificial victim he is not the Christ. A surer allegory is that of the struggle between the avenging angel, represented by the dark omnipresence of the RUC Head Constable (Denis O'Dea), who pursues MacQueen because he "belongs to the law", and the attempt at Johnny's salvation by Fr Tom.

But the music suggests a further level of meaning. At this juncture in Johnny's delirium, Shell interrupts the scene: "Have you heard tell of Father Tom?" he asks. The mention of the name diverts Johnny's delirium, and an image of Fr Tom appears amidst the paintings. Johnny leans forward: "Tell me, Father, like you used to tell us . . .", but the image smiles and mouths silently. "Louder, Father, speak louder — I can't hear you." The voices of Lukey and Tober break off abruptly, and cut-aways show them watching, but the music continues (knitting the shots together) while Johnny talks to the vision of Fr Tom: "Ah, we've always drowned your voice with our shouting . . ." At this point Alwyn introduces on horns the fanfare associated with Johnny's theme:

It is a sign that something significant is about to happen. Johnny declaims from St Paul's Letter to the Corinthians (1:13): "But I remember when I was a boy . . . I spoke as a child, I thought as a child, I understood as a child. But when I became a man I put away childish things." Cut to Fr Tom, smiling approval.

---

[21]   Actually by Roger Furse. Studio publicity shots of the paintings disclose that at least two are gross caricatures of the actors (Kathleen Ryan and Robert Newton) or the characters they portray.

[22]   Michael Voigt, "Sir Carol Reed", *Focus on Film*, 17 (Spring 1974), 24

Johnny stands, towering over a very low camera position, and, reversing the order of the Biblical text, continues, "Though I speak with the tongues of men and of angels and have not charity, I am become a sounding brass, or a tinkling cymbal. And though I have the gift of prophesy, and understand all mysteries, and all knowledge; and though I have all faith, so that I could remove mountains, and have no charity I am nothing." Alwyn's score illuminates the sequence: as Johnny rises to his feet, the music (voice matching) becomes an inspiring reworking of the Johnny theme. Fanfares are heard, *lontano*, as from a distance — reflecting the words "sounding brass" and recalling the brass fanfares that heralded Johnny's theme throughout the film:

Johnny has at last seen a truth he was groping for from the start, when he said, "I believe in everything we are doing, but this violence isn't getting us anywhere . . . If only we could throw the guns away and make our cause in Parliament instead of in the back streets." The film's message is therefore double-edged: it is a cry for pity, and we remember all those by whom Johnny has been used. More importantly, Johnny — the leader of an IRA cell — has at last grasped the meaning of humility and love, and is faced with the terrible realisation that power and violence are as nothing. Its mood sets up the bleak finale, which follows almost immediately.

Odd Man Out was given its London premiere on 30 January 1947 at the Odeon, Leicester Square, to critical acclaim. Some considered it to be the best British film ever made. "My boats are all burnt and my trumpets are ready for sounding", wrote Paul Dehn, perhaps thinking of Johnny's sounding brass; "this is the best picture I have ever seen." [23] It received the British Film of the Year Award, and Reed's reputation seemed made.[24] But unwittingly Reed had exposed a major flaw in his artistry. In *The Finest Years*, a study of British filmmakers of the period, Charles Drazin writes disparagingly of the "grandiloquence of William Alwyn's biblical-epic score" and suggests that Reed may have regarded the music as, in Drazin's words, "heavy-handed". In an unreferenced footnote he quotes the critic W. J. Weatherby: "I remember that when *Odd Man Out* had just been released and was being hailed as a masterpiece,

[23] Paul Dehn, in *The Sunday Chronicle* (2 Feb. 1947).

[24] A few months later Hugh Stewart produced a radio adaptation for the BBC Light Programme (30 June 1947). It presumably utilised the film's music track, since Alwyn's score was played by the London Symphony Orchestra, as in the film. James McKechnie and Joyce Redman played Johnny and Kathleen.

I criticised the soundtrack in parts for underlining the drama too heavily. Sir Carol wrote to me that he quite agreed but that, alas, it was too late to do anything about it!"[25] Considering the background to the making of the film, this sounds like hypocrisy. By not putting Weatherby firmly in his place, Reed not only washed his hands of a creative colleague but revealed a lack of confidence, masked in his three consecutive masterpieces, *Odd Man Out*, *The Fallen Idol*, and *The Third Man* (1949), and only too sadly exposed in his later films.

William Alwyn himself was proud of what he called his "big score"[26] for *Odd Man Out*. He liked it so much that he stated the film's major theme briefly in the first movement of his First Symphony, and the film's long emotional climax was a stunning conclusion to his memorable lecture at the Edinburgh Festival and the National Film Theatre in London in 1958.

---

[25] Charles Drazin, *The Finest Years* (London: Andre Deutsch, 1998), 65.

[26] Alwyn, *Winged Chariot*, 11.

14
Outcasts and Idioms

ODD *Man Out* was generally released on 17 March 1947, St Patrick's Day. A week earlier Sidney Gilliat's *Green for Danger* went the rounds with another score by Alwyn. The film was well received, although later Gilliat wrote that "it mortified me somewhat that nobody at all spotted that it was, so to speak, a film presented in quotation marks, dotted with stereotypes of half a century of detective fiction, with an affectionate side-swipe at the arrogantly omniscient Detective figure of the genre".[1] If the critics had paid more attention to the musical clues, they might have picked up on Gilliat's stratagem.

The plot, based on a Christianna Brand detective yarn, is set in a temporary wartime hospital during the days of the V-1 bomb. The narrator is Inspector Cockrill (Alastair Sim), a conceited, sadistic buffoon called in to investigate two murders, the first a patient under anaesthetic, the second a stabbed nurse. Mood is established by Alwyn's title music, an exhilarating fugue, but lacking the determined menace of a thriller. Gilliat explained how it came to be written:

> I had to leave for America immediately after seeing the assembly with him [Alwyn] and so would have no opportunity of hearing his sketches of the music, a great delight always with Bill. He asked if I had any particular notion in mind as to the character of the music and I said, "Only that I don't see it all as Micky Mouse", meaning that I felt the score should deliberately not point up the action too much. Feeling that this was a bit negative, I added facetiously, "I mean, write a fugue, Bill." And that, when I got back, I found was precisely what he had done.[2]

There is an even stronger early clue to the film's idiom. A pan around an operating table pauses on each of the five doctor and nurse suspects. Alwyn matches each camera movement with a short scale, interrupted by plucked strings — a semi-humorous, mocking effect. In a later scene the plucked strings are replaced by a celesta, which is funnier. Indeed, as the plot advances the music takes on an increasingly mocking tone. A descending discordant, scratchy violin phrase marks the chalking of the first fatal operation schedule

---

[1] Geoff Brown, *Launder and Gilliat*, 119.

[2] NFT programme note (BFI microjacket).

on a blackboard: a warning. When the second operation is chalked up, the scratchier repeat of the phrase is flippant.

A key scene takes place at a party, in which the hospital staff excitedly change partners in a seemingly interminable "mixer" dance called the "Paul Jones" (*c.*1910). The tune is "Here We Go Round the Mulberry Bush" (traditional) – apt in a film where the viewer is continually led up the wrong garden path. It is arranged here in dance-band style by Norrie Paramor, but when the next murder victim, Sister Bates (Judy Campbell), leaves the dance to run through dark and windy woods to the operating theatre, Alwyn himself siezes the tune and weaves it with whirling ascending and descending strings and declamatory brass to suggest menace and hysteria. When Bates arrives at the darkened theatre, slow strings and flute and celesta suggest frightening dangers in the shadows. Nevertheless, memory of the "Paul Jones" persists, caught on apprehensive woodwind and crescendoing via harp, trumpet, and xylophone to a blood-curdling (and surely tongue-in-cheek) scream.

At over four minutes, that cue is the longest. They tend to be short in *Green for Danger*, which relies as much upon sound-effects as on music. There is a dry institutional diegesis: footsteps on concrete or bare floorboards, slowly closing spring-loaded theatre doors . . .

Musically the film is structured by the main theme and the "Paul Jones". But the repetitive buzz-bombs structure, too, their throb frightening at first, but funny by the end when Inspector Cockrill shelters from a "bomb" that turns out to be a passing motor-cycle. The bombs produce a tension analogous to Alwyn's illustration of the trapeze artist, silent on his trapeze until followed by the "roll" on the side drum.[3] Like the circus drum, the sound of the bomb increases until the tension becomes almost unendurable; there follows the heart-stopping silence, and the final explosion. Alwyn had worked closely with Rotha on the sophisticated soundtrack of *Total War in Britain* and would have remembered how Rotha had attempted there to exploit the tripartite sound of the buzz bomb. Rotha's success was only partial because, restricted to library shots, he was unable to convey the emotional freeze of the long silence between the dying of the drone and the explosion.

Alwyn also deploys the device of sustained sequencing. The second operation scene commences with natural effects – quiet breathing to shots of the palpitating rubber bag, the eyes of the medical team, hands on the instruments. Quietly, ostinato violins on C and B are introduced, constant in volume and pitch, against which a cello descends the chromatic scale as the patient appears to be dying, until the strings are finally lost in crescendoing celesta chords and full orchestral climax to silence, the tension broken by Cockrill screaming: "Cut

---

[3] Alwyn, "Film Music: Sound or Silence", 3. See Introduction.

it off! Cut off the oxygen!" Similar effects have been noted elsewhere, notably in the tension leading up to the barrage in *Desert Victory*.

The spate of "man on the run" scenarios, films about society's outsiders, of which *Odd Man Out* was one, reflected society's unsettled postwar condition. Less well known is Ronald Neame's *Take My Life*. It was Neame's first experience as director, despite a long career in the industry, which included co-producing at Cineguild with David Lean and Anthony Havelock-Allan. The film is an accomplished neo-Hitchcockian thriller, centring around the trial of Nicholas Talbot (Hugh Williams) for the murder of his old flame, violinist Elizabeth Rusman (Rosalie Crutchley). With the circumstantial evidence loaded heavily against him, Talbot is saved by the determination of his diva wife Philippa (Greta Gynt), who ferrets out the real murderer — Rusman's husband, head-teacher Sidney Fleming (Marius Goring). The scenario is anchored in the courtroom, and it sustains tension by roaming from that point both chronologically and geographically.

It commences with a voice-over narration by the prosecuting counsel (Francis L. Sullivan), flashing back to the hours before the killing: first night at the opera and Philippa singing her heart out to the aria "Take My Life". That aria was especially composed by Alwyn in the style of Puccini and sung for the track by Victoria Sladen, the principal soprano in the Sadler's Wells Opera Company. It is one of two motifs that not only take the foreground, but are essential to the plot structure:

The other is a school song, alleged by the script to be adapted from a Dutch folk song, and by implication scored by Rusman:

Philippa's discovery of the manuscript leads her to Fleming's school in Scotland and to his entrapment. For a film composer, structurally important music that is incorporated into the film's diegesis is a godsend: here are two pieces, easily distinguishable, firmly established as plot devices, visibly performed to the audience, and with the potential for instant recall as creative leitmotifs.

The aria is Philippa's motif and represents her changing moods. Although it swamps the titles and the opulent first night triumph that follows, by the time its key scene is reached Talbot has been arrested. Now, as Philippa plays the aria on a piano, it has a slow, nostalgic rhythm, reflecting her mood of quiet despair. At this point the second musical theme emerges strongly. For, still idling at the piano, she doodles the melody of the as-yet unidentified school song.

9 Stage One, Denham, during a music session in 1947. Muir Mathieson is conducting, and Alwyn stands to the left of the podium. The stage had been converted
   from a "sound stage" to a music recording theatre in the summer of the previous
   year.

When Talbot's young nephew identifies it, the plot is freed up, and from this
point on the school song dominates.

As the second major musical theme, the school song carries more weight
than simple character motif: it is part of the nuts and bolts of the plot construction. Its use is nearly always diegetic: on the two occasions (apart from the
end titles) when it is played non-diegetically, it represents a motif for Fleming.
Thus, as Philippa returns to London from Scotland after confronting Fleming
in Scotland, it is prominent as he follows her in the corridor of the train, brass
dominating a panicky string ostinato that echoes the rhythm of the wheels. In
this way, her journey south contrasts with her earlier hopeful journey north,
when the "Take My Life" motif was hinted at behind the ostinato rhythm of
the train.

Alwyn's compositional techniques are extensive and often in complex variants, for reasons which are illuminating. The score for the flashback to the
crime, for example, portrays a mix of emotions: the ethereal, dreamlike sensation of the flashback itself; menace and fear; the unbalanced psychological state

of the murderer. Moreover the scene is overlaid with a troubling double effect: events are narrated by the prosecutor, but his surmising of the crime ("It is the Crown's submission . . .") is sometimes at variance with the pictures, which show what really happened. The sequence commences with a noir-style rain-swept seedy corner of town, its street lamps casting contrasting shadows across the wet pavement. A figure crosses the street. Alwyn introduces a quiet double bass and cello ostinato, not unlike the similar dark, wet, and ominous scene of *I See a Dark Stranger*. After a few bars it becomes dissonant as the action follows the figure through a doorway. The instruments are predominantly strings, but the piano has a brief moment. Those few piano chords (partially picked up a few bars later on the woodwind) represent an attention to detail, a composer's fancy, which a cinema audience would have to be impossibly alert to grasp. For Alwyn introduces here the theme of the school song, in a minor key. At this point in the drama the audience has no knowledge of the school song, so (had it but ears to hear!) Alwyn is offering a clue to the identity of the murderer.

The figure ascends the stairs to Rusman's flat, the tread of his feet emphasised and threatening. The mood resonates with impending evil, a feeling owing not a little to the dissonance of the score. It is well known that dissonance produces tension, said to be the brain's attempting to restore consonance and normality. A cut to the flat's elderly landlord, having a pint at the local, substitutes pub chatter for underscore: anti-climax. By the time the action returns to the lonely flat, the dark mood is climaxing and even more disturbing by contrast with the everyday. The breathing space has also given the composer the opportunity to change from dissonance to consonance, with full orchestra, although ostinato strings still predominate. The camera passes through a half-open door into the bedroom and, resting behind Rusman's visitor, faces her as she talks agitatedly. But although her raised voice can be heard, the orchestra is louder, the voice-over louder still, and her words are obscured. Tension is thus fused with frustration — the audience is observer, watching a drama it does not understand. The mystery and thickening of the mood is created mainly by the soundtrack. The man attacks Rusman, and the music climaxes: timpani and stressful rising orchestra tutti. A pencil Rusman borrowed earlier from Talbot falls to the floor. The strings return to tremolo, almost suspending the drama, breathlessly drawing our attention to the significance of the pencil. But a second, louder climax ensues: as Rusman and the man struggle she strikes him on the head with a table lamp (orchestra tutti) and the strings continue alone, still tremolo and climbing in volume, until Rusman's hands loosen on her assailant's shoulder. A moment later on another chord from the full orchestra, her hands fall: thus the climax, followed by . . . silence; time freezes. We hear the sound of a body falling.

More silence. The camera position remains behind the assailant's head. Then the prosecutor's voice breaks in: "In the submission of the crown that man was Nicholas Talbot." A cut, delayed by a perfect half-second, to the face of the murderer, and the prosecutor is shown to be wrong, for we are looking at a stranger (Fleming). Our reaction is shock. In the quietness we hear a passing train. So does the murderer, who is clearly shaken but in control of his actions, and moves swiftly to close the door and draw the blinds. His movements are followed, until the sight of a bottle of lighter-fuel decides him to set fire to the scene of the crime. The effectiveness of this sequence relies upon the contrast of musical silence with the preceding passion of the orchestral climax. It vindicates two of Alwyn's fundamental beliefs: the value of silence, and the value of careful pre-planning between director and composer.

Church bells sound: a cut from the isolated room back to normality. The bells add tension, stress the importance of time, and their funereal tone is a reminder of death. The landlord crosses from the pub carefully nursing a jug of beer. He reaches the stairs and Fleming, shielding his face, passes him. The bells, no longer serving a dramatic purpose, have ceased: we hardly notice. As the men cross, orchestral strings strike a chord. The landlord (audibly) sniffs burning, and high ethereal strings suggest his puzzlement as he cautiously climbs the stairs. The theme, now joined by the oboe and busily ostinato, crescendos to full orchestra by the time he opens the bedroom door and rushes in. Often a climax is followed by a sudden silence, stressing a climax. But on this occasion Alwyn's purpose is to release the tension from the previous horror, and the increasing speed and volume of the orchestra leads not to silence but to staccato repeated chords and xylophone ascending glissando, matching a close-up dialling of the police emergency call. There follows a quick montage of the landlord's call to the police, matched by the orchestra, tutti, climaxing on an audible police radio message.

The sound editing by Winston Ryder and Jack Slade is also intelligent and meticulous. In a sequence memorable by any standards, the murderer Fleming, all suppressed emotion, shows Philippa around his school; both visitor and teacher act out roles, mutually suspicious. Only diegetic sound is used, and it is chilling. With the school empty because of the vacation, their curt questions and answers echo about the empty corridors and rooms. Every sound is amplified: footsteps on the bare boards, stone corridors and steps, keys jangling, blinds swishing, doors closing. Even Fleming's dropping the keys into his pocket is sound-spotted. The scene climaxes as Philippa plays the school song on the chapel organ, her back to Fleming standing at the steps below her. She asks him who composed the song, he fails to reply, she asks again and watches him in the organ's mirror. When she looks again, he has gone. His approach up the steps behind her as the organ increases in volume and tempo manages by a hair's breadth not to tip into the ludicrous — saved by another sound, a school servant's cough as he enters the chapel.

Just as the rhythmic sound of the railway carriage was effective in *I See a Dark Stranger*, so here. Returning from Scotland, Philippa by chance shares a compartment with Fleming. Alone with her, Fleming confesses. As he talks he leans towards the camera menacingly: his account of the crime is accompanied solely by the urgent sound of the train wheels — which continues on a flashback to occasion of the murder. The rhythm of the wheels sustains the tension: music is unnecessary. In the first depiction of the murder scene, mystery was created by drowning Rusman's words with orchestra and voice-over: now is revealed her fatal threat: "By the time I've done with the divorce no school on earth will employ you." Enraged, Fleming strangles her, and the scene climaxes with the diegetic scream of the train whistle in "real" time as the pictures cut from flashback to a large close-up of Fleming in the railway carriage. Melodramatic, hackneyed, or Hitchcockian in concept?

Alwyn attempted to have the aria published,[4] but nothing came of the plan A year after the film's release it was performed by the soprano Gwen Catley on a television programme devoted to film music.[5]

In April 1947 Alwyn again set off for Ireland to gather local colour for the score for Frank Launder's *Captain Boycott* (1947). It was a fairly novel idea, perhaps the inspiration for Mathieson's suggestion shortly afterwards that film composers should investigate the potential of folk music.[6] Launder wanted to make a film about the "plight of the Irish peasants in the days of absentee landlordism",[7] and his vehicle was the story of the ostracism of the English landlord Captain Boycott (Cecil Parker) in the 1880s. A subplot was introduced of the love between Hugh Davin (Stewart Granger), a leader of the local rebels, and Anne (Kathleen Ryan), whose father rashly takes over an evicted farm.

The film had production problems, the worst being one of those moist Irish summers, which resulted in more than a hundred extras in period army uniform waiting around on a Wicklow mountain for the rain to stop. Launder recalled hearing their song at night: "Everytime it rains, it rains pennies from Denham . . ."[8]

Much of the location filming was in Wicklow, but the story is set in Mayo, so it was to there and Connemara that Alwyn travelled for his research. His jottings covered five sheets of music manuscript, as he scribbled away at one time in Ballinrobe and also at O'Malley's pub in Cornamona on the shore of Lough Corrib. These sheets are all that remain on paper of his score (Plate 10).

---

[4] Letter in Alwyn Archive to Chappell & Co. Ltd.

[5] *Film Music*, BBC Television (8 Oct. 1948). Arranged by James Hartley with the co-operation of John Huntley. Muir Mathieson conducted. The programme also included music from *The Rake's Progress*.

[6] *The Studio*, 1:9 (26 May 1948), 16.

[7] Geoff Brown, *Launder and Gilliat*, 121.

[8] Ibid.

Alwyn had an interest in Irish music that dated from his youth. While still in his teens, he arranged "The Boys of Wexford" (early 1920s) for violin and piano and an overture for orchestra, *Derrybeg Fair* (1925). Other "Irish" pieces followed, including *King of the Mists*, a ballet performed at Dublin's Abbey Thea-

10 A page from Alwyn's scribbled notes made during the trip to Mayo in 1947 for *Captain Boycott*.

tre in 1935 or 1936.[9] More recently, during the war, Alwyn had rearranged some Irish music for George Stratton's Westminster Players. Stratton was the leader of the LSO and a good friend.[10] Alwyn would therefore have jumped at the chance of a trip to the West, and it's easy to surmise this from his Mayo notes. The staves are peppered with terse comments; in one margin is a clumsy copy of the Irish for Nicholas against a stave of "A Prayer for Nicholas" (unknown). Practically all the tunes he noted down originated in the Boycott region, and most are better known by their original Irish titles — that Alwyn turned them into English implies that somebody was translating for him.

These expressions of Alwyn's earliest ideas for a score are a rare find among his papers. True, for several scores piano sketches exist — for some it is all that does exist — but by the time he penned most of these he had already passed through his initial decisions. Although Alwyn later abandoned some of the tunes noted on the *Boycott* manuscript, most of the major themes of the completed film are there in one form or another. It is revealing to compare the sketches with the completed film.

One theme not in his notes is the surprising start to the film, a clear reference on horn to the main (Johnny's) theme from *Odd Man Out*. *Odd Man Out* was still fresh in the memory, and it too dealt with Irish politics. Perhaps the echo is no more than Alwyn's personal conceit, but perhaps he hoped the alert filmgoer would make a political connection too. A mix from the producers' logo to a high shot of a mountain landscape concludes the theme. Then, menacing chords cue the significance of a mail coach coming into view from the edge of screen, a warning soon forgotten, however, as the score turns to a beautiful keening melody as the coach passes through the mountains and glens of Mayo.

The keen, or *caoineadh*, is an Irish lament, wailed or cried by the *bean chaointe* or keening-woman, and can be harrowing. That Alwyn listened to authentic keening at O'Malley's pub or elsewhere is surprising. The problems of documenting the music are illustrated by the experience of one folk-song researcher, who at first considered not publishing a tape recording of a keening "for reasons of sensitivity". The researcher recalled that the singer first "went round the house to peer up and down the road, and then she barred the door against unexpected callers. It is of course risking bad luck to 'wail' or 'cry' at random what is a solemn ceremonial expression of grief". The writer goes on to mention there was also a question of payment for these professional singing mourners.[11] Nevertheless, experts at the Irish Traditional Music Archive in

[9] Craggs and Poulton, *William Alwyn: A Catalogue of his Music*, 13.

[10] Mary Alwyn, in conversation with the writer.

[11] Insert to the tape cassette *Songs of Aran: Gaelic Singing from the West of Ireland* (Ossian OSS-16).

Dublin believe that the two staves of "keening" noted by Alwyn look genuine, remarking that "the shape of the tune looks right".[12]

In *Captain Boycott* the keening solo is performed (uncredited) by soprano Joan Cross of the Sadler's Wells. This can only be described as "concert-hall" keening, using a voiced trained in the classical manner and the use of vibrato — a far cry from the Irish tradition. Alwyn managed to note two separate sketches for the keening melody, initially[13]

and later

In the final version he combined the two, something well within the Irish tradition:

Later he transposed the key to C-sharp minor, which gives the air a plaintive feel:

Over a year later, Ralph Vaughan Williams depicted the Polar waste by a wordless soprano solo and women's chorus in *Scott of the Antarctic* (1948), which he later reworked into his Seventh Symphony (*Sinfonia Antartica*, 1953). Vaughan Williams's wordless soprano solo is close cousin to Alwyn's keening music, and it would seem that not only were Alwyn and Vaughan Williams at-

---

[12] Letter to the writer, dated 10 Sept. 1999, from Maeve Gebruers, Printed Materials Officer of the Irish Traditional Materials Archive. I am indebted to Miss Gebruers and her colleagues for help with these paragraphs.

[13] The bar markings are amended.

tempting similar film music techniques, but that Alwyn anticipated Vaughan Williams by a year. However, the verdict on the question of originality must remain open when one also considers Vaughan Williams's poignant Finale to his Third Symphony (*A Pastoral Symphony*), completed in 1921, where the soprano solo is accompanied by a string pedal point using a startlingly similar technique to Alwyn's keening theme.

It is bathetic, but also worth consideration, to mention here Richard Addinsell's score for Ralph Keene's *Ulster* (1940), with "its haunting melody sung by a female voice".[14] Although not wordless (it includes the traditional song "I Know Where I'm Going"), and musically unworthy of consideration with either Vaughan Williams's or Alwyn's compositions, its juxtaposition of the "female voice" with pictures from Ireland may have been the germ, perhaps unconscious, of Alwyn's idea.

Alwyn was obviously attracted to keening. In July 1947 he was commissioned by Gainsborough to write the score for Michael Chorlton's *Miranda* (1948), including the songs for Glynis Johns to "sing" as Miranda the mermaid.[15] In the event Ken Annakin took over the direction, and the score was taken on by Temple Abady, with an early example of a specially written pop song to back the title credits, a dreary number by Jack Fishman and Peter Hart, sung by Jean Sabbon. Nevertheless, before handing on the commission, Alwyn appears to have precomposed a piece for soprano and piano for Glynis Johns to mime to,[16] in much the same way as James Mason limped to a pre-recording in *Odd Man Out*. The scenes were recorded by an unnamed soprano, and they are unconvincing and out of synch. A sketch entitled "Mermaid's Song (Miranda)" resides in the Alwyn Archive, and its phrasing partially reflects the soundtrack, while key, rhythm, and verse patterns are the same. I am convinced it is the basis of the song from the film. The piano harmonies evoke a feeling of the mysterious ocean depths, while the verse is a wordless sequence of vowels: "ee oh eeyah ee oh ee oh eeyah eeh-oh . . .", and so on. There is an instruction on the sketch, the "syllables to be run into one another and not clearly articulated — final phrase to end on a closed O sound — almost humming". It would have been composed within a few months of Alwyn's return from Mayo, and its similarity to the keening of *Captain Boycott* is remarkable.

Alwyn's keening theme for *Captain Boycott* is evocative in the true meaning of the word, a calling up from the dead, a foreboding of the shadows of affliction and suffering. The mood is deepened by the pedal point on low strings and the black-and-white photography as the opening continues and the camera escorts

[14] *DNL* 2:1 (Jan. 1941), 9.
[15] *The Cinema*, 69:5516 (9 July 1947), 31.
[16] Unusually for the period, but I think not post-synched as a review in *Film Industry*, 4:23 (May 1948), 18, suggests.

the coach through the Mayo landscape. After a while, woodwind, harp, and high strings gently enter, take up and develop the theme until a horn fanfare echoing the initial triad rouses us from the dreamlike state, and a voice-over takes up a narration. The background melody nevertheless continues, although we now hear the sound of the hoofs, and shot by shot the carriage fills more of the screen as we are brought closer to the action. The coach stops at the scene of a body being lifted from a bog, and the music cuts abruptly as the bullying voice cue of the police guard, employed by the crown, breaks in: "What's happened there?" The violence of Alwyn's cut gives the audience all the clues it needs about where its sympathies should lie.

Alwyn's plan for the opening sequence are scribbled on his manuscript notes: "voice heard singing in distance. / followed by statement on orchestra with Harp. / coach theme announced by solo ob. or flute." Although Alwyn sketched out a "coach tune", he later abandoned the plan to introduce a new theme here and relied solely on the development of the keening melody. Nevertheless his "coach tune" sketch was not wasted. A couple of scenes later the action returns to the coach, where Anne as a passenger discovers a gun hidden in sack of seed; it is now that the coach tune comes into its own.

Drafts of most of the film's melodies are in these jottings, and — like the coach theme — they are not necessarily in an Irish vein. They include a diegetic waltz as background to a society dance, and a "Boycott theme", used just once in the film, where Boycott airs his grievances in a note to the editor of the London *Times*.

However, to create atmosphere, an Irish idiom is vital both diegetically and non-diegetically. Diegetic opportunities occur throughout. Hugh meets Anne at a dance, to which a lively performance of "Miss McLeod's Reel" (1772 or earlier) forms the background. Originally a Scottish tune, but played in Ireland since at least the beginning of the nineteenth century, "Miss McLeod's Reel" is still popular; Alwyn noted a variation of this tune when he was in Ballinrobe. Near the end of the film Joan Cross's "concert" keening is used diegetically to accompany a scene of a death. The arrival of the British army is a successful blend on pipes and drums of "The Girl I Left Behind Me", an English song popular in Ireland since the end of the eighteenth century,[17] and "The Heights of Alma", an Ulster song with Crimean connections, as Alwyn noted. When the diegetic march finishes he echoes "Alma" non-diegetically as the soldiers dig in.

Another, potent use of diegetic music occurs later in the film before the start of a political meeting addressed by Parnell (Robert Donat), where a band plays "The Boys of Wexford", an appropriate song from the 1798 rising, although the

---

[17]　Played also, I notice, by the British army in Sergei Bondarchuk's *Waterloo* (1970). It must be very common in historic British army scenes.

words are not recorded in the film. The song is too well known for Alwyn to need a reminder in his notes; besides, he had already arranged it 25 years earlier. But there is a faint pencil *aide-mémoire* of its title in a margin with "Michael Davitt" noted below. Davitt was a Parnellite from Mayo, and so Alwyn may have been told of a tradition linking the man and the song.

Despite such a brave attempt, the film fails to create a truly authentic sound, for the reason that other feature films fail. The band plays "The Boys of Wexford" with pipes, tambourines, drums, and strings, but the strings above all lack authenticity: they play vibrato where Irish traditional fiddles never would, and the playing is too bright, too smooth, too "concert hall" for a small Irish band. Moreover in Parnell's day (especially) fiddlers would usually play "off the chest" — these strings have the control of the chin rest.[18] Of course, the point is that the "Irish band" is really a studio orchestra with string players trained in the classical school, an important point when we consider the Irish themes worked into Alwyn's non-diegetic music. Thus, in a long cue for Hugh galloping home that would not be out of place in a Western, Alwyn weaves an Irish-sounding cascading string rhythm. But those classical violins can never sound other than what they are: instruments in a film recording studio.

Sometimes this is acceptable, as here, and as in the beautiful non-diegetic love motif on (vibrato) violin for Anne and Hugh, the two lovers:

Initially, too, the lively, humorous, jig rhythm as the people rush from Mass, heading in traps and carriages for Parnell's Land League meeting is quite delightful:

Its fast descending strings are quickly sketched on a single stave of Alwyn's memoranda, followed by its contrasting rising rhythm:

However, one questions the wisdom of its reuse at the film's conclusion. The narrative ends with a battle won: the departure of both English army and Boycott.

---

[18] For some reason the fiddles of "Miss Mcleod's Reel" at the dance where Hugh and Anne meet avoid vibrato and sound authentic.

As they leave, the local priest and supporter of the Land League, played by Alastair Sim, spells out to the peasants the benefit of non-violent resistance: "In the future if any man offends against the community you can ostracise him, you can isolate him — you can boycott him." His close-up is a peculiarly inept final image. Nevertheless, Alwyn's triumphantly dignified horn fanfare over the legend "The End" strikes an appropriate mood. Alas! As the rolling credit titles follow, the jig repeats. With its concert-hall instrumentation the mood becomes "Hollywood" Irish — a musical feeling akin to "stage Irish". The depth of the film's descent is to be measured by contrasting one's final impression — Sim's sly grin and a humorous jig — with the mood of the opening sequence, the lovely keening melody against the Mayo countryside. What Launder had hoped to be a serious film about "the plight of the Irish peasants" is nearly a music-hall comic act, no less because of its ill-considered closing music theme.

In June 1947 Alwyn was "preparing the score" for another promising Irish subject, Lance Comfort's *Daughter of Darkness* (1948),[19] a highly-charged psychological melodrama in which Siobhan McKenna plays a nymphomaniac Irish servant girl who wreaks vengeance on the men she arouses. The subject was ideal for Alwyn's talents, but he passed on the contract to Clifton Parker, together with another for Rotha's acclaimed *The World is Rich* (1947).[20]

While *Captain Boycott* was filming at the reopened Pinewood, at Denham Roy Baker was directing his first feature, *The October Man*, for Filippo del Giudice. The score was assigned to Kenneth Pakeman, whose film experience was a couple of documentaries for Rotha and another for Greenpark. Pakeman wrote three sketches before the film went into production, but his music was dropped, and Alwyn, who had previously worked with Baker on the AKS short *What's the Next Job?*, was called in to compose the entire score from scratch.[21] It was another pressure: at the end of May Alwyn, Mathieson, recordist Desmond Dew, and music mixer Ted Drake finished recording *The October Man* with the LSO at Denham; a week later they were back again with the Philharmonia Orchestra to record the score for *Captain Boycott*.[22] Despite the pressures, *The October Man* was a good composition — good enough for Baker to

[19] *Today's Cinema*, 68:5504 (11 June 1947), 42. The working title was *They Walk Alone*.
[20] Rotha to Alwyn, 30 Nov. 1973, in Alwyn Archive.
[21] John Huntley, letter to *DNL* 6:59 (Oct. 1947), 148.
[22] *The October Man* finished on 27 May, when a combination provided by Harry Gold recorded the music for the dance scenes and the record player. John Hollingsworth assisted Mathieson on this film; see *The Cinema*, 68:5501 (4 June 1947), 39. Recordings for *Captain Boycott* started on 5 June and finished on 26 June, when the title music, including Joan Cross's keening, was recorded; see *The Cinema*, 68:5510 (25 June 1947), 33. Alwyn also wrote some special hurdy-gurdy music for woodwind, brass, and percussion (see *The Cinema*, 68:5507 (18 June 1947), 38), which was used in a country-fair sequence in the early part of the film.

recycle, without a credit, for the titles and a short sequence in his submarine tale *Morning Departure* (1950), and thus to support Alwyn's axiom that film music is not descriptive.

The October Man was one of the period's run of noir psychological thrillers. Eric Ambler both produced and wrote the story of Jim Ackland (John Mills), who blames himself for the death in a bus crash of a little girl, his psychological inadequacy acerbated by a long seclusion in hospital with a severe head injury. He returns to work as a research chemist, taking a room in a small residential hotel. When fellow guest Molly (Kay Walsh) is strangled on the local common, the police believe Jim's mental instability has led him to commit the crime. They refuse to listen to him even when he discovers the real murderer, another guest named Peachey (Edward Chapman). He becomes a fugitive with only his girlfriend Jenny (Joan Greenwood) to support him.

Alwyn, not long from *Odd Man Out* and with a growing reputation for depicting unstable mental states, was the obvious choice as composer, and much of its success depends on his laying in of mood. To sustain the motif of Ackland's emotional stress, Ambler introduces two major psychological symbols, which are sufficiently suggestive to not require musical reinforcement. What Alwyn does is to probe behind them to explore Jim's confused inner mind. Two early scenes, in which both plot background and symbolism are established, serve as illustration.

The opening credit cards, plain lettering against a plain background, are matched by what we discover later to be the love motif. As such it affords no real intimation of the ensuing drama. However, as the titles near their close it becomes clear that the purpose of the tranquil beginning is to contrast with the dissonant melody that now follows: against a celesta background, foreboding descending strings enter with a constantly repeated motif:

The descending rhythm suggests (impending) misfortune, and here the gradual quickening of the ostinato theme induces a sense of panic, until it finally slows to introduce the first scene, like a theatre curtain drawing back, revealing a bus struggling in driving rain along a country lane at night.

Bassoons enter and grumble ostinato. Sound-effects mix in: the rumble of the bus and the sound of wind. Other instruments take up the ostinato theme, *agitato*, which continues throughout the sequence. Flutes point up the driver straining at the wheel, joined by strings and clarinets as the we stare past the windscreen wipers, into the rain and the short headlight beam. A sweet contrasting oboe lightens the mood briefly as the camera cuts to two passengers, a man (Jim) and a young girl talking together; but the menacing theme returns, and the man folds his handkerchief into the shape of a rabbit: the first psychological symbol. The gentle *dolce* theme makes a brief reappearance until trumpets sound a four-note warning fanfare and the return of *agitato*. Woodwind repeats the terse fanfare, signalling a cut to the driver. Still whirling instruments continue the repetitive, menacing theme, which, after a moment of calm, becomes *furioso*: beneath the bus a steering rod works loose. The music calms again to mere *agitato*, but the sound of the bus has grown louder, equal partner now with the orchestra. Violins repeat the *dolce* theme as man and girl continue to play with the "rabbit", short staccato flutes and piccolo reflecting the image of the man wiggling its ears. The bus approaches a railway bridge, a train rushes along the embankment in the opposite direction: with an abrupt chord the music ceases as the engine's whistle prolongs into a long wail: the second psychological symbol, the train and its whistle. The steering rod breaks, the driver loses control, Jim shields the child's face, a fast zoom to his face is followed by a second to the "rabbit" on his lap. The orchestra returns with crashing chords to match the sound of the bus plunging into the embankment.

Into these first two minutes are worked the symbols of Jim's neurosis. The first, the handkerchief "rabbit", is as much dependent on its visual impact as upon any musical embellishment, its whiteness often emphasised by dark shadows behind it. Alwyn points it up in the opening sequence, however, by short staccato "twitches" on the flutes and piccolo. The handkerchief is associated both with Jim's tragic past in which the child is killed and later with the scarf used by the murderer. The second psychological symbol, the train, is mainly dependent upon the sound effect of its whistle. So, although the whistle is announced by a short orchestral chord, the few seconds leading to the crash are held by that long screaming whistle. Thus the whistle serves a dual purpose: as a tension device that cannot be improved by music, and as emphasis to its ensuing psychological importance. Later, the scream of the engine whistle becomes associated with moments of tension, even fears of suicide.

Even though the whistle is potent enough to stand alone, it does not thereby render redundant Alwyn's more subtle musical suggestions: later whenever the whistle is heard it is followed by non-diegetic music as interpretation of Ackland's current mood.

There is another consideration. Somebody, probably Ambler, reduced the psychological emphasis of the film between the completion of the shooting script and the release version Thus, like Johnny's light-headedness as he is driven to the mill in *Odd Man Out*, in the shooting script Jim's departure from the hospital is depicted by his light-headed, detached state amongst the clamour of people, trains, stations, and streets. These sequences were certainly filmed,[23] but in the final cut only a single shot remains: a passing express train with whistle sounding, linking the hospital to Jim's arrival at his destination.

---

[23] *The Cinema*, 68:5476 (9 May 1947), 24.

Therefore, at this point much of the suggestion of Jim's mental state devolves upon Alwyn's score. It is dusk, and as Jim, suitcase in hand, walks to his hotel, Alwyn's repeated string and woodwind motives in unison, the drab scenes of the small town, and the miserable state of Jim's mind cross-reflect the mood. Coming to a railway bridge, Jim pauses to rest, causing a couple following to collide with him; the music ceases. There is a structural convenience in establishing the bridge at this point because of its importance later. Just as important, though, it recalls Jim's sickness and his potentially suicidal state, emphasised by an express train screaming beneath the bridge and covering Jim in a cloud of steam. But the whistle can only remind the viewer of Jim's state of mind: to show it depends upon Alwyn's music, which as the steam clears eddies in with light strings and horns, a celesta scale, more swirling and counterpointing strings, ostinato horns, woodwind scales . . . Jim stares across the gloomy common, turns, and enters the hotel as a lamplighter turns up a street lamp. The total feeling is almost atonal in its fluidity.

The symbol of the express train and its whistle returns again and again, but each time Ackland's cast of mind is asserted by non-diegetic orchestral melodies and harmonies. They are not always negative: on one occasion they reflect Jim's resolution to confront Peachey about the crime, and in the final scene the love motif confirms Jim's release from his mental turmoil and his freedom to affirm his love for Jenny.

Alwyn himself laid careful stress upon

> the remarkable faculty of music for portraying something which is happening in the actor's mind, and not what you see in his face or in his actions. In the old, silent film the actor had to rely on exaggerated gestures, the art of mime, to express his emotions: in the sound film he can behave naturally with the aid of words — the "method" came into its own — but he can also remain silent and poker-faced while music expresses for him the emotion which is to be shared by his audience. (Incidentally I like to cherish the idea that many an actor's reputation I have made or marred by the surreptitious use of music).[24]

He went on by illustrating the point by quoting (but not screening) a scene from *The October Man*:

> This is an entirely new weapon in the film director's armoury — with imagination he can shoot on two planes. I remember using a different version of this technique in a film called *October Man*. The actor is suspected of murder — in all the bustle of CID questioning and investigation he is utterly detached and thinking only of the girl he has just left. You

[24] Alwyn, "Film Music: Sound or Silence", 5.

realise this, not because of anything he says, but because you can hear remotely and intensely, high up on a solo violin, the persistent sound of the tune you have already learned earlier on in the picture to associate with the girl. Music then can operate on a plane completely contrary to the visuals — there is still a wide field for experiment in this. One of the fascination of composing for the cinema is that it is the youngest art, and to pioneer in any aspect of it is rewarding and stimulating to the creative artist.[25]

Although the scene does not seem quite the same as the mental picture conjured by Alwyn — he is almost certainly referring to the walk Ackland took, after kissing Jenny, back across the common past the police investigation — the point is a good one. One recalls the well-known scene in Otto Preminger's *Laura* (1944) where, alone with her picture, a detective falls in love with a dead girl he has never met, the emotion felt totally through composer David Raksin's "haunting" theme.[26]

---

[25] Alwyn, "Film Music: Sound or Silence", 5.

[26] Raksin's own adjective. Fred Karlin, *Listening to the Movies: The Film Lover's Guide to Film Music* (New York: Schirmer Books, 1994), 27.

15

Pennies from Hollywood

ESPITE a sublime confidence in their craft and artistic skills, the British studios were nevertheless unbalanced by a shaky financial superstructure. Having lost £1,667,000 on production in 1946, J. Arthur Rank could hardly afford to have his distribution negotiations with the United States ruined the following year by the government's *ad valorem* duty on American films. A subsequent crash production programme to compensate for the shortage of American product came to grief after the spring of 1948, when the duty was removed and cinemas were swamped by the backlog. At the same time the government encouraged American companies to invest in filmmaking in Britain as a way of releasing their "blocked" earnings. The result was an American invasion of the British studios; and as government and studio decisions trickled down to the man on the studio floor, Alwyn found himself paid in American-sourced money and working with American directors.

Oddly, his first two commissions for American-financed productions preceded, by a nicety, the tax-settlement agreement. By the middle of January 1948 Alwyn was scoring for 20th Century–Fox British. The film was *Escape* (1948), directed by the visiting American Joseph L. Mankiewicz. Rex Harrison took on the role, which Gerald du Maurier had performed in the 1930 film version, of convict Matt Denant, who, unjustly convicted of murder, escapes into the fog of Dartmoor with police inspector Harris (William Hartnell) in close pursuit. It is yet another man-on-the-run narrative and must have reminded Alwyn of *Odd Man Out*, especially after Denant injures his arm in a plane crash and staggers between locations weak and in pain. Despite the temptation, the score only echoes for a few bars the rhythmic beat of *Odd Man Out*'s concluding funeral march.

Those newspaper critics who were concerned that Hollywood screenwriter Philip Dunne did not stay faithful to Galsworthy's stage drama failed to recognise that Mankiewicz was instead expressing cinematic virtues. Turning to account the landscape, the bracken, bogs, rocks, and hills of the moors, Mankiewicz reinforced Denant's despair that his past actions have stripped him of the thing he values most, his freedom. It is this statement that Alwyn reinforces musically, and it is strongly conveyed in the opening.

Setting the mood as early as the censor card, an optimistic rising four-note motive on strings is all too quickly inverted into a fast descending pattern, creating an atmosphere of tension and desperation. As the screen preliminaries continue, the strings settle to a brief ostinato of the descending motive as brass in competition struggles to rise, only to be constantly pulled back, as it were, by the strings. Suddenly, aided by flute trill, the brass breaks loose into a fanfare as the camera commences a slow pan across the moor. When the title "John Galsworthy's *Escape*" appears, a cymbal clash releases the strings freely into a full romantic theme. Horns and trombones join in to whirl into an almost unrestrained exuberance against pictures of the open moor, until strings alone reach a high pitch and repeat on a high octave the four-note motive heard near the start. Its repetition again creates tension and expectation, until from the edge of the screen a dark image of Dartmoor Prison creeps into and finally dominates the frame. Now, the tall prison walls are reflected by low ominous strings, slowing until a chord in orchestral unison creates an organ-like colour. It is held until *staccato* strings accentuated by drums stress the beat to create the effect of the toll of a funeral bell, counterpointed against another rhythm that ascends jerkily and menacingly into a high, nerve-stretching pitch. This theme, as it continues to ascend and descend the scale, creates almost unbearable tension until a real prison bell chimes in, and the camera shows a warder passing from cell to cell, leaving open the door to Denant's cell. Our first sight of his face is a cliché: a pained close-up as he stares through the bars of his cell window.

For Denant, freedom is above all the open sky and flight, and the pitiful strings against his close-up rise to a sustained high tremolo as he gazes at a flock of birds passing overhead. There follows a zoom into his anguished face, a change to a more reassuring musical key, and a picture mix to flashback as Denant recalls sitting in the cockpit in happier times. Now Alwyn draws on experience to create the sensation of flight, soaring bright brass counterpointed by flute and string trills giving way to climbing strings in complex fugal patterns. To find the musical inspiration of this exuberant passage we need to look to the past, beyond Amy Johnson's excited harp arpeggios in the cockpit in *They Flew Alone*, as far back, in fact, as Alwyn's first commission, *The Future's in the Air*.

Faced by the dual frustrations of union pernicketiness and rain-soakings on Dartmoor, Manciewicz was overjoyed to complete *Escape* and to return to Hollywood. Not long afterwards Alwyn found himself on another Hollywood-financed project, Lewis Allen's *So Evil My Love*.

So Evil My Love has been described accurately by one modern film historian as "a minor masterpiece" and "superb melodrama".[1] At the time of its release, however, its reception was mixed, and negative epithets such as "drab", "mediocre", "plodding", and "stodgy"[2] were not untypical. The opprobrium was partly

---

[1] McFarlane, *An Autobiography of British Cinema*, 139, 561.
[2] "Culling the Critics", *The Cinema Studio*, 1:10 (2 June 1948), 26.

due to a mediocre performance from one of its stars, Ray Milland. More often it was the response to what was regarded as a sordid and occasionally meandering narrative about a missionary's widow, Olivia Harwood (Ann Todd), who becomes morally corrupted through her infatuation for the scheming Mark Bellis (Milland), a thief, blackmailer, and murderer. Seen today, the film contains much to relish, above all its exuberent melodrama and a compelling, lived performance by Ann Todd. It has musical virtues, too, which are revealed by a careful "reading". First, however, one has to disentangle the score's accreditation.

Alwyn is given an on-screen credit as composer, with Muir Mathieson (as usual, the music director) as conductor of the Philharmonia Orchestra of London. It is followed, worryingly, by another, smaller accreditation: "Additional music by Victor Young / Recorded by The Paramount Symphony Orchestra". It is probably now too late to confirm the full story behind those credits, but a reasonable guess may be made.

Although the film was financed by Paramount, and both producer Hal Wallis and director Lewis Allen were from Hollywood, it was made by a British crew at Denham. There would certainly have been no reason to involve Victor Young, Paramount's contract composer and conductor, far away in Hollywood. Once the film reached the composition stage, both Wallis and Allen seem to have thought their work was over: Wallis sailed back in the *Queen Elizabeth* to New York, and Allen and Milland went on to Nuremberg to shoot exteriors for their next film.[3]

Apparently, Mathieson and Alwyn proceeded with the musical arrangements in the accustomed manner, carefully spotting the music and judging where "silence" could make its best impact. I suggest, however, that when the film was viewed with its music track in Hollywood, somebody was so panicked by this cheerless film that, thinking to salvage it at the box office, they reached for the traditional sticking-plaster — more music. It would have been at this stage that Young and the Paramount Symphony Orchestra were called in. It is also possible that Alwyn's love motif was expunged and replaced by a sweetly melodic composition of Young's.

Perhaps the "somebody" who gave the orders to Young was Wallis, but Miklós Rózsa, writing from experience, leads one to believe it may have been somebody else. Rózsa narrates how when he was composing for Paramount's *Desert Fury* (1947) he was "intimidated by the head of the music department, who gave me long lectures about lovely main titles with swooning violins and the rest . . . A few days later he rang with a voice of doom to tell me that Wallis didn't like it, no doubt because the music wasn't melodious enough — the studio wanted hit tunes in the manner of Victor Young." When Rózsa spoke

---

[3] *The Cinema*, 69:5540 (3 Sept. 1947), 22.

to Wallis, his complaint turned out to be the opposite: he wanted "strong, gripping, powerful" music. Rózsa, who had other disputes with the music department, concludes,

> the producers and directors themselves were hardly ever to blame. The trouble stemmed from the heads of the music departments, men from jazz bands and theatre pits who hadn't the faintest notion of music as an adjunct to drama, and always wanted to "play it safe" (literally). They were the arbiters of musical taste in Hollywood, and since they employed hacks when real composers were available they caused the ruin of many potentially good films.[4]

Rózsa tactfully refrains from naming the Head of Paramount's music department. He was Louis Lipstone, and he ruled from 1939 until 1954. Victor Young was a mainstay of the department, under contract as composer and conductor from 1935 until 1949, after which he freelanced until an early death in 1956. His film career, therefore, spanned roughly the same period as Alwyn's. Like Alwyn, he was remarkable for the quantity of his film compositions, amounting to some 350 titles.

Unlike Alwyn, however, Young gave his orchestrators a lot of power. Bill Stinson, who was both a Paramount executive and a music editor, recalled, "Young had a couple of orchestrators[5] who knew his style and they really were his sound. You would turn lead lines over to them and tell them to score the picture, then he'd come in and conduct it."[6] Young had his failings, a major one being that his music sequences rarely fitted the pictures, but he was forgiven because he was a writer of great melodies. Many of his songs and themes are still played, "Sweet Sue" (1928), "Love Me Tonight" (1932), "My Foolish Heart" (1949), and so on. He was composer Henry Mancini's "hero" with "the gift of melody".[7] More prosaically, Miklós Rózsa called it the "Broadway-cum-Rachmaninoff idiom which was then the accepted Hollywood style".[8]

So Evil My Love ended up with an orchestrally overloaded soundtrack, which is in general uncharacteristic of Alwyn (although a thickly scored musical accompaniment could be thought appropriate to the film's melodramatic idiom). Moreover, the sound balance of music and dialogue favours the orchestra more than in British mixes of the period; this is Hollywood style, and suggests that, to incorporate Young's additions, the tracks were re-mixed in Hollywood.

---

[4] Rózsa, *Double Life*, 142.
[5] Leo Shuken and Sidney Cutner, according to Clifford McCarty, *Film and TV Music*, 16:5 (Summer 1957), 21.
[6] Karlin, *Listening to the Movies*, 36–7.
[7] Karlin, *Listening to the Movies*, 73.
[8] Rózsa, *Double Life*, 199.

An examination of the cue sheet[9] reveals that about one-third of the film score is attributable to Young. By and large the composers' styles are distinctive, although Young and his orchestrators seem at times to have matched Alwyn's style for the sake of homogeneity. Moreover, on a few occasions where the score passes from Young to Alwyn or vice-versa, the transition is well disguised. But as a whole, Young's cues are far sweeter in colour, place less emphasis on distinctive instrumentation, less on the brass and woodwind, and contain fewer repetitive motives within a short span.

In a report of an interview with Mathieson, *The Cinema* of 3 September 1947 states that the "theme tune is 'Cherry Ripe', which will form a motif for the musical score now being composed".[10] "Cherry Ripe" is a distinctive and light-hearted song contributed by Charles Edward Horn (1786–1849) to John Poole's comedy *Paul Pry* in 1826, supposedly based on a London street call. It is well known and has been adopted by other composers, including Roger Quilter and E. J. Moeran. Its special popularity in the 1930s and 1940s stemmed from Eric Coates's arrangement "Covent Garden" in his successful *London Suite* (1933). But its very familiarity as a piece of light music would seem to make it unsuited to the dark melodrama of *So Evil My Love*, unless as ironic comment. The song, immediately familiar from its first bars:

is woven, without any special emphasis, by both Young and Alwyn into some scenes between Olivia and Bellis. Young goes further, however. He takes a short development of the original "Cherry Ripe" song,

and expands it into the major love motif, a lush, schmaltzy "melody" insisted upon until it cloys the viewer:

The relationship between the motif and "Cherry Ripe" is openly exhibited only once, in a scene where Bellis at the piano breaks off from the earlier bars of the song at exactly the point where the orchestra takes up the motif as underscore. Since the motif occurs only in cues composed by Young, it is not unreasonable to believe it may replace one composed by Alwyn. Certainly it is

[9] Kindly given to me by Eldridge Walker, Vice President of Paramount's Music Clearance section.
[10] *The Cinema*, 69:5540 (3 Sept. 1947), 22.

over-worked in the earlier part of the film, often on a higher octave by a sickly violin. Worse, as a love theme suggestive of a "Romeo and Juliet" romance and plainly unsuited to the unsympathetic characters of this film, it weakens the impulse of the plot. After it has served its purpose of emphasising the growth of Olivia's infatuation, and as the film becomes increasingly ominous, it is forgotten until the end-credit roller caption, where as coda it assumes a (perhaps unintentionally) ironic role.

A motif by Alwyn starts the titles, a coldly aggressive theme played by strings in unison, stabbed by brass chords, and developing into a fugal pattern.

The passage suggests the bleak drama to follow, and it is saved for the film's climax and for a grisly final scene where Olivia stabs Mark, not from remorse but because of his sexual betrayal. Thus the motif becomes a frame to the overall drama.

Another cue of Alwyn's occurs in a scene set in a Parisian café, where an orchestra plays the polka from reel one of *On Approval!* In general, Hollywood left alone Alwyn's action scenes, too. A mood of stealth and mystery in a night raid on an art gallery is created through harmonic combinations characteristic of Alwyn. Flutes and very high, slowly descending strings in unison, against a long-bowed constant ground bass, are interrupted by intermittent plucked strings and later contrasted by rising basses, low cellos and contrasting woodwind. The subsequent chase, all tremolo strings and repeated fast clarinet phrases before dissolving inconclusively, is also representative of Alwyn's style. Characteristic, too, is a sequence that starts with rain dashing against a window to brass fanfares, flute tremolos, and ostinato clarinet at the top of its register. A cut inside shows Olivia on her bed while voice-overs (passed through an echo chamber) crowd her mind in a battle between good and evil choices, in much the same way as Johnny hears voices while he stares at his beer puddle in *Odd Man Out.* As in that film, inner tensions are reflected by rising and falling strings, harp arpeggios, and stabbing brass fanfares. Olivia rises from the bed, a significant movement suggestive of impatience with her conscience and emphasised by whirling strings and loud brass fanfares. Brass fanfares again sound as she lights the gas lamp in the drawing room. There is a pause — a dramatic gesture typical of Alwyn — and a second fanfare as Mark is revealed in the shadows of the door. The tone then modulates chromatically, offering up a feeling of relief as Olivia rushes to his arms — she has chosen Mark, and evil.

Music must always support the drama of a film, always be true to its idiom. That Alwyn's composition touches the heart of *So Evil My Love* can be established by examining in detail the vortex of the melodrama, its crisis. It is in the scenes showing Olivia's murder of the lawyer Henry Courtney (Raymond Huntley) that the musical composition reaches its most extreme: a whirl of passion almost Wagnerian in its intensity, and by Alwyn alone. The scenes, a series of linked sequences that almost could be called an act, commence as Olivia faces the coldly arrogant Courtney in his study. They barter: he wants letters sexually incriminating his wife Susan (Geraldine Fitzgerald); she wants the written evidence he possesses of Mark's crimes. The deal done, Courtney locks his drawer, casually remarking "By the way, you were quite right, it is just a copy". As Olivia realises she has been cheated, the orchestra shockingly bursts in, tutti, with the motif established at the start of the titles: whirling and quickly repeated strings joined by loud brass, until both strings and brass vie in a repeated three-note descending motive. With strings representing the female, brass the male, Olivia and Courtney struggle, he restraining her wrists, she beating his chest. Courtney, whose heart is weak, has an attack, and as he twists in pain stridently repeated strings are punctuated by abrupt and distinct bass drum beats that reflect the heartbeat. His fall is off-camera, conveyed by Olivia's reaction and rolling timpani as he hits the floor. The music calms, and, as Olivia kneels to search the body for the keys to his desk drawer, the ominous main theme enters, low pitched and in slow measure, its oppression intensified by the louring growl of a pedal point, almost inaudible, on the kettledrum. Two manservants approach the study, a dramatist's trick to increase anticipation at their discovery of Olivia with the body, but the musical motif continues unchanged, retaining our concern for Olivia inside the room. The men enter to a sudden drumbeat and rising string motive reflecting Olivia's surprise, echoed by a pause in the music which breaks the tension: quick-wittedly she pretends to be caring for the body: "Mr Courtney's had another attack, a bad one." As she speaks strings supplant the leitmotif and descend slowly down the scale: this over an emoting shot, a handy cinematic cut-away device enabling both manservants and body to be extinguished without distracting the main interest, which is — what Olivia will do now?

Alone again, she runs her hand over the drawer of the desk, the movement reflected by a beautiful sentence on the oboe reflecting her attachment to the letters inside. To tremolo strings and mounting brass and woodwind she reluctantly walks towards the doorway (repeated motives represent her indecision). She resolves on a plan of action, locks the door, and the musical rhythm crescendoes to greet the re-entry of the main theme with full melodramatic orchestral force, repeated again and again, forcing tension to an almost unbearable pitch as Olivia passes to the conservatory and removes a poisonous insect killer. The main theme pursues her up the sweeping staircase, but dissipates as a servant reminds her that she is travelling tonight: a secret arrangement to join Mark for the boat train to Ireland — an added tension, reflected in rising strings as she completes her journey up the stairs. At the top she meets another manservant: a repeated motive suspends both action and tension as they talk and hear the cries of Susan locked in her room by Courtney. Olivia inveigles the keys from the servant. She enters the bathroom to musical tension of another kind as suspended strings, vibraphone, and slow violins create an ethereal mix. A shadow on the wall shows her opening the medical cabinet to adulterate Courtney's medicine with the poison, given significance by a short rising vibraphone glissando.

Now excited climbing strings ensue as Olivia approaches Susan's room, and she is met by a hysterical outburst ("I hope he dies!") in a cacophony of screams and strings. Olivia calms Susan, and as she is encouraged to believe that the (now poisoned) medicine could help her husband the music ceases: it is a moment of calm that will intensify the impact of the ensuing music. The main theme recurs, uneasily and slowly, as Olivia seems to realise that she is committing a perfect murder, and Susan leaves the room. A flute hysterically takes up the main motive, and the vibraphone glissando is repeated as Susan reflects Olivia's previous action and removes the poisoned bottle from the bathroom cabinet. Now, as she carries the bottle confidently through the bedroom to her husband, Alwyn unleashes all his powers of depiction of an unbalanced, trance-like, state: low strings now descending, now rising, contrast with a violin *sul ponticello*. The vibraphone enters and resonates uneasily as Olivia peers through a crack and spies on Susan's shadow on the curtain, spooning the poison to her husband. An excited string passage follows immediately as Olivia is shown retrieving the letters from the drawer and dropping them on the fire to a twice-repeated triumphant fanfare, but the strings rise hysterically as she both awaits news of Courtney's death and watches the clock (the meeting with Mark). A pedal point increases in volume to stretch the tension to near breaking-point (like the pre-battle tension of *Desert Victory*, here dynamics replacing pitch), to be released when the door opens and Susan arrives with the doctor. "It's over . . . heart failure was not the cause of death . . ." Now the dark main theme again insinuates itself. "Not heart?" "No, Mrs Harwood . . ." As Olivia comforts Susan, her eyes widen with fear and wander to the clock, the main motif is continually repeated — until the scream of a train whistle cuts it off.

Alwyn's skill in structuring these scenes was consummate, but by now Hollywood's interference with the work of the creative artist would have been plain to him:

> I had many offers from Hollywood, but remembering those once fa-
> mous composers who had responded to its lures, only to have their tal-
> ents dimmed and even obliterated by the demands of the film world,
> I resisted the temptation. In spite of my interest in filmmaking, I was
> first and foremost a serious composer and each film score I had written
> was an opportunity for experiment and an exceptional chance, given
> the splendid orchestras who played my score, to improve and polish my
> technique and widen my dramatic range.[11]

[11] Alwyn, *Winged Chariot*, 11. See also a review by "W.A.", *Documentary Film News*, 7:66 (June 1948), 71, of Hanns Eisler's *Composing for the Film*, published shortly after the release of *So Evil My Love*, in which the writer "rejoice[s] in the freedom of action and thought that is the right of the composer in this country — the freedom to compose for films without the sur-render of artistic integrity."

16

Reed Again, and Asquith

CAROL Reed had left Two Cities Films and Rank in early 1947 after a quarrel over the budget and final edit of *Odd Man Out*. He joined Korda's new London Films set-up at Shepperton, where (bolstered by a loan from the National Film Finance Corporation, and a distribution deal with 20th Century–Fox) accountants had lower priority, and the atmosphere was more creative. An invitation to score Reed's first Korda production, *The Fallen Idol*, as well as Anthony Asquith's *The Winslow Boy* (1949), meant Alwyn now worked without his usual ally Mathieson, who was under contract to Rank. At London Films, the music director was Hubert Clifford, recently appointed in late 1946. Clifford had written his first score in 1943, for a documentary, and like Alwyn was a professor of composition at the RAM. By the time of *The Fallen Idol* he was fresh from a trip to Hollywood to study film music and sound recording techniques. Clifford had strong views about the subject of leitmotif, believing it made little impression on audiences.[1] Leitmotif is of no great significance to either *The Fallen Idol* or *The Winslow Boy*.

It was Korda's inspiration to join the creative talents of Graham Greene and Carol Reed.[2] Together they constructed from Greene's pre-war short story "The Basement Room" (1935) a screenplay about three days in the life of young Phillipe or "Phil" (Bobby Henrey), an eight-year-old ambassador's son living in a large mansion in Belgrave Square. A major part of Reed's achievement was to draw from Henrey a memorably unselfconscious performance of a child who, deprived of parental affection, worships the butler Baines as surrogate father. As the kind, self-sacrificing Baines, Ralph Richardson's performance rings true: he is trapped between his love for Julie (Michèle Morgan), a young secretary at the embassy, and his marriage to a wife he dislikes (Sonia Dresdel). Dresdel gives a truly cankerous performance as Mrs Baines, whose suspicions turn her from an unfeeling, cold woman into a desperately spiteful one. Left alone with Baines and Julie for a weekend, Phil misunderstands the repressed adult relationships. When Mrs Baines is accidentally killed, Phil believes Baines has murdered her and lies to save him from arrest.

Themes are interlinked, and lie-telling structures the plot. Lies start early and gain momentum, every major character practising deception of one kind

---

[1] Clifford, *Tempo* 11, 24. Quoted in the discussion of *Our Country*.
[2] Kulik, *Alexander Korda*, 301–2, 311.

or another, Baines, Julie, Mrs Baines, and especially Phil as he tries to save his friend, until finally Baines bitterly confesses, "Trouble is, we've told a fearful lot of lies." Another element is the film's Jamesian affinities with *The Turn of the Screw* (1898), *The Pupil* (1890), *What Maisie Knew* (1897),[3] and *The Awkward Age* (1899). Greene was an admirer of James, and James's lonely half-alien rootlessness, his depictions of indefinable menace, the corruption of innocence, and his insight into the child's vision of the adult world are all unquestionably powerful elements in the screenplay.

There is, too, the film's indebtedness to the fairy tale and the tradition of the wicked stepmother.[4] In this interpretation, Baines is seen as a surrogate "good" father, Mrs Baines as the wicked stepmother. It is not improbable that Reed and Greene intended such an interpretation.[5] There is the unreal world of the embassy setting, for example: Vincent Korda's set centres around an expansive hallway. Its chequered flooring suggests the deceptions and guile of the chess game, while its dominating high staircase enables Reed to emphasis Phil's smallness with carefully-chosen camera angles. A prison-like atmosphere is suggested by the bars on the staircase, a metal fire-escape, and a visit to the zoo. The feel of the film owes much, too, to Georges Périnal's high contrast black-and-white cinematography, especially in the scenes of terror, or in Phil's panic-stricken run in pyjamas (suggesting a dream) through cobbled London streets. Périnal's craftsmanship also contributes to the Continental ambience (the best fairy stories originate from the Continent), aided by the presence of Michèle Morgan and the setting of a foreign embassy. The product of these ingredients — morality tale, James, fairy-tale, and European ambience — is a film of unique character, which demanded a delicate touch of its composer.

The main titles are accompanied by orchestra tutti, luxuriously romantic, in a theme that is later restated in other harmonic and rhythmic guises, principally (but not exclusively) to represent the affair between Baines and Julie.

---

[3] Phillipe Horne, "The James Gang", *Sight and Sound*, 8:1 (Jan. 1998), 18.

[4] Referred to, but not explored, by Ana Laura Zambrano, "Greene's Visions of Childhood: *The Basement Room* and *The Fallen Idol*", *Literature Film Quarterly*, 2:4 (Autumn 1974), 324–31.

[5] Both Reed and Greene deploy symbolism. Reed intended the great staircase to be a symbol of growing up (Voigt, "Sir Carol Reed", 26), but it was Greene's idea to introduce McGregor the snake. Greene, Preface to *The Third Man and The Fallen Idol* (London: Penguin, 1971), 11, wrote of *The Third Man*, their next collaboration, that he and Reed "had no desire to move people's political emotions; we wanted to entertain them, to frighten them a little, to make them laugh. Reality, in fact, was only the background to a *fairy tale*". My emphasis.

Opening title music can serve as an insight into the ensuing drama, but here its languorous mood, punctuated by cymbal crashes, establishes an aspect of the drama, but offers no suspicion of the suspense, or indeed of the horror, of *The Fallen Idol*. It lulls, just as a fairy story often soothes its audience with a comfortable beginning.

Phil has no specific musical motif. In the opening sequence, his personality is expressed by a restless mix of short melodies and phrases, sometimes breathlessly cascading, sometimes thoughtful and curious, even occasionally faintly reminiscent of *Playtime*. Alwyn originally incorporated snatches of the latter light-hearted theme into the opening titles. Curiously, it can be heard in Christopher Palmer's arrangement of the "Prelude" for *The Fallen Idol Suite*,[6] which is based on the discarded manuscript. Another manuscript holds the revised opening titles, which cut out all suggestions of playfulness. As a result the title cue fell short of picture length, and the main theme is repeated to compensate.

One can only guess at the reasons for these changes. Perhaps Reed wanted to heighten the dramatic significance of the opening shot, a strong image of Phil in close-up gazing down through the prison-like bars on the stairway landing. The visual symbolism of the bars, stressed by the lighting photography, is however unstressed by the musical composition which whirls into even lighter mood with the excitement of the Ambassador's departure. The question therefore hovers: was Alwyn right not to emphasise, perhaps with a hint of "*con dolore*", the ominous significance of the first shot? The answer is in the affirmative: the opening sequence is a fine portrayal of the child's innocent perspective. The already strong pictorial symbolism of the bars is sufficient to make the point of his isolation; musical stress could have tipped the balance to melodrama and corrupted the overall structure.

In this establishing scene Reed calls attention to the spaciousness of the hallway, and to relationships. Both photography and music accentuate the spaciousness. A mixture of rhythms and melodies articulate the bustle of the scene, while passages of cascading strings accentuate the height of the stairway — a shot of a servant scuttling down the stairs, luggage in hands, against a descending scale across more than two octaves combines both purposes.

It is also important to contrast the freemasonry between Phil and Baines against the Ambassador's neglect of his son. Reed signposts the first relationship by cross-cutting Baines smiling conspiratorially at Phil with the boy's delighted response. It helps to know that Reed achieved this shot by ingeniously filming Henrey as he watched a children's conjuror.[7] The music, which almost

[6] *The Film Music of William Alwyn, Vol. 1*, London Symphony Orchestra, cond. Richard Hickox (Chandos CHAN 9243, 1993).
[7] Nicholas Wapshott, *The Man Between* (London: Chatto & Windus, 1990), 201; papers in the BFI Special Collection.

mickey-mouses but does not rigidly mirror the action, successfully catches the mood; shortly afterwards an exaggerated wink from Baines is accompanied by a witty arpeggio on the piccolo. (Compare this with the dream sequence in *On Approval*).

The Ambassador's contemptuous neglect of Phil is established more swiftly. As the Ambassador is on the point of departing, Baines is shown as caring enough to remind him to say goodbye to his son, and farewells are shouted across the extent of the hallway. Even now the Ambassador disparages his son to the aides: "He should have had his hair cut, he looks excessively neglected — any messages to your mother, Phillipe?" "Tell her I've got something to show her." "That should bring her home", this last comment delivered sarcastically. During this sequence we hear two very different string phrases, one short breathless ostinato as Phil runs to the stairway to say farewell, and the other (very idiomatic of Alwyn) a constantly repeated "holding" phrase, almost pausing, over the dialogue between the Ambassador and Phil. Played sequentially, they contrast and impart a tense impatience — the Ambassador is already late and is anxious to be gone. To establish the emotional distance between father and son, Reed stages the scene with a wide establishing shot but by so doing nearly loses the significance of the Ambassador's asides. Moreover, since they are delivered in a loud voice they appear to be heard by the boy, and the viewer is left slightly puzzled at his failure to react. To have matched the dialogue with underscore would have tipped the sequence into melodrama and sabotaged the overall mood. The composer cannot compensate for every weakness: perhaps the undercurrents of the dialogue could have been made clearer by intercutting the ambassador's asides in a closer shot. Later, Alwyn's warm musical reflection of the boy's response to Baines will be adequate contrast with his cool relationship with his father.

The emotional distance is re-emphasised when Phil waves from a far-off high balcony as his father steps into his limousine. Here the music repeats the earlier short ostinato phrase, but on this occasion it climaxes as the car drives away. The embassy flag is lowered to a descending phrase: and the Ambassador has gone. The excitement withers. Single notes on a horn create a feeling of indecision before the entry of a plaintive violin theme, and Phil, remembering a friend, removes his pet grass snake McGregor from its hiding place. It is tempting to comment that McGregor is one of the few cinematic snakes to depart from the "reptilian" musical conventions; but of course the touching McGregor theme is not really McGregor's at all but represents a displacement of Phil's own loneliness. Moreover, the melody is a modulation of the main theme, with the harmony and rhythm now invested with an East-European idiom.[8]

---

[8] The snake was originally called, rather exotically, Voojoo (see BFI Special Collection). The change of name to McGregor, with its overtones of Beatrice Potter's *Tale of Peter Rabbit*,

This gypsy-like passage on solo violin, as Phil gently handles and kisses McGregor, has nomadic redolence.

"Look! London!" says Phil, holding McGregor up to see a foreign place, but in words and action the boy could be simply showing the snake the view. It therefore falls upon the underscore to reinforce the affinity between boy and snake, both aliens, both separated from a rooted environment. (Later, when Mrs Baines secretly incinerates McGregor, she symbolically kills more than a snake. That action is performed in cruel silence; a repetition of McGregor's lovely harmonies without Phil's presence would be inappropriate, anything else melodramatic and unsubtle. Before that however, the theme is heard once more: passing ethereal bars as Baines slides him, concealed in a box, across the lunch table to Phil. The music continues as Phil takes him to his room, but the gypsy feel, no longer appropriate, evaporates.)

Discussion of *The Fallen Idol* cannot ignore the delicately managed scene where Phil stumbles upon Baines and Julie's clandestine meeting in a shabby teashop. His discovery concludes a long musical passage as he roams the streets in search of Baines. His cry of "Baines!" in jokey imitation of Mrs Baines, as he enters the shop, pierces the music and throws into relief the horrified and embarrassed silence that ensues. Gently, Alwyn recapitulates the main motif, but now in a very different mood. The scene is full of repressed passion, subdued conversation, quick glances, and concealed meanings. As Baines begins to talk gently to Julie in coded language ("This is how I see it, Julie, this girl you're talking about, this friend of yours . . ."), a soft compassionate texture is woven by solo cello, answered by solo violin, and developed as an interplay between the two instruments, male and female, tenderly accompanied by muted strings.[9] The music fades as Baines asks Phil for his handkerchief, the boy's

a story of a child hiding from its enemy, suggests interesting parallels. The score was also rewritten prior to recording. Alwyn's original concept was to represent McGregor with Middle- or Far-Eastern clarinets and bassoon (original MS in the Alwyn Archive). Evidently Reed wanted to suggest nothing further East than Phil's European roots.

[9] The music, partially concealed by the dialogue and intended to be "unheard" in this scene, can be fully appreciated on *The Film Music of William Alwyn, Vol. 1.*

half-knowing, half-innocent looks and questions now, and throughout the sequence, in Jamesian character. The pause allows emphasis for a dark chord to strike in, strings rising to a climax and joined by brass, as Julie rises to her feet and leaves the teashop, and the rendezvous is concluded unsatisfactorily. The passionate strings return to reflect Baines's misery as through the window he watches Julie walk away ("The cup that cheers", he ironically declaims as he drains his teacup). He and Phil leave the shop. Outside, however, the couple meet again and (waited for by a bored Phil) their relationship takes a more hopeful turn, the score matching the delicate changes of emotion to finally surge *molto appassionata*. It is a romanticism excelled only in *Odd Man Out*, when Kathleen's desperate search for Johnny is rewarded. But the observant will note that in *The Fallen Idol* the music belies the visual imagery and favours Baines's point of view only: as Julie turns to leave, in close-up, her expression is one of hopelessness.

The scenario of repressed passion in a seedy teashop recalls the better-known *Brief Encounter*, especially the scene, re-enacted near the close of the film, where the guilty couple are interrupted by a garrulous acquaintance. A comparison is revealing. Juxtaposed with *The Fallen Idol*, the dialogue of *Brief Encounter* seems trite, its characters emotionally immature. Lean's camera angles are stilted and limited compared with Reed's fluid positioning, movement within the frame, close-ups, and perfectly judged edits. Moreover, the soundtrack further disables Lean. *Brief Encounter*'s inflexibly lush Rachmaninoff score gives way to the aimless chatter of the intruder, which becomes itself a background accompaniment, especially as it fades unintelligibly behind a voice-over. Constrained by slabs of Rachmaninoff's score and by sound-effects, Lean is deprived of subtlety. He cannot modulate the interplay of emotions as Alwyn does for Reed, matching mood changes, suggesting repressed passion, the ebb and flow of emotion. It is a warning against the modern reliance on temp tracks, and an illustration of the weakness in Vaughan Williams's argument for composing film music as " a continuous stream . . . modified . . . by points of colour imposed on the flow".[10]

One sequence in *The Fallen Idol* pleased Alwyn particularly. In his lectures he described it as an

> illustration of . . . [the] primary function of film music — the dramatic heightening of atmosphere, already indicated in the visuals, but made more frightening by the addition of cumulative musical sounds . . . A little boy is playing hide-and-seek in the deserted, dust-sheeted Embassy — he becomes more and more excitable and frightened until the tension is broken by his scream . . . the music follows the rhythmic cutting of the

[10] Vaughan Williams, "Director's Address", 6.

shots, and the effect of the natural "break-off" of music with the boy's shout. The music is scored for muted strings and muted brass, both playing *fortissimo* but held down in the dubbing to add a sense of strain to the soundtrack — almost like trying to scream in a whisper.[11]

The sequence as a whole contains several individual tension points. By alternately relaxing and tightening these points, director and composer together create a heightening of the overall suspense. Alwyn achieves part of the trick by mickey-mousing — the only way to handle action that looks like a cartoon chase. There is the other part to the trick, however: the musical viewpoint is ambiguous. If Baines, Julie, and Phil (in some sort of strange diegetic fantasy-world) could hear the music track, they would think that it mirrors their game: but they would be puzzled, for its mood is not the cheerful music of a children's lark but dark and edgy. The audience, guided by the filmmakers, is more aware than the characters, apprehensive that the three players are unknowingly joined by a fourth, Mrs Baines.

The terror of the scene is quickened by every child's fears of the dark, accentuated by contrasty black-and-white photography, deep shadows, and low camera angles from the child's viewpoint. Our feelings of unease commence with a small, easily-missed detail: just before the start of the game, a light extinguishes in an upstairs window. Then, with a flourishing chord, the dust-sheets are swirled off the furniture, and skittish strings chase Phil across the hallway. When he crawls under the table, suspense is held by a pedal point on the vibraphone harmonising with string tremolos and dabbed by a convulsive clarinet. He sees what he thinks are Julie's shoes. The audience knows differently, but the shoes retreat when Phil makes mouse squeaks. Baines and Julie enter, and a tersely repeated musical motive accentuates the suspense that Baines playfully stokes up before sweeping the sheets off the table and entangling the child in them. The music agitates again as, freed from the sheets, Phil runs to the stairs, but the suspenseful chords return as the couple creep in search of him in the dark. A door closes, and a perfect example of the score's ambiguity ensues: Baines and Julie believe Phil has hidden himself in the room and prepare to seize him — the audience, on the other hand, knowing Phil is crouched at the top of the stairs, fear they will uncover Mrs Baines. The music works for both. As the couple enters, the strings climax. Then a brief, breathless silence points the surprise as Phil calls from behind, the music speeds again, all run away from the room. Back in the hallway Baines frenetically switches the lights on and off, and beats a gong, a whirlwind of light, noise, and especially music. Exhausted, the three climb the stairs, the excitement disperses, and the action slows; the music wings to full romantic flight as, now alone, Baines and Julie embrace.

---

[11] Alwyn, "Film Music: Sound or Silence", 4.

The tension is not fully released, however, for we know that Mrs Baines is still somewhere in the house, and we are aware that Phil is looking through the upstairs window. He sees a shadow beneath, dark frightening chords lunge in, he recoils with a scream, and there is silence: all the more telling by its contrast with the long sequence of music that has preceded it.

With this key sequence the ambience of the film is changed, and its fairy-tale scenario revealed. From her initial appearance as a cold-hearted, spiteful woman, a lover of carbolic, who resents the boy, Mrs Baines is magnified into the wicked stepmother, the bad fairy or witch. Baines can now be seen as the good (surrogate) father of the fairy tale. (Note how he always addresses the boy as "Phil", while Mrs Baines adopts the formal "Master Phillipe".) What other viewpoint can one take? For logic cannot justify the polarisation of Mrs Baines into this monster of terror, even though we hate her because she has killed the snake (with any symbolism, political or psychological, one may wish to attach to that). Only by shifting the scenario into a bizarre nightmare fantasy can one smile upon the adultery of Baines and Julie, excuse the death of Mrs Baines (the bad sorceress who always loses out), and find the happy ending. In fact, just before her death she is revealed as much a pathetic, unhappy woman, as the powerful witch or cunning queen, justifying Baines'st Jamesian comment: "Faults on both sides, Phil. We don't have any call to judge. Perhaps she was what she was because I am what I am. We have to be very careful, Phil, because we make one another."

The moment of her death lies at the centre of the film's remaining sustained musical sequence. Phil climbs from his bed to discover her prowling around the house in search of Baines and Julie. It is an eerie moment, in which slow vibrating alternations of *e* and *f* on the vibraphone are followed by ostinato violins and cellos briefly quoting a motive from the tritone, the *diabolus in musica*, of the wheelchair sequence of *I See a Dark Stranger*. Phil shouts a warning to Baines and is shaken and slapped by Mrs Baines, who rushes downstairs to challenge her husband. To orchestra tutti but with brass predominating, the boy runs to the fire escape and from descending levels watches three stages of the row between Baines and his wife, which he mistakenly supposes to end in murder. Alwyn himself describes what happens next, and the purpose of the music:

> He turns, runs down the fire-escape and tears through the deserted London streets as if all the devils in hell were after him — until eventually he is stopped by a night-patrolling policeman. Carol Reed is a master of technique of convincing his audience of the actuality of a scene which could not possibly hold water in real life. Here he wanted to build a huge emotional climax in order to start the second part of his film of a flat unemotional level — so he turned to music:

1. The little boy could not possibly have heard the sounds of the quarrel through a closed window and, 2. there are few sounds to be heard in the dead of night in the London streets — so Reed was only able to shoot this long and most effective visual sequence, and build to an emotional climax followed by silence, if he knew that the music would supply both the drama and the tension suggesting the nightmare fear in the child's mind. This was a sequence carefully planned to make its visual effect in terms of musical sound. Without music it could not have been shot in this way.[12]

The last part of *The Fallen Idol* is sparingly scored, for, as Alwyn hints, musical support would be deleterious to the psychological interplay between police, Baines, and Phil. An important moment hinges around an incriminating telegram folded into a dart, which Baines is anxious to recover. Left alone, Phil retrieves it from a display of flowers at the head of the stairs. His action is emphasised by a rise in the orchestral temperature, a melodramatic moment that could have been stolen from a second-rate "B" film. However, the strings continue to add to a worrying tension over police cross-questioning, even though whatever Phil is doing with the dart is out of sight. It lasts until the moment when the dart is taken from Phil by an adult who flies it from the balcony, allowing us to watch it float down, down across the hallway accompanied by a solo violin, to land at the feet of the police. It is one of the musical beauties of the film, which even the dots on the score seem to picture:

To end the film, Phil's mother (Bobby Henrey's real-life mother) arrives like the good mother of the fairy tale. Phil, in close-up, walks out of frame as he descends the stairs towards her. The actor Henrey's face is emotionally bland. The character Phil's feelings are contributed solely by the music, which is climbing towards the happy ending, an awakening from a nightmare. The music and the movement out of frame also express a stride towards maturity — emotionally this is a very different child from the one we saw in shot one. A child psychiatrist sums up what Greene, Reed, and Alwyn are illustrating probably instinc-

[12] Alwyn, "Film Music: Sound or Silence", 4.

tively: "The fairy-tale is future-orientated and guides the child — in terms he can understand in both his conscious and unconscious mind — to relinquish his infantile dependency wishes and achieve a more satisfying independent existence."[13]

There was a sad postscript to *The Fallen Idol*. In 1949 Reed promised Alwyn the composition of *The Third Man*, but during his researches in Vienna he heard the zither music of Anton Karas. There and then, Reed decided this would better evoke the atmosphere of the post-war city. It was a mistake. The music became popular because of the novelty of the instrument, but the subtle nuances of an Alwyn score — illuminating character, theme, and place — could not be matched by the repetitive gimmickry of the zither, and the film is the worse for it. Both Alwyn and Mathieson were bitterly disappointed; after *The Third Man*, Reed's reputation faltered and his later films were often indifferent. Fourteen years passed before Alwyn composed for him again.

Alwyn's other contract for Korda and Clifford, *The Winslow Boy*, was released in the same month as *The Fallen Idol* and is of a very different character. While *The Fallen Idol* has an insight into human relationships and an artistic quality that stamp it as one of the enduring classics of British cinema, *The Winslow Boy* seems caricatured and dated. It was a third collaboration between producer Anatole de Grunwald, director Anthony Asquith, and writer Terence Rattigan. Rattigan had adapted it from his play about a middle-class father who spends all his savings on legal fees to clear the name of his thirteen-year-old son, a naval cadet expelled for stealing a five-shilling postal order. It is essentially theatrical rather than filmic: the climactic courtroom scene is not even shown, but reported by one of the characters.

The artistic distance between *The Fallen Idol* and *The Winslow Boy* called for a different kind of music composition. In *The Fallen Idol* Reed had depended upon his composer to help structure the plot and for the emotional power of its bravura passages. In contrast, Asquith's *The Winslow Boy*, with its lack of real filmic creativity and often heavy dependence upon poorly-assimilated drawing-room dramatic conventions, comes with a predetermined structure and wordy emotions. Nevertheless, within even these limitations the music and effects tracks make real contributions to the film's structure.

Some contributions are obvious. Importantly, perhaps through Clifford's influence, perhaps to avoid dispersing the film's homogeneity with the introduction of a variety of leitmotifs, Alwyn relies on a single main theme upon which to hang changes in mood. In the title sequence, for example, hints of Elgarian ceremonial establish an ethos of the "rightness" of the British legal system.

---

[13] Bruno Bettelheim, *The Uses of Enchantment: The Meaning and Importance of Fairy Tales* (London: Thames and Hudson, 1976), 11.

In the details, too, music and sound-effects pull the plot together. The Winslow boy's short school career is swiftly sketched by a series of dissolves against a voiced-over letter home, together with not music but, imaginatively, the sound of the bugle and the parade ground. Again, a fine musical change points the misery of the disgraced Ronnie's arrival home: unknowingly the rest of the family is singing in church "All Things Bright and Beautiful" (1887); the scene cuts to the unhappy boy breaking off the hymn in mid-verse as Alwyn deftly echoes the note orchestrally, and shifts to a laconic violin solo:

In another dissolve sequence the spreading fame of the family is shown as the whole world (church, pub, club, train, middle-class men, middle-class women, working-class man, pavement artist) whispers the words "the Winslow boy". The sequence works because the musical score echoes and structures the rhythm of the whispered voices — a repeated four-note scheme commencing on the horns and rising to full orchestral climax.

Perhaps less obvious is the composer's skilful serving of the sometimes-lengthy dialogue scenes, matching the voice rhythms, and heightening their mood and meaning. The relationship of music to dialogue is one that Alwyn found of particular interest.

> You cannot have failed to notice that necessarily a considerable amount of film music is written as a background and as accompaniment to the spoken word. This is an art in itself, and one that is immensely fascinating to the composer. Unlike incidental music to the stage or radio play [in pre-recording days], where the pace of dialogue varies from performance to performance, the film composer knows to a split-second when any given word is to be said (this also applies, of course, to any fleeting visual action) and he can therefore plan to the split-second how and where to make his musical point. He learns to score in such a way that his music blends with the timbre of the voices — he can allow for punctuation and the breathing spaces and he can mould and influence the very performance of the actor himself.

Even the rhythm of the words can become pregnant with musical meaning. I myself have become increasingly intrigued with this reflection of a rhythmic word pattern with a rhythmic musical one. The tiniest phrase can be given significance in this way — I throw out this suggestion as a fruitful subject for experiment, made possible by the cinema but having obvious potentialities in the field of Opera — speech rhythm and its relation to music. The exciting thing about any Art is that somewhere, lurking round the corner, is something which has somehow escaped your attention, and that a trivial commonplace can conceal the germ of a whole world of new creativeness.[14]

The dialogue sequences of *The Winslow Boy* are visually near static. Alwyn heightens the drama by reflecting the voice patterns contrapuntally. This music, restrained behind virtually continuous dialogue, is certainly unnoticed by most of the audience. In one scene, typical of four or five in the film, Arthur Winslow (Cedric Hardwicke), the father, and his wife Grace (Marie Lohr) prepare for bed. The plot has reached a crisis where Arthur is determined to press on with his campaign, despite a near-calamitous drain on his finances, and the whole case is seeming to go nowhere. The orchestra enters gently with a slow, plaintive, unsettling, theme predominated by the strings. For a while the father talks about the unsteady state of his finances. The mother is more concerned with larger issues:

GRACE   I'm not talking about economics. I'm talking about ordinary common-or-garden facts. (*the musical temperature rises*) Things we took for granted a year ago. And which now (*the emotion continues to intensify, plaintive oboe and clarinet dominate*) don't seem to matter any more.

ARTHUR   Such as?

GRACE   Such as peace and quiet and a normal respectable life. Some sort of future for us and our children. (*the music intensifies*) A happy home, Arthur, (*the music surges*) a happy home. (*the orchestra resumes the plaintive mood*) But you've thrown that all overboard. I can only pray to God you know what you're doing.

ARTHUR   I know exactly what I'm doing, Grace. I'm going to publish my son's innocence before the world. (*a cello hints at the ceremonial, while the plaintive theme continues*)

GRACE   You talk about sacrificing everything for him. But when he's grown up he won't thank you for it, Arthur. Even though you've given your life to publish his innocence as you call

---

[14] Alwyn, "Film Music: Sound or Silence", 11–12.

it. Yes, Arthur, your life. You complain about arthritis and a touch of gout in your old age and all the rest of it. You know as well as any of the doctors what's really the matter with you. (*the music becomes increasingly plaintive*). You're destroying yourself, Arthur. And me, and your family. And for what I'd like to know. For what, Arthur?

ARTHUR For justice? — Grace? (*a light, mournful, trumpet fanfare*)

GRACE Are you sure it's not plain (*music pauses, lending emphasis to the following words*) pride and self-importance and (*music resumes*) sheer brute stubbornness? (*music briefly pauses again*)

The music resumes and continues in a similar manner to reflect the emotional interplay over the two following scenes, unifying the three scenes and casting a mood of despair even as it structures the dialogue. In later years Alwyn would find his experience of matching voice rhythms invaluable to the scoring of his two operas.

17
Pélissier, a Forgotten Talent

TOWARDS the end of the war, William Alwyn was elected to the commit- tee of the Composers' Section of the Society of Authors. It was initially a frustrating experience. Most of the board members were elderly and pomp- ous, and, according to Alwyn, its chairman ruled out of order everything that could further the cause of British music. So in 1947, with the help of colleagues, Alwyn initiated the Composers' Guild of Great Britain. Retaining its affiliation to the parent society, the Guild aimed to protect the legal rights of his fellow musicians (in which it hit), and to secure minimal concert performances of British works (in which it missed). Alwyn's election as chairman in 1949 was in the midst of what he called a McCarthyite "witch-hunt", and the Guild seemed likely to collapse under a threat of mass resignations. Fortunately, the affair calmed down, and Alwyn survived to serve again in 1950 and 1954.[1]

In the same busy period he helped to form the Society for the Promotion of New Music, offering new composers a chance to hear their works in perform- ance — not unlike the New Music Society he had founded in 1932. Committee work did not end there, for he was also elected to the council of the Performing Right Society, a position that led to the Executive Committee and, over the coming years, a number of international conferences.

There were also health worries. For two years doctors had diagnosed a persistent difficulty in swallowing as a "nervous affliction and . . . treated ac- cordingly in spite of increasing misery and frequent bouts of choking". Finally, Alwyn explained in his brief autobiography, "an 'X ray' revealed a pharyngeal pouch — a lesion of the muscles at the base of the gullet which necessitated a severe operation". Alwyn entered University College Hospital "calm and re- signed, glad to be finished with the fearful years of near suffocation and almost welcoming the knife".[2]

1949 also saw the completion of his First Symphony, so time must have been severely restricted, yet he managed two feature commissions for this year and five more for release in the first four months of the following year. The 1949 releases were produced by John Mills, the actor's star in the ascendant after

---

[1] Alwyn, "1066 and All That", 23–24.
[2] Alwyn, "Ariel to Miranda", 62–63.

Great Expectations (1946), and scripted and directed by Mills's close friend Anthony Pélissier.[3]

Pélissier, one of the forgotten talents of British cinema, had show business in the blood. The son of actress Gladys Cooper, in his younger days he had worked under people such as C. B. Cochran and Sir Alfred Butt, and he later became a dialogue writer for Korda. His films suggest a lively talent, but he spread himself too thinly, and throughout the late 1940s and 1950s he divided his talent between writing and directing for theatre and film, together with some radio and television work. He was a good friend of Alwyn, and for many years they shared company at that comfortable retreat for the arts fraternity, the Savile Club in Brook Street.[4]

Pélissier's script for *The History of Mr Polly* omits the first third of Wells's story, but is faithful to the rest, retaining some of the book's pathos and much of its pawkiness. It is a "man on the run" story in period costume. Briefly, the narrative tells of Alfred Polly (John Mills), who reaches middle age having achieved nothing except the disappointment of his romantic ideals, a near-bankrupt shop, and a nagging wife, Miriam (Betty Ann Davies). In desperation he sets fire to the shop, but forgets to slit his throat, and is hailed as a hero by the local community for his rescue of an old lady from the flames. Having failed again, he runs away and becomes handyman to the "plump woman" (Megs Jenkins), as Wells calls her, at the idyllic riverside Potwell Inn. Here, after ousting the savage and drunken Uncle Jim (Finlay Currie), he settles down to a life of idyllic contentment.

Polly was a product of the co-operation between crafts that Alwyn relished – in particular script, direction, film editing, sound editing, and musical composition. Nevertheless, since H. G. Wells was only two years dead and more widely read than today, a few critics misjudged the film through faulty comparison with the book. Nor was the importance of the music properly understood. Two respected critics, in particular, disparaged Alwyn's track. Richard Winnington talked of "the crashing sound track with its dollops of jolly Alwyn music especially being overstrained".[5] Worse was C. A. Lejeune's brutishly insensitive and negative review in *The Observer*, including in her bloodbath Alwyn's "obtrusive musical score" which was party to "the torture . . . directed to the ears of the audience which are subjected to a constant assault of chatter, sound-effects and music from what must be one of the noisiest sound-tracks ever used in a British film".[6] Other writers correctly responded to the film's

[3] John Mills, "I Produce Mr Polly", *Theatre Magazine* (24 July 1948), 14–15; John Mills, *Up in the Clouds, Gentlemen Please* (London: Weidenfeld and Nicolson, 1980), 206.
[4] Jonathan Alwyn, Interview.
[5] Richard Winnington, *News Chronicle* (14 Feb. 1949).
[6] C. A. Lejeune, *The Observer* (13 Feb. 1949).

caricature of male, middle-aged restlessness, its gentle comedy, its farce and its pathos, even though they may have been unaware of the several vital roles played by the music track.

To reduce the footage, many thematic and plot elements were restricted to a filmic shorthand that depended on musical composition to supply meaning. To this end Alwyn introduces three major motifs. It is convenient to label them the "Christabel theme" and "Polly themes" A and B. Two are established with the opening credits, and their meaning is unmistakable.

The Christabel theme represents Polly's romantic dreams. Like Don Quixote, Polly's head is turned by overindulgence in knights and armour. Here one meets up with one of Pélissier's valuable modifications of the original text, which does not specifically refer to the King Arthur and his Knights who fill Pélissier's Polly's daydreams. The central Christabel scene occurs as the young Polly, out sensing the freedom of his bicycle, the equivalent to Quixote's steed Rozinante, props his machine against an old stone wall and flops down. That the setting is idyllic is suggested mainly by Alwyn's pastoral composition — otherwise the audience might be persuaded it was just a corner of one of the Denham studios. The pastoral nature of this musical studio economy is represented by lyrical solo violin and harp chords. Two bursts of intermittent flute trills represent birdsong, perhaps even the novel's "little brown and gray bird" to whom Polly murmurs, "This is All Right. Business — later." In the film we hear those words but do not see the bird, which is another economy paid for with music. Suddenly Christabel appears on the wall, the dizzy summit of all Polly's dreams of romance, and the score, owing much to Delius, responds with her theme:

While Wells does not refer to Malory, he nevertheless permits Polly to woo with half-baked ideals of chivalry. There is talk of warhorses and dragons, and he kisses her finger in knightly fashion. Pélissier follows Wells closely, and Alwyn's musical motif matches the rhythms of speech. As Christabel reveals her name the music rises enchantingly ("It is rather pretty . . ." she confesses) and as Polly discloses his ("It's a girl's name!" she cries), poor Alfred looks disconcerted. Here Wells writes, "For a moment he went out of tune", and although Alwyn does not quite do that, he does allow a bassoon to lightly mock the silliness of the name with a few bars from the Polly theme.

When Polly's idealistic love is betrayed by the giggles of Christabel's friends behind the wall, the melody lingers like a dream in the air, until descending flute chords bring Polly down to earth. For — alas! — Polly's deficient education and his low social standing offer no hope in the sexual stakes. An ominously mocking low bassoon carries him off to his lowbred cousins the Larkins — and Miriam, whom he marries on the rebound.

Since the Christabel theme represents Polly's highest ideals, it is established early, as he stuffs his head with tales of Sir Lancelot. During the marriage ceremony with Miriam, a glance at an angel in a stained-glass window also brings memories of Christabel, one last glimpse of a radiant ideal. Fifteen years later, standing at a stile and contemplating a failed life ("I haven't done any of the things I really wanted to do, either . . .") the theme reappears in mourning dress, echoing Polly's sad contemplation of his lost youthful dreams. It is the last ostensible sounding of the theme, which is soon to be supplanted by the Polly motif. But there is a satisfying surprise in store. Much later, after Polly has deserted Miriam and met the Potwell's plump innkeeper, he runs away, fearing the dreadful Uncle Jim. His absence is for a single night, but a decisive one in which he resolves to return and face Jim's vengeance, and a few bars of Christabel's motif bridge a mix to the plump woman weeping at his desertion. Here the composer delivers a message sent by neither script nor direction: Polly's chivalric ideal is not quite dead. The plump woman is another Christabel, for whom he will do or die in his battle with Uncle Jim.[7]

The other main motifs, the Polly themes A and B, represent our hero's complicated headstrong determination which needs two motifs. Thus Polly theme A under the opening titles sets mood and period in lively music-hall style, and is hinted at as Polly dashes around the countryside on his bicycle.[8] At this stage Polly has youth and bravado but awaits his awakening. When that comes, the fast descending strings of Polly Theme A,

[7] As Polly returns to the inn there is also a final, and faint, hint of Polly theme A which represents his youthful bravado. He will need it in his confrontation with Uncle Jim.

[8] Alwyn labels the A theme as Polly's cycling theme.

are abandoned for the lyrical hue of Polly theme B (although both themes have some notation in common) as Polly deserts Miriam and strides through the countryside towards the Potwell Inn:

Afterwards the motif returns at key lyrical moments, including the film's ending where Polly and the plump woman enjoy what Alwyn describes as "Utopian sunset",[9] he painting and she sewing. Here, the scenario resembles the homestead scene of an American Western, strongly suggested by Alwyn's languorous music, flute solo and violins. As a contemporaneous comparison I would suggest Dimitri Tiomkin's main theme for Howard Hawks's *Red River* (1948). The comparison is entirely apt — for Polly's victory, freedom to make his own world, is the ideal and victory of the Western film.

Alwyn's old acquaintance Harry Miller was sound editor on Polly, and because they evidently enjoyed their collaboration, there are exciting discoveries in the soundtrack. An orchestration of door slams accompanies Polly and Miriam as they walk from the Larkins' house: mother's, the rejected sister Minnie's, and the front door — against the background of a street barrel organ playing "A Bicycle Built for Two" (1892). The slamming doors symbolise the ending of a stage in Polly's life: he is about to propose to Miriam ("give me your answer do . . ."). The pleasures of the soundtrack are often found in the detail: for example, the short oboe fanfare that accompanies Polly's decision to commit suicide, and sounds again to reflect the buzz in his memory when he remembers that he has forgotten. There is a significant funeral march in this film too, celebrating Polly's father's death, but compare its light satirical pathos with the tragic finale of *Odd Man Out*. Polly senior's funeral tea is intercut snatches of conversation and stuffing of food gradually rising to an unintelligible cacophony joined by whirling orchestral strings . . . from which Polly abruptly escapes into the stillness of the back garden, realising he hates all these unfeeling people. Here an echo of the funeral march reinforces what the book spells out but the filmscript only suggests, that Polly's thoughts remain with his dead father: "Funereal gigglers . . . funereal games". A year later Alwyn would recall the march in one of the funniest sequences of the Ealing comedy *The Magnet* (1950).

The merits of mickey-mousing, or hitting the action with music, compared with its opposite of playing through the action and hitting nothing specifically,

[9] The description on the score.

have been discussed extensively. As a proponent of the latter school Vaughan Williams claimed he liked to "ignore the details and to intensify the spirit of the whole situation by a continuous stream of music".[10] Max Steiner, with whose views Alwyn had much in common, described such film composers as "symphonists",[11] believing that a film ought to be a co-operative art.[12] In at least two of Vaughan Williams's films, *Coastal Command* (1942) and *Scott of the Antarctic*, sequences were extended to fit scores written with a genial disregard for the timings, resulting in an embarrassing *longeur* in *Coastal Command*. Steiner's opposite approach resulted in meticulous mickey-mousing. For his Oscar-winning score for *The Informer* (1935) he worked for days trying to persuade a water tank to drip in tempo. The importance of the emphases brought by composers to momentary emotional peaks in the drama was summarised in a review in *Film Music Notes*: "If the larger outlines of drama are accomplished by writer and director, the smaller undulations are almost entirely the work of the composer".[13] The film composer and teacher Fred Karlin suggests that the best course lies somewhere between the two extremes, sustaining the overall emotion of some sequences, hitting important moments in others.[14]

Alwyn was never afraid to enhance the action with his music. In *The History of Mr Polly* the style is established in the opening scene, as Polly rushes in a series of musical sequences from the basement of the draper's where he works to the shop floor. There he hides from the wrathful manager by stacking a pile of cardboard boxes one upon the other — the humour emerging from the dual unison of the rising pizzicato strings and wood blocks that accompany the action. In mickey-mousing it is important to maintain a line of musical continuity whilst avoiding monotony; this can be achieved by varying instrumental colour or technique. Thus in the scene that follows, Polly piles on more boxes, slides them across the counter, peers between them, and camouflages himself behind a dummy, accompanied by (amongst others) slurred triads progressing up the scale, a clarinet rising in hops and trailed by strings, various astutely-judged "plops" from the wood blocks, flute and horn solos, and a short burst of Polly theme A — before he trips and is discovered in a heap on the floor. Music and script conspire to manufacture the farce.

Alwyn partially mickey-moused in Polly's key set piece, the arson of his shop, perhaps the hardest to score. Something more is required here, something quite subtle: normal mickey-mousing that points up the action but is rooted

[10] Vaughan Williams, "Director's Address", 6.
[11] Isabel Morse Jones, "This Leitmotiv Music", *Film-Music Notes*, 4:8 (May 1945), unnumbered.
[12] Manvell and Huntley, *The Technique of Film-Music*, 221.
[13] Harold Brown, "Steiner has a Way", *Film-Music Notes*, 12:1 (Sept.–Oct. 1952), 4; also quoted in Karlin, *Listening to the Movies*, 80.
[14] Ibid., 81.

in reality and conveys human qualities and failings. The sequence falls into two parts. It starts with Polly's "arsonical" preparations. Again, Alwyn varies the orchestral textures, starting with ominously low bass and cellos (the same dark colour as in the night scene of *I See a Dark Stranger*), followed by trembling strings ascending both scale and tension as he sorts out his inflammable materials. As he trails paraffin up the stairs, Alwyn's wood block plops and amused clarinets render funny what is visually uninteresting, achieving a significance they had in the dream sequence of *On Approval*. A tottering funeral pyre, mainly of spindly chairs, is accompanied by a tiny fugal arrangement of the Polly theme A, now on bassoon, now on horn. As Polly sprinkles it liberally with paraffin, the oily sound of clarinets in dual unison, a characteristic Alwyn combination, accompanies the action.

The second part of the sequence starts as the fire accidentally ignites, commencing with strings on a six-note falling scale in the middle register to express the fanning flames. Increasing tempo and instrumental interjections (especially by rising flutes) pile on the urgency until — "It's all going too fast!" — Polly panics, and the orchestra leaps into tutti to embark on a theme that, through its speeding strings, suggests all is out of control, and which owes much to the animated cartoon. At first, as Polly attempts to motivate the bungling fire brigade, orchestral variety and effects — fanfares and bugles, bells, and a barking dog — ring sufficient sound changes. As the scene turns to Polly's rescue of a deaf old lady (Edie Martin) from the rooftops, the score eventually comes to owe something in tempo and orchestral colour to the "Ride of the Valkyries", the ostinato strings become faster, and the urgency becomes greater. It is a long sequence to sustain musically, and if towards its end the score begins to seem repetitive and tired, it is owing mainly to a lack of instrumental variety.

To discover Alwyn's real skill at mickey-mousing we must look at Polly's slapstick encounters with Uncle Jim. In his chronology of Mills's work, John Tanitch points out that "Finlay Currie's mad, drunken Uncle Jim was a comic version of his Magwitch and his first meeting with Polly paid homage to David Lean's *Great Expectations* and Pip's memorable first meeting with the convict on the marshes."[15] Pélissier deals with this in a delightful way, assisted, like Lean, by the soundtrack. Having heard about the fearsome Uncle, Jim Polly walks along a lane at twilight, whistling nervously. The audience, also warned against Uncle Jim, senses something happening and is nervous too. A sudden cut to a close-up of a hand grabbing Polly's shoulder startles the audience, but the shock is intensified because Alwyn's orchestral tutti slams in on the cut with a deafening and abrupt chord. As Tanitch suggests, the scene is a tribute to a well-known shock edit in *Great Expectations*.[16] But similar cuts and shock

---

[15] John Tanitch, *John Mills* (London: Collins & Brown, 1993), 66.
[16] Analysed in Reisz, *The Technique of Film Editing*, 240.

techniques had been performed time and again in the Hollywood animated cartoons. Their greatest exponent was Carl Stalling,[17] who had extensive experience in silent cinema and with Walt Disney and Ub Iwerks — literally Mickey Mouse-ing! He joined Warner Brothers in 1936 and until 1958 was responsible for *Bugs Bunny*, *Daffy Duck*, *The Roadrunner*, and other series. The opportunity to indulge in cartoon slapstick rarely comes the way of the feature film composer, but Alwyn siezed the chance in 1948 in the depiction of Polly's David to Uncle Jim's Goliath. Alwyn, the lover of cinema, must surely have included watching cartoons among his pleasures, for his battle score adopts many of the inventions, and conventions, of Stalling.

The major slapstick sequence takes the form of an *entr'acte*, confirmed by shots of the innkeeper and her niece watching from an upstairs window, and cuts to the scene from that viewpoint — a topshot that resembles a stage. The fight commences slowly, and rightly so. Polly grasps the neck of a beer bottle and approaches a drunken singing Jim. There is a pregnant pause as Jim sees Polly: "You! — scoot!" he declares, waving his arm about. "Your job", retorts Polly. A trombone stutters to a climax (as Polly elevates both courage and bottle) and ends with a satisfying wood block "bop" as Polly hits Jim on the head with the bottle, followed by a descending flute, and ending tutti as Polly quickly jumps out of Jim's way: pure Hollywood animation scoring. Jim staggers into the inn, swaying to a drunken trombone — a musical invention attributed to Stalling[18] — and Alwyn's familiar sleazy clarinets in unison join in as Polly stares at the broken bottle-neck in his hand, until in fright he throws it away, accompanied by skidding *sul ponticello* (*forte*), and dashes off.

The action speeds up like a Mack Sennett short. But, as in the cartoons, no harm comes to Uncle Jim however hard he is hit. When he emerges from the inn, *marcato* strings, crescendoing on a constant note, build suspense as we wait for Polly, standing round the corner with a paddle boathook, to thump him. He does so to a loud orchestral chord. Then strings, exhilaratingly Stalling-like, rush with Polly round the inn, scaring the hens, while Jim chases and throws bottles at him. A little piccolo motive interjects on a cut-away to the bedroom to see the little niece excitedly running from window to window. Back at the chase Polly rushes offscreen-right, Jim enters from screen-left and rests, and Polly catches up with Jim again from screen-left (an old gag). Some familiar slapstick follows: a bucket of pigswill ends up on Uncle Jim's head, followed by more chasing strings, until Polly hides in an outhouse and finds a broom. Bugles now faintly sound the final skirmish of the battle (if not the war) and one of the film's delights follows. Polly and Jim at each end of the broom tug and push, swing and pull, to a quickening Viennese waltz — until Polly manoeuvres Uncle

---

[17] Scott Bradley, who scored MGM's *Tom and Jerry* series, was a close competitor.
[18] John Zom, *A Corny Concerto: The Music of Carl Stalling*, BBC Radio 3 (18 Feb. 1996).

Jim to the water's edge and pushes him backwards into the river. We shall not again see such sustained mickey-mousing. But Uncle Jim is not yet defeated, and Alwyn is given several more, though shorter, chances at the genre.

One cannot finish discussion of the film without mention of Polly's first try at punting. His attempt to ferry an elderly gentleman (Miles Malleson) results in much wobbling, unsteady running up and down, entanglements, desperation, near loss of the pole, and drifting all over the river. For all its choreography, however, it would be as nothing but for Alwyn's *allegro scherzoso* fugal accompaniment, which starts with an honest bassoon, is quickly joined by oboe and flute, and rounded by clarinet, horn, woodblocks, and xylophone in a perfectly-judged musical partner to a sequence of light-hearted visual mayhem.

If as a whole *The History of Mr Polly* seems a little sprawling and not totally structured, the cause may be in its almost literal fidelity to Wells's novel. As compensation the film offers life, imagination, and freshness: qualities deriving as much from its cinematic treatment, to which the music is a major partner, as from the book. In later years, as Alwyn searched for his own Utopian sunset in which to compose his symphonies, operas, poetry, and paintings, perhaps he cast his mind back to Alfred Polly and saw something of himself in that idealistic, confused, but very human character.

For Mills's next production, Pélissier suggested bringing D. H. Lawrence to the cinema screen for the first time with an adaptation of *The Rocking-Horse Winner*, a complex and ambiguous story that touches on the paranormal, psychological, and moral, and is not fully understood in either novella or cinematic form. To Pélissier's text and direction Alwyn brings a thoughtful, fertile score that both illuminates and imposes fresh and exciting perceptions and interpretations.

The film's inner meanings, as in Lawrence's story, are ambiguous and worrying. A sensitive child, Paul (John Howard Davies), is obsessed with the financial difficulties of his father Richard (Hugh Sinclair) and especially of his spendthrift mother Hester (Valerie Hobson). Secretly colluding with the handyman Bassett (John Mills) and his uncle Oscar (Ronald Squire), the boy discovers he can pick winners during frenzied rides on his rocking-horse. He passes on his winnings to his mother, who, unaware of their true source, squanders them. The boy dies during a final brainstorm as he tries to pick the Derby winner.

In a careful study of the film, Henry Becker III looks at some psychological analyses of the novella and reaches the conclusion that Pélissier has simplified his adaptation by removing its masturbatory and Oedipal suggestions.[19] While for censorship reasons Pélissier would have been unable to stress such

---

[19] Henry Becker III, "*The Rockinghorse Winner*: Film as Parable", *Literature Film Quarterly*, 1:1 (Jan. 1973), 55–63. Becker's insights are occasionally marred by faulty recall.

elements, Becker's conclusion is not entirely correct: both masturbation and Oedipal love are suggested in the visual imagery and in Paul's neurotic anxiety to give his mother his savings. Other elements of Lawrence's novel — the moral parable of greed, and the fantasy elements — are well represented. Any consideration of the musical contribution to these elements must be mindful of considerable complexities and ambiguities in their expression.

Alwyn's exploration of the film's text makes it quite plain that he is aware of these difficulties. Moreover his composition goes far to express inner meanings that cannot be implied by the imagery alone. At the time his score received high praise. The music critic Hans Keller wrote that "Alwyn has created a revolutionary form of dramatic music."[20] Unfortunately Keller's review is undermined by its opacity, its writer's brag that for analysis he is relying on his "memory and some notes of a distant, single session", and his ignorance that some of what he is lauding had been achieved already in Alwyn's previous feature films. Puzzlingly, both Keller and Gordon Hendricks eighteen months later[21] were impressed by the incorporation of the film's motif under the title credits, a not unusual concept.

The credits sequence that so impressed Keller and Hendricks displays considerable harmonic complexity and introduces the film's two major motifs. Most determined is a four-note fanfare motif which opens the sequence, on high strings, partially perhaps to distinguish it from the clash of the Rank gong. It is expressed by variations of $g\sharp''-g\sharp''-c\sharp''-g\sharp''$ or $g\sharp''-g\sharp''-c\sharp''-c\sharp''$ or with other variations such as $g\sharp'-g\sharp'-c\sharp'-c\sharp''$. Later, the first three notes of the motif, short as it is, suffice, and other divisions and modulations of it are employed.

Once the gong is succeeded by the Two Cities production credit the motif is taken up on trumpet,[22]

This is repeated in various forms, almost fugato, in which can be recognised clarinets and horn. After cymbal and timpani clash in unison, it descends to a minor key by oboes in unison where it is joined by the regular beat of two alternating kettle drums, tuned perhaps to C and G-flat, suggesting the rocking motion of the horse.

As the timpani fade, strings slowly fall down the scale, a suggestion of the supernatural enhanced by a ground of low ostinato strings, until precedence is taken by a bassoon descending in *acciaccatura* semitones. This galloping rhythm is the film's other major motif. Here the rhythm speeds to a gallop

[20] H[ans] K[eller], "Film Music and Beyond: William Alwyn — Bad and Great Work, Part II", *Music Review* (Aug. 1950), 216–7.
[21] Gordon Hendricks, "Film Music Comes of Age", *Films in Review*, 3:1 (Jan. 1952), 23.
[22] The score is no longer extant.

and crescendoes until — enhanced by oboes — the whole is taken up by whirl-ing high ostinato strings enhanced by harp glissandos, punctuated by repeated sounding of the fanfare motif, finally subsiding until a peaceful oboe and strings slow to the fanfare theme, all energy spent, to introduce the action as the boy Paul is seen walking through the snow.

Against all this musical activity, the visual background is an aerial shot of a snow-covered house at night, towards which the camera slowly zooms. The "creepy" feeling attached to the house finds its source principally in the ostinato strings, but the incessant fanfare motif also links itself to the house, although in a way that, at this stage, is unclear to the viewer. So far, therefore, although we "pre-hear" the motifs, their exact meanings are by no means understood.

In fact, the meanings are meticulously precise, and because this precision must not be allowed to become unfocussed, Alwyn's composition is spare. Becker puts his finger on one element. "The house in which the Grahames live", he writes, "is in itself an important member of the cast, audibly echoing the moods and thoughts of the family."[23] To the audible construction of the "pres-ence" of this extra character Alwyn's composition is a key component and can only make its entry on cue. Paul's psyche, where it is represented by musical el-ements, is absorbed and reflected back by the house — like a kind of resonating supernatural sounding board. Linked to this esoteric element, but by no means easily separated and identified, are two further primary and persistent musical metaphors, neither explained nor resolved until near the end. One we shall mention in its place; for clarity the other must be interpreted from the start: the fanfare motif. For the major part of the film it seems as if this is a motif for Paul's emotions. We are, however, misled: by its concern with the racetrack and gambling, the narrative deafens us to persistent reminders of the hunt. What we hear as a fanfare for Paul is a hunting horn; it sounds throughout the film, and its quarry, the hunted, is Paul himself.

A grasp of these crucial points illuminates the second music cue, some ten minutes into the film. It is Christmas Eve, night, and Paul is awakened by a church bell. The camera watches through the bars of the landing balustrade, a shot that lays emphasis on the physical presence of the house. The bell's toll is echoed by the fanfare motif on horn and taken up by the oboe: the hunt commences, and the boy is lured — ambiguously, however, for it seems to the viewer that the fanfare represents Paul's heightened emotional state. Against slow strings the motif repeats as Paul gets up and descends the stairs. A sudden stress on the final note of the fanfare, tutti, emphasises a cut to a wide shot that shows just the boy and the staircase, the child dwarfed by a vast darkness: his emotions of anticipation and fear both absorbed and reflected by the house. Now as the boy descends slow, high strings and flute impart a mysterious

---

[23] Becker, "*The Rockinghorse Winner*", 59.

atmosphere, without crushing the motif. He looks suddenly across the hall-way, and the hunting-horn motif crystallises the situation: his fears, observed by the house, justified by the music. As he approaches the sitting-room door, short-bowed strings crescendo, and the tension increases until the orchestra climaxes on the fanfare; the hunt is closer as he enters the Christmassy room, his excitement the greater. An ethereal vibraphone colours the mood, which is joined by an echo of carol singers heard earlier singing "Silent Night" (1818), and a high sweet violin (*sul ponticello* at one point) while he examines the Christmas tree and the presents, but his absorption is in the tree; there is no motif. However, as he sees the wrapped rocking-horse the orchestra peaks with both his excitement and the excitement that the trap is nearly sprung; the motif is repeated against a ground of ostinato strings and a harp glissando. When in a visual mix to the same camera position the next day the horse is unwrapped and exposed, the music is replaced by sound-effects. In other words, the motif does not belong to the horse — yet.

Paul is a prisoner — the bars at the top of the stairs trap him as much as they trap Phil in *The Fallen Idol*. He is prisoner to his ignorance about adult things (his questions are naïve), to his mother's obsession with material goods and his Oedipal need to pay off her debts, to his sensitivity to the house that he fears. He is also prisoner to its spirit voices. Just as the house reflects Paul's emo-tions, signalled by the musical motif, so it catches and reflects the emotions of others — indeed, in this way, Paul's sensitive psychic antenna senses his moth-er's money worries. In conveying this moment in the film's third music cue, di-rector and composer achieve an almost perfect congruity. It is still Christmas Day. In the sitting room Hester's brother Oscar lectures father and mother about their extravagance. Hester stubbornly repeats her need for money, clos-ing the door with a determined, "There must be more money!" A loud orches-tral chord accents the closing of the door, as if shutting off Hester physically, but leaving her spirit in the hallway. Now, her statement is echoed by secret whispering voices as the camera, subjective of the ghostly voices themselves, creeps up the staircase in a series of dissolves. Between each whisper Alwyn echoes the phrase rhythmically on clarinet and flute in unison. Dissonance, together with ostinato short-bowed strings, creates a disturbing sensation that increases as the whispers fall away, the orchestra crescendos, and tempo quickens as more instruments (including an understated vibraphone) join in until the camera reaches the topmost floor — the nursery, where the camera glances at clumsily framed toys, as if the voices have difficulty in orientat-ing themselves, or are examining the expensive Christmas presents: a doll, a doll's house, a teddy bear. The whisper returns and reaches Paul, standing by the rocking-horse. The music is very loud now, but without an echo so that it seems close, in the head, Paul's head. Hearing it and chilled, he glances at his small sisters playing with Nanny by the window. They hear nothing. The whisper fights with the orchestra to be heard, matching the boy's confusion. Stricken, the boy looks at the leering face of the rocking-horse, and the house's whisper and horse seem linked in a macabre union. Whisper and music now fade together, repeating "more money, more money . . ." Corruption, conveyed largely by the soundtrack, has spread out from the mother's greed to the very nursery and to Paul, who reacts to the house's whispering and to his mother's needs.

In the next cue the "money" motif (the rhythmic pattern of "There must be more money") and hunting motif are tellingly contrasted to reveal his increasing distress. Away from the house, the motif is freed from its sinister overtones and leaps into a carefree melody on flute as he greets his Uncle Oscar, who presents him with a horsewhip as a gift. The house is too far away to exert an influence; however, as Paul rushes off with his new toy, the parents and uncle talk serious money matters, and the "money" motif enters on a dark cello, to be replaced by passionate violins as the child, now distressed, observes from a distance.

It is a decisive moment: from now on, Paul becomes obsessed with winning money for his mother. But since he is a prisoner, he can only go "to where there is luck" by psychically removing himself from the house. The manner in which he succeeds, and thereby successfully predicts race winners, depends on not only the visual but also the musical content manifested in a key scene. Riding his horse in a frenzy, Paul still cannot discover the winner. He dismounts, whips the horse, and shouts "Now take me to where there's luck!" As he rides again, the music whips itself into a frenzied gallop, the *acciaccatura* gallop motif introduced in the titles, orchestra tutti, while Paul's sisters crouch in the corner, and outside a storm is raging. Hester, Oscar, and Nanny enter. Nanny rushes to close the window, Oscar and Hester stay at the door and talk. The scene cross-cuts between Paul's view-point of both doorway and window zooming to near pinpoint and growing large again through a special lens, and his sweating and hysterical face; but although Paul sees them he does not hear them: their lips move mutely beneath the fevered music,[24] as — possessed — he gallops and whips and sweats. Their shrinking and — more significantly — the crushing of their dialogue by the music proves Paul's success in removing himself from the room to "where there is luck". Ultimately, to thunder roll and dwindling bugle motif on horn, the action calms, Paul has achieved fulfilment, and the music dies to thunder roll: "Well, I got there." His words help understand Oscar's words to Hester in the final scene: "He's best gone out of a life where he rides a rocking-horse to find a winner."

Pélissier's plot structure quickly disposes of various loose ends and moves the film towards its tragic conclusion through one pivotal episode. To begin

---

[24] Becker, "*The Rockinghorse Winner*", 59.

with, it is the one scene in which non-diegetic music has no association with that extra character, the house. By the episode's end the house has returned, for the house cannot be escaped. The scene commences at the riverside, away from the house. Paul proves his "luck" to Uncle Oscar by correctly predicting an outsider; he tells Oscar about the whispers and his plans to present his mother with £1000 on each birthday. As they talk, background music is faintly introduced — the term "background" applied purposely here, for the mix is at such a low level that the ear can scarcely distinguish the melody. The composition is a waltz, and because Hester is the topic of conversation it is a motif for her. As the boy and man finish chatting ("I hope it makes her happy, uncle. Just lately the house's been whispering worse than ever"), the waltz dances in loudly to commence one of the most musically complex sequences of the whole film, described by Keller as "artful in its fabric and artless in its effect".[25] The waltz plays against a montage demonstrating Hester's extravagance: dresses, invitations, jewellery, bills, a cheque. Within the waltz pattern is inserted the hunting motif, elaborated and suggesting that the mother's luck is sourced in Paul's. Quickly, however, shots are superimposed of Paul rocking furiously to pay for his mother's extravagances, and the two elements of mother's improvidence and the child's neurotic ride compete both visually and musically: an important dramatic linking of child and mother. At first the rhythm of the timpani with a bugle call on the hunting motif counterpoints then acquiesces to a resurgence of the waltz. But a more determined image of the horse returns, and this time the much stronger hunting fanfare counterpoints the waltz in a complicated dissonance, into which the galloping *acciaccatura* rhythm is then introduced to all but crush the waltz. The waltz nevertheless resurges over pictures of house decorators (the mother is spending money), but the reintroduction of the house allows it to commandeer, the gallop motif vanquishes the waltz, and the camera again climbs the stairs as the whispers return: "there must be more money, money, money . . ." It is to no avail: gallop and whispers dwindle as we see Paul through the doorway of the nursery ceasing his rocking, shaking his head, and dismounting. For all his gallopings, and despite the urgings of the whispers, his "luck" has run out.

The inevitably tragic climax is a masterpiece of composition, sound editing, and mixing in a sequence that parallels and reverses Paul's descent to the drawing room on Christmas Eve. Mother and father are at a charity ball. A plucked string reveals Paul, in open pyjama top, looking through the window at the moonlit sky. To these pictures a ground of tremolo strings and flute suggest enchantment as wind instruments repeatedly descend in stabbing *acciaccatura* gallop phrases, finally to climax with an interrupted cadence joined by a rising harp glissando as we see, on a cut, that the clouds racing across the face of the

---

[25] Keller, "Film Music and Beyond, Part II", 217.

moon are in the shapes of horses. We recall Bassett's statement, "He's no ordinary horse but one you could ride halfway to the moon and back if you tried." Shifting to Paul's point of view the camera stares around the moonlit room as the whispers are heard again ("There must be more money") accompanied by rising and falling strings, flute and harp glissandos and declining clarinets. Trance-like, he walks across the room to the gallop rhythm, now slowed and hesitant: bassoons predominate, oboes, horns, and flutes marking time. As he approaches and climbs the stairs, the sound of hoofs on the turf becomes mixed into the soundtrack, joined soon by all the cacophony of the meeting, which almost smothers the orchestra. The gallop motif returns beneath the natural effects, growing faster and faster, horns sound a fanfare, and the gallop proceeds at several fugal levels, a confusion beneath the noise of the racetrack, but mounting to a climax — all this as Paul slowly climbs the staircase, now passing into velvet darkness, now silhouetted, now fringed with moonlight. The music rushes to a climax — three notes of his fanfare motif repeat against the galloping theme, strings cascade, others play ostinato, amidst the clamour of the race course a voice cries "More money! more money!" As Paul reaches the nursery door, the orchestra reaches a frenetic climax, and Paul's fanfare sounds — no longer for Paul, but on a shot of the rocking-horse with its hideous Lucifer's grin. The hunt motif has at last been seized by the horse — its triumph, the kill, its possession of Paul, is close. Now, shockingly, we understand what Alwyn has been shouting at us from the first note of his score, but we have been too obtuse to understand. As Paul stands at the nursery door, the sound of hoofs races away. The music, galloping with the hoofs, re-enters and crescendos as Paul enters (a parallel to entering the sitting room at Christmas). He approaches the horse: "I've got to know for the Derby."

At the ball a rush of extrasensory anxiety grips Hester, and the parents return early to the house. Their entry to the house is watched through the bars of the balustrade above, reminding us of the living presence of the house. Hester runs up the stairs to a fast two-note descending phrase, a treatment of the gallop, the orchestra following and pausing with her fearful hesitations, but reflecting her panic by increasing in tempo until, as she reaches the nursery landing, it suddenly falls silent. The cold fearful silence, reflected by black shadows from the position of the nursery, is a variation of Alwyn's familiar — but entirely satisfactory — device to augment tension. Low in key, and slowly in tempo, the gallop recommences as Hester advances towards the room, speeding until it reaches an almost unbearable climax as she opens the door. The cut to a viewpoint from the far side of the nursery reveals a huge shadow of Paul, rocking frenziedly, cast by the moon on the wall — next to the horrified Hester. The juxtaposition of the shadow with the elegantly dressed mother recalls the earlier montage sequence. Then boy's obsession and mother's obsession were separated, conflated only by an optical trick of the cinematographic mix and by a musical gallop and a waltz. Now the mother physically confronts the full hysteria of the horse's rocking gallop. The furious tempo speeds until it seems to run out of control, with cymbal clashes and whip cracks. The boy cries out the winner of the Derby "It's Malabar! It's Malabar!" and falls to the floor. The fanfare sounds the motif — but its rhythm echoes the rhythm of the boy's cry ("It's Mal–a–bar!"). The pivot of the motif is achieved, for at this crucial point it not only sounds the horse's — or the boy's — victory, the victory of the kill, but also echoes backwards in time, weaving the motif into the texture of the scenario like a fateful omen, the justification and meaning of all those earlier occasions on which it was heard.

Hester runs to Paul. The orchestra falls silent. But the score brings one last horror: as the camera cuts suddenly to a low angle of the leering face of the horse, a single sour chord blares out its triumph.

The film has a coda, extraneous to Lawrence's story, to show Hester's crushing realisation of her guilt. According to contemporary reports, it was requested by the censor, although Valerie Hobson has claimed it for her and Pélissier.[26] Hans Keller believed that it spoiled the story by its "supreme Kitsch", but that, nevertheless, "had this not been doomed by its existence, Alwyn's continued exploration of his dramatic-thematic material would have saved it".[27] He was right. By manipulating the visual and musical elements, Pélissier and Alwyn turn the film into a frightening parable of a child's mental abuse. It commences as Bassett sets fire to the horse: as the flames leap up the fanfare motif — now owned by the horse — leaps with them. Bassett looks at the tin box containing the winnings and a plaintive violin enters, based upon a note pattern of the waltz, until a phrase enters loudly and shockingly on trombone to announce the presence of the mother:

She pleads with Bassett to burn the money, but he refuses, saying he cannot burn "good money". "How can you call it 'good money'", she replies. "Blood money, dreadful, evil money." Bassett is unmoveable: "Might be able to save a few lives with it. Cost one to get it." He leaves and the film ends on a single shot of the mother confronting the flaming rocking-horse: its fanfare motif is repeated,

and superseded by a chilling solo violin that descends to two low plucked chords:

[26] MacFarland, *British Cinema*, 305.
[27] Keller, "Film Music and Beyond, Part II", 217.

There is nothing more.

The fanfare represents a triumph, its juxtaposition with the leaping flames of the burning horse suggest the triumph of Mephistopheles, revealing the film in its final moments as Faustian parable.[28] The fanfare motif has imparted all along that Paul was hunted by Satan. Religious intimations have been carefully planted: Paul kneeling in prayer before his fateful descent on Christmas Eve; the Christmas carol echoed by Alwyn in the same scene; an ironic (blasphemous?) comment by Bassett on Paul's powers: "Just like he had it from Heaven . . ." Even as Paul lies dying, Oscar sins by betting on Paul's tip: the musical hunting motif continually repeated as the telephone tempts with its line to the bookie's. But Paul was a child Faust, selling his soul in innocence: learning he has won £1000, he asks "Is that a lot?"[29] while his dying words, "I told you I was lucky", plumb the depths of irony. In his naïvety Paul sells his soul, not for himself but for his mother, who is also in a way, an innocent victim: now we see the meaning of the visual and musical linking of child and mother in the waltz montage and the moonlit rocking scene. "If you were me and I were you, I wonder what we'd do", Hester says to Paul in another scene. The film's final descending chords recall the abyss of Gounod's *Faust* (1859). Hester's guilt and horror as she watches the flames licking about the victorious horse to condemn to Hell both her son and (later) herself, is one of the most frightening conjunctions of music and image in the cinema of the 1940s.

Feature work was absorbing most of Alwyn's attention, but he never relinquished his love for documentary. In 1949 he was associated with three notable travel films. They were made by filmmakers at the peak of their profession, concerned to express authentic regional identities, and the opposite of those despised tourist puffs, the travelogues, musically no more demanding than a trip to the pre-recorded music library.

Working on *Three Dawns to Sydney* (1949) must have seemed like old times. The film was produced by two colleagues, Ralph Keene and Paul Fletcher, and script and direction were by John Eldridge of *Our Country*, who had made films with Alwyn since 1940. Like the old Imperial Airways documentaries,

---

[28] Becker, "*The Rockinghorse Winner*", 57, refers to the horse's "Mephistophelean grin", but fails to explore his fleeting insight.

[29] Another request by the censor, quoted by Keller, "Film Music and Beyond, Part II", 217, to make clear "his innocence and lack of appreciation of the value of money for its own sake", which unwittingly corrupts Paul even further.

the narrative was dictated by the film's sponsor, the British Overseas Airways Corporation (BOAC), an account of a three-day flight from London to Sydney to arrive in time for Christmas Day. En route the script pauses to narrate short tales about some of the places passed over, in which Eldridge shows a sensitivity that bears comparison with his eye for the British regional differences captured in *Our Country*.

The musical content demands two veins: first, a depiction of the journey with its trappings of airports, flight, and so on, which recall Alwyn's earliest film compositions, *The Future's in the Air* and *Air Outpost*. The flight itself, for example, is enlivened by fugal strings and brass, or ostinato high strings counterpointed by brass fanfares.

These sequences create a lively and distinctive contrast to a variety of indigenous musical styles, both folk and modern, to accompany the local dramas. Today we are accustomed to regional idioms, but in 1949 they were unusual. Antony Hopkins, a film composer himself, wrote of *Three Dawns to Sydney*'s

> refreshing quality of unusual sound. We heard strange evocative Indian and Chinese music; music which, especially in the Indian childbirth sequence, made my hair stand on end with excitement, such was the extraordinary novelty and mystery. It was an odd coincidence that this film should have gone the rounds with *The Third Man*.[30] What with Anton Karas' zither and the unidentified instruments of the East, it was quite an evening. My ears have not so pricked since the animal-like screams of the clanging sinuous drills in *Louisiana Story* [Robert Flaherty, 1948].[31]

In these episodes Alwyn is called upon only where Western music is appropriate, or to supply a rare deficit. At the start of the first foreign location, a few seconds of wide general shots of the mountains and archaeological ruins of Sicily, he hints at an Italian atmosphere with a slow variation of the little tune he composed for the sailors' stroll around the Italian dock town in *Soldier–Sailor*. The linking cue is essential, but for just this once there is an uncomfortable inching towards the travelogue. It is brief and forgotten by the time authentic folk music is heard, which if it were anticipated would spoil the story — shepherds descend from the hills at Christmas to play their pipes at the village of Castel Mola. Next the plane passes "the Dead Sea, the waterless deserts, and ruined cities how many histories deep . . .", where Bedouins search for pasture and water. Again, Alwyn has to fill a gap, this time to evoke nonmetrical Arabic rhythmic patterns, which he does by calling upon slow strings, clarinet, and flute. A similar passage later is heralded by a fanfare on the oboe, perhaps in

---

[30] Ironically, the film that spurned Alwyn for Karas.
[31] Anthony Hopkins, "Music", *Sight and Sound*, 18:71 (Dec. 1949), 23.

an attempted replication of an end-blown flute known as the *nây*. Again, one recalls the compositions for *The Future's in the Air* and *Air Outpost*. Here, too close a juxtaposition with real national idioms, especially a genuine recording of a *muezzin* that closely follows, draws attention to the European symphony orchestra's inability to recreate authentic-sounding Arabic instrumental colour and melodic intervals.

In the remainder of the local sequences the music is solely authentic, including the *sirangi, sita*, and other Indian instruments, in a remarkably sympathetic and true study, for a European director, of a village woman's time of giving birth. Its voice-over recalls the girl's narration in *Our Country*, and its mood and pacing anticipates Satyajit Ray's *Pather Panchali* (1955).

Once freed from the need to replicate, Alwyn's score shows respect and careful co-operation with the indigenous. An episode set in Singapore is noteworthy for its variety of authentic musical sounds, in which a cabaret sequence calling for Western dance music was probably arranged by Alwyn.[32] Later, to reflect the tension between tradition and innovation, cabaret and temple are cross-cut with close matching of their very different musical idioms at the cutting points. In Australia, only pure *didjeridu* and natural sounds accompany an aboriginal fishing sequence; while Western music is perfectly appropriate to illustrate mail being collected for delivery to the outback — the occasion, in fact, for Alwyn to have fun with a comic, laconic harmonic descent down the scale picked up in turn from strings to oboe and from oboe to bassoon.

Anthony Hopkins's delight with the "unusual sound" of non-Western music reflects the insularity of Western musical taste at the time. There is a scene in *Under One Roof* where a young Egyptian, in the common room at Loughborough College, tunes the radio to an Islamic song. Although the room is filled with students of all nationalities, looks of distaste cross their faces until somebody throws a ball of paper at the Egyptian, who is obliged to retune to a waltz. By 1949 a century and more of colonial occupation and military expeditions should have opened ears to non-European music, but appreciation of the musical world beyond Europe and America was for the few. Radio was just twenty years old, foreign holidays were for a minority, record companies could not be expected to explore uncommercial fields. Folk song meant Western folk song. *Under One Roof* was sponsored by the United Nations Film Board and has a message that "the things we have in common are more important than the things in which we differ". Despite this sentiment, the film's score interprets Islamic musical forms through a European filter, and the scenario concludes with students from 36 nations sharing traditional British tea and cakes.

It was Lewis Gilbert's fourth documentary before embarking on a successful career in features, and produced by Brian Smith, whose creative relationship

---

[32] No scores exist for the travel documentaries discussed here.

with Alwyn was long-standing. Perhaps the film's odd construction was the result of Smith and Gilbert's collaboration on the script: it commences with two long episodes about life in Norway and Egypt before reaching its subject matter — the variety of nationalities among the students at the engineering college, all keen to learn skills for use in their home countries.

A Norwegian sunrise accompanies the titles, which Alwyn matches by a horn motif counterpointed by high strings. There is a Norwegian feel about these harmonies, and soon plucked strings representing melted snow dripping from a rooftop descend in seconds and thirds, intervals typical of Norwegian folk music. Alwyn had been attracted by "Grieg's subtle harmonisation of folk songs" since childhood.[33] In 1954 his *Autumn Legend* for cor anglais and strings would be partially inspired by a visit to Grieg's house in the company of the poet Christopher Hassell.[34] Now, in his brief cues for this Norwegian episode of *Under One Roof*, Alwyn catches Grieg's love of nature, the fresh air, his sensitivity to the seasons. There are illuminating comparisons to be made between his horns with Grieg's "Morning" from the *Peer Gynt* Suite no. 1 (1888), the overture *In Autumn* (1866), and the descending opening chords of the first movement of the Piano Concerto in A minor (1869). When later the scenario moves to a Norwegian family enjoying their own company at the table, harmony and simplicity of melody and rhythm bring to mind the Russian domestic scene of *Our Film* (where it is marked "*più tranquillo*"). A parallel between Russian and Scandinavian idioms, and a familiarity with Grieg, are implied by the Russian pianist Emil Gilels's remark that "In Russia only teachers and children knew Grieg's *Lyric Pieces*."[35] Here, violins and cellos in unison is a characteristic of Grieg's doublings. The delicacy of touch about this whole Norwegian episode leaps with a delightful little childlike dance by flute solo matching a young boy's running through the snow to school, which afterwards Alwyn reworks as a tiny motif.

In *Under One Roof* Alwyn's European interpretation of Muslim musical idioms does not suffer from the disadvantage of juxtaposition with genuine folk music found in *Three Dawns to Sydney*. Here the music is sufficiently flexible to retain overall mood while using instrumental colour to stipple in texture. Scenes of Egyptian village life are enlivened by, at first, bassoon and slow regu-

---

[33] Letter to Elizabeth Lutyens, quoted in *Dear Bill, Dear Liz, Programme 1*, arranged by Andrew Palmer, BBC Radio 3 (19 May 1995). The original letters are in the Alwyn Archive.

[34] Alwyn, "Ariel to Miranda", 16. Elsewhere Alwyn claimed inspiration also from the painting and poetry of Dante Gabriel Rossetti ("Ariel to Miranda", 80; *Winged Chariot*, 15–16), and even that Rossetti was "the onlie begetter": Lewis Foreman, case note for *Alwyn conducts Alwyn: Concerto Grosso No. 2; Autumn Legend; Lyra Angelica* (Lyrita SRCD230, 1992; LP 1979).

[35] Ursula von Rauchhaupt, case note to *Emil Gilels Plays Grieg* (Deutsche Grammophon, 1987).

lar drum beat as the women of the community carry the morning water jugs on their heads, a flute catches father and son finishing breakfast, and jolly chickens peck around to a clarinet. The boys set off with donkey and ox to a reedy oboe, and a little girl runs to school chased by a perky flute. Later in 1949 Alwyn's capability for suggesting Arabic rhythms and textures would again be put to use in the Tunisian setting of *The Golden Salamander* (1950).

The integration of Alwyn's composition and indigenous music is at its most successful in *Daybreak in Udi* (1949), which won an Academy Award as the best documentary feature of 1949. Alwyn had worked with its director Terry Bishop on several Merton Park productions dating back to 1941. The story is set in Eastern Nigeria, where two teachers call on the help of the local district commissioner to build a maternity home and install a midwife. Their plans are opposed by a village elder, who attempts to frighten away the midwife. The film's larger theme is the emergence of the people, by their own effort, out of the darkness of superstition into the daybreak of civilisation.

Alwyn's music is perfectly integrated with the native idioms because, by and large, he picks up the local rhythms without attempting to develop them into more complex themes or melodies in the Western style. He is helped by the differentiation of the authentic Nigerian music from orchestral music through predominantly (although not exclusively) percussion instruments and the human voice, and because the local rhythms and melodies are based on repetition, either through drum beat or through chanting.

The chant is a tool dating back to ancient times not only in ritual and festival, but for the co-ordination of heavy communal work: in the West the old sailors' shanties still linger in recent folk memory; in *Under One Roof* Egyptians chant as they move huge stones, build, and saw. The chant predominates in *Daybreak in Udi* both to lighten the burden of manual work and as festive dance. Alwyn catches at the repetitive character of the Nigerian music, thus beginning the film with an imposing timpani roll repeated as wind instruments twice repeat a seven-note phrase as motif, before moving to a variation that is again repeated twice. More variations are introduced, but each is subjected to repetitions until these opening titles end with clarinet and bassoon repeatedly answering each other, echoed by a high violin and concluding with a gong.

Later, as local men dig at the ground, producing a cloud of dust, their unvarying chant is counterpointed by orchestral timpani until the chant itself is supplanted by woodwind, and the film's constantly repeated motif speeds the action. The matching of voice actuality with imposed orchestral scoring in this sequence is impressive. In a later sequence, the workmen spin and dance as they fling mud into moulds to harden as bricks for the walls of the maternity home. The sequence becomes one of whirling feet, slopping clay, and burgeoning bricks as the motif is seized with exhilaration by clarinet and what appears to be a jangling luthéal piano. One is reminded that Terry Bishop wrote the scenario of *Queen Cotton*, with its dizzy spinning and weaving musical sequences.

The film's core scene is set in the maternity home on the night of the expected birth of its first child. Here, the use of close scoring to create tension and atmosphere is impressive, and although largely Western-based, Alwyn attempts to catch African rhythms and mood. At first, the fears of the midwife, alone with the expectant mother, are suggested by frighteningly low double-bass, cellos and woodwind, punctuated by an owl hoot: this music of fear could come from a Western scenario. But, gradually, repetitive chords with a fast African rhythmic beat make their presence known, plucked on strings in the very lowest register, almost like drumbeats, but contrasted by quiet woodwind and horns in a higher pitch. From the window the midwife sees a figure approaching: the repetitive African rhythm is now taken up by the piano in its very lowest octave doubling in unison with hushed timpani, accompanied by an eerie clarinet. Tension increases with rising dynamics until suddenly it suddenly cuts off to silence and a knock on the door. In one form or another (rhythmic speed, pitch, dynamics) it is an old Alwyn trick, but it always works. Tension now relaxes as we discover that the visitor is the teacher, come to keep the midwife company.

Later, the maternity home is attacked by men in frightening ceremonial masks. Again, Alwyn utilises dark rhythms on the low keys of the piano, punctuated by a rapid flute trill on the cut to a mask representing a spirit of the dead. Gradually all the instruments of the orchestra join in, rising in pitch and tempo but retaining the constant repetitive African rhythm. The music climaxes with a repeated rising piano phrase and deafening trill on flutes and piccolo, and pauses — not to silence as before — but to a scream of pain as the nurse throws a pot of boiling water over a masked attacker. This time tension is allowed to fall gradually, and stressed phrases and trills see the attackers off into the forest. The birth of the baby next morning is represented by a simple, barely elaborated five-note flute passage. It is a refreshing, unsentimental contrast.

The perfect integration of pure folk sounds with the dramatic demands of film music and the timbres of the Western orchestra is a difficult problem for the film-maker working in the traditional studio, and one that not many are called upon to solve. In *Daybreak in Udi* Alwyn, unpretentiously and through a thorough absorption of the vernacular, achieves that integration.

18
Kitsch or Art?

I N the spring of 1950 Hans Keller saw *The Cure for Love* and expressed himself in the pugnacious manner for which he was notorious:

> I have seen or heard no comment, let alone the overdue outcry, about
> the alarming fact that a leading member of our official musical institu-
> tion par excellence, a professor of composition at the Royal Academy
> of Music who has quite rightly earned himself the reputation of being
> one of our most important film composers, has of late turned out not
> merely such indifferent scores as *Golden Salamander* and *Madeleine*
> [1949], but also the reeking Kitsch that forms, if form is the word, the
> admittedly sparing background to *Cure for Love* . . .[1]

Keller's criticism was indicative of the stigma to which Alwyn was becoming
increasingly sensitive. And like any such criticism it ignored the cultural context of the film medium.

Robert Donat had long dreamt of bringing Walter Greenwood's play about
Lancastrian life, *The Cure for Love,* to the screen. Rank, trying to reduce his
debts by pleasing both British and American box-offices, was uninterested in
a narrative of a local character and dialect, and in the end Korda came up with
the finance. Donat's co-director was Alwyn's old friend Alexander Shaw, on his
first feature film, which probably explains Alwyn's commission. Shaw collaborated with Donat, Greenwood, and Arthur Fennell on the screenplay, about
the soldier Jack Hardacre (Donat) who returns from the wars to his small Lancashire hometown and the brassy embrace of his fiancée Janey Jenkins (Dora
Bryan). Hardacre falls in love with a charming London girl, Milly Southern
(Renée Asherson) who has been billeted on his home, and he is faced with
casting off the unwanted Janey and prising Milly from the attentions of a local
romeo, Sam Balcome (John Stratton). Several of the actors were repeating their
stage roles, and the production is theatrical. Despite this, the film has warmth
and charm, is funny and often tender: it is a naïve painting rather than an Old
Master.

Alwyn's contribution must be considered with that idiom in mind: Northern, farcical, warm and sentimental. There is one major motif, the love motif:
for Milly alone and for Milly and Jack together. In the credit titles it perfectly

---

[1] Hans Keller, "Film Music and Beyond, Part 1", *Music Review* (May 1950), 145.

expresses the film's content, starting with the rhythm and harmony of a Northern music-hall, proceeding to the harmonies of a mechanical fairground organ, and finishing as a romantic slow waltz. Particularly effective is the diegetic use of the motif on the wireless, first to introduce the lovely Milly, later to suggest a potential romance as the couple makes small talk.

There is much else of musical interest. In a bravura scene, Jack and Janey, Milly and Sam do the town. But Jack and Milly are unhappily coupled with the wrong partners. The situation is summarised in a montage, starting with a close-up of Janey and Jack on the big dipper, she chattering incessantly, he looking distraught. The music, a fast theme distinguished not so much by its melody as by harmonies reminiscent of the sound of travelling showmen, commences simultaneously with a high-pitched and unintelligible babble representing Janey's stream of conversation. To the audience of the pre-tape-recorder period it must have seemed both adventurous and funny. The body language of mating, as Jack and Milly drift together in successive scenes, is accompanied by appropriate style changes to the motif, from mechanical organ harmonies to the foxtrot. Finally, on the train home, with Jack and Milly obviously unhappy at being reclaimed by their original partners, the strings sound passionately in harmonies that in a few years would be discovered by Nino Rota.[2]

Despite his fulmination and his obsession with "reeking Kitsch", Keller was fighting the current of time. Alwyn, who loved the culture of the one-and-ninepennies, had a real empathy with popularism and is here matching the idiom of his medium. He was before his time: towards the close of the century even the *Carry On* films (1958–1978) had cultural revivals. By then, Alwyn's once-recognised achievements in sensitising a popular nerve were long forgotten.

Keller's ground was no surer with his passing sideswipes at the "indifferent scores" of *The Golden Salamander* and *Madeleine*, where he fails to discover the extent to which Alwyn penetrates beneath the surface of the drama. *The Golden Salamander* was a second commission from Ronald Neame. Based on a story by Victor Canning, it tells of an archaeologist, David (Trevor Howard), who arrives in Tunisia to arrange a collection of antiquities for dispatch to England. He stumbles on a ring of gun-smugglers and falls in love with a sister of one of them, Anna (Anouk Aimée). The climax is a boar-hunt, which turns into a hunt for human quarry as the couple are chased through the scrub and hills of the Tunisian coast.

Alwyn's score jolts from the start. After two strikes of the Rank gong, Alwyn introduces a third "gong" of his own, which modulates the logo into the key

[2] Rota's passionate combination of trumpets and strings is associated with the circus or funfair in e.g. Fellini's *La Strada* (1954) and *Le Notti di Cabiria* (*Nights of Cabiria*, 1956).

of E-flat major. From there he proceeds by four rising plucked chords against a shimmering mysterious-sounding tremolo to the four-note phrase that is the basis of the film's motif. Regrettably the score no longer survives, but the idea is something as follows:

Startlingly, the motif is immediately taken up by a low sonorous bassoon, perfectly catching the dark mood illustrated by the figurine of a menacing golden salamander behind the titles — "every creeping thing that creepeth upon the earth".[3] The solo bassoon continues to develop the motif, seized by agitatedly stabbing strings but always returning to the repulsive creeping bassoon.

About this time Alwyn had composed a four-note motif for *The Rocking Horse Winner* as metaphor for the hunting of the boy Paul. To interpret the four-note salamander motif in the same way is by no means fanciful, for however much it metamorphosises under Alwyn's pen it never represents less than a threat to the hero David. When David handles the figurine, Alwyn's harmonies of the low bassoon and ostinato strings (in a higher key) introduce the uncanny. Two scenes later, the film recaptures the same eerie mood, at first by the bassoon and vibraphone chords. Both occasions are rendered more chilling by David's quiet translation of the statuette's Greek motto: "Not by ignoring evil does one overcome it, but by going to meet it." To recall Keller, this is most certainly kitsch, but its kitschiness is here emphasised because neither statue nor the mood of prescience is followed up. Presumably it has served its pivotal purpose of hardening David's resolution to investigate the crime ring — triumphal horns echoed by oboe in the manner of the motif — but the audience is disappointed in its expectation of a bigger role for the title prop. This is hardly the fault of the composer, and Alwyn contrives to sustain the motif with its metaphor of the hunt in later scenes.

Creative inspiration is often difficult to uncover, but we may suspect a likely origin for this hunting motif. About 40 minutes of the finished film was shot on location in Tunis, and much of the footage was devoted to the boar hunt, in which the sighting of the boar is sounded twice by four repeated notes (short-long-short-long) on an authentic Arab horn. It would seem at least possible that this inspired Alwyn's motif, which is heard no more after the introduction of this diegetic horn. Moreover, it is not entirely fanciful to suggest that it may also have inspired the four-note hunting motif of *The Rocking Horse Winner.*

---

[3] Genesis 1:26.

Alwyn had several films simultaneously on the boil towards the end of 1949, and cross-fertilisation under the pressure of deadlines is not an impossibility — another surprise is to hear a close cousin of the "I must have more money" theme from *The Rocking Horse Winner* as the motif for *The Golden Salamander*'s master criminal Serafis (Walter Rilla).

A piano, played *Casablanca*-style by a barfly, Agno (Wilfred Hyde-White), introduces the film's second major motif. The tune is "Clopin Clopart" ("Hobbling Along"), a well-known tune prominent in Robert Nesbitt's musical *Latin Quarter* (1949), which had recently opened at the London Casino. It was composed in 1947 by the French composer Bruno Coquatrix, and one cannot help but feel that its use as a love motif may have been prompted by the composer's surname. What better in a film about a mythical golden salamander than a tune by a composer named after the *coquatrix*, the mythical reptilian cockatrice or basilisk whose very look and breath could kill. The motif is effective both diegetically and descriptively, especially as colouring to the musical structure of the boar hunt.

Despite all the composer's efforts to impose homogeneity, *The Golden Salamander* lacks overall pace and a determined plotline. A lack of dramatic structure (contributed to by serious location problems) in what is, or ought to be, the climactic episode of the hunt fatally weakens the film. While Alwyn uses his familiar musical devices to raise and maintain tension — repetitive ostinato and stabbing and rising strings, the climax of the silent pause, and so on — they fail to compensate, and by its ending the film feels tired and clichéd. Nevertheless, it received mainly excellent reviews, even to the honour of being compared with *The Third Man*.[4]

Certainly, the notices were better than those for *Madeleine*, which David Lean had been directing on an adjacent stage at Pinewood. *Madeleine* is a reconstruction of the true story of Madeleine Smith (Ann Todd), the daughter of a middle-class Victorian Glaswegian family, put on trial for the murder of her lover. As the film opens, she is well into her affair with the penniless French clerk Émile (Ivan Desny); while behaving with respectability upstairs, she borrows her maid's bedroom below stairs for clandestine meetings. But Émile has seduced Madeleine to entrap her into a lucrative marriage. When, terrified of her cruelly severe father, Madeleine refuses him and becomes engaged to the local businessman Minnoch (Norman Wooland), Émile attempts blackmail and later dies from poisoning. In Madeleine's subsequent trial for murder, the jury return a verdict of "not proven", a Scottish verdict not allowable under

---

[4] Jympson Harmon in *The Evening News* and Jack Davies in the *Sunday Graphic. The Times* critic thought it did "not equal *The Third Man*", which is still a compliment. Review extracts in "Culling the Critics", *The Cinema Studio*, 4:98 (8 Feb. 1950), 17.

English law. Lean sides with that verdict, and leaves the question of Madeleine's guilt unresolved.

Madeleine had much in its favour — Lean's own hard work, Guy Green's atmospheric gaslit period photography, Geoffrey Foot's immaculate editing — yet years later Lean described it as "the worst film I ever made".[5] Almost unanimously the critics agreed.[6] One factor was, as Noel Coward told Lean, he could not make a film, "in which you, the writer-director, don't know in your own mind what was the outcome. In other words, did she do it or didn't she?"[7] The enigma is reflected in Ann Todd's Madeleine, who is at one time naïve, trusting, and girlish, at other times frightened, scheming, and lying: her complex motivation is hardly to be understood, let alone empathised with. Lean himself blamed the script, which, after it had passed through three previous hands, he rewrote at nights between directing. The rough cut was edited and re-edited; a narration was tacked on to the front and end.

Nobody looked at the musical composition, yet examination of the music track suggests another reason for failure. Lean clearly intended to start the film with high romance. The opening titles fall into a syrupy lyrical main theme, which continues into the opening action as the Smith family moves into its new home and Madeleine secretly approves the basement's potential for dalliance. In another early scene, Madeleine happily descends to the basement to a waltz. Only rarely does the underscore suggest a hint of darkness.

Yet, by the standards of her time, Madeleine is a shameless hypocrite. Her reckless infatuation with Émile is not a fairy-tale romance but a furtive affair in which her character is redeemed only by its naïvety. While, clearly, the film-makers did not wish to portray her in such strong terms, to contrast her upstairs and downstairs persona would have expunged some of the ambiguities in her character. Thus, an early opportunity is thrown away in a sequence where Émile waits to be secretly admitted to the basement, accompanied by nothing more sinister than flute and clarinet in a light, tripping theme; in the drawing room above Madeleine sings (ironically) Amédée de Beauplan's "La Parjure" (1857), an equally light *chansonette*.

It looks as if in these early scenes Lean wanted to establish a young romantic woman's suffocation by her environment, then to contrast this mood with Émile's brutality in the second part of the film. But the continual musical emphasis on romanticism in the first part, even as the action and dialogue spell out Émile's cruelty, confuses the message and undermines the structure. For Madeleine, the shock comes as she rehearses with Émile the words she must use to her father ("we wish to be married, papa"), and her sudden apprehension

---

[5] Kevin Brownlow, *David Lean* (London: Richard Cohen, 1996), 275.

[6] "Culling the Critics", *The Cinema Studio*, 4:100 (22 Feb. 1950), 16–17.

[7] Brownlow, *David Lean*, 275.

of her cruel father's likely reaction. The moment is superbly conveyed by a long-bowed high B-flat, which increases in dynamics and intensity. It is brilliant, but it is not enough: the earlier scenes needed brushing with darker hues.

Of course, attempts are made at structuring — for example the contrast between Émile and Minnoch, a local businessman to whom Madeleine becomes engaged. When Madeleine and Émile meet clandestinely on a hilltop, the romantic motif gives way to the diegetic sound of nearby locals dancing to a traditional reel ("Miss McLeod's Reel"). In a scene of intense eroticism Madeleine dances to the music and encourages Émile to join her, which he does clumsily. This scene structurally relates to a later one in which Madeleine accepts Minnoch's proposal of marriage in a ballroom as a pipe band plays the same reel: the secret relationship and Émile's gaucheness is therefore contrasted with the public event and Minnoch's confidence. Thereafter, Alwyn echoes the reel orchestrally as leitmotif for Minnoch, contrasting Émile's Frenchness with Minnoch's Scottishness. The device, a clever one, collapses because it is difficult to think of Minnoch, with his Mayfair accent, as Scottish (in this film Scots accents are reserved for the lower classes).

"One of the essentials in the movies", said Lean," is for the audience to feel that they are in the hands of a good story-teller; they are being led, and what leads them is the intention of the scene . . . We didn't have real intention on *Madeleine*."[8] That lack of intention is epitomised in a single scene. After Madeleine and Émile make love on the lonely hilltop at night, they watch the moonlit clouds: Alwyn introduces ethereal celesta chords, while Madeleine appears to foresee future troubles. To Madeleine's already perplexing personality is added the gift of occult prophecy: it is all too much for an already overloaded character.

The confusion of purpose in Alwyn's score reflects Lean's own confusion of purpose. A sense of destination is not lacking in Alwyn's work for *State Secret* (1950), which marked a welcome return to Launder and Gilliat's Individual Pictures, now financed by Korda after wrangles with Rank. *State Secret* is a tense, witty thriller with a close affinity to John Buchan's and Hitchcock's *The Thirty-Nine Steps* (1935) and Philip Hope's and John Cromwell's *The Prisoner of Zenda* (1937).

The scenario, which in its day was considered topical, even satirical, is set in the mythical East-European dictatorship of Vosnia, to which an American surgeon John Marlowe (Douglas Fairbanks jr) is invited to receive an award. During his visit, he performs an operation, discovering as he completes it that the patient is (secretly) the country's president General Niva (Walter Rilla). When the dictator dies, Marlowe is held captive, but he escapes in the company of

---

[8] Brownlow, *David Lean*, 275.

a music-hall singer, Lisa (Glynis Johns), pursued by the militia and climaxing in a mountain chase.

State Secret was directed by Sidney Gilliat, who was so determined his film should both look and sound authentic that he hired a language teacher to invent Vosnian and drill the actors in the tongue. In similar spirit Alwyn invented a delightfully burlesqued Vosnian national anthem. Codded national anthems are not rare in the cinema, but Alwyn captures nicely the rhythm of the second-rate; in particular the pattern of minim, quaver, and dotted crotchet (in common time) is especially characteristic:

etc

Having introduced a motif not only to open and close the film but also to be used diegetically in scenes of state occasions, Alwyn characteristically weaves it into the score wherever else it is appropriate. Indeed, it becomes a motif for the president, thus musically bonding both state and dictator.

The attention to detail is revealed throughout the score. In one scene, for example, Marlowe dashes from a hospital into a waiting car. The orchestra mirrors the urgency of the moment, but as the car pulls away a long-bowed cadence matches the pitch of the car's engine, enabling the score to hand over invisibly to the ensuing diegetic sound-effects. The surgical operation, with its masked faces, quiet voices, controlled gestures, and emotional undertones, is a perfect cinematic setting for chilling scenes of foreboding.

Here, the sequence commences on a light, ethereal high B-flat. After a few seconds, the tension is sustained by cello and clarinet joining in contrast. Eerie harmonies follow, in which strings and clarinet collude to create a mood of quiet indeterminate menace. Later, chords descending chromatically through the scale create a mood of sinking menace, of helplessness. In the operation sequence for Gilliat's *Green for Danger*, Alwyn utilises a similar descending rhythm, the cello contrasting with a sustaining ostinato rhythm on the high strings.

The most sustained scoring is demanded for the mountain pursuit. Alwyn supports the overall structure by varying the tension: this he achieves by counterpointing the action in the finer detail, and by contrasting whole sequences with each other, either by musical contrast or with natural effects. Thus, at first, stately brass chords and ethereal strings represent the grandeur of the mountains — and, by extension, freedom for Marlowe and Lisa. Yet the major musical phrase is a reiteration of the national anthem (with a change of key), thus maintaining musical cohesion and functioning as a reminder that the hunted are still in perilous territory. The first sequence is cross-cut with the natural sound of the military convoy in pursuit on motorcycles and a car Later, Alwyn contrasts the laborious rhythms of the dangers of the climb with a fast rhythm for the pursuing militia. Key contrast represents the dangers and triumphs of the climb. The sequence concludes on a stunning example of the latter: as the couple run (as they believe) across the border to freedom, the score lightens to a triumphant roll with trilling and optimistic strings, only to be reversed as the national anthem strikes up when they spot a poster of president Niva and realise they have been tricked.

Charles Frend's *The Magnet* was the first of four assignments for Ealing. It was well-received on release, and has since been cruelly treated by the two major histories of Ealing Studios. George Perry describes it as "oddly charmless",[9] while Charles Barr lazily dismisses "an elaborate whimsical plot which resists economical summary and does not merit a full one".[10] On the contrary, the screenplay by T. E. B. Clarke, mainstay of the Ealing comedies, is inventive and witty, and bursting with a wry symbolism that lends itself to exploration and study.

Superficially, the narrative tells of a ten-year-old Merseyside boy, Johnny Brent (William Fox), who tricks another little boy, Kit (Michael Brooke jr), into exchanging a superb magnet for an "invisible watch". Seized by guilt feelings, Johnny gives up the magnet as a donation to a Mr Harper (Meredith Edwards), who is raising funds towards the cost of an iron lung. After Johnny leaves for boarding school, he becomes an unknown hero by his action. By the time he returns at the end of term, he believes Kit has died and that he is guilty of his death. Convinced he is pursued by the police, he ends up in another part of town and becomes involved with a gang of boys, one of whom he saves from drowning. He receives a civic award for his donation of the magnet, and by chance again meets Kit, with whom he exchanges his medal for the "invisible watch".

To tell this story Frend drew wonderful, natural performances from his child actors, shooting much of the footage on location in Merseyside. The result is a freshness that also characterises many of the Children's Film Foundation titles of the period. That quality is matched by Alwyn's perfectly-judged score, which both reinforces the dramatic construction and — since the narrative often depends on action rather than dialogue — enhances the visuals.

The mood of the exposition is established by the title music, and shows Johnny inventive and endlessly enquiring. To this Alwyn provides a fresh-sounding lyrical background — strings, brass, celesta, flute bird trills, wood-blocks to match a tramp's footsteps, and so on — at times harmonies akin to

[9] George Perry, *Forever Ealing: A Celebration of the Great British Film Studio* (London: Pavilion, 1981), 125.
[10] Charles Barr, *Ealing Studios* (London: Cameron & Tayleur, 1977), 190.

the descending strings of the opening morning sequence of *Fires Were Started*, elsewhere phrases and motives and harmonies that could have sprung from *Great Day* or *The History of Mr Polly*. However, once Johnny discovers the magnet, we join a realm of fable and myth in which director and composer unite to provide the clues. A three-note fanfare ("the–mag–net"?) sounds on our first sight of the magnet as, playing on the beach, Kit clunks it, full frame, on to a seaside bucket. A violin high up in the register at first ascends and descends as the magnet at first exerts its attraction on Johnny, then descends the scale, with cello pedal-point, as the magnet draws him towards the camera until his face fills the frame. That we are not simply watching Johnny's desire for the magnet, but that the magnet itself is exerting the attraction, is made clear by cutting to behind the toy in large close-up with Johnny in the background — the magnet's POV as Kit lifts it higher into the frame. High violins echo the three-note fanfare, which is taken up on the cor anglais. Magic is sustained as Johnny now barters the magnet for the "invisible watch". The magnet is a talisman, a magic charm with powers of attraction, and the three-note fanfare is its motif. Several later sequences demand Alwyn's talent for ethereal harmonies, but only where the talisman exerts its powers does the fanfare motif sound: the motif, and its purpose, is therefore cousin to the hunting motifs in *The Rocking Horse Winner* and *The Golden Salamander*. How many would notice it at a single viewing, however? Nobody: but there it is. Alwyn was exploring a whole new form of musical expression, a coalescence of sound and visuals. One would not expect to understand a symphony from a single hearing; similarly many a film in which Alwyn had a hand yields its rewards from more than a single viewing.

Clarke's screenplay suggests that after Johnny gains the magnet he is the agent of the magnet' predestined purpose for good — it resists his own attempts at disposal, or for others to take it from him — but permits itself to be handed over to Harper. Even when he has shed it, it continues to exert its pull: Johnny is worried and frightened by the wrong he has done to Kit. To convey this psychological state Alwyn creates intangible, ethereal sounds. Sometimes he freely ascends and descends the chromatic scale in unsettling instrumental combinations: vibraphone and strings, vibraphone and cello, vibraphone and oboe, often interspersed by woodwind. The harmonies sound strange, with elements of contrast (sometimes dissonance) and of tension. At other times the scale intervals communicate primitive, unrestrained associations, especially when (as often) Alwyn builds his intervals upon the tritone. Again, in one sequence fluctuating orchestral dynamics alone convey Johnny's night terrors. Unexpectedly interjected chords, in all the examples, heighten the tension. Both Johnny's terrors and his father's crassness recall sequences in the information films by Brian Smith, *Your Children and You* and *Your Children's Sleep*, although theirs was a surer psychiatry, and Alwyn's ethereal effects more chilling than in *The Magnet*. But never is relief more true than when, at the film's end, his theft of the magnet redeemed and his conscience clear, Johnny skips along the sands to Alwyn's singing strings.

Albert Schweitzer asserted that there are two types of composer: the subjective composer whose music is drawn from his own inner resources, and the objective composer who adopts the inspirations of others.[11] The totally subjective composer is a rarity, and like most composers Alwyn displays characteristics from both camps. His music for *The Magnet*, however, is predominantly subjective, revealing an intelligence and originality that explore and extend the art of film; notwithstanding which, by his contribution to a group craft, Alwyn relinquishes — and is pleased to relinquish — much of his unique individuality.

Yet, as a jobbing composer, required to formulate scores for a mixture of film styles, and always under pressure of time, it was inevitable that at times Alwyn became a *pasticheur*. Thus, given the subject and style of *The Mudlark* (1950), Alwyn could hardly have done other than devise a pomp and circumstance. The pastiche sets the mood under titles and reoccurs later. Resourcefully Alwyn enfolds a reworking of his William Penn motif from *Penn of Pennsylvania* as a leitmotif for Queen Victoria.

One of two 20th Century–Fox films offered to Alwyn in this year,[12] and made by Korda's offspring British Lion at their Shepperton Studios, *The Mudlark*'s producer and scriptwriter (Nunnally Johnson), director (Jean Negulesco), and leading star (Irene Dunne as Queen Victoria) were American. Set in the 1870s, the scenario relates the adventures of Wheeler (Andrew Ray), an orphan boy who scrapes a bare living grubbing in the Thameside mud. He takes a fancy to Queen Victoria and manages to enter Windsor Castle, where his meeting with the queen persuades her to end her long seclusion since Prince Albert's death. Pompous, sentimental, and dull, the film is tourist-board history rather than creative cinema. Nevertheless, Alwyn's score is one of the more appealing and subtle elements — indeed it is crucial to the framework and supports at least two long action sequences. Wheeler's secret exploration of the castle is delicate mickey-mousing and sustains and comments on the action and, as John Huntley has noted, "becomes subjective and expresses the mood and character of the people rather than the grandeur of the building. Woodwind delicately pick out the thoughts of the boy; they concentrate attention on him."[13] Yet, the resultant empathy with the appealingly dirty little ragamuffin results in a more

---

[11] Albert Schweitzer, *J. S. Bach*, Vol. 1 (London: A. & C. Black, 1923), 1. Cited in Francis Routh, *Contemporary Music: An Introduction* (London: The English Universities Press, 1968), 63.

[12] According to Sir Malcolm Arnold, Alwyn was also offered Henry Hathaways's *The Black Rose* (1950), subsequently scored by Addinsell. Interview, 25 Feb. 2000

[13] John Huntley, "The Music in the Mudlark", *Film-Music Notes*, 10:3 (Jan.–Feb. 1951), 10–11;

complicated transference than perhaps Huntley allows. Wheeler's wide-eyed awe at the luxury of the royal apartments is concomitantly expressed through the score and transferred (as the filmmakers presumably hope) to a similarly impressed cinema audience.

Of greater interest from a filmic point of view is *Night Without Stars* (1951), directed and scripted by Anthony Pélissier, and produced by Hugh Stewart, who as a hands-on producer also had some input. The story, which is not easily summarised, concerns the near-blind lawyer Giles (David Farrar), who while holidaying in the South of France falls in love with Alix (Nadia Gray), the widow of a Resistance leader. Giles discovers the dead body of another suitor, Pierre (Gerard Landry), in her flat, and both woman and body disappear. An operation in London fully restores Giles's sight. He returns to France to discover that Alix's brother Louis (Maurice Teynac) is the head of a smuggling ring, and that Pierre was killed because he was a wartime traitor. Louis, who is sister-fixated, attempts to murder Giles to prevent his marrying Alix.

"*Night Without Stars*", complained the anonymous reviewer in the *Monthly Film Bulletin*, "is lacking in form or style (a symptom of this is the strange use of loud background music played indiscriminately over the most trivial happenings on the screen)".[14] Certainly there a great deal of music, much of it diegetic, but, far from its being "strange" or "indiscriminate", close examination suggests an intent to use music to structure form, as is only to be expected from the director and composer of *The History of Mr Polly* and *The Rocking Horse Winner.*

The film's main subject is blindness. While it is a weakness that the degree of Giles's blindness varies confusingly from scene to scene, nevertheless the director takes pains to emphasise it both visually and aurally. A distinctive feature of blindness is a heightened sensitivity to sound. A blind man would be more aware of casual music — the noise from radios, gramophones, and bands — than would a seeing man. Alwyn had always shown an interest in "source" music, often using it to underline a story point, and there is much diegetic music in this film.

Cleverly, it serves also as motif. Thus, the chatter of Giles's garrulous friend Claire (June Clyde) is always accompanied by annoyingly insistent jazz. A Latin-American rhythm represents Pierre, to be heard no more after a knife strikes him between the shoulder blades precisely as a number finishes on the radio. Louis plays chamber music on his radiogram; in one scene his music matches Alix's agitation as she paces backwards and forwards. There is also meaningful

repr. in James L Limbacher, *Film Music: From Violins to Video* (Metuchen, NJ: The Scarecrow Press, 1974), 96.

[14] *MFB* 19:208 (May 1951), 266.

radio dialogue: as Alix rests after Pierre's failed attempt to strangle her, the radio chatters away and the phrase "Calmez-vous, calmez-vous" is heard.

For the leading characters, leitmotif is more complicated. There are two major motifs, both stated in the main titles, commencing with the old French nursery song "Au clair de la lune" and moving to the main motif. Both are love motifs. The main motif is built upon a six-note scheme from the French song:

"Au clair de la lune" is introduced first, diegetically, as a song enjoyed between Giles and Alix at the piano and merges into a montage sequence depicting the whirling romance of the couple. It appears to represent a more carefree aspect of their love. The other motif, the major love theme, is also introduced as source music as Giles explains his blindness to Alix at their first restaurant date (when Pierre enters the music changes to the rumba, Pierre's motif). Later, as the two stand talking on a terrace, the motif returns on French accordion and mandolin, a French-sounding instrumentation. No instrumentalists are shown, but the assumption is that this is diegetic music, especially when the couple's kiss is segued by the full non-diegetic orchestral strings of the motif in a contrasting musical colour. A few scenes later, however, the couple are again on the terrace, again the "diegetic" French instruments are playing, and again Giles takes Alix into his arms. This time, however, the music does not depart from the diegetic illusion, for to introduce the love theme in a non-diegetic way the composer would lend his authority to a wrong message: for the couple are deciding to break off their relationship.

The change in the relationship between the two love motifs is reflected in the key sequence to which the second terrace scene leads. It is the turning point in the relationship of Giles and Alix and is a fine choreography of direction, camera movement, editing, and musical composition. Having agreed to break their connection, the couple return to Alix's flat. As they cross the street and enter the doorway, poignant strings followed by a plaintive cello suggest an end to their romance. As Alix brushes past Giles and starts to mount the stairs, the theme changes to the "Au clair de la lune" motif, its minor key expressing

Giles's loneliness and feeling of rejection. He calls to Alix who suddenly turns, saying "Yes, I'm here", and a sweet violin breaks in. "I thought I'd lost you", replies the blind man left behind in the shadows. Giles approaches her, and they slowly and affectionately nuzzle each other. "Au clair de la lune" re-enters, now in a major key, but in slow measure. As resolution crumbles and the couple kiss, "Au clair de la lune" gives way to a full emotional surge of the main theme, which gains supremacy. "Au clair de la lune" is allowed one dying spurt, but henceforth (apart from a minor re-entry in a slightly different role) is never heard again. The infant love has been replaced by the mature love of the main theme.

Weaknesses of plot, dialogue, and performance in *Night Without Stars* obscure isolated examples of fine cinema craft. Two prolonged musical sequences, Giles's secret investigation of the Café Gambetta and his climb up the dark mountainside after Louis's failed murder attempt, display Alwyn's adept creation of irrational, unsettling musical hues. In the first, we are not unfamiliar with his simultaneous mickey-mousing and creation of tension by contrasting his strings, both ostinato and falling through the chromatic scale, with brass and woodwind fanfares and diegetic noises (people talking, the breaking bottles, a cat mewing). In the second sequence, Alwyn's formidably textured underscore holds a variety of messages. Anxiety is created by commencing without any sense of tonal centre or resolution, beginning with low tremolo strings which rise on a minor scale over a scene of Alix and Louis at their house. As we cut to Giles stunned on a ledge overhanging a gully, double basses and cellos contrast with high tremolo strings and celesta representing Giles's dazed state of mind, while three-note brass fanfares repeated at intervals represent his danger. Alwyn now creates anticipation and suspense as he moves through a mixture of vertical combinations in minor mode, changing themes and motives, unresolved cadences. Scratchy strings represent unease, rising strings shot through with fanfares represent triumph, high tremolo strings represent height. The strings climb to support Giles's struggle against sliding scree, followed by a passage from the major motif. The motif is a reminder of Giles's wider cause of meeting up with Alix, and is anticlimax, lulling the audience into a sense that safety is not far off — betrayed when Giles is faced with an even greater danger: slipping down a sheer face without any sign of hope. Here the music is a reference to the last triumphant ride (including the fanfare) of the rocking-horse in Pélissier's previous film, and proof of Alwyn's assertion that music is not representational. After a sideways leap (with one bound, Jack . . .) and successful hold, Giles pulls himself to safety, and following a suggestion of a partial phrase from "Au clair de la lune" (another suggestion that relief is not far off), the musical key resolves to a major tonality, a sense of stability, and both Giles and the audience feel fairly secure.

19
"Choosing my Palette"

DESPITE a heavy feature schedule, there was time for a television score — William Alwyn's first — for John Read's *Henry Moore: Sculptor*, transmitted in April 1951. Filmed documentaries were uncommon, and critical praise went to Alan Lawson's fluid circling camera movement of Moore at work on an eight-foot reclining bronze figure for the Festival of Britain. The film went on to win a prize at the Venice Film Festival, although its viewer reaction was the lowest of the period.[1] For the music Alwyn composed a *Passacaglia* for string quartet, bass clarinet, and vibraphone, linked to the sculptor's actions. Moore commented to Alwyn afterwards, "I am glad you didn't write ultra-modern music for my film. I regard myself as a classic sculptor."[2]

Many film composers prefer a small orchestra — Alwyn and Malcolm Arnold among them. Alwyn put the matter succinctly:

> I would often far rather use a small group of players than a full symphony orchestra — primarily because I like to choose my palette to fit my canvas. Unhappily the Symphony Orchestra is like the All-Star cast, it provides a sort of Hollywood gloss and a pseudo-prestige value to the Film. To put it at its worst — important sounding title music makes the picture sound important (How often I've had that said to me). However, if I am hoist with the symphonic petard, I can tactfully disband it during the action of the film. Of course, there are some films which demand a large orchestra — a massive effect can only be obtained by massive means (*The Fallen Idol* for instance).
>
> Why do I like few players rather than many? Simply because, on the whole, it records better, and because one can make a small body really "tell". I am sure that it was for reasons not entirely economic that such a practised dramatic composer as Benjamin Britten chose to score his operas *The Rape of Lucretia* (1946) and *The Turn of the Screw* (1954) for a chamber ensemble. Britten, like myself, was trained in the cinema in the early years of documentary under the inspiration of people like Grierson, Rotha and Basil Wright. A limited budget led to unlimited ingenuity, and taught us to search for our effects by the simplest means.

---

[1] John Read, lecture at National Film Theatre, 16 Sept. 1997.
[2] Alwyn, "Film Music: Sound or Silence", 7.

I remember scoring one complete documentary for flute and drum — I played the flute myself and drummed away happily on soap boxes. It seemed to work . . .

It is rarely now that one is allowed to use economic means to secure one's intentions in the feature film. In the last ten years I can think of two only in which I have been given this opportunity: Ronald Neame's *The Card* [1952] in which a separate instrument was associated with each character — Alec Guinness as "The Card" himself was a solo clarinet — and Rotha's *No Resting Place* [1951].[3]

No Resting Place, with roots in Italian neo-realism, was a logical development of the documentary ideal. Based on a story by Ian Niall, it was directed by Paul Rotha — his first feature film — entirely on location in Wicklow. The tale is a simple one about a headstrong tinker, Alec Kyle (Michael Gough), who accidentally kills a gamekeeper. Too frightened to confess, he is suspected and pursued by a civil guard, Mannigan (Noel Purcell), in the obsessed manner of Jauvert in Victor Hugo's *Les Miserables* (1862).[4]

Rotha aimed for authenticity, recruiting all the actors except Purcell and Gough from the Abbey and Gate Theatres and Radio Éireann, while Wolfgang Suschitzky's photography caught much of the wildness and beauty of the Wicklow countryside. Although emotionally the film has moments of touching clarity, its authenticity is undercut by inept scripting and an implausible conclusion (probably imposed by the censor).[5] It was Alwyn's last commission from Rotha, and, as Alwyn pointed out, it was as much the rare opportunity as budgetary considerations that impelled him to work with a tiny ensemble in the most simple of styles. The instruments he chose were characteristically Irish: harp, flute, and violin. The music's translucent, fresh texture is entirely appropriate and establishes the film's mood from the start. The title sequence shows the family preparing to move on, commencing on harp and flute trills, in the Alwyn manner, and here suggestive of birdsong and the countryside. After a few bars the composition takes up a pastoral style, subsequently progresses to a jig rhythm, and returns to a melancholic lyrical mood. It is perhaps the jig that impresses an Irish character on to both composition and film: the otherwise plaintive fragrance of mood could as easily step from the English pastoral school. Rather than adopting a folk idiom, the style is English, pitched to the classical chromatic scale based on equal temperament, and with vibrato violin.

Later, some happier scenes recall the wartime documentaries showing children at play, which also employed small musical ensembles: Alec tickling and catching a fish to present to his wife for breakfast, while their son takes his tea

[3]   Ibid., 7–8.
[4]   HH, *Films in Review*, 3:5 (May 1952), 244.
[5]   *The Cinema Studio*, 6:124 (Aug. 1951), 17.

quietly nearby; or husband and wife happily scything and stooking the hay. The solo flute of another scene of tender intimacy between Alec and his wife as their child sleeps recalls the similarly tender "Love in a Cottage" for solo oboe in *The Harvest Shall Come*. Alwyn's score for *No Resting Place* is spare, unobtrusively positioned within the dynamics of the overall scenario, and compassionately expressive of the rough, sad life of the illiterate itinerant.

In 1951 Alwyn temporarily gave up the Chair of the Composers' Guild while remaining on the council, and in this same year he was elected to the Council of the British Film Academy. He had important work, too, for the Festival of Britain, which, as the country struggled to pull itself from the mire of austerity, shaped itself around an exhibition on London's South Bank. Today, one of its few remnants is the Royal Festival Hall, solemnly opened by King George VI on 3 May 1951. For the occasion Alwyn composed a $\frac{12}{8}$ *Festival March* owing much to Elgar's *Pomp and Circumstance* (1901–7, 1929–30) in inspiration and tone, and based on the rhythm of a march he remembered from boyhood.[6] Regrettably it was not performed at the opening ceremony, its performance delayed until 21 May, when it was played by Sir Malcolm Sargent conducting the LSO. Later the march became the score for Philip Leacock's ten-minute *Festival in London* (1951), evoking patriotic pride in his impression of the South Bank Exhibition and the nearby Festival Pleasure Gardens.

Under the arches of Waterloo Bridge, in the heart of the exhibition, was the Telekinema, built and equipped by the BFI to show off the latest audio-visual developments. Its programmes demonstrating three-dimensional and stereophonic techniques were a popular attraction, and during the five-month run of the Festival from May until September 1951 they were projected 1,200 times. They included a ten-minute short, *Royal River* (1951), believed to be the first actuality 3-D colour film with a specially composed stereophonic music track. The film, hastily directed by Brian Smith and composed by Alwyn, was beset by technical problems, mainly resulting from a fault in the BFI's specially constructed 3-D camera. In the end two standard Technicolor cameras were lashed together, and the rushes were speeded through the laboratories in Los Angeles to meet the deadline.[7] The cameras had been mounted on a boat travelling down the Thames from Windsor to the Festival Pleasure Dome, and as a special BFI Festival publication explained, the result is "a cameraman's picture . . . showing how complex movements of planes can lend a new beauty to scenery when viewed through the twin lens of the stereocamera".[8]

[6] William Llewellyn, "Obituary, William Alwyn 1905–85", *RAM Magazine* (Autumn 1985), 24.
[7] Charles W. Smith, introduction to a screening of short films from the Festival of Britain at the NFT, 12 Sept. 1997.
[8] Raymond Spottiswoode, "Three Dimensions — or Two", *Films in 1951*, 45.

On the soundtrack natural sound is nearly absent, and while the beauty revealed by the "stereocamera" is crystallised by Alwyn's score, his beautiful tone poem is not at all reliant upon the camera for a reciprocal enhancement. "Flow on sweet Thames . . ." quotes the commentary, and the music, flowing over edits and changes in location, is mainly unspecific, only occasionally illustrating precise pictures: royal swans are heralded by a courtly fanfare, so characteristic of the early 1950s, crows' nests starkly silhouetted against the sky evoke a menace matched by a high violin descending in a minor key. The caw of the crows and, later, a bird chorus are the film's sole natural sound-effects.

The ebb and flow of the waters are painted with musical colour and instrumental contrast: dripping strings and brass, harp and cor anglais, harp and brass. The harp is important to this score, its mellifluous chords and rippling arpeggios anticipating sections of *Lyra Angelica* (1953–4), Alwyn's sensuous concerto for harp and string orchestra. After nearly ten minutes, pictures and music reach journey's end: London, the Pleasure Dome and Skylon, horns and orchestra tutti, as the commentary honours the "spirit of the Festival".

Not to be left out of the celebrations, the feature-film industry pooled its resources into the prestigious *The Magic Box* (1951), produced by Ronald Neame and directed by John Boulting for half fees. It says much for William Alwyn's reputation that he was its chosen composer.

A biography of William Friese-Greene, a British inventor of moving pictures, must have seemed particularly apt. It reflected all the Festival's biases: the Victorian era, British technical ingenuity, hints of artistry, and a glance towards the future (Friese-Greene was developing a colour system when he died). For the titles, therefore, Alwyn strengthens the opening shot of the Festival logo with an appropriately ceremonial fanfare and theme, before turning to a motif based on a passionate descending four-note theme for strings, hinting at disaster, perhaps even tragedy.

Alwyn was correct to alert the audience, for *The Magic Box* is not a happy story. Eric Ambler's script depicts "Willy" Friese-Greene (Robert Donat) as a dull, obsessed individual, and introduces a double flashback device that spells out from the beginning — first through the recollections of Willy's second wife (Margaret Johnston), then through those of the inventor himself — that this is a story of a failure.

The flashback device and a weakness in properly exploring Friese-Greene's family relationships reduce the plot to a series of vignettes, a formula permitting the introduction of over 60 British stars. In the film's structure, therefore, music assumes a particularly important role, which Alwyn handles with particular subtlety.

One way is through his consummate skill in guiding musical themes into natural sound. As Friese-Greene, disillusioned by a lack of public recognition, wanders out into a lonely lamplit street, the scene mixes to a war-recruitment parade whistling "Tipperary" (1912), Alwyn's strings exactly matching the first note of the song.[9] Elsewhere, as an expectant Willy rushes for the doctor, the neigh of a waiting horse blends orchestrally — like a musical instrument — to heighten the tension. Moments later, the anxious father watches a dancing image on a zoëtrope: ethereal celesta (or vibraphone) and tremolo strings mingle with the mechanical clatter of the toy to climax in the cry of the new-born baby.

Sometimes no music at all creates greater effect: a quiet conversation between Willy and a son who has been bullied at school is given an emotional intensity through a lack of musical comment. At other times music makes an impact through contrast. In an extended sequence, Friese-Greene is beset by the dual problems of his wife (Maria Schell), about to give birth, and a shortage of cash. He decides to pawn all his photographic plates, his deliberations expertly mickey-moused. But when he arrives at the pawnbroker's, all music ceases, pointing up both the significance of the broker's shop and Willy's separation from the stressful domestic scene. On his return home he finds a customer requesting a sitting, but since he now he has no plates more mickey-mousing leads to a return visit to the pawnbroker's, and a second absence of music as Willy negotiates the return of a packet of plates. Thus the repeated scenes at the pawnbroker's are given a unity, and the whole extended sequence of selling and retrieving is structured by the musical composition.

A masterly music sequence culminating in the highly significant scene of Friese-Greene's first projection of a moving image depends for its effect on both the combination of music with natural sound and the contrast of music with silence. At night church bells strike the hour as Willy works on in his dark laboratory developing his first moving film. Low and high strings briefly initiate a short, mysterious fugal theme until soon the orchestra joins in, emphasising the passage of time by echoing the chime of the church bells, and counterpointing the diegetic sounds of the rhythmic click of a handle on the developer frame, and the drips of liquids. All is slow and mysterious harmonies. A developer timer ticks, its sound enhanced by vibraphone and woodwind. The developer plops; an oboe takes up a poignant theme high in its register. The scene cuts back to two policemen in the alley outside, their conversation given a nervous, tense feeling by a low pedal point. Back in the laboratory tension mounts, the orchestra continually speeding, until reaching tutti as Willy, beads of sweat on his forehead, hesitantly turns the handle on his projector. But the music does not even achieve a natural climax, as the scene returns abruptly to the silent alleyway outside — silent but for a single, faint, sustained note, suggesting something happening inside the building. The climax follows

---

[9] Slightly marred by a bad sound edit, masked by the voice-over.

through as Friese-Greene bursts out, his feet clattering on the cobbled alley-way, a screeching cat running out his path. The orchestra and its parts, diegetic sound, and silence have been carefully synthesised in the attainment of an ascending tension and ultimate crescendo of natural sound.

Alwyn's music director was, as usual, Muir Mathieson. The pair must have had a great deal of fun with one sequence, in which Friese-Greene and his first wife take part in a gala programme of the Bath Choral Society with Sir Arthur Sullivan conducting. Alwyn wrote a skilled pastiche of a Sullivan oratorio, and Mathieson took on the role of Sullivan — with appropriate sidewhiskers and macassared hair, the likeness is a good one. In the film, Friese-Green arranges a meeting with the great William Fox Talbot (Basil Sydney) for the same day as the concert. Absorbed, he forgets the concert in which he has the only chorus solo. A buxom soloist (Oda Slobodskaya) continually bewails her absent lover while the chorus asks repeatedly "Where has he gone; oh, where is he?", emphasised by shots of Friese-Greene's vacant chair. When the solo part arrives his embarrassed wife substitutes for him, to Sullivan's annoyed surprise. Not only is Alwyn's pastiche in perfect keeping with Sullivan's musical style, but it works as film music. For in the cut-away from the concert to the meeting of Friese-Greene with Fox Talbot, the absence of music contrasts boldly with the concert hall, with only the faint crackling of the flames in the fireplace to suggest Willy's forthcoming damnation.

In the oratorio — "Where has he gone; oh, where is he?" — the four-note motif, which sounded so tunelessly under the titles, is discovered again and revealed as something more than Alwyn's fancy. The words and the empty chair symbolise Friese-Greene's failure. For all that the film applauds Willy's obsession with moving pictures, it also suggests that, because of it, he failed in his family relationships, as his second wife bitterly laments near the start of the film. He failed, too, to receive recognition. Alwyn concludes *The Magic Box* with the ceremonial march that opened it; the British film industry's choice of a failure to depict its achievement exposes the strength of the Dunkirk spirit in the early 1950s.

The nationwide dimension to the Festival of Britain was reflected in *Lady Godiva Rides Again* (1951), a mixture of comedy and satire from Launder and Gilliat Productions, a new company replacing their Individual Pictures. Here, a pretty nineteen-year-old, Marjorie (Pauline Stroud), rides as Godiva in a pageant organised by a Festival Committee in the Midlands, and subsequently wins both a beauty contest and a film contract. Although the tale becomes a familiar one, as poor Marjorie's dreams are dashed and she takes to nude work in a touring revue, this is no tale of degradation and shame! Frank Launder, who both directed and co-wrote the script, keeps tongue in cheek and lets loose a few satirical digs, although the film also unconsciously mirrors some contemporary patronising attitudes towards women. Amidst the jokes and asides, Alwyn seizes a chance with some scratchy violin chords, no doubt representing "new music", heard diegetically on a radio. ("I'm waiting for *Take it From Here*",[10] explains the listener. "Can't you take it somewhere else?" comes the retort.)

Alwyn's light-hearted score stresses an ironic mood signalled at the start by a title caption of Lady Godiva on horseback joined by coconut hoofs and a Western film rhythm. Very fast strings and piano, in the style of Carl Stalling, complete the message. As the first act opens, plucked strings with staccato orchestral chords represent both the raindrops and the tedium of a wet English Sunday. Later, as Launder joins the miserable queue for the Sunday afternoon pictures, Alwyn decorates his irony with unearthly strings and, in turn, a mournful trombone and a sad horn.

Launder and Alwyn never talk down. They trust their audience to recognise the irony of the crowds on Blackpool beach ruling the waves as Alwyn crashes in with "Rule Britannia" (1740), while the humour of a shot of a pawnbroker's sign matched by the first three chords of a clock chime is almost subliminal. Marjorie's visit to the local cinema to see *The Shadow of the Orient* permits Alwyn to have fun with his Arabic-sounding strings, gongs, and cymbals during the love scene of a Valentino lookalike and a sultry princess (Dennis Price with Googie Withers). As the legend "THE END" floats on to the screen, the musical climax is abruptly interrupted by the cry of "Ices!", a crude advertisement for ice cream, and the sound of jingling muzak: Alwyn's ear for the tone of both music and moment is perfect and creates the comedy, while the sequence looks forward to Launder and Gilliat's production of *The Smallest Show on Earth*. The composer evidently had no illusions about what happened to his own hardworked compositions once they reached the local fleapit.

---

[10] A popular radio programme.

20
Seeing Another Meaning

I N a scene in *Lady Godiva Rides Again*, Alistair Sim as a bankrupt film producer cynically reflects that, "What with television to the left of us, Hollywood to the right of us, and the government behind us, our industry — laughable term — is forever on the blink." It was a cry from the heart: by 1952, the independent companies formerly under Rank's umbrella had found the rain getting in, several of the major studios had been disposed of, the Crown Film Unit was closed, and the "X" certificate was introduced to tempt audiences to the previously forbidden. Yet, while television and Hollywood seemed a threat to the studios, for an adaptable composer like Alwyn they could be an opportunity. Already he had composed for a television film, and, of the four features bearing his credit in 1952, the first was Hollywood-financed.

Stuart Heisler's *Saturday Island* (1952) was released by RKO-Radio in March. An episodic, improbable, and often ludicrous curiosity notable for its kitsch, the film explores the relationship between a Canadian nurse (Linda Darnell) and a US marine (Tab Hunter), shipwrecked together on a desert island. The performance of the one-armed actor Donald Gray, who arrives late in the film as a crashed RAF pilot, strips it of any vestiges of dignity. Alwyn made some attempt at rescue, compensating for inadequacies in the direction through his own interpretations of mood and emotions, at its most extreme amounting to a kind of musical doodling. At other times the composition seems too polished for the uninspired direction and camerawork.

The film's main theme, a calypso by full symphony orchestra, lacks the robust rhythmic mix of calypso and rumba of its predecessor in *The Rake's Progress*. There is also a surprise: among the orchestral instruments is what sounds like a theremin. Although the instrument had been used successfully by Miklós Rózsa in *Spellbound* (1945) and Roy Webb in *The Spiral Staircase* (1945), Alwyn usually relied on fairly standard orchestral instruments for his vertiginous harmonies. However, here it is, joined by the vibraphone to flashback to the experiences of a crazed, shipwrecked poor-man's Ben Gunn (John Laurie). The combination of the two instruments, especially in one passage where they are preceded by contrasting low double basses and cellos, is effective in context, although in a passage in which the theremin rises and descends wildly and unnervingly to suggest an approaching storm, the performance is clumsily executed and sounds inexperienced.

Also in March, Ronald Neame's new film for British Filmmakers (in other
words, the Rank Organisation) was released, Eric Ambler's adaptation of Arnold Bennett's "Five Towns" comedy *The Card*. Set in the late Victorian period,
it light-heartedly narrates the rise of "Denry" Machin (Alec Guinness), the re-
sourceful son of a washerwoman, whose climb to the top begins with forged
scholarship results and ends in the Mayor's regalia. "He's a card, that one —
a proper card!" says somebody of Machin, and his character is reflected by Alwyn's engaging motif, starting under titles as a cheeky whistle (the whistler was
Neame himself[1]), and soon joined by equine coconuts, pre-echoing the card's
donkey-drawn light cart. The cheerful musical mood is sustained throughout
by the solo clarinet, solo flute (Alwyn's own instrument), or in duet, the high
register recalling the whistling card of the titles. It is the clarinet, however, that
dominates and even has the final say. The film ends on a parade to the new
Mayor and Mayoress, brass band playing the card motif as a full ceremonial
march with church bells ringing behind. After the end titles fade away a final,
cheeky, riposte of two rising notes ($c\#''$, $f\#''$) is the allegorical two fingers of both
instrument and Machin.

There is another major motif. The Countess of Chell (Valerie Hobson) and all
that is to do with her are unfailingly represented by variations of a fanfare motif, as is appropriate to her elevated situation. The fanfare sounds, baldly, when
she first bowls into the solicitor's office where Machin works, but it transmutes
into a waltz as Machin dreams, Walter Mitty- or Billy Liar-like, of taking the
dance floor with her. When dream becomes reality, the same waltz is playing. But Alwyn plays with the motifs of Machin and the Countess. Each time
Machin forges an invitation to the Countess's ball, a variation of his own motif dynamically submerges the Countess's fanfare theme; when the Countess
becomes patroness of Machin's "Five Towns Universal Thrift Club", shown by
huge lettering dominating its office building, and again as it grows even huger,
it is the Countess's motif that rings out: for her motif not only represents her,
but her power, which is now shared by Machin and his Club.

Alwyn's musical structuring is sophisticated. The film's introduction, for example, calls for a background sketch of the (Potteries) Five Towns and Burs-
ley and a résumé of Denry's early career. Alwyn shuns the obvious solution of
scoring continuously throughout and unites the separate scenes by constant
short musical phrases and mickey-mousings, which are punctuated by sound-
effects, thus sustaining interest by variety and contrast. This musical welding
of diverse scenes and ideas through a constant harmonic pattern is used again
in the film's penultimate act, where Machin snatches his future wife from the
jaws of embarkation for Canada, and against competition from her rival. Here
nostalgic violins supply the linking theme and represent our hero's love, ini-

---

[1] Ronald Neame, *Straight from the Horse's Mouth* (Lanham: Scarecrow Press, 2003), 138.

tially unrecognised by him — but signalled by the audience's friend, the composer.

The track is filled with imaginative touches, of which a few examples must suffice. Miss Earp (Glynis Johns), the local dancing teacher, is initially recognised by her piano and a veneer of respectability; when Machin discovers she is heavily in debt her sagging prestige is reflected by an untuned honky-tonk piano. Machin's car ride with the same lady, regretting the recent passing of her husband, commences with "oompah" brass (to match the car's horns) before moving to lighter chords; as Miss Earp attributes her husband's death to his "overtaxed strength", Machin's expression, plus the return of "oompah", is suggestive.

The film was nominated for a "Best Sound" Oscar. The sound editor was again Harry Miller, and the combination of sound-effects, silence, and music is particularly felicitous. A friendly footman protesting too late at being gulled into helping Denry is met by a horse's mocking neigh. When the wily gold-digging Miss Earp lures Denry into her room, his danger is underlined by a shot of the cuckoo clock and Alwyn's clarinet "cuckoo" call. Later, as Ruth Earp luxuriates in a shopping spree with Machin's purse, a shopkeeper asks his name. "Rockefeller", Machin cries disgustedly, the impropriety of his response emphasised by both Alwyn's clarinet and a sudden train whistle.

There is also a faultless example of the effective use of silence. Machin presents his mother with a top-hat box, which he says contains "pebbles". Tension builds up as she silently opens the lid, lifts a cloth wrapping, and uncovers over £1000 in coins. A pause of a few frames is judged to a nicety before the cut to her face. Her cry is a shocking and well-judged climax, accompanied by a rapidly climbing and falling clarinet and subsequent xylophone chimes as the coins are scattered across the stone floor.

Alexander Mackendrick's *Mandy* was released in July 1952. Mackendrick was a rising, perhaps even risen star at Ealing after his previous successes of *Whisky Galore* (1949) and *The Man in the White Suit* (1951). In his earlier career he had been involved in storyboarding, a training that shows in his grasp of symbolism and significant camera set-ups. The plot of *Mandy* concerns the six-year-old deaf-and-dumb Mandy (Mandy Miller), whose mother Christine (Phyllis Calvert) insists the child be sent to a school for oral education, against the will of her immature husband Harry (Terence Morgan) and the child's grandparents. At the school, the care of the teachers and especially the headmaster Searle (Jack Hawkins) stimulates Mandy's first attempts at speech and helps her to relate to other children, but Harry sees himself as being displaced by Searle as Mandy's father. Finally Harry's own "deafness" is cured, Christine and he are reconciled, and Mandy takes her first hesitating steps to communication with the wider world.

So much for the basic plot, but Mackendrick's films, as Alec Guinness pointed out, "were always about something".[2] What *Mandy* was about has been analysed by Charles Barr,[3] Pam Cook,[4] and Philip Kemp,[5] the last of whom synthesises and augments the earlier commentators. These writers find in *Mandy*, both the film and the child, a microcosm of British society at the turn of the 1950s, a representation of the failure of the older generation and the potential of a new generation to communicate and co-operate. In assessing the underscore for *Mandy*, therefore, it is useful not only to make the usual judgements, including an assessment of Alwyn's success at conveying the sensation and emotions of Mandy's education, but to explore whether he in any way captures the film's wider significance.

In a lecture to the National Film School in 1979, Mackendrick expressed the opinion that Alwyn "wrote awful film music, because when he saw a sentimental scene he'd say, 'Oh, isn't that lovely!', and write sentimental music for it. And when the music's doing the same thing as the picture, it never works because one of them's redundant. The good composer's the one who plays against the film and sees another meaning in it."[6] It is a harsh judgement: a half-moment's reflection reveals a glibness amounting to nonsense, for while it is true that music which "does the same thing as the picture" may be bad composition (as Alwyn himself often stressed), a good composition will do the same thing as the pictures yet enhance the meaning. The score of *The Rocking Horse Winner*, for example, intensifies the force of the frenzied riding scenes as well as imparting meanings impossible to convey by the pictures alone. Similarly, Alwyn augments the meaning of Mackendrick's film, although Mackendrick himself may have lacked the insight to read the message of the score.

In his study of Mackendrick's work, while commenting that Alwyn's score "never establishes much presence", Kemp makes an exception for a tense park scene that "gains from the addition of a mocking, repetitive little tune like a child's counting-rhyme. It's an imaginative touch from William Alwyn".[7] The tune to which Kemp refers had been established earlier under the titles and draws from actuality of an actual skipping rhyme (on the soundtrack one can hear the rope smacking the ground) immediately after the Rank gong and before the title music begins. The idea of starting in this way probably belongs to

[2] Philip Kemp, *Lethal Innocence: The Cinema of Alexander Mackendrick* (London: Methuen, 1991), p. ix.

[3] Barr, *Ealing Studios*, 152–7.

[4] Pam Cook, "Mandy: Daughter of Transition", in Charles Barr (ed.), *All Our Yesterdays* (London: BFI Publishing, 1986), 355–61.

[5] Kemp, *Lethal Innocence*, 68–97.

[6] Alexander Mackendrick, tape of lecture at National Film School, May–June 1979, quoted ibid., 85.

[7] Kemp, *Lethal Innocence*, 85.

Mackendrick, and it is most certainly an imaginative touch. Since the chanting children are not visually represented, depriving the audience of its sight draws its attention to the auditory sense. The impression is heightened by commencing the sound over black before the first caption. Moreover, in case the audience misses the point, the screen fades to black again after the first caption, which is incomplete ("An Ealing Studios"...). The dual senses of sight and hearing are closely allied in this film about lip-reading.

After a few moments, Alwyn's light strings pick up the easy rhythm of the actuality rhyme, but, before long, horns sweep in and the strings metamorphose to bold wave-like surges, which almost drown the skipping rhythm and introduce a feeling of emotional power. Nevertheless the skipping tune repeatedly attempts to break through — suggestive musical imagery in a film about a little girl who attempts, and finally manages, to break through her own disability and social exclusion. Soon the fast skipping rhythm discovers an equality with the slower passionate strings, counterpoints them, and finally subdues them to end the title sequence optimistically. Thus, from the start Alwyn has informed the viewer of the struggle and ultimate achievement in the societal sense, which the three commentators referred to above suggest is a part of the film's subtext.

It is the skipping music that is reintroduced in the park sequence approved by Kemp. While the parents are engrossed in conversation, Mandy wanders away and a light rhythmic beat on strings introduces a sense of apprehension, combined with our empathy for Mandy as she confronts the wide, misty (= impaired senses?) playing grounds. As she drops her ball and it rolls away, clarinets introduce the skipping tune. Now the ball is picked up by a boy, and Mackendrick's skilled framing stresses the (emotional) distance between the two children, the boy large in the foreground. Strings take up the melody, and despite the lightness of the skipping tune the atmosphere is menacing. Mandy becomes "piggy in the middle" as the boy and his sister toss the ball to each other. Terrified, unable to speak, unable to join in the play of the children, Mandy rushes back and forth, helplessly trying to retrieve her ball, until the music level is dipped as the girl, Dot, implores, "Dougie, give it to her." The underscore now drops to a long pedal point, suggesting partially the calming of Mandy's fears, but also holding and raising tension — just as a similar device did all those years ago in *Desert Victory* and other films. When Doug refuses to hand over the ball "until she says 'please'", the music cuts out altogether, all chance of reconciliation is abandoned, and diegetic sound proves more shocking by contrast as Mandy falls on Dougie, tearing and screaming at him with frustration. In this sequence music assumes an equal importance with direction, editing, and sound editing to create the effect of rising frustration. Later in the film, Mandy is goaded by Christine to show off her progress in front of Harry, and the skipping beat is again hinted at, crescendoing until cut off by

Harry's shout of "stop it!"; here the musical composition suggests that Christine is adopting the bullying tactics of Dougie. Of course, in making these musical references Alwyn is writing precisely as Mackendrick thought a "good composer" should, a composer who "plays against the film and sees another meaning in it".

Mackendrick is partially right, however, for Alwyn's heightening of emotionalism occasionally descends to bathos — ironically, less sophisticated than Alwyn's filmscoring of the second-rate *Saturday Island* the same year — which is a pity, for Mackendrick, with his artist's eye, plants visual messages throughout this film, and Alwyn at his most sensitive could have helped create a masterpiece with his musician's skills. As it is, Alwyn's infrequent lapses draw attention away from much fine composition — for example, the exquisite musical scaffolding of the cumulative interrelated sequences showing Mandy's first days and nights as a boarder at the school, which transcends the passing of time with a dark, dreamlike underlying tension.

As Reed in *The Fallen Idol*, so Mackendrick uses visual imagery to suggest barriers between Mandy and her family and imposed by her family. As she makes the first halting moves to escape from the imprisonment of her disability, Christine says, "It's like seeing the door of a cage beginning to open." One cage is the yard where Mandy peers — like Alice (herself disabled by her size) gazing at the beautiful unattainable garden in Wonderland — through a broken wall plugged with chicken wire, to watch children playing on an open bombed site beyond. The yard is crazy-paved as if representing Mandy's difficulty in making mental connections. Alwyn introduces a repetitive musical passage as motif to represent Mandy's entrapment, first with celesta chords, light strings, and plaintive oboe as a flashback uncovers the passing years in the prison-like yard. Shortly afterwards she runs from the yard, anxious about her dog sitting on the road in front of an approaching van. As she hesitates, trapped behind a parked car, and by her bewilderment at the normal world, the motif emerges in the lower, more powerful register of double-basses and cellos. Later, as she circles round the yard, imprisoned by both physical and psychiatric disabilities, her cycling is represented by the same slow, repetitive descending motif. When Mandy goes to the school she cannot at first cope with her first experience there, cannot relate to the other children, and is as much confined as in the yard. So in the school playground, surrounded by children swinging a rope in circles or playing on the roundabout, a variation of the motif and Mackendrick's parallel imagery, suggest the same circles of entrapment. The motif appears elsewhere and in other forms, but its final introduction near the end is significant to the film's resolution: Mandy enters her grandfather's room and peers through his window at that same pitiable yard, the children playing on the waste ground beyond. But this time she unconsciously reveals to her grandfather she is beginning to both read and speak, and at his discovery the motif becomes affirmatory, full orchestra communicating that the door of the cage is open.

A persistent motif is Alwyn's repeated use of chimes and chime-like chords. Their inspiration is the tuning-fork used by a doctor near the start of the film to test baby Mandy's hearing. The meaning of the chords is ambiguous. Mainly they represent the condition of deafness, as when a celesta chord conveys Christine's discovery that Jane Ellis (Nancy Price), the intelligent and articulate founder of the school, is herself deaf. But the chords also possess a positive element, an element of hope. Here, Christine was asking a question, unheard by Ellis, "Do they [the deaf children] ever get to the stage where they can lead a normal life?" — the question answers itself. The chime-like chords, especially in regular beats, also represent a passing of time. In the example just given, there is synthesis of both the representation of deafness, Christine's question about children, the image of the elderly woman, and the hope conveyed by that image. Again, faint celesta chords sound over an early general view of the school building: it is not under consideration for Mandy at this stage, hence the low dynamics, but the chords themselves convey the dual vibration of both deafness and future hope. In another example, as Christine listens through an open door to Mandy's governess failing in her instruction of finger speech, her thought, "Must be something, someone", is resonated by chimes that signal both the deafness of the unseen child and a future hope represented by her own continued efforts. Earlier, a shot of baby Mandy glumly trapped behind the bars of a playpen is introduced by a single celesta chord. The motif here has the same purpose: the shot precedes a voice-over that carries the passing of the following five years; the next shot shows Christine carrying the baby into the dismal back yard to a single celesta chord; a third shot shows an older child running in a snow-covered yard (the passing of the seasons) to harp chords. Sometimes the chimes seem solely to represent a spark in Mandy's brain. Hence the lively and excited celesta as she runs from the yard with her dog. Most often they sound as Mandy is being educated. Is it too fanciful to imagine that the chimes ultimately become the diegetic sound of the human voice as Mandy's attempt to say the letter "P" — a gentle high-pitched sound — enlightens her grandfather and leads to the resolution of the film?

Mackendrick considered the soundtrack important to all his films, and, no doubt because of its subject matter, he paid particular attention to *Mandy*. Diegetic sound, the squeak of doors, the echo of footsteps across an empty hall, and so on, are important in this film about the deaf. In three sequences Mackendrick also attempts to empathise with Mandy's deafness by suppressing the sound of speech altogether. He claimed that simply to fade away the sound did not work: "You have to have something much more complex: at the moment of fade-out have some ongoing sound, speech or whatever, put it on a variable-speed disc and introduce the Doppler effect. So it becomes intermittent, changes pitch and drops. Then people realise the sound is being taken away, leaving them with silence".[8] Nevertheless, he said, absolute silence could not be sustained for more than three or four seconds (actually, quite a long time in filmic terms), after which he found it preferable to replace the silence with "some sort of high-pitched ringing buzz".[9] It seems that by the time he gave this interview Mackendrick had forgotten the composer's contribution, because the three sequences in which he claims to have attempted what he called "sub-jective non-sound"[10] are highly dependent upon film music techniques. In the first a van-driver, alarmed that Mandy has run in front of his vehicle, descends from his cab to scold her. A celesta chord sounds (the motif for Mandy's deaf-ness) beneath the driver's angry tirade and about two seconds before a cut to Mandy's uncomprehending face. Here the sound dips and vanishes on a re-verse cut to a distorted extreme close-up of the man. There is no "Doppler effect" and the "high pitched ringing buzz" that Mackendrick talks of is a pedal point held by high violins, which give way to a full orchestral climax as Mandy picks up her dog in two-shot and runs off. Interestingly, once she reaches the interior of the house the "trapped" motif re-emerges, expressing her frustra-tion at being unable to tell the adults what happened.

The second attempt at "subjective non-sound" occurs where Mandy's teacher encourages her to understand the word "tiger". Here Mackendrick does attempt to distort the voice as it fades away. But Alwyn's underscore does not fade, indeed it crescendoes to create a rising tension which climaxes in Mandy's scream. Clearly, music was indispensable here.

In Mackendrick's third attempt, a crucial dramatic turning point, the teacher encourages Mandy to feel the vibrations of her vocal chords in a balloon held against the lips. "B-b-b-b . . ." repeats the teacher, and the camera cuts to Mandy as she attempts to comprehend and imitate. As the teacher's voice fades (no distortion of her voice here), a light string pedal point is introduced. This fades, and considerably more than four seconds elapse in total silence as Mandy struggles with the teacher and rushes to a sink. The pedal point re-emerges and grows in dynamics until crescendoing in the child's scream and crashing a cup on the floor. Again, it is the *Desert Victory* sequencing technique, and tellingly so, while both the first and third examples illustrate Alwyn's case for the power of silence in contrast with sound.

This film about a deaf-mute is crammed with messages about the healing of broken communications. Mandy is isolated from her family by her family and barred from the outside world. Yet she touches everyone: she confirms a young teacher in her vocation; she affirms the headmaster's determination

[8] Kemp, *Lethal Innocence*, 71.
[9] Ibid.
[10] Ibid.

to serve his pupils; she imparts courage to her mother and exposes the deafness of her father to her cry for help. The film approaches its end with an affirmation: Mandy has matured sufficiently in confidence to leave not only the restriction of the house for the open waste ground, but also to leave her parents for her peers and a more positive future. Mackendrick makes this clear by his camera set-ups: Mandy gives her ball and her name to a boy framed diametrically to her father; in a single shot Harry restrains Christine from following her daughter, for he now hears Mandy's needs, and Christine conveys that she both recognises this and will resume a wife's role. Mackendrick's final shot cranes to show mother and father watching their child join the children on the open space, as representation of the future.

Alwyn's opening response to these scenes is a phrase which has the flavour of a lyrical passage from "Nimrod" in Elgar's *Enigma Variations* (1899). Perhaps he sensed an enigma, for the composition's development to optimistic ascending chords is without deeply felt or memorable melody. A fanfare marks the words "The End" displayed on the screen.

But the film is not yet finished. Barr, Cook, and Kemp spell out the subtexts, the limitations of the characters and the culture: the future is precarious, much has still to be resolved, and much depends on a small disabled child. Pictures alone cannot convey this frailty: it is left to Alwyn to express the final uncertainty. As the "The End" title segues with a rolling credit list, the music also continues, but it has changed. Now, with the addition of regular chiming chords — conveying both "deafness" and the passing of time, the future — it descends quietly to a darker mood of uncertainty and premonition.

21

Swashbucklers and Noir

IN diametric contrast to *Mandy* was Robert Siodmak's buccaneering yarn, *The Crimson Pirate* (1952). Alwyn's enjoyment oozes from every stave of this score — one senses a relief from serious-minded assignments, a satisfaction of his romanticism and his sense of fun. Financed by Warner Brothers — director and stars Burt Lancaster and Nick Cravat were American, other actors and film crew were British — it found inspiration, as the title suggests, in the 1926 Douglas Fairbanks swashbuckler *The Black Pirate*: several stunts were alike, and both were irreverent extravaganzas typified by the fixed grins of their heroes.

Alwyn's often tongue-in-cheek composition lies in the tradition of Erich Wolfgang Korngold's swashbuckling action music, especially his composition for *The Sea Hawk* (1940). There is a great deal of music in the film, with the cues often separated by just a few seconds. But the film is not over-scored, even though this fast-moving dramatic structure, with frequent changes in direction and several fight and chase sequences, demands prolific scoring. Moreover, the composition supplies a thematic and motivic unity to the texture of the film, the themes often blending and maintaining a musical flow even as they mickey-mouse or hit split-second timings. Alwyn restricts the number of his motifs, a decision that helps his audience to familiarise itself with the tunes. At the same time, he allows himself a great deal of liberty in their handling by classical variations of harmony, melody, and rhythm.

Thus, Alwyn's vigorous main pirate anthem, which commences under titles, appears to be based on gypsy-like rhythms, complete with tambourine — appropriate for the rovers of the high seas. As important is another motif, encountered by our heroes Vallo (Burt Lancaster) and his mute companion Ojo (Nick Cravat, who communicates by whistles and mime like a swarthy Harpo Marx) as they reconnoitre an occupied island. Here they meet the island's grenadiers, strutting like clockwork soldiers and accompanied by a military-march motif appropriately scored for brass and flutes. When the militia chase the two pirates, the motif becomes a mocking recitation when the pirates win every round. Alwyn jumps this major motif through several stylistic hoops, transforming it into an anthem (like the brass-based anthem from *State Secret*) and a minuet, and in the ultimate fight sequence he somehow permits it to be seized by the pirates for their own motif. (Maybe that is something pirates do.)

Other motifs include a stirring symphonic sea motif and a fast-moving *furioso* theme sometimes called upon for the chase sequences, very much in the rhythm and harmonies of the animated cartoon. A love motif for Vallo and the rescued maiden Consuelo (Eva Bartok) is memorably melodic with a hint of melancholy, matched by the ethereally romantic harmonies of solo flute accompanied lightly by harp and high strings. But it's mainly schmaltz to poke fun at the budding infatuation of Vallo and Consuelo — like the passion in the rigging at the film's conclusion, justifiably ridiculed by Ojo.

Using the motifs as scaffolding frees the rest of the musical construction, and other themes are introduced in passing and where necessary. Thus, an orchestral echo of the sailors' sung shanty "What Shall We Do with the Drunken Sailor" (traditional), and even a fleeting hornpipe, become the composer's entertaining nods and winks without disturbing the overall structure. Diegetic music is unlikely to affect the structure, of course, but it is worth observing in passing that Alwyn devises a Spanish flamenco-inspired dance and a Basque-style folk dance, reminders that in this film we have descended to a more earthy, folksy musical culture. Previous to their film careers, Lancaster and Cravat worked together as circus acrobats, and for some of their stunts Alwyn introduces appropriate circus devices. When they are chased by the militia, Vallo and Ojo leap and jump to glissandi on the timpani and drum rolls, a whistle sounds somewhere, and Ojo tosses rocks at the militia, which rebound with satisfying wood-block claps. It is suggestive of clowns, of an ancient affinity between pirates, travellers, and the circus — and the roots of theatre and the cinema.

The following year, Alwyn was given another chance at a Warner Brothers swashbuckler with William Keighley's *The Master of Ballantrae* (1953). Appropriate to an Errol Flynn vehicle of derring-do and flowing action, Alwyn supplies a copious underscore, masterly matching rapidly-shifting moods, colour, action, and locations, in split second mickey-mousing and in closely paralleling voice rhythms. So generous is it that it becomes as unheard as the accompaniment to a silent movie.

It says much for Alwyn's adaptability that he is able to swing from the deep subtext of *Mandy*, to the exuberance and gags of *The Crimson Pirate*, to the bleak pessimism of Robert Hamer's film noir *The Long Memory* (1953). Comparing like for like, it is revealing to evaluate, say, the glitzy love motif of *The Crimson Pirate* with the love passage of *The Long Memory*, with its overtones of renounced revenge, and restrained to (just) this side of popular romanticism. Hamer's film, with its dark Dickensian, even Dostoyevskian overtones — some commentators have remarked on its affinity with Jacques Prévert's *Quai des Brumes* (1938)[1] — recounts the mental torment of Philip Davidson (John

---

[1] *MFB* 20:229 (Feb. 1953); Tanitch, *John Mills*, 76.

Mills). Wrongly convicted of murder, Davidson leaves prison intent on reveng-
ing himself on Pewsey (John Slater) and his former girl friend Fay (Elizabeth
Sellars), who perjured themselves at his trial; Fay has since married Lowther
(John McCallum), the detective in charge of the case. Davidson finds a home
in a derelict barge on the mudflats of the Thames Estuary and in a shabby riverside café meets a refugee, Elsa (Eva Burgh), whose undemanding love persuades him of the futility of revenge.

The film's joyless desolation is communicated best by natural sounds. Thus
the title theme dies on a six-note phrase (in C minor) on the oboe, which mixes
with the mournful cry of the curlew as the camera pans across the barren mudflats. A cut to a noisy, busy railway station serves to heighten the loneliness.
Soon we shall discover that the motif, a catch-all that appears in various for-
mulations, pre-echoes the folk-song of an elderly mudlark collecting tawdry
pieces of scrap-metal. Diegetic sound-effects sustain the air of loneliness and
neglect. Hooters in different pitches sound short and cold across the estuary.
As the police gather in the town to watch Davidson's visit to Pewsey's seedy
love-nest, a train puffs gloomily in the background. When night falls, a sequence of comings and goings is structured by the ring of footsteps on the cob-
bles, punctuated by forlorn ship sirens, train whistles, a dog's bark. Elsewhere,
the atmosphere of the grubby café is suggested as much by the sound of feet on
wooden floorboards, Elsa scrubbing the floor, and the clink of spoon against
tea mug, as by the set and camerawork. Sometimes silence alone is telling: at
night in the quiet of the barge Davidson revealing to Elsa his need for revenge
is significantly juxtaposed with Fay confessing to her husband in the quiet of
their comfortable bedroom.

Musical composition is carefully balanced with sound-effects, dialogue, and
moments of silence. The music spotting is immaculate and reflects dedicated
teamwork. In the narrow view music serves as punctuation, but in the broader
perspective it creates structure. At its simplest, this dual purpose is revealed
in the flashback to the court scene, where short stings punctuate the crucial
points of the trial represented by dialogue and culminate in a longer climaxing passage when Davidson is led off to prison. The complete sequence is thus
contained and unified by the music.

A more sophisticated sequence is Davidson's visit to Pewsey. Here, after carefully building up tension by sound-effects alone, Pewsey's discovery of Davidson at his doorway (as he puts the cat out) is met by a panicky and threatening
musical burst as he pushes Davidson back and bolts the door. Pewsey returns
to his room, and only Davidson's footsteps sound as he crosses to wait in an
entrance opposite, watched by the police. The shot of Davidson waiting in the
shadows is underscored by dark strings and a regular threatening drum beat,
suggesting the inevitability of fate, a glimpse of the Grim Reaper. Inside, the
house is quiet, the chiming of a clock and the sound of a church bell alluding

to Pewsey's entrapment and the passing of time, and again hinting at the patience of fate. Pewsey peers through the letterbox and his sighting of Davidson still waiting is stressed by a repeat of the menacing strings with the funereal underbeat. Yet again Pewsey returns to the room, time passes, again the clock chimes: it is daylight. But now the music has invaded the house, gradually rising in volume and speeding in tempo, the drum beat suggesting the beating of the heart, until in panic Pewsey rushes outside into the safe arms of the police. The sequence is an object lesson in the marrying of effects and music to construct a satisfying dramatic unity.

Later, the score similarly unites an even more disparate series of scenes, whilst simultaneously unfolding the drama's central moral precept. Davidson sets off from the marshes for Fay's house, his intention revenge, while the motif mounts to tutti. By the time he reaches her he has remembered Elsa and abandoned his revenge. When Fay comes to the door, the revenge motif returns fiercely with her recognition of him, but limps finally away as he enters the house. To background silence, he tells her he wants nothing from her, but after his departure the orchestra returns *furioso* to reveal her *Angst:* thus Davidson's mental anguish has been transferred to Fay. Both scene and music elide into Davidson's return to the barge where Elsa sits waiting; a lyrical passage ensues to represent their love and the purging of his conscience.

Much of the tension of the scenario is constructed from parallel action and cross-cutting. Its climax, as Davidson is chased across the mudflats by the man he was presumed to have murdered, is cross-cut with shots of the police (accompanied by the journalist and Elsa) rushing to the scene. The cutting here is sufficient to build suspense without aid of a non-diegetic score, but once the rescuers join in the chase the music seamlessly joins in, *furioso*, until rising strings lead suspensefully to the final gunshot — Davidson is saved not by the police, but by a gunshot from the old mudlark. With that the musical score finishes: the sound of the curlew and the folk-song of the mudlark contrast with the preceding orchestra *tutti*. The soundtrack expresses, therefore, much of the subtext of the film: for all their musical bombast, the police — as throughout the film — are ineffective. Their role is supplanted by an old man with a shotgun, and to Lowther's, and society's, heartfelt promise that, "I'm going to put everything as right for you as I can", Elsa replies for Davidson, "He doesn't need anything that you can do for him. He only needs to be left alone, to come back to life again." A few simple orchestral chords complete the end title: the film concludes with a musical asceticism.

The Long Memory was a brave attempt to escape from the mainstream of British cinema into a style at times indebted to the French or Italian, and to expose something of the sub-strata of English society. It failed from an uneasy mixture of realism, studio artifice, cinema cliché, and improbability. Nevertheless the working relationship between Hamer — who was ill for much of its filming — and Alwyn was a good one, and the result is an immaculate balance between musical score and diegetic sound.

The 1950s have been seen as a period of stagnation in the British film industry, yet home productions flowered at the box office. A genre to which audiences returned again and again was the war film, which contextualists have seen as both a nostalgic longing in a time of uncertainty about Britain's place in the world, and as defining popular concepts about the war. Significantly, the period was reassurance for the filmmakers themselves, too, for, as James Chapman has perceptively remarked, the war was also British cinema's finest hour.[2] For the composer of the scores for *Desert Victory*, *Tunisian Victory*, *The Way Ahead*, *The True Glory*, and so many war documentaries, Alwyn's contribution to the 1950s genre was comparatively slight. It included, however, Brian Desmond Hurst's *The Malta Story* (1953), a narrative of the island's struggle in 1942 under air threat from the Axis powers, and the role played by Flight-Lieutenant Peter Ross (Alec Guinness) in the successful destruction of a large German convoy. Its bland heroism (benefiting from hindsight and sure knowledge of victory) is characteristic of the early 1950s product, compared with the passionate desperation, even hysteria, of the features and documentaries produced during the war. Even the stiff upper lip lacks the passion of the wartime films.

As if reflecting the shift of emphasis within the genre, Alwyn's score sometimes seems less nervy and sparkling compared with his 1940s compositions. For instance, an early sequence depicting Ross alone in his cockpit lacks the musical exhilaration of the earlier flying films. Nevertheless the craftsmanship is faultless throughout, and in one prolonged and musically complicated sequence, a tour de force. In the control room, an announcement of the approach of long- and desperately-awaited Spitfire planes is followed by a high-pitched violin trill. This trill is an adhesive that binds together the whole sequence. At this early stage it suggests the use of radar (which is not yet depicted) and shapes a taut suspense. A cut to the artillery is marked by increasing dynamics, joined soon by the roar of Spitfires overhead. A fanfare seems to announce the consummation and relaxation of the suspense: the first planes have, after all, arrived. But the underscore continues, and trill and tension return, matching now a second wave of Spitfires passing over the town — to become a mixture of diegetic sound and non-diegetic fanfares, a second climax. On the tarmac the planes are moved to safety, an excitingly paced mix of natural sound, kettledrums, brass fanfares, and timpani, a hint of trill from time to time adding

---

[2] James Chapman, "Our Finest Hour Revisited", *Journal of Popular British Cinema*, 1 (1998), 63–75. For a near-contemporary survey, yet in embryonic form suggestive of Chapman's opinions, see also Ian Johnson, "The Decade: Britain — We're all right, Jack", *Films and Filming*, 8:12 (Sept. 1962), 44–8.

an edge of tension. Now motifs are defined, increasing suspense by contrast: between the high-pitched trill of control room and radar, the natural aero-engine noise, drums and fanfares on the tarmac. Finally fanfares and a ceremonial passage accompany the Spitfires as they take off once more for the attack.

Another sequence deserves comment. The film's climax, the defeat and death of Peter Ross, flying alone as he seeks out an enemy convoy, and the convoy's subsequent destruction by the air force using his radioed position, is depicted without music. As he takes off, the tragic outcome of Ross's flight is presaged by a brief passage of an ominous timpani rhythm used as a motif for an earlier tragedy. The score having set up the presentiment, sound-effects alone now carry the dramatic tension of Ross's death in the cockpit. The absolute silence of the loudspeaker in the control room — contrasting with a cross-cut to the rush of air and the sound of the plane as it twists and falls into the sea, and a last cut back to the continued still of the control room and the repressed emotion of the control crew — is eloquent. The subsequent bombardment of the enemy fleet is similarly depicted without music. The mayhem fulfils a cathartic need after the death of Ross, but by shunning the emotional heightening of a music score it is as if the filmmakers wish to make a factual statement, as if to make it plain that this destruction is not emotional, not revenge, but necessity. It is the equivalent in sound of the stiff upper lip. The composer returns only at the very close.

Between 1953 and 1954 Alwyn composed fifteen episodes of a television crime series starring Boris Karloff, *Colonel March of Scotland Yard* (shown on ITV in 1955–6). The title music was by Philip Green, a prolific composer with a film list almost as long as Alwyn's, and probably best known for his melody "Romance" in Bernard Knowles's life of Paganini, *The Magic Bow* (1946). Knowles directed several of the episodes of the *March* series, and other directors included Terence Fisher, Arthur Crabtree, and Paul Dickson.

The composer of *Odd Man Out* and *The Fallen Idol* was lending his hand to (what appears to be) a second-rate television series. No doubt Alwyn would have argued that a composer has to eat. But composition for such works could compromise his reputation: the stigma of the "mere" film composer is encouraged by assembly-line product.

Similar problems also arise when the composer is faced with an inept film with serious pretensions. Such was the case with *Personal Affair* (1953), produced by Anthony Darnborough, who had earlier working associations with Muir Mathieson (Mathieson married his sister). For Anthony Pélissier, the director, it was his final major feature, and it is a pity that his artistic co-operation with Alwyn ended with a creative disaster. Based on a two-act play by Lesley Storm, with an improbable plot, poor character motivation, and ludicrously artificial and over-written dialogue, it was an appalling choice for a film treatment without major rewriting. Presented with a self-evident cinematic failure, Alwyn has scant opportunity to do more than spot the dramatic highlights, in the manner of a stage-play, and to lubricate three major montages.

Another film in which the composer was cruelly used was Ealing's *The Rainbow Jacket* (1954), the first of four films for Basil Dearden. Scripted by T. E. B. Clarke, this tale of the ambitions of a failed jockey (Bill Owen) for the success of his young protégé (Fella Edmonds) contains little musical composition. Yet two short sequences reveal how more generous underscoring may have enhanced the film: a suspenseful moment before the start of one of the races is achieved by slowly climbing dark strings against bright tremolo strings with a repeated three-note motif on bassoon; and, later, the orchestra crescendoes to match an excited voice rhythm during the reading of a vital letter. Such examples, commonplace in other films, here stand alone. One other scene perhaps deserves mention. The dramatic impact of the low string tremolo and six-note horn motive at the start of the film's climactic last race is indebted to the old favourite "The Ride of the Valkyries".

In contrast, Alwyn's score shines in Ronald Neame's *The Million Pound Note* (1954), a charming, fresh little comedy based on a Mark Twain short story made, perhaps, with an eye to the American market. Henry Adams (Gregory Peck), an out-of-pocket American, newly arrived in London, is given a million-pound note for a month. He cannot cash it, but on the strength of the credit it brings he lives in luxury, wins a fortune, and weds a pretty heiress, Portia (Jane Griffith).

The score is abundant, filled with fun and musical wisecracks. Alwyn's delight is evident, and his techniques similar to *The Crimson Pirate*, shifted from eighteenth-century pirate ships to Edwardian London. Sometimes Alwyn italicises the visual jokes, but often the wit is in the musical score: when a hotel register is signed with an "X", the stroke up and the stroke down are mirrored by glissandi on the xylophone.

Three simple motifs form the musical framework: a waltz representing Portia and romantic love; a rather ponderous theme, usually on the trombone, for Adams's mute companion, the strongman Rock (Reginald Beckwith); and "Yankee Doodle". This motif fulfils an important psychological subtext, representing the novelty of Adams's arrival in London and his first experiments with the million-pound note. Midway in the film Adams has a bad dream (harp glissandi, string and flute trills, Adams's groans and minor brassy repetitions of the motif, crescendoing to orchestra tutti), which acts as catharsis; next morning a short passage of the motif on clarinet gives way to an airy violin solo with harp and real birdsong. The nightmare is over. Adams decides to stay in London — "we can't throw in the cards when the game is only halfway through". The "Yankee Doodle" theme is never heard again.

Having restricted his motifs, Alwyn is freed to mickey-mouse at will and to explore a myriad of rhythmic and harmonic variations, especially on the "Yankee Doodle" theme. Its most strident application is a bright and brassy march as a regiment of pages bear heaped-up tailors' boxes for Adams up the broad hotel stairway; in his room Adams takes up the motif, whistling as he dons hat and catches walking stick in time to the music. He breaks off whistling while the orchestra matches the phrasing perfectly as Adams and Rock strut to the doorway. They then proceed down the staircase, still in perfect step to the march. It is a clever example of co-operation between composer and director, obviously planned before the scenes were shot.

One scene, which draws its charm largely from mickey-mousing, has the banknote taken by the wind, chased along the street by a desperate Adams. In its two and a quarter minutes the sequence airily catches the whims of the paper as it floats, first fast, then slow, gets trapped and freed, and takes in *en route* a waltz, a galop as it sticks to a child's hoop, yet another waltz as Adams spins with an elderly nanny, a brassy suggestion of Sullivan's "Onward Christian Soldiers" ("St Gertrude", 1871) as it wafts past a religious pamphleteer, and skywards ascending strings when the pamphlets go whirling into the air to join the banknote. When, at the last, Adams reaches across the pavement for the note, in succession a plaintive solo violin takes pity on his predicament, a brass fanfare sounds his triumph as he grabs it, and a bassoon plays "Yankee Doodle" in mockery.

The problem of mixing Western musical traditions with authentic folk idioms is raised again with the score for Ken Annakin's *The Seekers* (1954), a film Annakin later described as "junk",[3] making an exception of its opening. Set in the early years of British settlement in New Zealand, with Jack Hawkins as Philip Wayne and Glynis Johns as his wife Marion, the film contains authentic Maori scenes, filmed during the location shoot. They include the *haka* (thrusting, stamping, and grimacing, to match alternate shouts of the leader and chorus response), the *waiata tangi* (a funeral lament), and the *poi* (a sung dance in which women swirl balls attached to strings).

Alwyn is less successful in integrating European and indigenous rhythms here than in, say, *Daybreak in Udi*. Certainly there is no attempt to imitate the folk rhythms or to escape from the customary underscore — perhaps from fear of disturbing audiences with the unfamiliar, but more likely from habit of thought. Yet some attempt is made to restrict the Western orchestral music to scenes involving the settlers. It fails because the task is impossible: settlers and Maoris often appear in the same scene, and to whom does one give musical preference? (Usually, the settlers.)

---

[3] McFarlane, *An Autobiography of British Cinema*, 26.

258   *William Alwyn*

The musical confusion expands with the presence of the Maori singer Inia Te Wiata in the role of the Maori chief Hongi Tepe. Te Wiata arrived in England in 1947 and by 1950 had made his debut as a principal singer with the Covent Garden Opera Company. With his deep bass baritone voice, his presence is reminiscent of a latter-day Paul Robeson. The result is theatrical Western-style Maori music, notably in the baby's baptism scene in which Te Wiata is accompanied by a European choir. An erotic "choral" dance by Laya Raki as Tepe's wife Moana is in the same bastardised mould. Both sequences were shot at Pinewood, in contrast with the authentic location chant sequences. Moana's temptation of Philip in the forest further muddies the musical waters, where the mix with "jungle" sound-effects is appropriate to a Tarzan film.

Underscoring is uneven, at times seeming half-hearted or rushed. Consider, for example, the sequence when the settlers await an attack, keeping lookout from pits in the ground. While they wait, Moana rushes through the forest, in a storm, beset by fear, danger, and an appropriately urgent and menacing underscore. Yet the underscore continues with the same freneticism when the scene cuts back to the patiently waiting settlers. In these shots there is a case for a quieter mood, or for no music at all. The resultant lack of tension can be profitably compared with the nervous intensity of the troops, similarly dug in, awaiting the German attack in *The Way Ahead*.

It remains to consider the film's opening, which Annakin considered "was all right". The titles open over a New Zealand landscape with a ponderous three-note introduction matching a succeeding passage by Te Wiata and the chorus. It is the track from the "baptism" music heard later in the film. As the titles conclude, the orchestra returns with a fanfare and a "thank you" caption. There follows voice-over narration of an "ancient Maori legend" ("Far back in time, beyond the borders of memory . . ."), joined by the wordless choir and singer. It lasts until the orchestra repeats the three-note theme as Chief Tepe paces in the night, troubled about keeping the peace between tribes ("his only answer the whispering of the wind in the great trees of the forest"). Thus the introduction supplies motive and structure, resolved at the film's conclusion by Tepe's commitment to Christianity. Unfortunately, the introduction's solemn pretentiousness belies the debilitated film in between. And, despite Annakin's limited approval, the sequence — music and script — is stark kitsch.

Noel Langley's *Svengali* (1954) avoids kitsch by a hairsbreadth to bring to the screen an acceptable adaptation of George du Maurier's novel *Trilby* (1894). In its depiction of the tone-deaf artist's model Trilby (Hildegarde Neff) hypnotised into becoming a prima donna by the sinister musician Svengali (Donald Wolfit), the film strives for authenticity. Located in the Parisian Latin Quarter in the 1890s, its sets and photography are copies of du Maurier's original il-lustrations.[4]

Yet authenticity lies not only in images. Struggling at an impression of Bohe-mia, the soundtrack unwraps musical lollipops, which Alwyn balances nicely with his own work, often blurring the distinction between the diegetic and the non-diegetic. Moreover, by eroding the diegetic/non-diegetic distinction, Svengali's almost Satanic presence, his mysterious extrasensory communica-tion, is demonstrated — even when he is absent from the scene. Thus at an art-ists' party Svengali reaches an angry climax at the piano precisely at the point where Trilby kisses her lover Billy (Terence Morgan). Later, as Billy declares his love to Trilby a rhapsodic piano solo is integrated into the underscore; on the exchange of a kiss the piano ends on a discordant and violent smash on the keys, and a cutaway shows Svengali rising angrily from his stool.

The crucial turning point in the film, Trilby's mental seduction by Svengali, owes much to musical structuring. Svengali enters her empty room: as he does so the underscore takes up an ominous theme, which foreshadows and intro-duces a short motif that Svengali takes up on the piano, "calling" Trilby to him. The orchestra responds with low strings, repeating the introductory theme. Svengali repeats the piano motif, which is now echoed by the strings accompa-nying a visual mix to Trilby approaching trance-like through the streets, pulled as it were by the piano now transmuted to strings. This is repeated twice more, first with full orchestra (the "power" thus increasing) and on the last occasion against a suspenseful high pedal point as her shadow announces her arrival.

As in *Take My Life*, Alwyn's brief included the composition of an operatic aria. All the songs were sung by Elisabeth Schwarzkopf and convincingly mimed by Neff.

Towards the end of 1954 Alwyn's second television documentary was transmit-ted, a meticulous history of the art of cartoon, *Black on White*. It was again directed by John Read, whose *Henry Moore* had been such a critical success, and because of a musicians' strike, Alwyn scored for musical effects of his own devising:

> The score was written for Piano, which I played myself, and — work-ing in the closes[t] collaboration with the Editor, we relied on such eminently simple sounds as a Toy Trumpet, a Barrel Organ, drums recorded at different pitches, [spinning] the record faster — a pi[e]ce of non-copyright jazz and carefully calculated natural sounds. We wanted to use an old, tinny recording of the "Charleston", but, at the last

---

[4] *MFB* 22:253 (Feb. 1955), 21.

moment this was found to be prohibitively expensive — so I wrote a new Charleston, played it myself and mixed it with surface noise from an old blank record disc.[5]

It was great fun, and for Alwyn it must have recalled the old experimental documentary-film days.

---

[5] Alwyn, "Film Music: Sound or Silence", 8. The lecture notes are hastily typed at this point.

22
Music and the Spoken Word

ACCORDING to Mary Alwyn,[1] William was particularly satisfied with the scores of *Odd Man Out*, *The Rocking Horse Winner*, and *The Ship that Died of Shame*. For Dearden's *The Ship that Died of Shame*, Alwyn's proportioned and complex score in 1955 is in contrast to his spare contribution to the same director's *The Rainbow Jacket* the previous year. The heroine of this excursion into the paranormal is motor gunboat number 1087, with a noble wartime history and commanded by Bill Randle (George Baker), whose young wife Helen (Virginia McKenna) is killed in an air raid. With the war finished, he enters a partnership with his wartime second-in-command, the spivvy George Hoskins (Richard Attenborough). They buy 1087 and refit her for smuggling. Hoskins, however, becomes involved with less pleasant contraband than nylons and watches, culminating in an attempt to smuggle a child murderer, Raines (John Chandos), out of the country. After her illustrious wartime career, 1087 increasingly balks at these activities, until in a storm Hoskins is drowned and the ship crashes to her death on the rocks.

The producer, Michael Relph, considered that 1087 "in a sense, represented what people had done with the country they had inherited after the war".[2] Modern commentators, too, have seen the film as a metaphor in which the wartime ideal of commitment to the community is demolished for the degrading quick buck. The metaphor is validated only by the anthropomorphic device of imbuing 1087 with a wilful soul. In the cinema such symbolism depends upon apt musical composition, a task for which Alwyn was at his best — one recalls the benign forces of *The Magnet* and the diabolic forces in *The Rocking Horse Winner*.

Like all ships, 1087 is feminine, and after the death of Helen she becomes the film's single female presence. Her importance is emphasised before the commencement of the title music, sweeping towards and past the camera, the prima donna, displaying her form visually and by the roar of her engines. To her, too, is awarded the film's major musical leitmotif, which bursts in exuberantly as the title music, based around a simple five-note motif:

---

[1] In conversation with the writer.
[2] McFarlane, *An Autobiography of British Cinema*, 482.

At the start, the score reflects with dignity the wartime achievements of 1087, but soon key, rhythm, and harmony are transformed to express her changing moods. The motif is plaintive when the ship is sighted in the breaker's yard, triumphant as her controls are displayed to recall her potential, elegant and relaxed as a montage conveys the innocence of the early postwar trade. Before long, as the business becomes increasingly sinister, the ship's feminine determination makes itself felt. As in much else, Hoskins is pernicious in his judgement of both women and 1087: "Like the ideal woman, eh? She does what you want, when you want it. If we knew the way and could set a course for Hell — she'd go!" But when Bill confronts Hoskins with smuggled counterfeit banknotes, the engines die, and 1087's motif, sung by an ethereal solo violin, suggests eerie eavesdropping. The contrast of the ensuing unpleasant animal-like throaty grumble of the failed engines conveys 1087's protest at her cargo. Soon, in high waves and bad weather, the ship becomes increasingly intractable: her wheel resists the hands of the crew, and her protest is conveyed by the passionate repetition of her motif on the cello, an instrument of liquid and feminine resonance.

In the *Musical Times,* Hans Keller wrote a short analysis of the score.[3] Alwyn was pleased with it and had it reprinted in Manvell and Huntley's *The Technique of Film Music,*[4] of which he was the editorial chairman. Writing for a musicians' magazine, Keller gives the impression of sitting in the cinema with his eyes closed, content to analyse the mechanics of the composition and ignore how the composer is relating music to the visual image. In his notice, Keller affects boredom with the score for the first half of the film, a boredom that apparently did not prevent his counting the musical cues. "The fifteenth entry with its consequences", he wrote, "made me jump."

What made Keller jump appears in the rendezvous of Hoskins and Bill with the child murderer, Raines. Mist swirls about the shore and the landing stage where they wait impatiently for the arrival of the "cargo". On an inspiration, Hoskins runs to a pillbox on the headland. A foghorn sounds in the distance, a C-sharp. The orchestra catches the note and repeats it in a motif, pre-echoing and echoing Hoskins's shout through the door of the pillbox: "Come on out!"

"Come on out!"

The three notes, if not exactly leitmotif for Raines himself, certainly become leitmotif for the dark episode of the rescue of a murderer from the police. With her cargo on board, 1087 moves into the mist. Raines stands alone on the deck,

---

[3] Hans Keller, "Film Music: Speech Rhythm", *Musical Times* (Sept. 1955), 486–7.
[4] Manvell and Huntley, *The Technique of Film-Music,* 288–90.

the mood tense and frightening from things unseen, or the shapes of things. The engine chokes and the "come on out" leitmotif sounds again, to become transformed into the 1087 leitmotif on plaintive solo violin, now in the key of F-sharp major. The ship recovers and continues to move through the water. She is challenged by a French coastguard, the 1087 motif on solo violin is repeated, and her wheel refuses to respond — "she's heavy on the helm again". A third time the solo violin plays, mixed this time with the sound of the coughing, failing motors. "She's losing heart", says Bill. The sequence ends with the final "come on out" cue. Bill comes on deck and senses that George, now a murderer, has pushed Raines into the sea.

Throughout this elegant, economically-scored sequence, the atmosphere of fear and guilt has been enhanced by the sound of fog-horns and the bells of buoys, in C-sharp, their note punctuating long silences and augmenting the underscore. When Raines emerges from the pillbox, his mute fear — like a hunted animal — at George's bullying shouts is reflected not by the underscore but by a plaintive fog-horn, thus eliciting the audience's sympathy for a character they know is evil (although they do not yet know his crime) — yet without (apparently) involving the complicity of the filmmakers.

Keller was excited by the "come on out" motif. He saw the sequence of the rescue of Raines as the turning point of the film, and considered Alwyn had given the sequence great significance by his musical adeptness. Keller referred back to the whispers in *The Rocking Horse Winner*, although he thought the present achievement the greater because the musical pattern *preceded* the verbal statement. Such patterns were not new to Alwyn, however, who had experimented with them earlier — we recall *The Winslow Boy* whispers, or the anticipation of Svengali's piano "call" to Trilby by an orchestral pre-echo. Keller, however, was thrilled by the unification of *speech* and music and compared Alwyn's achievement with examples from Britten's *The Turn of the Screw* and Schoenberg's *Pierrot lunaire* (1912). Alwyn's achievement, thought Keller, was the most revolutionary, impossible outside the cinema, and consisted in "unifying the two belligerent parties at the stage where their differences are at their acutest, where speech remains speech and music remains wordless; and the incisive contrast between the two sharpens our wits for the understanding of new musico-dramatic unities between them".

Composition for the film taught Alwyn much about the relationship between music and the spoken word. In August 1955 his radio opera, *The Farewell Companions* (1954–5), was performed on the BBC Third Programme. It was based on the tragic life of the Irish patriot Robert Emmet and was broadcast in Eire on the anniversary of the Easter Rising. After Alwyn retired from film composition, he set to work on his opera *Miss Julie* (1973–6), writing his own libretto based on Strindberg. Commenting on his technique, he wrote, "I frequently use the rhythm of a significant phrase or sentence *before* it is actually sung, to give extra stress to the words by anticipating them in the music. And again, I use the same device *after* the words have been sung".[5] In films like *Svengali* and *The Ship that Died of Shame* Alwyn was absorbing and refining techniques invaluable to the inspiration and creation of his opera.[6]

Geordie (1955), produced and written by Launder and Gilliat and directed by Launder, was filmed in haste on a shoestring because of financial worries at Korda's London Films.[7] It tells the story of a puny Scots lad (Paul Young), who following an intensive correspondence course grows into a muscular ham-mer-thrower (Bill Travers) who travels to Australia to win the Olympic Games. The film was a financial success in the United States, and not surprisingly in Scotland where it had extended runs. Its near jingoistic Scottish atmosphere, hovering this side of the twee, is swamped by Scottish folk-songs, suggestions of such, and fast reels. On at least two occasions the score is supplemented by a piper, although the music spotting is particularly intelligent, resulting in a tartan that both colours and controls the scenario. Alwyn's sense of humour seems always ready to break through — for example the hint of "The Ride of the Valkyries" as Geordie, in a fair imitation of Superman, lifts a car off a trapped man.

Whether conscious or not, the prominent love leitmotif for scenes between Geordie and his girl friend Jean (Norah Gorsen) is strongly suggestive of the main leitmotif (motif B) from *The History of Mr Polly:*

Geordie

The History of Mr Polly

---

[5] Alwyn, case notes to *Miss Julie* (Lyrita SRCD2218, 1992), 10.

[6] Sergio Leone's *C'era una volta il West* (*Once Upon a Time in the West*, 1968), with music by Ennio Morricone, resonates with the stylisations of Italian grand opera. A short musical phrase played repeatedly on the harmonica by the film's hero (Charles Bronson) reflects the villain (Henry Fonda)'s repeated question, "Who are you?" which rhythmically resembles *The Ship that Died of Shame*'s "Come on out!" In the Italian film, the phrase becomes a major ele-ment of the plot and is mainly diegetic, as opposed to Alwyn's subtle underscore.

[7] Brown, *Launder and Gilliat*, 136–7.

Their common theme is homesickness. The homeloving Geordie, loath to travel to Australia for the games, desires nothing more than to settle down with his beloved Jean, while Mr Polly seeks and finds a home for his restless soul. If one senses a suggestion of "Going Home" from Dvořák's Symphony no. 9 in E minor (*From the New World*, 1893), it is hardly surprising: bar four of the *Geordie* passage contains a motive from the Largo in retrograde.

The year is marked, too, by what seems to be Alwyn's unfortunate willingness to help out with a quick commission. Mitchell Leisen's *Bedevilled* (1955) is an odd melodrama about a seminarian (Steve Forrest) who becomes involved with a murderess (Anne Baxter) hunted by a Parisian gang. Direction and acting lack enthusiasm, pace, and credibility, and appearances suggest that the turn-round was so fast that Alwyn and Mathieson had time for no more than a quick and consequently pedestrian job. In the last reel the murderess is shot twice, but the music track does not even emphasise the climax.

23
"Music My Task-master"

O N 7 November 1955 William Alwyn's birthday was marked by a broadcast of his Festival March on the Home Service. He was 50 years old, and it was time to take stock. His diary, polished for publication in 1967, records his daily life for the twelve months following September 1955:[1] he had already retired from his professorship at the RAM, he started composing his Third Symphony (1955–6). There were meetings with Roger Manvell and John Huntley about a major book on film music,[2] and after much heart-searching he turned down the prestigious appointment of Head of Music for BBC Television — he could not face his "creative work reduced to a spare-time pursuit".[3] He undertook two major film scores to be completed within six weeks, one of which, *Safari*, he felt, "does not stimulate me to much enthusiasm, but difficult to reject as I shall need the money to pay for the time that must be devoted entirely to the symphony".[4]

Terence Young's film is an uneasily scripted, directed, and acted tale of a white Kenyan hunter, Duffield (Victor Mature), employed by the rich patron Brampton (Roland Culver) to hunt a famous lion. This familiar situation is complicated by the menace of the Mau-Mau and Duffield's determination to search out the murderer of his family. A romantic interest is provided by Brampton's fiancée Linda (Janet Leigh).

Alwyn's diary reveals the stress of composition. On 16 December he received the first editor's "lengths", and he started work on his sketches. He found the blank manuscript paper "a reproach and a demand — an urgent and frightening reminder that the Royal Philharmonic Orchestra has been engaged for three whole days in a few weeks time to perform and record this non-existent music". "Tense with anxiety and apprehension", Alwyn exhausted himself in the first two days, "ideas forced out like drops from a squeezed lemon".[5] By 27 December he was working at the orchestration, and on 11 January, having almost finished, he took time off to look at his symphony again, before starting work the next day on *The Black Tent*.

---

[1] Alwyn, "Ariel to Miranda".
[2] Manvell and Huntley, *The Technique of Film Music*.
[3] Alwyn, "Ariel to Miranda", 42.
[4] Ibid., 37.
[5] Ibid., 38–9.

A few days earlier, the stress of composing against the clock had brought worries of

> the suspicion that my work is deteriorating into mere mechanical processes; no consolation that these processes are technically ingenious. It is alarming, as one gets older, how inventiveness is replaced by a reliance on old formulae . . . I want desperately to say what I have to say in fresh colours and patterns . . . Perhaps, however, it is wrong to persist in a search for new methods. The mature artist should perhaps rest content to repeat himself, always providing that the substance of his repetition is worth repeating . . .[6]

It is hardly surprising that the composer betrays stylistic formulae. To have written, as Alwyn did, "during the last three weeks . . . nearly an hour's music for full symphony orchestra — twice the length of a symphony"[7] would demand experienced formulaic composition from anyone. Several passages in *Safari's* copious score are several minutes long and encompass a variety of moods and scene changes. One recognises more than once the cascading strings that accompanied Captain Ellis's suicidal night walk in *Great Day.* Or the funereal beat Alwyn cannot resist when death is close, here as Duffield returns to find his farmhouse burnt out by the Mau-Mau. The lyrical motif for Linda resonates with the love theme of *Our Country.*

What is remarkable is that Alwyn can take the familiar and make it sound fresh. The cascading strings are not lingered on, but exactly the right length to spice moments of tension and adventure; the funeral march is counterpointed poignantly by a solo violin when Duffield finds his dead son's toy tank on the ground; variations of Linda's motif convey yearnings unsuggested by the pictures or the actress. There is a sprinkling, too, of other motifs that seem entirely original, and Alwyn often suffuses the whole with African-sounding harmonies that match the scorched photography. The film does not neglect indigenous African music, but Alwyn devises his own, including a fast drum rhythm, enlivened and clarified by brass and woodwind. It is also remarkable that Alwyn can put so much effort into partially rescuing by his music a production he knew was near-rubbish. He was also compelled to write a tune to a trite and inappropriate title song (with lyrics by Paddy Roberts) "We're on Safari".

Alwyn was finally, and rightly, pleased with the technical aspects of his score, attributing "the clarity of effect"[8] to his familiar technique of scoring in three distinct planes of unison strings, woodwind, and brass in counterpoint to each

[6] Ibid., 45–6.
[7] Ibid., 46.
[8] Ibid., 49.

other. On the 19th, 25th, and 27th of January he joined Mathieson at Elstree for the recording sessions, and on the last day he was able to report:

> *Safari* brought to a successful conclusion. Musically it is not of much account, but it is the most consistently brilliant piece of scoring I have done so far, and it sustains its energy throughout the whole hour and a quarter — a considerable length of music! . . . There is nothing tentative about it and I am able to rejoice in my technical mastery. The new score for the second film, which is now well under way, is very different; where the first was positive, this is more delicate in texture. It is interesting how subconsciously one responds in different ways dramatically to each problem.[9]

Recording sessions for *The Black Tent* were booked for the end of the month, but the work was less strain:

> *January 12th*: Started work on the second film score, and immediately I was stimulated by its far more congenial and imaginative subject; ideas began to flow, and life took on a new sense of adventure and excitement . . .
> *January 13th*: Easy inspiration for the film *Black Tent*, I worked hot-foot all day.
> *January 14th*: Scribbled all day at the film.[10]

Alas! On Monday 16 January Alwyn could report that "I have felt far from well during the last few days", and "after a feverish day of work, I could hold out no longer and went to bed early with a pain in my chest and shoulders".[11]

On 30 January,

> First day of recording *Black Tent* at Denham. This has renewed my faith in myself after some of the near-banalities of the last film. The score is much more personal and blends romanticism with Arabian scale patterns in a new orchestral texture. The last few days of writing have been a great strain. Since the middle of December I have composed almost two hours of music for full orchestra of a quality of which I am not ashamed. For six weeks, Sundays included, I have laboured with hardly a day's break, and this excess is now beginning to tell on my nerves.[12]

A household catastrophe intervened before recording was finished — be-

[9] Alwyn, "Ariel to Miranda", 45–6.
[10] Ibid., 46–7.
[11] Ibid., 47.
[12] Ibid., 50.

cause of the freezing weather a 40-gallon water tank in the loft burst and deluged William's bedroom:

> The days which followed the flood were uncomfortable and my life was complicated by the urgency of work on the film. I completed this task on Sunday and the music was recorded next day.[13]

It is sometimes as well to remember that behind the film score is a human being with a domestic life.

The Black Tent was directed by Brian Desmond Hurst, for whom Alwyn had worked on *A Letter from Ulster* and *The Malta Story*. Hurst's best-known film is *Dangerous Moonlight*; during the recordings Mathieson jokingly asked if Hurst expected Alwyn's score to save this film as Addinsell's "Warsaw Concerto" had the earlier one.[14] The script by Robin Maugham and Bryan Forbes is exceptionally intelligent and unusual for its period. The film was photographed extensively on location in Libya; it narrates the story of Captain David Holland (Anthony Steel), wounded during the Libyan campaign in 1942. He is nursed back to health by Mabrouka (Anna Maria Sandri), the daughter of a Bedouin sheikh; they fall in love and marry, but Holland is killed before his son is born. The son could inherit a considerable fortune if he leaves his mother and grandfather for England, but he decides to stay with the people of the desert.

The Black Tent is unsatisfying because of its weak exploration both of character and of the implications, emotionally and culturally, of a sexual relationship between a European and an Arab. Nevertheless, its subject affords Alwyn considerable opportunity to suggest Arabian harmonic textures, scored — as Alwyn acknowledges in his diary — for a Western full symphony orchestra.

To write the film score Alwyn had interrupted work on his Third Symphony, in which he introduced a modification of Schoenberg's twelve-note system. Alwyn, the romantic, had never felt at ease with serialism, could never agree to the "loss of tonality, concord and discord and a 'singable' melodic line", which he "felt were the very foundations of western music".[15] In the symphony, he divides Schoenberg's twelve-note chromatic tone row into two groups. By using a form suggested to him by Indian classical music, he limits himself to eight notes in the first movement, four in the second, and an integration of both groups in the third. In this way, he believed he could still preserve consonance and dissonance, retain the "singable" melody, and — most important — not lose contact with the ordinary musical public.

Fascinatingly, work on the Third Symphony has leaked over into the film score. The correspondence of the film's major motif in "Arabian" scale patterns

---

[13] 8 Feb. 1956. Alwyn, "Ariel to Miranda", 51.
[14] MacQuitty, *A Life to Remember*, 321.
[15] Alwyn, *Winged Chariot*, 16.

with the four-note group of the second movement of the symphony is startling. A good comparison, for example, is the almost identical four-note statement at the commencement of the second movement of the symphony with the seventh film cue (in E-flat major). Alwyn's film score continues by counterpointing, evocatively, the diegetic chant of the tribe at prayer. Other resonances are the fast-descending scales, and a back-reference to *Odd Man Out* when a funereal drum and string theme accompanies the wounded David as he limps across the desert towards the Bedouin camp.

In previous productions, Alwyn's integration of Western film music with authentic indigenous folk music had had mixed success. In *The Black Tent*, European and Middle-Eastern traditions are interwoven in the wedding ceremony of Mabrouka and David without any sense of jarring. The native music is solely instrumental, although in real life a vocal "poet musician" would probably take a prominent role. The sequence commences as a procession conducts the shrouded bride beneath a canopy, accompanied by tambourines, a cylindrical drum, and bagpipes. Percussion instruments form the most important constituent of Arabic music, but even before the bagpipes fade Alwyn picks up their melody on the orchestral strings; if there is an incongruity in the counterpoint of the two traditions it goes unnoticed. Tambourines alone continue the rhythm as the scene changes to show Mabrouka being undressed by the women prior to being bathed and anointed in the pool; Alwyn's strings re-enter, in a slower rhythm, again with no sense of inappropriateness. The scene intercuts with a diegetic sequence of a belly dancer performing for the men, to a lute and cylindrical drum. Again the scene shifts to the pool, again back to the dancer. As her father leads Mabrouka into the bridal tent, a mixture of Western strings and folk instruments form a cacophony of sound. The cultural exchange between the two musical traditions is completed. After an intercut scene of horsemen riding through the village, David is led to the tent, to the same musical babble. Now, alone in the tent, David removes Mabrouka's veil, and a full Western romantic lyrical mode returns, in "Arabic" rhythms.

Alwyn's immaculate score for *The Black Tent* was followed by Anthony Kimmin's *Smiley* (1956), a story about a young Australian boy, which was warmly received by the critics, who found it authentic and refreshing. Regrettably, the film is no longer accessible. In keeping with its subject, the orchestra was to be the small chamber Sinfonia of London, which gave Alwyn difficulties of an unexpected kind in "acclimatising myself to a chamber orchestra after the symphonic orchestration that has occupied me recently to the exclusion of all else".[16] By the Autumn of 1956 Alwyn's Third Symphony was finished and performed at the Royal Festival Hall under the baton of Sir Thomas Beecham.

---

[16] Alwyn, "Ariel to Miranda", 67.

The work was well received, given some half-a-dozen further performances, and, Alwyn noted, "since then it has lain on the shelf awaiting a sponsor before the dust settles on it". With its completion came the end of the published diary, an invaluable insight into the pressures on a composer, especially a film composer. "I was the 'slave of music'", notes Alwyn, "and, with music my task-master, I labour on."[17]

[17] Ibid., 84.

24
I Labour On . . .

THUS the following March saw the release of *Fortune is a Woman* (1957), a *film noir* from Frank Launder, critically undervalued in its day and since slighted by its producer Sidney Gilliat, who hated its elements of the whodunnit[1] — which are precisely what sustain the tension. The script is intelligent yet complicated, involving an insurance assessor, Oliver Bramwell (Jack Hawkins), who investigates a fire at a country house where he meets Tracey Moreton (Dennis Price) and his wife Sarah (Arlene Dahl), with whom he has previously had an affair. When Oliver returns to the house alone, he finds Tracey dead and the house set on fire. He marries Sarah, but the mysteries of the house return to haunt them. Characterisation is robust and convincing, and direction polished and inventive.

The film commences with a brief introduction of the main leitmotif over the Columbia and Launder–Gilliat production credits, the six-note love motif reflecting exactly the accented stresses of the phrase "fór-tune-is-a-wó-man":

Launder and Gilliat were unhappy with the title but considered the American title *She Played with Fire* worse. When the film's adapter Val Valentine thought of the perfect title, *Red Sky at Night*, it was too late.[2] For the sake of concordance with the composer's leitmotif, perhaps it was just as well. It is significant that Alwyn was again playing with voice patterning, albeit an *unspoken* voice heard only in the musician's, and hopefully his audience's, head. Later in the film he would experiment in another way.

As soon as the production credits finish, the film swiftly propels the audience into a dream sequence, commencing with the relentless beat of a metronome. One recalls Launder's metronome in the dream sequence of *I See a Dark Stranger*: in neither case is the device's relevance obvious. Probably no more is implied than the "dumb remorseless beat of time", as Alwyn puts it in one of his poems.[3] In *Fortune is a Woman* the rhythm is caught by a car's windscreen wipers, a regular musical beat in which trumpets —

[1] Brown, *Launder and Gilliat*, 139–40.
[2] Ibid., 140.
[3] William Alwyn, "Metronome", in *Winter in Copenhagen* (Blythburgh: Southwold Press, 1971), 51.

— and xylophone predominate, counterpointed by tremolo woodwind and strings. Beyond the car windscreen, the headlamps reveal the heavy doors of a stately home: the music slows broodingly, horns sound menacingly. Soon, the camera zooms through the doorway into the dark interior of the house, up to a painting of the house and through its doorway, like the infinity of a reflection between two mirrors . . . The music becomes ethereal with tremolo strings prominent and (what may or may not be) an ondes martinot is introduced. Alwyn's orchestral score, still extant, is not scored for ondes martinot, and the strange sound is not indicated on the score: nevertheless its success is total as it mounts to a roaring, vibrating climax. Tubular bells, in a gothic-sounding chime —

— join the now crescendoing orchestra, and the sequence ends, as the pictures reach a dead man's hand, *con tutta forza* and with a jangle of bells:

Oliver sits up in bed, screaming. After the nightmare it is a relief to return to the romantic main motif as, under titles, Oliver leaves his bed and washes his face.

Despite his huge output, Alwyn had so far not scored a horror film as such — at this period Hammer films were just beginning to find their métier. But it is quite clear that his special talent for emotionally disturbing musical combinations (one recalls *Your Children's Sleep*, *The Fallen Idol*, *The Rocking Horse Winner*, and others) made him ideally suited to the genre. Nevertheless, his only real horror film would have to wait another five years.

All the same, *Fortune is a Woman* has a good share of heart-racing sequences. When Oliver returns to the deserted house on a moonlit night, tension is built first by the Foley mixer: the kicking of a bucket, feet on creaky stairs. When Oliver discovers faked paintings, music enters gently (***pp***) on woodwind and strings, later joined by the vibraphone. Its regular beat reflects the beating of the heart, crescendoing to a climax when Oliver discovers the dead body of Tracey. From here on Alwyn tells the story (virtually mickey-mousing) in music as Oliver moves about the house, illustrating each move, each fear, each

apprehension. Oliver drops his torch, and violins and violas moving mysteriously up the scale suggest the moon partially obscured by scuttling clouds:

He moves up the stairs, accompanied by music that by its gradual step up the
scale in semitones recalls the moonlit clouds, which we see again in a quick
cut-away:

A little later he detects the smell of a herbal cigarette, Tracey's brand, marked
by the horns —

— and then hears a tiny noise —

and, thinking Tracey is alive after all, calls to him, the music pointing his
cries:

When he detects smoke trails from underneath a door, a fanfare against trilling
strings introduces a new development:

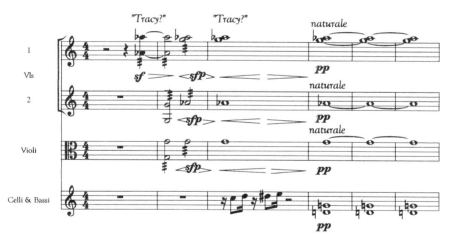

From now on the music illustrates Oliver's efforts to check the fire and call the
fire brigade. As he retreats towards the window the underscore recalls the regular beat associated with the opening nightmare sequence of the windscreen
wipers, and also the "ondes martinot". Oliver leaps from the window — on the
score to a xylophone arpeggio, but mistimed on the soundtrack by a second,
a rare slip-up that Mathieson (as conductor) let pass.

When, later, Oliver returns to the now burnt-out house to search for his wife
Sarah, the score repeats many of the motives of the earlier night sequence. But

at one point he hears the bark of her dog, and as he turns and follows its direction, woodwind imitate the sound, repeatedly:

Reflecting an animal's voice pattern is close to imitating a human voice pattern, and bears comparison with the "come out now" motif Hans Keller praised so highly in *The Ship that Died of Shame*. Alwyn has again achieved the unification of (dog) speech and musical motif — although in the earlier example the motif also preceded the voice. There is another significance in this example, for although he is imitating the dog's voice, Alwyn is still character-led, patterning and enhancing the key moment from Oliver's viewpoint.

The invitation to work on *The Smallest Show on Earth*, in which the leading player is an old picture-house, must have been irresistible for an enthusiastic cinemagoer like Alwyn. Several of his associates were connected with the film: Launder and Gilliat were producers (with Michael Relph), Basil Dearden was director, and John Eldridge collaborated on the script, although he was now in poor health and the major writing was by William Rose Commentators have observed a resemblance with the Ealing comedies, and indeed Relph and Dearden had recently moved on from Balcon, who had turned down an option on the script for reasons that puzzled Relph.[4] Its subject is attractive and amusing, a fantasy about the young couple Matt and Jean (Bill Travers and Virginia McKenna), who inherit a closed-down, ramshackle old Northern flea-pit, the Bijou. With the Bijou comes its ancient ticket lady Mrs Fazackalee (Margaret Rutherford), Old Tom the simple-minded janitor (Bernard Miles), and the alcoholic projectionist Mr Quill (Peter Sellers). Together they decide to reopen the cinema in order to secure a lucrative buy-out from the town's plush Grand cinema.

In a study of Dearden's work within the English comic tradition, Paul Wells has sensed an underlying tension in the film.[5] Wells suggests that *The Smallest Show on Earth* laughs "both with and at" its characters and culture. Laughing "with" the film is a "sociable" form of humour rooted in music-hall traditions, in which the audience identifies and participates. Wells argues, however, that within the changing cultural values of post-Festival England an American-influenced, detached, cynical humour sprang up in which sentiment and nostalgia were "both expressed and mocked". *The Smallest Show on Earth* laughs

---

[4] MacFarlane, *An Autobiography of British Cinema*, 483.

[5] Paul Wells, "Sociability, Sentimentality and Sensibility: Basil Dearden and the English Comic Tradition", in Alan Burton, Tim O'Suillivan, and Paul Wells (eds.), *Liberal Directions: Basil Dearden and Postwar British Film Culture* (Trowbridge: Flicks Books, 1997), 44–5, 50–53.

not only with, therefore, but also at, recognising that in the modern world there is hardly any place for old values or sentimentality. Wells attributes the humour to Dearden, but it may be significant that the American William Rose was largely responsible for the script.

In conspiracy with these tensions is the soundtrack, with music all-important. Thus the reopened cinema's first customer is a small boy, lured in by the sound of a cheap cowboy-and-Indian film: the whine of bullets, horse whinnies, and a breathless rhythm from Alwyn. Rhythm and orchestration closely resemble the main theme of *The Crimson Pirate*, a buccaneering film, proving yet again Alwyn's argument that film music is contextual. The scene ends as the camera tracks into the boy staring entranced at the screen, suggestive of a remembrance of times past. Similar resonances are expressed by the episode of Quill's private screening of *Comin' Thro' the Rye* (1923), accompanied by Mrs Fazackalee playing Alwyn's silent film score on the piano, while Old Tom and the cat view it comfortably from the stalls. In these scenes and in others, including some passionate musical passages as parched victims crawl across the desert (and Old Tom stokes up the boilers to enhance the sales of ice-cream), the music is at the same time both non-diegetic and diegetic — as underscore to scenes on the Bijou's screen, but extended to the "real-life" scenes in the cinema auditorium.

Non-diegetic underscore expresses the composer's evaluation of the Grand and the Bijou. The first sight of the Grand is expressed by a fanfare. But as a fanfare, on a repeated *d'*, it is boring: perfect expression of the impressive, huge, clean, but uninteresting modern architectural lines of the Grand. In contrast, first sight of the Bijou is alarming and vulnerable — a declining clarinet as the camera pans down the building from its globe roof to the pavement below, ending in some trombone diversions and a few emaciated xylophone chords. Alarming, vulnerable, but interesting.

The Bijou even has its own motif. Near the start of the opening titles, this fast rhythmic tune is permitted its solo piccolo — Alwyn's own first instrument and apt for the smallest show on earth. As the closing music it is all-important in stating the film's message. Here, in conjunction with the visuals, it confirms Paul Wells's claim that *The Smallest Show on Earth* represents a transition from sociable and sentimental humour to a cynical denial of its place in modern thinking. The scene works like this: Matt and Jean board a train, and suddenly grasp the significance of Tom's final words, that he burned down the Grand. Their initial instinct is to refund the £10,000 paid by the Grand's management for the Bijou while their cinema is being rebuilt. But after some soul-searching they decide to write — which Jean's voice-over informs us, they did: "We sent him a postcard from Samarkand." Matt and Jean have given way to the modern expedience of the quick buck, have abandoned traditional morality. At this Alwyn introduces a harsh unpleasant brassy chord, darkly cynical. Over the succeeding rolling credits the jaunty Bijou motif sets forth, but the final shot of the Bijou is in gloomy shadow. The juxtaposition of music and image evokes a nostalgia for a bright past (expressed by the music) dichotomised against an unhappy present (expressed by the image). Nor will it escape audiences enjoying the film in a cinema like the Grand, that the Bijou's victory is pyrrhic — the Bijou's demolishment is only postponed, until the day it can be pulled down to make a car park entrance for a rebuilt Grand.

In 1957 there were still plenty of small independent flea-pits, but bowling alleys and bingo were a growing cloud on the horizon. Exhibitors and studios were entwined in a drowning man's clasp, the story of the Bijou's plight (the studios' old comfortable ways) and its threat from the Grand (John Davis's position of veto at Rank) was too close to the filmmakers' own fears — which was perhaps why Balcon turned the script down in the first place. As for Alwyn, if he felt any insecurity or dissatisfaction, for the time being he may have decided — like the Bijou's owners — to take the money and run.

There is a Continental feeling about *Manuela*, which its director Guy Hamilton attributes to "all the films I'd seen in my childhood in France (and shouldn't have seen, because of my age)".[6] There are moments when one could believe one is watching a French or Italian film of the period. Partly this is due to its sensuality, and partly to its unwavering depiction of real working sailors with all their roughness and kindliness — remarkable for a British film and for this period. It is also partly a result of strong characterisation and performances, and the harsh immediacy of Otto Heller's black and white photography. Much is also due to William Alwyn's music.

Based on a novel by William Woods, the narrative is mainly set on a battered old tramp steamer, whose master Prothero (Trevor Howard) is "44 years old and up to the ears in alcohol". When at a South American port, his brutish Chief Engineer Mario Costanza (Pedro Armendáriz) brings on board the seventeen-year-old half-caste girl Manuela (Elsa Martinelli); Prothero becomes infatuated and talks of marriage. But while captain and girl make love below decks, a fire in the hold gets out of control, and the ship is ultimately destroyed. Prothero and Manuela are saved in separate boats, where he finally decides he is too old and set in his ways for marriage.

As composer, Alwyn's role was to create atmosphere, overall dramatic colour, and mood. Partly he achieves this through a highly sensual score, partly by knowing when musical silence serves best. At these times sound-effects alone create a documentary, neo-realist atmosphere. Thus in the opening sequence the captain takes a coffin to shore in a boat, silent except for the sound of a distant siren, and the sound of oars dipping in the water and groaning on

---

[6] MacFarlane, *An Autobiography of British Cinema*, 274.

the rowlocks. In such tightly-observed scenes, much is suggested by the tiniest dramatic gesture: here the quick disapproving side-glance of the sanctimonious Presbyterian mate, Evans (Donald Pleasance), as Prothero lights a cigar. Later, when the crew assemble in their quarters, one of them fails to see the girl. His prattle about "spirituous liquor not being allowed on board . . ." forms a tension almost like music, as his shipmates stare with unbelieving joy at the girl (even less "allowed on board") in their midst.

The balance between music and natural sound is rarely overdone, the matching of speech patterns subtle, the matching of mood changes within a few frames and bars adroit. The script is economical, driving towards a bitter conclusion yet never hurried. Thus a scene where Prothero, drawing on his cigar and brooding on a futile life, begins to realise his attraction towards the girl as he listens to her chatting to an elderly mate. Barely heard snatches of conversation ("do you have tomatoes at home, Miss?") drift through the still night air, mixing with the plaintive main leitmotif on a high solo violin: it is a key scene, yet the moment is almost unbearably poignant. *Manuela*'s characters are defined sufficiently strongly not to require individual motifs. Instead Alwyn depends on a single melodic main motif, which broods thickly and sensually throughout the scenario. Perhaps it is based on a slow tango rhythm, appropriately for a ship sailing from South America and appropriate to this tale of passionate attachment. If so, Alwyn never allows it to gather the momentum of the tango, slow as that dance is. Instead, it assumes slow rhythms and harmonies of bittersweet character, and runs like a thread through the length of the drama, suggestive of bruised, fragile emotions, which contrast with the imagery of the ship's hard ironwork.

At the film's end Costanza lies to Manuela that Prothero is dead, and together the men set off to sea in the night. As Costanza upbraids Prothero — "You should have told her yourself!" — a guitar plucks the motif, reflecting Prothero's heartbreak at his doomed passion: "It wouldn't have changed anything." The theme is taken up by the full orchestra, but finishes quickly as the cast credits fade. It is not unusual in this period for films to end swiftly, but here one is left with a feeling of unresolved passion, dissatisfaction, loss. In this final scene, camera set-up, lighting, dialogue — Costanza's final cry, "Hey Capitano, wait for Mario!" — and music combine in counterfeit of a late-1950s Fellini film, with a score by Nino Rota.

Lewis Gilbert's *Carve Her Name With Pride* (1958) was one of the most popular war films of the 1950s. The very title suggests its reverential treatment of its real-life heroine, Violette Szabo (Virginia McKenna), who after the death of her French husband (Alain Saury) is parachuted into France to fight with the Resistance, caught and tortured, and executed at Ravensbrück. There are no psychological insights: the British are good, the Germans bad. Virginia

McKenna, miscast as the cockney shop-girl, portrays goodness and fortitude but little else. One yearns for some of the passion of Ann Dvorak's performance in *There's a Future in It.*

Alwyn's workmanlike score aptly matches the general tenor of the film with a familiar technique: fanfares announce parachute jumps, descending strings accompany the parachute falls and landings, and a funereal drumbeat follows Violette down the street as she says farewell to her family for the final time. Nor would the accomplished battle sequence have offered any great challenge to Alwyn, with his experience of war documentaries.

But familiarity does not preclude craftmanship. Her courtship, a three-day affair marked by a montage, metamorphoses from a waltz, through rhythmic and key transitions, to pre-echo and merge almost invisibly with Chopin's Prelude no. 15 in D-flat major ("Raindrop", 1838–9). This is played diegetically by her lover in a darkened room. The emotional association of a doomed hero or heroine with a tender piano piece was discovered by Addinsell in *Dangerous Moonlight*, and Alwyn's evocative "Nocturne" for *They Flew Alone* sought a similar effect. His skill at "ethereal" musical effects is called into play, too, in a sequence where Violette is tortured by the enemy to force her to reveal a poem containing the key to the British code. The film pretends the poem[7] was by her dead husband. His voice uttering the verse through an echo chamber is effectively counterpointed by a dual tonality of high violins and brooding ostinato cellos and basses.

José Ferrer's *I Accuse* (1958) was the cinema's fourth attempt to narrate the complicated story of the Dreyfus Affair. A scandal of passion, intrigue, injustice, pathos, and honour, it demands in its portrayal a panache and fire not to be found in this pallid retelling. The story had been handled with more imagination and pace in William Dieterle's award-winning *The Life of Émile Zola* (1937). There, one particular musical sting by Max Steiner stands out. Based on the first phrase of "La Marseillaise", it concludes with a shockingly sharpened final chord as if tarnishing the anthem's honour. Alwyn's title music for *I Accuse* discovers a similar idea: opening fanfares resolve themselves into variations of the same first phrase of the "Marseillaise" in military style (with kettle drums), but flattened and dishonoured. A later phrase from the "Marseillaise" supplies the inspiration for the slow motif that follows (which textually represents Dreyfus's love for his family), and the sequence ends with march variations of the opening theme. From all this it is not surprising to discover the "Marseillaise" as the basis of almost the entire underscore. Since the honour of France is at stake, it is apt but simplistic: would Alwyn have based his motifs for a film about a British scandal on a phrase from "God Save the Queen"?

---

[7] Actually by Leo Marks, then working for the Secret Service.

Nevertheless the score is conscientious and workmanlike, and the film's lack of vitality cannot be attributed to Alwyn. In one particularly accomplished working of musical transitions, the music carries a scene of intense suffering on Devil's Island, changes to a street scene in Paris, is followed by a reunion of Dreyfus with his wife and brother, and (without having paused) concludes with sensitive matching of the emotional interplay between Dreyfus and his wife. In another scene the newspaper proprietor Clemenceau (Peter Illing) is asked for a headline for his lead story. After a moment's thought he suggests "I Accuse". An immediate cut shows newspapers streaming from the presses — with the headline — while the music catches the speech rhythm with a three-note motif.

Speech rhythm appears to form the basis of the title motif of *The Silent Enemy* (1958), too. This competent war film, written and directed by William Fairchild, recounts the attempts by Lieutenant Lionel Crabb (Laurence Harvey) to prevent Italian frogmen from attaching mines to the hulls of British ships at anchor in Gibraltar harbour. It commences with menacing slow brass in fugal patterning, brass answering brass, over sinister frogmen in an inky sea. The three notes commencing the phrase suggest the words "The Si-lent . . .", but the completing motif varies, and never with a simple three notes to complete the spoken phrase ". . . En-e-my". The closest is a two-note phrase ("En-my"?), but a three-plus-four note theme soon predominates, brought in loudly over the title:

This seven-note phrase is subconsciously worrying, for as soon as the brain has echoed the words "The Silent . . ." against the first three notes, the four-note elaboration that follows, which does not quite fit the word "Enemy", suggests the devious, secretive role of the frogman, and perhaps the swirling movement of the sea.

The opening titles are incorporated into a short scene-setter of two Italian frogmen attaching mines to British ships at Alexandria. Within the sequence the title motif, especially the seven-note phrase, becomes the established motif for the Italian frogmen — its unsettling feeling of menace soon to be set against the general, happy and light-hearted motif for the British. As Crabb first visits the quayside he meets his future colleague Knowles (Michael Craig) singing: "In the Atlantic or the Med / Diver, diver, keep your 'ead . . ." Developed by Alwyn, the song is immediately established as the British motif when Crabb takes his first joyous underwater swim into the sea.

Underwater scenes suggest an opportunity for Alwyn's ethereal effects, which he creates in moderation and appositely. In Crabb's first serious underwater dive, to release a mine from a ship laden with explosives, cascading strings and rising woodwind are important, but just as important are the sounds of Crabb's breathing apparatus and the tick of the mine's clockwork timer. In another scene, as a group of divers plunge below the surface, a harp arpeggio emphasises the muffled bubble effect of water against the eardrum. Then, plaintive woodwind and harp with ostinato celesta, and a modest use of strings, are sufficient to express the remoteness of the underwater world.

Subtlety is not a strong point in the musical structure of Roy Baker's *A Night to Remember* (1958), a narration of the *Titanic* disaster based on Walter Lord's history of the same name. Baker does not seem to have had a great interest in the music of his films (his *Morning Departure* reused old library tracks), and, despite *A Night to Remember*'s high production values, it looks as though the composer was called in almost as an afterthought.[8]

It opens well. Baker and his producer William McQuitty were anxious to establish the authenticity of their film, and they start with what purports to be the launch of the *Titanic*. Library shots of a Belfast launch from the 1940s,[9] carefully avoiding any full view of the ship, are intercut with an unconvincing studio set-up of the launch platform, initially over diegetic effects. Only as the ship slips into the water does Alwyn's score, initially ceremonial, mix in. As the pictures dissolve to a ship's view of the horizon at sunset, so the score changes to a broad string passage that glows with the beauty of the sea. All the same, it is undermined by an intensifying sense of foreboding that turns military in its feeling: the rattle of the kettledrum and a plaintive military bugle to end the cue. It is as if Alwyn appears to be setting the scene for a war film. The closing credits are moving: an orchestral arrangement of "Nearer My God to Thee" (Horbury, 1861), recalling the last moments of the ship's tiny orchestra, over shots of assorted flotsam (a rocking-horse, a lifebelt labelled *Titanic*).

Between the outstanding opening and closing cues, and a short fanfare to set the *Titanic* forth on her voyage, Baker — backed by Mathieson as music director[10] — shuns underscore for most of the film's length, as if to validate its "documentary" feel. Music is used solely in four separated cues in which Alwyn repeats the same passage, or something closely similar, to heighten scenes of excitement. Alwyn claimed in his Edinburgh and National Film Theatre lectures later in the year that film music "should be sensed and not predominant

---

[8] However, in his autobiography Baker expresses admiration for Alwyn: "William Alwyn was one of the people I am proud to have worked with. Quiet, sensitive and wonderfully responsive to the style of the film and the varying moods of the scenes within it. And in compete control of the means of expressing them. Mad on cricket. A charming man and a gent." Roy Ward Baker, *The Director's Cut* (London: Reynolds & Hearn, 2000), 62.

[9] In the crowd of shipyard workers a woman in 1940s outfit is a give-away.

[10] Baker, *The Director's Cut*, 103.

— predominant and only sensed".[11] If he is right — and I believe he is — then the first two of these severely obtrusive cues are failures. The third is less so, helped by its introduction on a punctuation point, a general view of the *Titanic* settled low in the water. The fourth cue, chronicling the final moments of the *Titanic*, up-ended and sliding into the water, enters with a sharp chord on a shot of shocked survivors watching from a boat and thus encourages the cinema audience to respond similarly. Without any change of pace in the underscore, the scene cuts to the panic on the decks, to passengers leaping into the sea, and back to the view from the boats, where the Lord's Prayer is recited and to which Alwyn adds an arrangement of "Nearer My God to Thee".

While the excited strings and brass mixed with the cries of the passengers do create a sense of distress and panic, nevertheless the underscore is unnecessarily slavish to the action in these final scenes. One cannot help feel that a depiction of the death throes of the *Titanic* deserves more than a rehash of the previous three cues: it needs music to counterpoint the action, perhaps something ceremonial. After a succession of sharp chords (a musical phrase that in context is hackneyed), the sequence ends as the ship sinks from sight to an absence of music. The roar and clouds of steam is impressive, but not enough: the moment is robbed of its full awesomeness. A ship's final moments were handled better in *The Way Ahead*.

Alwyn felt more comfortable with the Irish ambience of Michael Anderson's *Shake Hands with the Devil* (1959), shot at Dublin's Ardmore Studios and on location. Set in the period of the IRA's guerrilla war against the Black and Tans just prior to the settlement of 1921, the plot recounts how a pacifist American student, Kerry O'Shea (Don Murray), is drawn by events to enrol into an IRA cell led by Sean Lenihan (James Cagney). Much seems authentic: Dublin's seedy back streets, the expansive Wicklow countryside, the IRA soldiers who are depicted as ordinary people fired by patriotism. Even Glynis Johns settles believably into the role of Kitty, a small-town prostitute. It is Cagney's part that goes awry, changing from a surgeon single-mindedly devoted to the Irish cause to a sexually-inhibited psychopathic killer standing against partition. By suggesting that, because of that stand, he was an odd man out, the film denies the core of resistance to the establishment of the Free State in 1921. It thus exposes its political agenda of the 1950s.

The film's affinities with *Odd Man Out* in thematic material, background, and characters, as well as the opportunity to work in the Irish idiom he loved, undoubtedly ignited a spark in Alwyn. He joined the crew and recalled how,

On a shiveringly cold day while on film location in the Wicklow Hills,

---

[11] Alwyn, "Film Music: Sound or Silence", 5.

I sheltered in a ditch with James Cagney. The tough gangster actor whiled away the time by singing Irish folk-songs and ballads for me in the traditional manner of the Irish folk singer, drawing on a seemingly inexhaustible memory. These were taught to him by his grandmother during his childhood on New York East-side. The native ear survived the Atlantic crossing.[12]

The result is a fine composition. The opening cue introduces Alwyn's two main leitmotifs, starting with a brass fanfare counterpointed by a furious woodwind five-note figure: this is the leitmotif representing the Black and Tans, who, as the titles commence, are shown driving a sinister military vehicle along a dark Dublin street. It is only the secondary motif, however, and soon the score shifts to the main motif, later shown to represent the IRA. The theme is a grim repetition of a single seven-note figure, endlessly repeated — in the title sequence slowly against the funereal beat of the timpani. Its basis is said to be an Irish melody.[13]

As much of the film is set in the Wicklow countryside as in the city, and it is here that one would expect a breath of folk music. In one scene O'Shea passes by a colleague sitting in the evening calm, singing "Eileen Oge" (1908), an air by the Irish song-writing partnership of Percy French and Houston Collisson. At the cliff edge he chats with another IRA volunteer, a poet (Cyril Cusack). Alwyn now picks up the song and, by arranging it lightly on barely audible strings, enhances a peaceful and tender atmosphere. Much later Kitty tiptoes at dawn from a guarded light-house, past sleeping IRA volunteers, to a slow arrangement of the same air — on clarinet against contrasting high and low string pedal points, suggesting an "Irish" and plaintive feel to the moment. She walks by the sea, and Alwyn develops the figure, mainly on oboe, in the style of Delius The lightness of touch, both in direction and score, is a delightful confirmation of Kitty's Irishness, winning our affection and deepening our sense of injustice when she is shot as a "traitor" to the cause.

Both lightness and darkness are portrayed in short musical cues. In a short scene near the start, O'Shea is diverted from a lecture by a dove on the window ledge. As the dove flutters down, a clarinet near the top of is register reacts with a flurry, the sound mixed with the cooing of the bird. Soon the cue develops into the main motif on a slow meditative solo violin. The scene is a strange foreshadowing of the film's closing scene. The lecturer, Lenihan himself, now upbraids O'Shea: if he were on the operating table "with my life in your hands, I would not rest easy" knowing a pigeon "would have more of your attention than my exposed inside". In the final scene with Lenihan's inner motivations

[12] Alwyn, "Ariel to Miranda", 33–4.
[13] *New Zealand Film-Music Bulletin*, 52 (Nov. 1985), 9–10.

exposed, his life indeed rests in O'Shea's hands, who does give more attention to the pigeon (peace) and shoots Lenihan dead. In contrasting colour to the dove scene is the sombre cruelty of O'Shea's beating in a prison cell by the colonel of the Black and Tans, Smithson (Christopher Rhodes). With the camera in O'Shea's POV the fist repeatedly thrusts at the lens, the beat marked by a discordant flute and timpani, while between each beat rising timpani and brass heighten the expectation of the blow.

The structure of the film's closing moments compares with *Odd Man Out*. Perhaps the resemblance occurred to Alwyn, whose score stresses the similarities and underlines them with a colour also reminiscent of the earlier film. In *Shake Hands with the Devil*, Lenihan drags the daughter of an English official, Jennifer Curtis (Dana Wynter), to the cliff top to shoot her. As he takes her from the lighthouse, a chord parallels the start of Johnny's painful trek through the snow in *Odd Man Out*. The ensuing funeral marches of both films, with their strong regular timpani beat, are directly comparable. In *Odd Man Out*, Tom and Shell pursue Johnny and Kathleen, while in *Shake Hands with the Devil*, O'Shea and a companion run in pursuit of Lenihan and Curtis. By the time O'Shea catches up with Lenihan, he is joined by other IRA men: their confrontation with the couple trapped against the cliff edge compares with the police facing Kathleen and Johnny trapped against the dockyard railing. At this point there is a difference: O'Shea calls to Lenihan, explains the truce, and there is a dispute. Lenihan calls on his former subordinates to support him, but as the camera cuts from face to face and each refuses, each cut is punctuated by a sharp orchestral chord; in *Odd Man Out* the main theme is unceasing, Kathleen murmurs her farewell to Johnny against the funeral march. Afterwards, however, the films again move in parallel towards their resolutions. Kathleen fires two shots and is answered by the guns of the Royal Ulster Constabulary; Lenihan turns on O'Shea who shoots and kills him first. Anderson's scene is the more melodramatic: Lenihan topples down almost on top of a low angle camera, whereas Reed's characters die off camera. In *Odd Man Out*, there is no pause, the gunshots followed by the mounting roar of a timpani roll. In *Shake Hands with the Devil*, a shocked silence follows. In Belfast the police and Father Tom quickly examine the bodies, again with the underscore in resolution, and the film ends swiftly as Father Tom takes Shell away, the camera panning to the city's ironic clockface; in the South the music resumes as O'Shea examines the body briefly and throws his gun over the cliff edge, the underscore in resolution and a fanfare as a final shot reveals the gun ironically on the sands below.

25

And On . . .

THE paths of Alwyn and Peter Graham Scott had crossed as early as 1942, when Scott was the young editor of *A Modern Miracle* (1942). Scott remembers working with Alwyn after the war on *Proud City*: "Bill and I had to run through each sequence on the Moviola, a rackety and noisy viewing machine then universally used for editing . . . many many times until he had the precise footage and action written down, and impressed on his fertile brain."[1] By the end of the 1950s Scott was carving a successful career in television, but he made a rare return to the cinema to direct a B-picture, *Devil's Bait* (1959). Though cheap, *Devil's Bait* has considerable merit: tight scripting and direction and convincing characters and relationships, in a tense drama of less than an hour's length. Its director now tends to disclaim it — "I've done much better work since"[2] — but Alwyn nevertheless took the trouble to compose an original, meticulous, and well-structured score. The story, an unusual one by Peter Johnston and Diana K. Watson, concerns the baker Frisby (Geoffrey Keen), a gruff, unloving husband to his wife Ellen (Jane Hylton), who takes on the alcoholic rat-catcher Love (Dermot Kelly). As a result of Love's impatience for a drink, cyanide is baked into a single loaf, which is sold on before Frisby and Ellen discover what's happened. There ensues a panicky chase to retrieve the loaf.

This was not Alwyn's first film about rats. His wartime instructional film, *Rat Destruction*, contains a little *moto perpetuo* for woodwind (and no strings). The opening mood of *Devil's Bait* is equally fast, but these rats squeal with clarinet and flute trills, short appoggiaturas, and arpeggios against ostinato strings. A dark mood is created, entirely missing in the earlier documentary, heightened by a dissonance in the woodwind, encouraged by the use of tonics with seconds and sevenths.

In the crucial scene where Love mixes and lays his deadly bait, suspense is tightened by a mixture of musical techniques: low brooding cellos and basses, rising scales, sequencing, trembling dissonant chords, ostinato, pedal points, and rubato. It contains one of the oldest tricks of the cinema, the shock of an unexpected alarm (the baker's wife's dough timer) with the crash as Love drops a saucer in surprise. Sound-effects intelligently enhance the drama of

---

[1] Peter Graham Scott, letter to the writer, 9 June 1998.
[2] Peter Graham Scott, letter to the writer, 3 July 1998.

this second feature throughout. As the rat-catcher Love's landlady discovers his cyanide bottle, a train passes the window; another passes as she pours him a whiskey. Thus the train forewarns of both the danger of the cyanide and the manner of Love's death.

Devil's Bait also contains several scenes of unsettling mental disorientation. One scene finds Love, the worse for drink, all ostinato strings and brass fanfare. As he totters home along a dark road, the strings quicken and mix with the sound of an approaching bus. The jumble of music and effects, and dark and confused pictures, is a good depiction of Love's drunken state. In another scene, Frisby's shock at discovering the label to the cyanide bottle is marked by ostinato celesta chords, counterpointed by rising strings, to climax; his subsequent despondency is appropriately depicted by the same strings declining down the scale.

Scott, who has a developed sense of music, rightly thinks the film is "considerably aided by Bill's deliberately melodramatic score, which 'pongs' the danger of the poisoned loaf very effectively all the way to a quite powerful climax".[3] It is the score that adds structure and screws tension in the final scenes, as a police car carrying Frisby and his wife seeks the young mother Barbara (Eileen Moore), her baby, and her girlfriend Shirley (Shirley Lawrence) on a picnic carrying — unknowingly — the poisoned loaf. The climax comes when Shirley, who has temporarily left Barbara and the child, learns that their bread is poisoned and rushes back to the picnic spot, wading waist-deep through muddy water in her panic. Alwyn saves his climax for when Shirley, all tears and streaming mascara, reaches Barbara and believes her dead. The music stops: in the abrupt silence Barbara (who was merely sleeping) opens her eyes and says "Oh you haven't fallen in!" The striking contrast of the sudden silence after the crescendoing musical climax is one of Alwyn's favourite dramatic devices.

Ken Annakin's Disney production *Third Man on the Mountain* (1959) contains the line: "A man must do what he feels he must do. Or he isn't a man." The cliché distils the message of an intelligent script — by Eleanore Griffin from James Ramsey Ullman's novel — which takes the challenge of a mountain as metaphor for the indomitability of man's spirit.[4] Alwyn's music often suggests subtexts beyond pictorial content, but here he has merely to suggest the power of the mountain for the metaphor to take care of itself. Thus the film opens with impressive views of the mountain wrapped in clouds, and the feeling of menace is suggested by two minor triads bridged by bassoon and low cellos.[5]

Although the struggle, the danger, and the triumph of the climb are a gift

---

[3] Ibid.
[4] The film is of its period in its delineation of gender roles.
[5] Alwyn's three Disney films and *The Running Man* were orchestrated by Mathieson.

to the composer, it could have been only too easy to become carried away by the dramatic tension and overdo the musical charge. Alwyn, however, achieves his effects by a deceptive simplicity, and it is illuminating to compare the complicated themes and motives that accompany Giles's scramble up the mountainside in *Night Without Stars* with the spareness of the struggle of this hero (James MacArthur) through a narrow funnel in the rocks: a repeated four-note rising motif on low strings, interspersed with brass fanfares.

There is a commercial formula to Alwyn's Disney scores. The main motif is based on a title song by a second composer, arranged by Alwyn and incorporated into his own cues. The song can be exploited in sheet music and recordings, and for *Third Man on the Mountain* Franklyn Marks composed a piece entitled "Climb the Mountain".

In his second Disney film for Annakin, Alwyn faced a theoretical ambivalence of style. *The Swiss Family Robinson* (1960) relates Johann Wyss's children's yarn of a shipwrecked family on a deserted tropical island. Desert islands suggest strange and exotic happenings, a child's excitement and wonder, which Alwyn more than adequately evokes. But the family's German Swiss nationality (pointedly established by the furniture and costume) deserves expression, too. The problem is resolved by the Disney formula of importing specially composed numbers: "The Swissapolka" by Bob Jackman (the words by Buddy Baker were only used for the sheet-music sales), arranged by Alwyn for a Christmas dance and an animal race, and the traditional Christmas song "O Tannenbaum".

In addition, Disney provided a special main theme, "My Heart was an Island", with words and music by Terry Gilkyson. Using arrangements of this motif as a framework, Alwyn is free to score at will — in one of those imaginative bravura displays of musical fertility earlier exemplified in *The Crimson Pirate*, in which fluid, spontaneous rhythms suggest comedy, romance, and spectacular adventure. Of special interest is Alwyn's depiction of the animals. One recalls the witty suggestions of animal characteristics by other composers — Saint-Saëns and Sir Malcolm Arnold in their respective *Carnival of the Animals* (1886, 1960), Prokofiev's *Peter and the Wolf* (1936), and Miklós Rózsa's menagerie in Zoltan Korda's *The Jungle Book* (1942). But Alwyn is no less comic, and his score sparkles with animal vignettes. Geese gaggle to a smart staccato jazz rhythm; monkeys swing to a worried oboe and staccato strings; an ostrich speeds around to zipping violins; trembling strings and cautioning brass warn of a prowling tiger; a contrabass (of course) is a fat porker; a huge snake in the water rises and falls with trumpets, then strings and flute; and an overall bitonality makes our flesh creep and crawl at the hidden menace of the jungle.

26
Dark Themes

THE director Michael Anderson's penchant for melodrama, already noticed in *Shake Hands with the Devil*, led in 1961 to almost unanimous critical disdain for *The Naked Edge*. The composer received brickbats too: the anonymous *Guardian* critic wrote of "so insistent a weight of background music",[1] while *Time* magazine observed that the "cellos groan ominously in what ought to be called the film's foreground music".[2] Background, foreground . . . Alwyn's defiantly confrontational cues seem to fly in the face of his maxim that music should be "sensed and not predominant — predominant but only sensed".[3]

Yet Anderson, Alwyn, and photographer Erwin Hillier were simply attempting the fashionable. *Dragnet* had first appeared on American television screens in 1951, compensating for its small black-and-white image with strident dialogue, camera work, editing techniques — and orchestral cues. Since then both small and large screens on each side of the Atlantic had discovered the fast style. *The Naked Edge* also hung onto the coat-tails of Hitchcock's popular *Psycho*, its publicity stressing that the screenplay was by the same writer (Joseph Stefano), and adapting a similar gimmick of refusing admission during the last thirteen minutes of the film. The tale concerns George Radcliffe (Gary Cooper), a businessman whose "killing" on the stock market at the same time as the murder of his employer arouses the suspicions of his wife Martha (Deborah Kerr) and her fear that he plans the same for her. Like its publicity, the plot is gimmicky, and, like *Psycho*, it is built on a confidence trick.

The film's stridency not only contributed to its critical and artistic failure but masks a genuine attempt to explore the couple's relationship. The performances are sensitive: Gary Cooper as Radcliffe portrays a helpless dismay at the suspicions of his wife, played by Deborah Kerr, who herself ranges subtly through the emotions of doubt, fear, despair, panic, and submission; Eric Portman offers a discerning portrait of the real murderer. Where the script fails is in its failure to establish early on the couple's close relationship, for which a single scene would have sufficed. The film's failure to cohere, nevertheless, derives not solely from a script deficiency but partly from a fault in the score.

The Naked Edge is a film about daggers, razors, and the emotional edging

---

[1] The Manchester *Guardian* (26 Aug. 1961).

[2] *Time* (21 July 1961).

[3] Alwyn, "Film Music: Sound or Silence", 5.

forward, little by little, of the two surfaces of a relationship, the breakdown of trust. Alwyn captures well the consistently edgy tone; his underscore is filled with sharp, biting rising chords, brassy interjections, and nonharmonic tones. There are over thirty separate cues in this film: only one is a genuine "sting" (defined as a single chord), but several are remarkably short punctuation — stabbing — cues. But by acceding to the overheightened melodrama, the underscore concentrates too much on separate sequences and insufficiently delineates the broader structure. The main motif to express the relationship between Radcliffe and Martha is poorly defined melodically and lacks prominence where it should be felt.

Nevertheless, there are times when the musical composition suggests deeper feelings where the script offers none. And occasionally a whole drama is worth the few seconds in which its elements fuse in a memorable moment. In this film, it is the moment when Martha's remorse suddenly breaks through as, believing him to be on the other side of the bathroom door, she cries against it "Cliff! Oh Cliff, I'm so sorry. It breaks my heart!" Here Kerr's performance, blended with strings reminiscent of that other female with a broken heart, the ship that died of shame, produces a moment exquisite in its poignancy — only to be ruined by the immediately ensuing melodrama as, together with a loud brass-dominated chord, the door is flung open, and Martha is grabbed by the real murderer, razor between his teeth. Ruined? One winces at the coarseness, but the intrusion of the sharp edge is what this film is all about.

Alwyn professed to prefer moods more subtle than the stridency of *The Naked Edge*. In his lecture of 1958 he commented:

> a function of film music, more obvious because of familiarity, is its use to secure dramatic tension. This has now become rather a commonplace of the television thriller — but you are only too conscious of it because little attempt is made to use it with subtlety. Generally it is a blatant use of the circus performer's drum roll already mentioned, but to me it loses its effect when it becomes a cliché and I know that I am being cheated emotionally by an extraneous device — blowing single dramatic chords which I believe are called, believe it or not — stings.[4]

The Naked Edge cannot be dismissed without reference to a scene where Martha, unknowingly left alone in the house with the murderer, flicks on the television to calm her nerves. Lo! on the screen appears what sounds rhythmically and harmonically like Addinsell's "Warsaw Concerto", and there is Muir Mathieson conducting. But the melody has changed. What we are watching is Alwyn's clever pastiche of Addinsell's pastiche of Rachmaninoff, truly a "worser" concerto. With this music as both diegetic companion and as non-diegetic un-

---

[4] Alwyn, "Film Music: Sound or Silence", 5.

derscore in the style of, for example, Hitchcock's Albert Hall sequence in *The Man who Knew Too Much* (1934), we cut away to a man's feet on the stairs, Martha nervously pouring a whisky in close-up and mixing in water, the man turning on the bathroom hot-water tap, his slow and deliberate cleansing of the razor, his slicing a strip of wide sticky tape, and back to Martha's troubled face. A clever intensification of the drama occurs when Martha nervously switches channels to a football match as the music mounts to a climax, then flicks back again to catch its blazing conclusion. Afterwards she turns off the set altogether and all is ominous silence: dangerous moonlight indeed.

By the early 1960s the horror genre, led by Hammer Films (the "House of Horror"), was well established. Alwyn's talents were ideal for the medium, and it is claimed that some of his music was recycled in the Hammer production *The Abominable Snowman* (1957).[5] But although his contracts had several times touched on the supernatural, only Sidney Hayers's *Night of the Eagle* (1962) was in the true Gothic medium.

The Gothic genre has a long history. At the turn of the nineteenth century it was popular enough to be ridiculed by Jane Austen in *Northanger Abbey* (1818) and to sustain several "Gothick" melodramas on the stage. Some of the musical devices from that period are to be discovered in film-music techniques. They have been usefully summarised by David Huckvale,[6] who isolates: very short phrases, fragments of melody, "agitated semi-quaver figures", ostinati, and sequencing. These techniques are common enough in Alwyn's filmscores, especially in his depiction of scenes of melodrama, terror, or tension, while Huckvale's reference to "dialogue to be declaimed over recitative-style accompaniment" has obvious affinities with Alwyn's matching of underscore to speech patterns.

It is not surprising to discover these techniques in Alwyn's contribution to *Night of the Eagle*, an excursion into the occult within the suffocating confines of academia. The opening title sequence illustrates the first three of the techniques described by Huckvale: short phrases, fragments of melody, and fast agitated figures. Against the image of a single staring eye, a nine-note fanfare is followed by a short ascending and descending motive on woodwind, swept away by mounting strings in a mysterious wind-like figure, the main theme. It is repeated, but the colour of the passage changes with the introduction of two continuous single vibraphone notes, in a minor second interval, to suggest

---

[5] Randall D. Larson, *Music from the House of Hammer* (Lanham: The Scarecrow Press, 1996), 15. *The Abominable Snowman* was also a title transmitted on ITV on 8 October 1955 in the television series *Colonel March of Scotland Yard*, produced by Panda Productions and scored by Alwyn.

[6] David Huckvale, "Hammerscore", *Journal of Popular British Cinema*, 1 (1998), 116–17.

the passage of time or suspense. This grows in dynamics as woodwind join in, until a dissonant six-note brass phrase (minor second chords) intercedes, with a response by deep cellos and basses. Again the windy string ascent returns, but before it can be repeated it is joined now by an asymmetric orchestral beat, the breath-stopping opening of "Mars" from Gustav Holst's *The Planets*. The brass repeat their scratchy phrase, the vibraphone rejoins, and a distant fanfare sounds, echoed nearby by a plaintive violin. It need hardly be said that the whole passage is casting around for a tonal centre.

In another sequence, the ingredients of ostinato and sequencing from Huck-vale's menu are represented. The professor's wife Tansy (Janet Blair) searches for a protective charm she has misplaced. She finds it by spinning the shade of a table lamp that seems to ignite in a blaze of sparks. To this Alwyn sets a passage reminiscent of the scene in *Daybreak in Udi*, where men, dressed as the spirits of the dead, attack at night. What passes for a strong African beat there becomes here the powerful yet nervous beat of the heart, rising in climax as a ten-note phrase is sequenced, accompanied by a strong ostinato rhythm, first on strings, but taken up by the timpani until reaching a climax as the spell flares. The power of the passage is intensified by an overall textural complexity of instruments and phrasing

The *Dies irae* (Latin for "day of wrath"), a thirteenth-century plainsong forming part of the Requiem Mass, has been seized on by several composers — Liszt, Berlioz, Rachmaninoff, Prokofiev, and Saint-Säens, among them — to represent the horror of death following a life of sin. In the cinema the musical sequence has been a fertile source for horror scenes, although in Ingmar Berg-man's *Det sjunde inseglet* (*The Seventh Seal*, 1957), which is set in the period of the Black Death, its diegetic chant is an appropriate historic context. There is a suggestion that Alwyn's use of the theme in *Night of the Eagle* is amongst the earliest in the horror genre.[7] His working of the motif, which is by no means straightforward, occurs when the main character, Professor Norman Taylor (Peter Wyngarde), reaches a lonely sea setting where his wife intends to commit suicide. Panicking because he cannot find her, and the midnight hour of her doom approaching, he ransacks the house for light to search the clifftops. Throughout Alwyn has often used musical sequencing to raise tension. With variations, a frequent sequence has been

etc

Now, as Taylor searches, a descending four-note scale on the vibraphone is caught up by the strings, which is a phrase from the sequence in retrograde:

---

[7] Larson, *Music from the House of Hammer*, 25.

etc

The notes are preparation, for suddenly Taylor sees a book opened at a chapter entitled "The Devil", and — developing the preceding passage — Alwyn's arrangement from *Dies irae* enters loudly and startlingly —

— but combined with the brutal ostinato of Holst's opening passage of "Mars, the Bringer of War", famous for its threatening and uncanny vibrations, and briefly established earlier in the film. The frightening counterpoint continues as Taylor discovers a black magic spell to save his wife. In a flurry of wild strings and brass, Taylor struggles across cliffs, rocks, and sands towards the cemetery. Xylophone chords repeat the *Dies irae* in the interval of the tritone, the *diabolus in musica*; and the theme is repeated several times until making a final call after the midnight chime as Taylor recalls Tansy from the dead. Holst's "Mars" passage also makes its last appearance as Taylor releases a significant recording tape from her fingers, before bearing her away to a heavy repetitive thud of the orchestra tutti in the main theme.

Musical suggestion is one of the most powerful components of the horror film. In *Night of the Eagle* Alwyn often cuts across his rising suspenseful moments with a climax of musical silence, a favoured technique dating back at least to *Desert Victory*, and appropriately more frequent here than in probably any other film. The underscore also at times interiorises Taylor's thought processes, even to influencing plot development in one scene. Here, Tansy, sick after her recent recall from the dead, becomes possessed again and rises from her bed as Taylor slumbers in an easy chair. She takes a kitchen knife and proceeds towards the bedroom. Accompanying is a reiterated asymmetric three-note syncopated theme,

sequencing and forcibly inflaming the tension. She enters the bedroom and stabs an empty chair: Taylor has awoken and he switches on the light. As Tansy, knife raised, approaches him, he sees that she has taken on a heavy limp similar to that of club-footed Flora (Margaret Johnston), the school secretary. A sequenced two-note appoggiatura rhythm, a shortening of the previous three-note motive, limps in time to her dragged foot. Taylor overcomes Tansy in the ensuing struggle, but after he has returned her to bed, his recall of the limp and its link with Flora (now revealed as the witch who possesses Tansy) is depicted by his close-up in deep thought coupled with the return of the two-note motive. Only the music, however, can confirm his mental process. Subsequently, in variation, it insistently reiterates the message as he prepares to expose Flora.

27
Endings

V ery different from *Night of the Eagle* was Alwyn's final work for Disney, recorded at the beginning of March 1962. His first plan for *In Search of the Castaways* (1962) was a chorus "sung like a sea shanty",[1] based on Richard M. and Robert B. Sherman's main theme "Castaway". The plan was later abandoned in favour of an orchestral arrangement, but it was a sensible one for what was billed as "Jules Verne's fantasy-adventure". It is a tale of a young girl, Mary Grant (Hayley Mills), who sets off with her brother Robert (Keith Hamshere), the eccentric Professor Paganel (Maurice Chevalier), and Lord Glenarven and his son John (Wilfred Hyde-White and Michael Anderson jr respectively) in search of her lost sea-captain father.

As in earlier whimsical yarns such as *The Crimson Pirate* and *The Million Pound Note*, Alwyn's music track is brim-full with fertile inventiveness, spontaneity, and energy. Thus the sequence in which our characters are hurtled on a toboggan-like boulder down a snow slope is accompanied by brassy circus music. When their rocky carriage enters an icy tunnel, with delicate glass-like stalactites and stalagmites, an echoing trumpet sounds a fanfare (based on the "Castaway" motif), which gives way to light bells when Paganel tests the echo with his yodel. Re-emerging from the tunnel, the circus refrains leap in again on a breathlessly fast piccolo solo — until the party crash and, via some Latin American chords as they pick themselves up, gives way to a "palm court" waltz when a giant condor takes Robert off. Or there is the short but humorous sequence of crotchety Lord Glenarven dubiously tasting an omelette concocted by Paganel to a halting bassoon and tremulous strings, a sequence that is nothing without its musical score. Just as impressive is the Viennese waltz accompanying Robert as, held by a home-made rope around his feet, he swings upside down across a wide and frighteningly deep chasm.

Apart from "Castaway", the Shermans composed three other songs, all except one incorporated by Alwyn into the underscore. There are also sequences of natural native chanting. The music track thus presents a rich diversity, to which Alwyn's score, consciously and artfully moulded, contributes the major share.

Alwyn evidently found satisfaction in layering his filmscores with meaning,

---

[1] Alwyn's note to Mathieson on the sketch. Alwyn Archive.

enjoying this influence over a film's emphasis. Of a different genre from *In Search of the Castaways*, but permitting a similar fluidity, was Michael Relph and Basil Dearden's *Life for Ruth*. The team have become known for their socially aware films: postwar social changes in *The Ship that Died of Shame*, the dichotomy between old and new values in *The Smallest Show on Earth*; and, in films with which Alwyn was not concerned, juvenile delinquency (*The Blue Lamp*, 1950), racial prejudice (*Sapphire*, 1959), and homosexuality (*Victim*, 1961). The subject of *Life for Ruth* is of minority interest, the torment of the husband and wife John and Pat Harris (Michael Craig and Janet Munro), forbidden by their religious scruples to permit a blood transfusion that will save their eight-year-old daughter's life. As a result their marriage is devastated and the husband charged with manslaughter.

In an outstanding analysis,[2] Brian McFarlane differentiates Dearden and Relph's films from their "new wave" contemporaries such as *Saturday Night and Sunday Morning* (1960) or *A Taste of Honey* (1961). He suggests that their narrative structures, including "set-pieces" such as the court scene in *Life for Ruth*, place them closer to the genre of American melodrama. Such melodramatic structuring is underlined in *Life for Ruth* by its "boldly polarised performances . . . a turbulent score by William Alwyn, [Otto] Heller's often striking low-key lighting, [Alex] Vetchinsky's skill in creating an oppressive production design, and John Guthridge's eloquent cross-cutting".[3]

It suggests teamwork, Alwyn's preferred method. Early on, probably after a discussion with Dearden or a first viewing, he pencilled out his two leitmotifs on a scrap of manuscript paper.[4] "Theme A" he called "Conviction of Belief Theme", "Theme B" expressed "Bewilderment . . . Love . . . and conflict". As an afterthought between "Bewilderment" and "Love" he added "Mother". For Pat, the mother, who has adopted her husband's beliefs but whose roots are in non-literal Anglicanism, attempts too late to reverse the withholding of the transfusion and is divided between her grief for her daughter and her love for her husband. Thus in his two themes Alwyn distils the major, and conflicting, emotional elements of the film.

The conflict is stated in the opening titles. The film starts with a scene of crashing waves, over which a brief passage from Theme B is heard. But very quickly Theme A makes itself known, gravely and religiously moving as the camera, firm on the rock of the cliff top, pans across the seascape:

---

[2] Brian McFarlane, "*Life for Ruth*: Con/Texts", in Burton, O'Sullivan, and Wells, *Liberal Directions*, 203–12.

[3] Ibid., 210.

[4] Alwyn Archive.

But as soon as the camera reaches the grey houses of the city (Durham) with all its possibilities of alternative — or lack of — religious observances, Theme B reasserts itself:

Alwyn's choice of these two themes is imaginative. McFarlane identifies Theme A as an arrangement of the fundamental chorale from Bach's cantata *Ein feste Burg ist unser Gott* (*A Mighty Fortress is Our God*, BWV 80, 1727–31, rev. *c*.1744–7), but that seems incorrect. A closer identification is with a chorale motif used in a funeral motet by Johann Hermann Schein (1586–1630), *Mach's mit mir Gott nach deiner Güt* (1628), moved from D major to the mournfully "wrong" key of C major,

In some English hymnals the tune is identified as *Eisenach*, to be used with the words of Francis R. Havergal's hymn "Lord, speak to me that I may speak" (1872).[5] Theme A is most often used to represent the unyielding fundamentalism of John, the father, and against his brief sketch Alwyn has noted "Diatonic".

The anguished Theme B, however, with its non-traditional form that shakes the rigidity of Theme A, is, as Alwyn also notes, "based on 12 tone series". Oddly, nobody noticed, and it became almost a private cryptogram, which provided Alwyn with some amusement. Even Muir Mathieson, the music director conducting the Sinfonia of London, failed to spot the cipher.[6]

It is interesting to observe that Doctor Brown (Patrick McGoohan) the third protagonist of the film, the non-believing doctor who pursues John to the court, is offered no leitmotif at all; thus his attitude is objectified, seen as scientific and almost unemotional.

The team craft elements integrate to heighten the film's emotional impact. McFarlane, who is sensitive to the contribution of the composer, contrasts two

---

[5] Several lines from Havergal's verse, based on Isaiah, are remarkably apt. For example, "Lord, speak to me, that I may speak / In living echoes of Thy tone; / As Thou has sought, so let me seek / Thy erring children lost and lone. / . . . O strengthen me, that while I stand / Firm on the Rock, and strong in Thee, / I may stretch out a loving hand / To wrestlers with the troubled sea. / . . . O use me, Lord, use even me, / Just as Thou wilt, and when, and where; / Until thy blessed face I see, / Thy rest, Thy joy, Thy glory share."

[6] "Writing Music for Films", William Alwyn interviewed by Ken Emrys Roberts, BBC Third Programme, 25 Feb. 1964

illustrations.[7] In the scene in which Dr Brown first announces the need for the transfusion, the camera moves from a three-shot to track in to John's face in close-up, thus — as John refuses the transfusion — emphasising the separateness between the doctor and the father. Subsequent cutting, framing Brown and Pat together and John by himself, also suggests that Pat will later find difficulty in standing by John's faith. The scene is conducted in musical silence, which, as McFarlane points out, "heightens the melodramatic power of the moment". McFarlane's second example occurs towards the end of the film, after the verdict is given of "not guilty" and the court clears. John suddenly shouts from the dock "No, I'm guilty!", realising that he had believed a miracle would save Ruth's life. As he finishes and bows his head the music crashes in melodramatically over Pat's face in helpless pain. The device is the reverse of the one we have several times noticed, of cutting off the music in climax to a melodramatic shout: here the music cuts in shockingly *after* the speech is narrated in an absence of music. In such intensely melodramatic moments, McFarlane applauds "the deployment of a range of the cinema's narrational strategies, in which the verbal is but one".[8]

But, of course, by isolating Alwyn's film music, a single element of the craft structure, his cinematic achievement has been acknowledged throughout this study. *Life for Ruth* is rich in such moments. After Pat, unknown to John, begs the doctor to give the transfusion, Brown brings her home in his car. We hope that Ruth has been saved — but the underscore, a funeral march, suggests otherwise, just as a funeral march towards the end of the film warns of John's attempt at suicide. In the earlier scene, the music ends with the car door slam. As Pat enters the house, John's shadow passes across her as he comes down the stairs, and his reception of the news of Ruth's death, still on the stairs, again emphasises their separation. When the real funeral is depicted, it is in the absence of music, cold and brief.

In a film of disturbing dialectic, the final resolution is of paramount importance. The core of the argument is that John's tenacious belief takes precedence over his wife. Thus, when Pat pleads with him to take on legal council rather than to conduct his own defence, he ignores her. However, when his father points out that "You are not the only one to be tried, it's everyone who believes as you do, we are all on trial", the argument is settled, stressed by the underscore which enters with Theme A in ceremonial form. When Pat balks at a chapel service in Ruth's memory, John chooses chapel rather than her, the choice again underscored by Theme A. By the film's ending John's faith has been so considerably undermined that he attempts suicide, from which he is rescued

---

[7] McFarlane, "*Life for Ruth*", 207.

[8] Ibid., 210, quoting David Bordwell, *Narration on the Fiction Film* (Madison: University of Wisconsin Press, 1985), 57.

by Brown. Three key statements follow. Brown advises him to "find your God again, and this time don't load him with the whole responsibility"; John says he cannot stay with Pat because "Ruth will always stand between us"; and Pat will not follow him, saying "If he's going to come back, he must come by himself". John makes his way to the cliffs overlooking the scene where Ruth was injured. He inherited his belief from his father, and he from his father before him: now the lighthouse of which his father is the keeper reflects its light over the town and across a group of children playing at the town's edge. As a symbol the light-house traditionally offers Christian salvation for souls in distress. When John looks into the sea the score turns again to Theme A ("Lord speak to me . . ."), the tone ominous, a camera shot from behind hinting that he may yet throw him-self off the cliffs. But the music calms, strings entering in colour contrast to the preceding brass; murmuring "Ruth", John looks to the sky, and the underscore confirms that his faith is reaffirmed and he believes that Ruth is safe in Heaven. He glances at the children playing in the street, a statement of affirmation, and turns back towards the town, passing the children, the lighthouse still casting its light across the town. Theme A now resolves positively to a brassy church style. The combination of lighthouse, children, editing, and acting contributes to the affirmatory conclusion to *Life for Ruth*. But it is especially the underscore that informs us that — whatever opinions we may hold — John has rediscovered his faith and his self-confidence, and is returning to his old values, and "by himself" perhaps to Pat.

After his significant contribution to *Life for Ruth,* Alwyn could have expected a similarly rewarding relationship when he rejoined Carol Reed for *The Run-ning Man*. It was ironic, therefore, that Reed was at a low creative level. It was not for the lack of a gifted team: Reed himself, John Mortimer (who adapted Shelley Smith's original novel), Krasker, and Alwyn. In his biography of Reed, Nicholas Wapshott suggests that Reed had received a severe bruising from Marlon Brando over the direction of *Mutiny on the Bounty* (1962), which left him suffering from a crisis of self-confidence, and dithery.[9]

Most of the film was shot on location in Spain. It tells the story of Rex (Lau-rence Harvey), a commercial pilot who fakes his death by crashing his plane in order to make an insurance claim. In Spain, he is joined by his wife Stella (Lee Remick) and also by an insurance investigator, Stephen (Alan Bates), whom he suspects of following them, although Stella is romantically drawn to him. Rex attempts to murder Stephen but dies in another plane crash as he escapes from the police. The film lacks tension, and its gaudy photography lacks atmos-phere; its positive virtues lie in its subtext about national culture and personal

---

[9] Wapshott, *The Man Between*, 317–18.

relationships, suggested largely through the script and the musical score (again orchestrated by Mathieson).

Once the action crosses to the continent, the accumulation of warm continental musical rhythms, one virtually after another, creates a hard structural break with the earlier English environment as well as imposing local atmosphere through a succession of national clichés. The device is common enough, used famously with the calypso sequence of *The Rake's Progress*, while Reed believed decaying post-war Vienna could be evoked by a zither tune in *The Third Man*. The clichés commence in Paris, with a predominant accordion solo, and in Spain are represented by a Spanish brass band, a Spanish guitar, and three different forms of dance music (of which the latter two are more Italian than Spanish in harmonies). Apart from the band, no visual musical sources are depicted, but loud dynamics imply their presence somewhere off-camera. Thus while the music is not exactly diegetic, neither is it underscore.

The regional music reinforces the subtext. First, Reed appears to attempt to distinguish between a more simple native Spanish culture and the flashy, shallow style of the tourists and expats. Thus, when Stella arrives at the airport and waits for Rex, Alwyn's original notes for "lively and gaudy" music as from a loudspeaker[10] were abandoned for a Spanish guitar solo, reflecting her aloneness and the germ of her later separation from Rex. When shortly afterwards she is swept into a lively cocktail party, with Continental-sounding muzac, the contrast is startling. The dichotomy between the simple native Spanish ways and the influx of moneyed foreigners becomes a reflection of Rex's growing obsession with money and his mounting recklessness. Rex lacks sympathy with anything Spanish, except once where it coincides with his own interests: two boys pull him into a bullring and rehearse a bullfight. Alwyn introduces a rhythmic bullring atmosphere while Rex struts and boasts that "They make a fortune these bullfighters, thousands and thousands of pounds. You know what? They don't do it for the money. They do it to show all these stupid people that they just don't care!"

More representative of the contrast between the cultures is a scene where local gypsies dance near to where Rex, Stephen, and Stella sit drinking. Suddenly all quietens. "Gypsies with television", sniggers Stephen as the gypsy guitarist stares bemusedly at ballroom dancers on the screen. Stephen asks Stella to join him for a slow foxtrot. The scene is significant, and introduces the film's second message, a statement about the institution of marriage. Rex, Stella's supposedly dead husband, has assumed a new identity in Spain — and now she must pretend not to be his wife. "I don't know who I'm married to", sighs Stella. And the theme of marriage is always present. In a pivotal scene Stephen and Stella enter a church, where a wedding mass is being conducted. The authentic wed-

---

[10] *The Running Man*, music summary. Alwyn Archive.

ding song, sung in guttural Spanish by a boys' choir, becomes the foundation of a musical motif to represent the love of Stella and Stephen, and it dominates the remainder of the film.

When they leave the church a plaintive guitar picks up the song while they talk of Stella's marriage to Rex. As the mood swerves to their own relationship, a solo violin takes up the motif. Thus the motif is transformed from a sturdy indigenous hymn, to "Hollywood" kitsch; perhaps in a film that has more than enough directorial kitsch, the lapse may pass. From this moment onwards, the motif — and Alwyn takes care to reduce its saccharine content later — is a strength of the film, continually reinforcing Stephen's and Stella's attraction to each other.

The film ends as Stella watches a police launch take away the body of her husband. It is unclear from Mortimer's script whether her relationship with Stephen will be cemented. Yet the audience may be certain, for the underscore is the love motif.

Reed's lack of confidence showed in his choice of title music. His original opening sequence was substituted by silhouetted graphics in imitation of the James Bond box-office success *Dr No* (1962). Alwyn's title score disappeared too, to be replaced by a jazzy composition by Ron Grainer, an Australian composer new to the film scene. The replacement gives every wrong signal about the nature of the ensuing drama. The film is destabilised from the first frame.

28
Utopian Sunset

A LWYN may have regarded the scrapping of his title music to *The Running Man* as a quid pro quo of working for the film industry. Perhaps, though, it was a blow to his pride in a stressful employment, which he was coming to think he no longer needed. It was time to get out; the pop titles of *The Running Man* were the writing on the wall: pop, jazz, and electronic underscores were proving that expensive orchestras could be dispensed with. The classic film with the large orchestral music track was about to be eclipsed.

In any case he was becoming severely depressed. Relationships at home had been tense, and in the spring of 1963,[1] on his doctor's advice, he left his family and moved to Blythburgh, a small village on the Suffolk coast, where he settled in a newly-built house called "Lark Rise", evoking both his mother's birthplace in Flora Thompson's countryside and Vaughan Williams's *Lark Ascending*. There his grand piano was housed in a custom-built soundproofed studio, facing away from the window because he thought the bleak beauty of the river estuary would distract him from his work. To balance his reduced income, his collection of Pre-Raphaelite pictures, then unfashionable and acquired for comparatively minute sums, were auctioned at Sotheby's. Doreen Mary Carwithen set up house with him changing her surname to "Alwyn" by deed poll, pending their marriage in 1975 after William's divorce.

Carwithen was seventeen years junior to Alwyn, whom she had met as a student of his composition classes at the RAM. She was a composer of talent; two of her early pieces included an exquisitely lyrical First String Quartet (1945) and the colourful *ODTAA Overture* (1945). In 1948 she was chosen as one of two RAM representatives under a new scheme to train students in writing for film, and she spent three days a week at Denham with Mathieson. In time she contributed to over 30 films in some way or another, including full scores for Anthony Darnborough's *Boys in Brown* (1949), described by Antony Hopkins as "a score of which even William Alwyn would not be ashamed",[2] and Wendy Toye's *The Stranger Left No Card* (1953), which won a Cannes Film Festival award. She assisted Adrian Boult in arranging the score for ABPC's official film of the Coronation, *Elizabeth is Queen* (1953). In addition she claimed to have

---

[1] In *Winged Chariot*, 21–2, Alwyn charts an impossible chronology for the years 1961–3. He was notoriously unreliable about dates, and I have assumed a more likely time-scheme.

[2] Anthony Hopkins, "Music", *Sight and Sound*, 19:3 (May 1950), 127.

made several unacknowledged contributions, including help with Arnold Bax on his score for Lean's *Oliver Twist* (1948), and the composition of the "Spanish Dance" in David Macdonald's *Christopher Columbus* (1949) for which Arthur Bliss wrote the underscore.[3]

Once recovered, Alwyn set to work again, but with his film work behind him he had time for prose, poetry, and painting[4] — different ways of expression. For a few years he devoted himself to realising his dream of writing opera. Alwyn was convinced that the composer should also write his own libretti, matching his own text to music, avoiding too many sibilants, overcoming the need for programme notes and soliloquies, and using techniques of voice rhythm and inflection he had explored in his film compositions. His effort culminated in the five-act *Juan, or The Libertine* (1965–71) and the two-act *Miss Julie* (1973–6).

He took breaks in his opera composition to write and translate poetry, paint, and compose other works, importantly his Concerto Grosso no. 3 (1964), a Sinfonietta for strings (1970), which he later felt should have been called "Symphony no. 5", an actual Fifth Symphony (*Hydriotaphia*, 1972–3) — a one-movement work in four sections — and a second String Quartet (1975). He took an interest in the Suffolk music scene, and a song-cycle set to his own poems, *Mirages* (1970), was performed at Snape.

In 1979 *A Leave-Taking* (1978) for tenor and piano, composed for Anthony Rolfe Johnson, was performed at Aldeburgh. Alwyn planned it as his own leave-taking, a farewell to musical composition: osteoarthritis in his right hand made the writing of musical scores increasingly painful and difficult. He said he did not mind: he was engrossed in his oils and chalks. Alwyn had always had a sharp visual sense, inherited from his family and revealed in his film work. In his youth he had studied, as he said, "unofficially"[5] at the Slade School. Now he was happy for painting to take over his life.

It was a mental relief, too. He had been deeply disappointed at being passed over as president of the RAM, with the knighthood that came with it, and although the award of a CBE in 1978 was some recompense, he continued to fret that his work had not been sufficiently recognised. His "leave-taking" was premature, however, and a few more works followed — he could not help himself. In April 1981 he suffered a stroke, but recovered in time to accept an honorary degree of Doctor of Music from the University of Leicester. Then, during the Aldeburgh Festival in 1985, Sir Peter Pears arranged the first performance of Alwyn's new Third String Quartet (1984) at nearby Blythburgh Church in

---

[3] Mary Alwyn, in conversation with the author.
[4] And cricket. Alwyn had a lifetime's enthusiasm for cricket, stemming perhaps from the proximity of his childhood home to the local cricket-ground. He loved to listen to matches on the radio — tolerated by Mary Alwyn, who regarded them as a feat of the listener's imagination.
[5] Vanson, "Profile No. 13: William Alwyn", 6.

"A Celebration of William Alwyn's 80th Year". Not long afterwards, on 11 September, Alwyn died from a tumour on the brain.

To an extent Alwyn was a self-made person: he had no family background in music, no benefit of a public school education, and no contacts in the film world. There was luck, of course, but he happily combined a real musical gift with an intelligent adeptness at everything he attempted, and there was also something attractive about his personality: McEwen became a firm friend and gave him a prestigious appointment when he was only 21, and Rotha took to him and offered him one contract after another following his first lucky film chance.

By survivors of those best of times in British films he is remembered with affection. Alwyn was no musical snob; he fitted in, and he respected fellow craftsmen. In return, he earned respect not only as a composer (an awe-inspiring profession) but also as a superb technician. It is what John Huntley, who worked with Alwyn on several major features including *Odd Man Out*, admired him for.[6] On the other hand, the musician Trevor Hold suggests that "for Alwyn writing music for films was musical journalism, no more, no less".[7]

Technical proficiency, yes; journalism, yes — surely two sides of the same coin — and also versatility. A versatility that enabled him, in the company of only the most gifted of film composers, to get to the heart of his films, whether they were destined for working-class halls (*The Cure for Love*), had serious pretensions (*Odd Man Out*), or were simply rubbish (*Saturday Island*).

With versatility came an unfailing ear for rhythm: whether the rhythm of music, the spoken word, or the edited moving image. He had a talent for invention, for individuality, for the use of radical devices in an unobtrusive way. In his concert works he constantly self-reviewed and self-renewed, with an inevitable influence on his cinema style — as musical interpretation of the film text, *Life for Ruth* is as rewarding as *Odd Man Out* (superb as that is) ten years earlier.

There was another gift: a gift of taste and good proportion. A piece of music, poetry, writing, sculpture, architecture, painting — whatever art form — demands proportion, a correctness, a sense of form. So too does the moving image, whether a thirty-second sequence or a three-hour feature. Alwyn understood this, and 99% of the time his sense of proportion between picture and music was judged to a nicety, despite the constrictions and pressures of the industry, the deadline, and earning a living.

As Hugh Ottaway appositely puts it, Alwyn was " by nature both an aesthete and an artisan".[8] It was as the *aesthete* that he reviewed his life "as a long search

---

[6] Huntley, interview, 13 May 1998.
[7] Hold, "William Alwyn — A Profile", 8.
[8] Hugh Ottaway, "William Alwyn", in Stanlie Sadie (ed.), *The New Grove Dictionary of Music and Musicians*, 1st edn (London: Macmillan, 1980), 300.

for the meaning of beauty, that elusive quality which like Daphne to Apollo is just within one's grasp but always escapes the clutch, the quality of which motivates all my creative efforts".[9] Alwyn searched for beauty in his concert works, his poetry, and his paintings. Would it have surprised him to learn, however, that his cinema audience, the *hoi polloi* in the one-and-ninepennies, could also discover that elusive beauty through the magical fusion of his music with pictures and text? Could it be that by giving of his best as an *artisan* that his craftsmanship passed into a major contribution to the collective *art* of the cinema?

A montage of memories passes through my mind: sunlight on the Thames before the tragic night of *Fires Were Started*; an "ordinary" sailor and girl kissing farewell in *Our Country*; the exhilaration of the kestrel's flight in *Great Day*; the anguish of a child in *Your Children and You*; Bridie's dark walk in *I See a Dark Stranger*; the chillingly lovely countryside of *Captain Boycott*; Kathleen's uneasy parting from Johnny in *Odd Man Out*; a brief encounter between a small boy and two unhappy lovers in a teashop in *The Fallen Idol*; the slapstick timing of *The History of Mr Polly*; the diabolism of a child's rocking horse; the high jinks of *The Crimson Pirate*; the feminine Ship that Died of Shame; Mandy's hesitant steps into the great world; and so many evocations of meaning and emotion illuminated by Alwyn's music.

To the complex coalescence of talent that is sound film Alwyn brought flair, intelligence, imagination, and an immaculate attention to detail. He discovered the techniques of submerged persuasion and meaning, he pioneered a grammar of film composition, and — yes — he created an art form.

That is the achievement of William Alwyn. Recognition is overdue.

---

[9] William Alwyn, unidentified lecture (MS in Alwyn Archive, *c.*1975).

Glossary of Musical Terms

[Cross-references within this glossary are indicated by SMALL CAPITALS.]

acciaccatura. a short APPOGGIATURA.

appoggiatura. an unaccented ornamental extra ("grace") note struck almost simultaneously with the main note or chord.

arpeggio. the notes of a chord played in succession instead of simultaneously.

atonality. without the traditional tonal key. Systematised by Schönberg in TWELVE-TONE (SERIAL) TECHNIQUE.

cadence. a progression of chords to convey a feeling of rest or closure at the end of a musical sentence.

cadenza. an opportunity for the soloist to show off while the orchestra remains in silence.

canon. a melody stated in one instrument exactly imitated and overlapped by one or more other instruments.

chromatic scale. a scale entirely of the twelve semitones in an octave (i.e. including all the black and white notes of the piano); see DIATONIC SCALE.

coda. a flourish added to the end of a passage to round it off.

colour. also called "timbre" or "tone-colour"; the sound quality of different instruments.

con sordini. "with mutes"; for example, on strings a mute is clipped to the bridge of the instrument to reduce the vibrations and produce a muffled, "nasal" tone; a mute is placed in the bell of wind instruments such as trumpets and horns, altering the timbre.

con tutta forza. with all force the musician can muster.

concord. CONSONANCE; opposite of DISCORD.

consonance. a chord producing a pleasant effect suggesting stability and harmony; opposite of DISSONANCE.

contrapuntal. pertaining to COUNTERPOINT.

counterpoint. two or more melodic lines stated simultaneously.

crescendo. getting louder.

cuivré. the harsh "brassy" sound, especially on the horn, produced by extra tension on the player's lips.

diabolus in musica. "the devil in music", an expression for the TRITONE.

diatonic scale. a scale of seven notes to the octave, some separated by whole tones and some by semitones (as on the white notes of the piano alone), as in the major or minor scale; to be distinguished from the CHROMATIC SCALE.

diegetic music. music or sound that derives from a visible action on the screen (as opposed to the UNDERSCORE).

discord. DISSONANCE; opposite of CONCORD.

dissonance. simultaneous tones that produce an unpleasant effect; opposite of CONSONANCE.

dynamics. loudness and softness of sound.

equal temperament. Western system of tuning keyboards, which deviates from the acoustically "correct" intervals.

fugato. passage in the style of a FUGUE in a non-fugal composition.

fugue. development of a short melodic subject by "voices" of different harmonies and pitches, successively in imitation of each other.

furioso. furiously.

galop. a lively dance, dating from the mid nineteenth century, in $\frac{2}{4}$ time with hopping and frequently-changing steps.

giocoso. jocose, joyfully.

glissando. a rapid gliding from note to note.

interval. distance in PITCH between two notes; *see also* SEMITONE.

leitmotif. "leading motif"; a theme or musical idea associated with a character, place, object, or plot idea; invented by Richard Wagner (1813–1883).

lontano. as from a distance.

luthéal piano. obsolete upright piano with an extra pedal to convert the sound into a jangling quality; a similar sound can be achieved by putting a sheet of paper over the strings of an ordinary piano.

maestoso. majestically.

major. a scale, triad, or key distinguished by the "major" third, comprising two whole tones, also the major sixth and seventh, a whole tone above the fifth and a semitone below the octave respectively; *see also* MINOR.

martellato. "hammered" strokes at the tip of the bow on stringed instruments.

mickey-mouse (*vb*). to closely co-ordinate film music to the action on the screen; a familiar technique in cartoon films, hence named after the Disney superstar.

minor. a scale, triad, or key distinguished by the "minor" third, comprising a whole tone and a semitone; the sixth and seventh are variable according to context; see also MAJOR.

motif. a short rhythmic figure: the smallest unit of musical composition, sometimes consisting of no more than two notes.

molto appasionato. with great passion.

moto perpetuo. "perpetual motion", used for pieces with almost repetitive rapid notes.

musique concrète. "concrete music", music that uses recordings of sounds and noises rather than musical instruments; developed in France from the late 1940s.

nobilmente. in a noble manner.

nocturne. a short instrumental piece of a reflective character, typically for the piano.

note row. see TWELVE-TONE (SERIAL) TECHNIQUE.

orchestration. the art of writing for an orchestra utilising the COLOUR and characteristics of the individual instruments.

ostinato. persistently repeated; a melodic phrase so treated.

p. *piano*, Italian for "soft". Hence, **pp** signifies *pianissimo*, "very soft", ***ppp*** *molto pianissimo*, "softer still".

pedal point. an elongated note, normally in the bass, originally characteristic of organ music; in concert music it is sustained against changing harmonies in the upper parts, although in the cinema it sometimes stands alone; strictly speaking, a pedal not in the bass is termed an "inverted pedal".

pentatonic. a five-note scale used in early music and folk cultures.

phrase. a small group of notes, like a clause in language; one or more motifs.

pitch. the "highness" and "lowness" of a musical sound, determined by its frequency, or number of vibrations a second. The pitch is often indicated by: c = middle C; c' = an octave high than middle C; c'' = two octaves higher than middle c; c''' = three octaves higher than middle C; and so on. Pitches lower than middle C are not referred to in this way in this book.

pizzicato. plucked stringed intruments.

resolution. the passing from DISSONANCE to CONSONANCE.

retrograde. to present a theme backwards.

rubato. flexible tempo; slight speeding up or slowing down according to the musical expression.

scherzando. playfully.

semitone the smallest INTERVAL between two notes in most Western music; on the piano between two adjacent notes.

sempre agitato. all the time agitated.

sentence. a group of PHRASES that together make a musical statement.

sequencing. the immediate repetition of a passage at a higher or lower PITCH; a rising sequence increases excitement.

serialism. see TWELVE-TONE (SERIAL) TECHNIQUE.

sonata. a work usually in three or four movements for one or two players.

spiccato. short, rapid bowing, bouncing on the strings.

staccato. a note sustained for less than its normal value, a mere moment; produces a short, pinched sound.

sul ponticello. played "on the bridge" of a stringed instrument, producing a thin, "nasal" sound quality.

syncopation. abnormal metric pattern accenting the normally weak beats.

timbre. COLOUR.

tonality. key; the deciding note of a composition and all the notes related to this central note, e.g. C major, C minor, etc.

tone-colour. COLOUR.

tremolando. with a *TREMOLO*.

tremolo. on strings the quick reiteration of the same note; on most other instruments the rapid alternation between two notes.

triad. a three-note chord consisting of any note with its upper third and fifth; *see also* MAJOR, MINOR.

trill. the rapid alternation of a note with its upper neighbour.

tritone. an interval of three tones; i.e. an interval on the scale in which the fourth note is sharpened ("augmented"), e.g. c to *f-sharp*. Because it is an awkward interval to sing, it was prohibited in the Middle Ages and called the *DIABOLUS IN MUSICA*; some prefer to think, however, that it is so called because of its sinister sound.

tutti. the whole orchestra.

twelve-tone (serial) technique. a compositional method devised by Arnold Schoen-berg (1874–1951), in which the twelve notes of the chromatic scale are arranged in a succession ("note row", "series") chosen by the composer according to specific rules; now unfashionable.

unison. at the same PITCH; sometimes loosely applied to notes or parts an octave apart.

vertical combination. "vertical" notes on a score represent harmony, "horizontal" melody.

vibrato. a rapid regular fluctuation in pitch; produced on stringed instruments by a shaking motion of the left hand.

vivace. lively, vivaciously.

Filmography

In order to place Alwyn's film composition in a broader context, television, radio, and other works are briefly noted in this filmography. Dates indicate year of film release or the best assumption thereof. Feature films and titles over an hour in length are in bold face. Timings are rounded to nearest minute. Credits are noted only where verified (for example, Mathieson was more often musical director than he is credited).

Abbreviations

WA:	William Alwyn
Arr:	Arranged.
Comm:	Commentary
D:	Director
Ed:	Editor
LPO:	London Philharmonic Orchestra
LSO:	London Symphony Orchestra
m:	minutes
MD:	Music Director
MM:	Muir Mathieson
P:	Producer
ph:	photographer
PO:	Philharmonia Orchestra
RPO:	Royal Philharmonic Orchestra
Sc:	Script/Screenplay
Sd Ed:	Sound Editor
SOL:	Sinfonia of London
Tx:	Transmitted

1937

The Future's in the Air. P: Paul Rotha. D: Alexander Shaw. Joint credit with Raymond Bennell, although WA wrote the entire score. Composed autumn 1936. 45m.
Air Outpost. P: Paul Rotha. D: Ralph Keene, John Taylor. 16m.
Of All the Gay Places. P: Donald Taylor. D: W. B. Pollard. Rereleased in 1940 as *Healing Waters*. 12m.

Other Works

Mountain Scenes: suite for cello and piano. *Two Russian Folk Tunes* (arr. for flute quartet).

Overture for flute, clarinet, violin, cello, and piano. Nocturne for flute, clarinet, violin, cello, and piano. March for flute, clarinet, violin, cello, and piano. Two Pieces for piano. *Harlequin's Child*: incidental music to a play (flute and cello).

1938

Behind the Scenes. Part of *The Animal Kingdom* series. P: Stuart Legg. D: Evelyn Spice. Made in 1937. 17m.

Zoo Babies. Part of *The Animal Kingdom* series. P: Stuart Legg. D: Evelyn Spice. Score (working title *Care of the Young*) dated Oct. 1937. 15m.

Birth of the Year. Part of *The Animal Kingdom* series. P: Stuart Legg. D: Evelyn Spice. Score (working title *Spring at the Zoo*) dated Oct. 1937. 14m.

Free to Roam. Part of *The Animal Kingdom* series. P: Stuart Legg. D: Paul Burnford. Score (working title *Whipsnade Freedom*) dated Dec. 1937. 14m.

Monkey into Man. Part of *The Animal Kingdom* series. P: Stuart Legg. D: Stanley Hawes (uncredited: Evelyn Spice, Donald Alexander). Score dated Dec. 1937. 17m 30s.

Mites and Monsters. Part of *The Animal Kingdom* series. P: Stuart Legg. D: Donald Alexander. 17m.

The Zoo and You. (Working title *Animals Looking at You*). Part of *The Animal Kingdom* series. P: Stuart Legg. D: Ruby Grierson. 17m.

Fingers and Thumbs. Part of *The Animal Kingdom*, second series. P: Stuart Legg. D: Evelyn Spice. 15m.

New Worlds for Old. P: Paul Rotha. D: Frank Sainsbury. 28m.

Other Works

The Marriage of Heaven and Hell (oratorio). Numbers from *Album for the Young* (arr. from Tchaikovsky). *March of the Little Folk* (arr. from *Nugae* by John McEwen). *Siciliano* (arr. from J. S. Bach). *Bourée* (arr. from Handel). *Two Irish Folk Songs* (arr. for cello quartet). *Novelette* (for string quartet). *From Town and Countryside*: eight little pieces for piano. *Harvest Home*: easy pieces for piano). *Shut the Window Please!*: music for a mime (piano).

1939

Roads Across Britain. P: John Taylor. D: Sidney Cole, Paul Rotha. 14m.

Wings over Empire. Devised, P: Stuart Legg. Score (working title *Air Routes*) dated Feb. 1938. 25m.

Other Works

Suite for small orchestra. Rhapsody for piano quartet. Prelude and Fugue for string orchestra (arr. from Beethoven). Movement for string trio. Two Irish Pieces (arr for string quartet). *Sonata quasi Fantasia* for violin and viola. *Pastoral Fantasia* for violin and string orchestra. Concerto for violin and orchestra (1937–9).

1940

These Children Are Safe. P: Donald Taylor. D: Alexander Shaw. 20m.
The New Britain. P: Alexander Shaw. D: Ralph Keene. "Music Advisor": MM. 7m.
Big City. P: Alexander Shaw. D: Ralph Bond. "Music Advisor": MM. 12m.
It Comes from Coal. P: Edgar Anstey. D: Paul Fletcher. 11m.

Other Works

Overture to a Masque (orchestra). Divertimento for solo flute. *Down by the Riverside* (piano). *Night Thoughts* (piano). Three Songs for voice and piano. *Irish Suite* for string quartet (1939–40).

1941

SOS. P, D: John Eldridge. Completed by June 1940. 12m 30s.
Architects of England. P: Donald Taylor. D: John Eldridge. MD: MM. Score (working title *British Architecture*) dated November 1940. 13m.
Salute to Farmers. P: A. R. Taylor. D: Montgomery Tully. Score dated Dec. 1940. 17m.
Living With Strangers. P: John Taylor. D: Frank Sainsbury. (WA uncredited). 12m.
Night Watch. (Working title *Footsteps in the Night*). P, D: Donald Taylor. "Musical Advisor": MM. A "Five Minute Film". 8m.
HMS Minelayer. P: Sydney Box, James Carr. D: Henry Cass. A "Five Minute Film". 8m.
Steel Goes to Sea. P: Cecil Musk. D: John E. Lewis. LSO conducted by WA. 17m.
Queen Cotton. D: Cecil Musk. LSO conducted by WA. 14m.
Playtime. D, ph: S Raymond Elton. 9m.
The English Inn. D: Muriel Baker. Score dated Sept. 1941. 10m.
Green Girdle. P: Basil Wright. D: Ralph Keene. MD: MM. (Credited to Richard Addinsell; WA's score dated June 1941; working title *Green Belt*). 11m.
Penn of Pennsylvania (US title: *The Courageous Mr Penn*). P: Richard Vernon. D: Lance Comfort. MD: MM (LSO). 93m.
Jane Brown Changes her Job. P: Sydney Box and James Carr D: Harold Cooper. (WA uncredited; working title *Women in Industry*). 9m.
Post 23. P: Donald Taylor. D: Ralph Bond. *ARP Advisor*: WA. (no music credit). 10m.

Other Works

Short Suite for viola and piano. *The Londonderry Air* (flute, clarinet, violin, cello, and piano).

1942

WVS. P: Sydney Box, James Carr. D: Louise Birt. Played by section of LSO. (1941 for US distribution; revised 1942 for UK release). 22m.

They Flew Alone (US title: *Wings and the Woman*). P, D: Herbert Wilcox. MD: MM
    (LSO). 103m.

Trinity House. D: John Eldridge. Score dated Oct. 1941. 9m.

Western Isles. D: Terry Bishop. 14m.

Border Weave. P: George E. Turner. D: John L. Curthoys. 16m.

Rat Destruction. P: Paul Rotha. D: Budge Cooper. 10m.

Winter on the Farm. Part of *Winter/Spring/Summer on the Farm* series. Assoc. P:
    Edgar Anstey. D: Ralph Keene. LSO conducted by WA. 15m.

The Battle for Freedom. P: Basil Wright. D: Alan Orbiston. 15m.

Squadron Leader X. P: Victor Hanbury. D: Lance Comfort. MD: MM (LSO). 99m.

Life Begins Again. P: Paul Rotha. D: Donald Alexander. 20m.

Lift Your Head, Comrade. P: Basil Wright. D: Michael Hankinson. 14m.

British News. (Newsreels). Newsreel Association for British Council. For overseas
    use. Ran from 1940 to 1948, and continued by Movietone and Pathé until Sept.
    1966 (when it was retitled). WA composed various versions of the titles and end
    titles music. Dated 1942 in Craggs and Poulton, *William Alwyn: A Catalogue of
    His Music*, 37; whether this should be backdated to 1940 is uncertain.

Man of Science. Turner Film Productions. A film about Faraday. No further details.

Our Film. Production Manager: Charles Permaine. D: Harold French. MD: MM
    (LSO). 14m.

The Harvest Shall Come. P: Basil Wright. D: Max Anderson. 35m.

A Modern Miracle. P: Donald Taylor. D: Desmond Dickinson. MD: MM. 23m.

Worker and Warfront. D: Paul Rotha, Duncan Ross and others. The series ran from
    1942 to 1945. WA contributed titles and series of breaks to cover background
    themes: fanfares, comedy, landscapes, Eastern, and so on.

Radio

Britain to America. P: D. G. Bridson. Tx: NBC (North America), 26 July 1942; BBC
    Home Service, 14 Aug. 1942. WA may have contributed to others in the series.

Other Works

Land of Our Birth (baritone, chorus, and orchestra). Rhapsody for piano, violin, and cello.

1943

Spring on the Farm. Part of *Winter/Spring/Summer on the Farm* series. Assoc. P:
    Edgar Anstey. LSO conducted by WA. 15m.

Wales: Green Mountain, Black Mountain. P: Donald Taylor. D: John Eldridge. MD:
    MM. English- and Welsh-language versions. 12m.

A Letter from Ulster. P: Ian Dalrymple. D: Brian Desmond Hurst. MD: MM. (WA
    uncredited). 35m.

Desert Victory. P: David Macdonald. D: Roy Boulting MD: MM (BBC Northern
    Orchestra). *March* published by Chappell. 60m.

I Was a Fireman. P: Ian Dalrymple. D: Humphrey Jennings. MD: MM (BBC Northern Orchestra). 74m. (Short cinema version: *Fires were Started*: 63m).

Crown of the Year. Part of *Winter/Spring/Summer on the Farm* series. Assoc. P: Edgar Anstey. D: Ralph Keene. LSO conducted by WA. 20m non-theatrical; 15m theatrical.

Summer on the Farm. Part of *Winter/Spring/Summer on the Farm* series. Assoc. P: Edgar Anstey. D: Ralph Keene. LSO conducted by WA. 12m.

World of Plenty. P, D: Paul Rotha. 46m.

Escape to Danger. P: Victor Hanbury. D: Lance Comfort, Victor Hanbury, Mutz Greenbaum (Max Greene). "Special Sound Effects": Harry Miller. MD: MM. 92m.

A Welcome to Britain. P: Arthur Elton. D: Anthony Asquith, Burgess Meredith. 60m.

The Royal Mile, Edinburgh. D: Terence Egan Bishop. 14m.

Africa Freed. P, D: Hugh St Clair Stewart. Supervising Editor: Roy Boulting. 70m (not released).

Citizens of Tomorrow. D: Brian Smith. Production company: Realist for MoI and Latin-American distribution. 18m. No further information, but its working title may have been *Child Welfare* (score in Alwyn Archive).

ABCA: The Story of the Army Bureau of Current Affairs. P, D: Ronald H Riley. (WA uncredited). 15m.

ABCA Magazine. (Series of seven). P, D: Ronald H Riley. WA composed titles and breaks.

Radio

Transatlantic Call: People to People. Supervisor: D. G. Bridson. 10 Feb. 1943.

Made in Britain. Arr: Donald Stokes. P: John Glyn-Jones. 1 June 1943.

Four Years at War. Sc: Louis MacNeice. P: Laurence Gilliam. 3 Sept. 1943.

Pulse of Britain. No details.

Other Works

Desert Victory: concert suite. *Air Force*: march for brass/wind. *The Fraternity of Fellows*: march for brass/wind. *Women of the Empire*: march for brass/wind. Concerto Grosso no. 1 in B-flat major for chamber orchestra.

1944

There's a Future in It. P, D: Leslie Fenton. Sound supervisor: Harold King. MD: MM. 43m.

Tunisian Victory. P: Hugh Stewart, Roy Boulting, Frank Capra. MD: MM. 79m.

Potato Blight. P: John Taylor. D: Rosanne Hunter. 20m.

On Approval. P: Sydney Box, Clive Brook. D: Clive Brook. MD: MM. 80m.

The Grassy Shires. P: Edgar Anstey. D: Ralph Keene. (First in series: *The Pattern of Britain.* Working title *Midland Shires*). 15m.

A Start in Life. P: John Taylor. D: Brian Smith. English version of film originally for Latin American distribution. 22m.

Eve of Battle. P: David Macdonald. 17m.

A Medal for the General. P: Louis H. Jackson. D: Maurice Elvey. Orchestra directed by Charles Williams. 90m.

The Way Ahead (US title: *The Immortal Battalion*). P: John Sutro, Norman Walker. D: Carol Reed. MD: MM. "Blues" number composed by Denis Blood. Sheet music published by Chappell (1945). 115m.

Atlantic Trawler: P: John Taylor. D, scenario: Frank Sainsbury. 22m.

Accident Service. D: A. Reginald Dobson. For medical and nursing audiences only. 42m. (Version for general audiences: *They Live Again,* 18m.)

The Gen. RAF Newsreel. 1944/5. Music played by RAF Symphony Orchestra conducted by MM.

Radio

The Spirit of '76. Sc, P: D. G. Bridson. 4 July 1944.
The Chimes. P: D. G. Bridson. 30 Dec. 1944.

Other Works

Sonatina for viola and piano.

1945

Our Country. P: Alexander Shaw. D: John Eldridge. MD: MM. 45m.

Penicillin: P: John Taylor. D: Alexander Shaw. 20m.

French Town: September 1944. P: John Taylor. D: Alexander Shaw. 12m.

Great Day. P: Victor Hanbury. D: Lance Comfort. SE: Harry Miller. MD: MM (LSO). Band of Irish Guards directed by G. H. Willcocks. 79m.

Country Town. (Working title *Our Town*). P: Max Munden. D: Julian Wintle. LSO conducted by WA. 16m.

What's the Next Job? (Working title *Employment Exchange*). Exec. P: Ray Pitt. D: Roy Baker. SE: Ray Palmer. "Music Supervisor": Alan Rawsthorne. 22m.

Peace Thanksgiving. D: N. Walker. Duration unknown.

Soldier, Sailor. P: John Taylor. D: Alexander Shaw. MD: MM. 61m.

Your Children and You. P: John Taylor, Alexander Shaw. D: Brian Smith. 28m.

Your Children's Eyes. P: John Taylor. D, ph: Alex Strasser. Sc: Carleton Hobbs. 19m.

Your Children's Ears. P: Margaret Thomson. D: Albert Pearl. 17m.

Your Children's Teeth. P: Margaret Thomson. D: Jane Massy. 15m.

The True Glory. D: Carol Reed, Garson Kanin. MD: MM. Sheet music published by Chappell. 87m.

Today and Tomorrow. P: Ralph Bond. D: Robin Carruthers. MD: MM. 42m.

The Proud City: A Plan for London. P: Edgar Anstey. D: Ralph Keene. LSO conducted by WA. 20m.

The Rake's Progress (US title: *Notorious Gentleman*). P: Frank Launder, Sidney Gilliat. D: Sidney Gilliat. SE: Eric Wood. MD: MM (National Symphony Orchestra). 123m.

Radio

Britain's Our Doorstep. Sc, P: Leonard Cottrell. 3 episodes: 12, 19, 26 Jan. 1945.
Their Finest Hour, 5: *The People of Britain.* Sc, P: Leonard Cottrell. 17 May 1945.
London Victorious. Sc, P: Louis MacNeice. 18 May 1945.
Ex-Corporal Wilf. Sc, P: D. G. Bridson. 6 parts: Programme 1, 31 Oct. 1945.
City Set on a Hill. P: Louis MacNeice. Sc: W. R. Rodgers. NI Home Service, 15 Nov. 1945.
Atlantic Flight. Sc, P: Leonard Cottrell. 2 parts: 23 Nov., 7 Dec. 1945.
Wherever You May Be: Christmas Feature. Arr, P: Laurence Gilliam, Leonard Cottrell. 25 Dec. 1945.
Threshold of the New. Sc, P: Louis MacNeice. 31 Dec. 1945.

Other Works

Prelude and Fugue for piano, formed on an Indian scale. *The Tree* for voice and harp. Suite for oboe and harp (1944–5). Concerto for oboe, harp, and string orchestra (1944–5).

1946

Land of Promise. P, D: Paul Rotha. Made in 1944/5. 67m.
Total War in Britain. P, Ed: Paul Rotha. 21m.
Each for All. (Working title *Trade Unions*). D: Montgomery Tully. 11m.
I See a Dark Stranger (US title: *The Adventuress*). P: Frank Launder, Sidney Gilliat. D: Frank Launder. Sound supervisor: Brian Sewell. MD: MM (NSO). 123m.

Radio

Nalinakanti: Indian Folk Tune. Contribution to a features production (March 1946). Untraced. Recorded 21 March 1946.
Flying Visit. Contribution to a features production (Jan.–June 1946). Untraced.
Man from Belsen. Sc, P: Leonard Cottrell. 1 April 1946.
The Careerist: A Psycho-Morality Play of Modern Life. Sc, P: Louis MacNeice. 18 Oct. 1946.
Home Again (Christmas feature). Arr, P: Laurence Gilliam, Leonard Cottrell. 25 Dec. 1946.

Other Works

Suite of Scottish Dances for small orchestra. *Overture in the Form of a Serenade: Men of Gloucester* for wordless chorus and orchestra. *Sonata alla Toccata* for piano.

1947

Home and School. P: Alexander Shaw. D: Gerry Bryant. MD: MM. Made in 1946. 20m.
Approach to Science. P: Geoffrey Bell, Edgar Anstey. D: Bill Mason. 28m.
Odd Man Out. P, D: Carol Reed. SE: Harry Miller. MD: MM (LSO). 115m.
Green for Danger. P: Frank Launder, Sidney Gilliat. D: Frank Launder. MD: MM
  (LSO). "Paul Jones" and WA's quickstep and waltz arranged for dance orchestra
  by Norrie Paramor. 93m
A City Speaks. P: Paul Rotha. D: Francis Gysin. Hallé Orchestra conducted by John
  Barbirolli. 69m.
Take My Life. P: Anthony Havelock-Allan. D: Ronald Neame. SE: Winston Ryder,
  Jack Slade. MD: MM (LSO). 79m.
The October Man. P: Eric Ambler. D: Roy Baker. SE: Harry Miller. MD: MM (LSO).
  Harry Gold collaborated on scoring of dance music, played by Harry Gold and his
  Pieces of Eight. 95m.
Captain Boycott. P: Frank Launder, Sidney Gilliat. D: Frank Launder. SE: Charlie
  Crafford, Arthur Southgate. MD: MM (PO). 93m.

Radio

The Hare. P: Louis MacNeice. Recorded 18 Feb. 1947. Transmission date untraced.
The Pharaoh Akhnaton. Sc, P: Leonard Cottrell. 6 July 1947.
The Moon in the Yellow River. Sc, P: Denis Johnston. 14 July 1947.

Other Works

Suite: *Manchester* for orchestra. *Slum Song* for voice and piano, words by Louis MacNeice.
  Three Songs.

1948

City Government. A shortened version of *A City Speaks* (1947) for general circulation
  (omitting the centre reels). Approximate length 45m.
Your Children's Sleep. P: Brian Smith. D: Jane Massy. Made in 1947. 23m.
One Man's Story. D: Dennis Shand, Maxwell Munden. MD: John Hollingsworth
  (LPO). 26m.
Three Dawns to Sydney. P: Ralph Keene, Paul Fletcher. D: John Eldridge. MD: John
  Hollingsworth (String section of PO). 58m.
Escape. P: William Perlberg. D: Joseph L. Mankiewicz. SE: K. Heeley-Ray. MD: MM
  (PO). 78m.
So Evil My Love. P: Hal B. Wallis. D: Lewis Allen. SE: Leonard Trumn. MD: MM
  (PO). "Additional Music": Victor Young (Paramount Symphony Orchestra).
  109m.
The Fallen Idol (Working title and US title: *The Lost Illusion*). P: David O. Selznick,

Carol Reed. D: Carol Reed. SE: Ben Hipkins. MD: Hubert Clifford (London Film Symphony Orchestra). BFA: Best British Film, 1948. 94m.

The Winslow Boy. P: Anatole de Grunwald. D: Anthony Asquith. SE: B. H. Hipkins. MD: Hubert Clifford (London Film Symphony Orchestra). 117m

Other Works

Fanfare for a Joyful Occasion for brass and percussion. Concerto Grosso no. 2 in G major for string orchestra. *Three Winter Poems* for string quartet. Sonata for flute and piano.

1949

Under One Roof. P: Brian Smith. D: Lewis Gilbert. 25m.

The History of Mr Polly. P: John Mills. D: Anthony Pélissier. SE: Harry Miller. MD: MM (RPO). 94m.

Daybreak in Udi. P: Max Anderson. D: Terry Bishop. SE: Jean Mackenzie. MD: John Hollingsworth (LPO). Academy Award Winner 1948. 40m.

The Rocking Horse Winner. P: John Mills. D: Anthony Pélissier. SE: Harry Miller. MD: MM (RPO). 90m.

The Cure for Love. D: Robert Donat. MD: MM (LSO). Sheet music published by Chappell (1950). 98m.

Other Works

Symphony no. 1 in D major.

1950

Madeleine. P: Stanley Haynes. D: David Lean. MD: MM (RPO). 114m. Sheet music published by Chappell.

The Golden Salamander. P: Ronald Neame, Alexander Galperson. D: Ronald Neame. SE: Gordon Pilkington. MD: MM (LSO). Music *Clopin Clopart* by Bruno Coquatrix. 87m.

State Secret (US title: *The Great Manhunt*). P: Frank Launder, Sidney Gilliat. D: Sidney Gilliat. SE: Lee Doig. MD: MM (RPO). 104m.

The Magnet. P: Sidney Cole. D: Charles Frend. MD Ernest Irving (PO). 79m.

The Mudlark. P: Nunnally Johnson. D: Jean Negulesco. SE: Eric Wood. MD: MM. 79m.

Radio

Christmas Journey (Christmas feature). Arr and P: Laurence Gilliam, Leonard Cottrell. 25 Dec. 1950.

Other Works

Conversations: suite for violin, clarinet, and piano (original title: *Music for Three Players*).

1951

Night Without Stars. P: Hugh Stewart. D: Anthony Pélissier. SE: Harry Miller. MD: MM (RPO). 86m.

Royal River (US title: *Distant Thames*; aka: *Distant River*). D: Brian Smith. 10m. Technicolor, 3D, and stereoscopic sound for the Festival of Britain.

Henry Moore: Sculptor. P: John Read. Tx: BBC Television, 30 April 1951. 13m.

No Resting Place. P: Colin Leslie. D: Paul Rotha. 77m.

The Magic Box. P: Ronald Neame. D: John Boulting. MD: MM. 118m.

The House in the Square (US title: *I'll Never Forget You*). P: Sol C. Siegel. D: Roy Baker. MD: MM. 91m.

Lady Godiva Rides Again. P: Sidney Gilliat, Frank Launder. D: Frank Launder. MD: MM. Songs: *How Long is Always* by Leo Towers and Frankie Russell; *If I Painted a Picture* by Tommy Duggan and David Heneker; *Comedian's Dance* by Walford Hyden. 90m.

Festival in London. P: Frederick Wilson. D: Phil Leacock. Technicolor. 10m.

Radio

The Gifts of Christmas (Christmas feature). Arr and P: Laurence Gilliam and R. D. Smith. 25 Dec. 1951.

Other Works

Festival March for orchestra; *Festival March* for brass band. Trio for flute, cello, and piano.

1952

Alliance for Peace. Production for Supreme Headquarters, Allied Powers, Europe (SHAPE). Comm: Edward R. Murrow. (No further details). 25m.

Royal Heritage. P: Ian Dalrymple. D: Diana Pine. 27m.

The Card (US title: *The Promoter*). P: John Bryan. D: Ronald Neame. SE: Harry Miller. MD: MM (LSO). 91m.

Saturday Island (US title: *Island of Desire*). P: David E. Rose. D: Stuart Heisler. SE: Tom Simpson. MD: MM. 102m.

Mandy (US title: *The Crash of Silence*). P: Leslie Norman. D: Alexander Mackendrick. SE: Mary Habberfield. MD: Ernest Irving (PO). 93m.

The Crimson Pirate. P: Harold Hecht. D: Robert Siodmak. MD: MM (LSO). 104m.

Radio

The Queen's Inheritance (Christmas feature). Arr, P: Laurence Gilliam, Alan Burgess. 25 Dec. 1952.

Other Works

Symphonic Prelude: *The Magic Island*. Nine Children's Piano Pieces.

1953

The Long Memory. P: Hugh Stewart. D: Robert Hamer. SE: Winston Ryder. MD: MM. 96m.
The Malta Story. P: Peter de Sarigny. D: Brian Desmond Hurst. SE: Eric Wood. MD: MM (LSO). 103m.
The Master of Ballantrae. D: William Keighley. SE: Arthur Ridout. MD: MM. 89m.
A Personal Affair. P: Anthony Darnborough. D: Anthony Pélissier. SE: Harry Miller. MD: MM. 83m.

Radio

Long Live the Queen (Coronation programme*)*. Arr, P: Laurence Gilliam, Alan Burgess. 2 June 1953.
Coronation Across the World. Arr, P: Laurence Gilliam, Michael Barsley. 2 June 1953.

Other Works

Symphony no. 2. String Quartet no. 1 in D minor. *Lyra Angelica*: Concerto for harp and string orchestra.

1954

The Million Pound Note (US title: *The Man with a Million*). P: John Bryan. D: Ronald Neame. MD: MM. 91m.
The Rainbow Jacket. P: Michael Relph. D: Basil Dearden. MD: Dock MM (PO). 99m.
The Seekers (US title: *Land of Fury*). P: George H Brown. D: Ken Annakin. SE: Roger Cherrill. MD: MM (PO). 90m.
War in the Air. 2 episodes for BBC Television. Series D: Philip Dorté. *No. 3: Fifty North*. P: John Elliot. Tx: 22 Nov. 1954. *No. 13: Eastern Victory*. P: John Elliot. Tx: 31 Jan. 1955.
Black on White. D: John Read. 27m. BBC Television: 28 November 1954.
Svengali. P: James George Minter. D: Noel Langley. MD: MM (RPO). 82m.

Other Works

Autumn Legend for cor anglais and string orchestra.

1955

Bedevilled. P: Henry Berman. D: Mitchell Leisen. MD: MM. Song *Embrasse-moi bien*: Paul Durand (English lyrics Richard Driscoll). 86m.

The Ship that Died of Shame (US title: *PT Raiders*). P: Michael Relph. D: Basil Dearden. SE: Gordon Stone. MD: Dock MM (RPO). 91m.

Geordie (US title: *Wee Geordie*). P, D: Frank Launder. MD: MM (LSO). Olympic Games music played by HM Royal Marines (Plymouth Group), conductor Capt. K. A. McLean RM. 99m.

Colonel March of Scotland Yard. 26 episodes of television series of 25m each. P: Hannah Weinstein 1953–4. Title music by Philip Green. WA contributed to the following 15 episodes (dates of first tx by the ITV companies): *The Abominable Snowman* (8 Oct. 1955). *Present Tense* (15 Oct. 1955). *At Night All Cats are Grey.* D: Phil Brown. (22 Oct. 1955). *The Invisible Knife.* D: Terence Fisher. (29 Oct. 1955). *The Headless Hat.* D: Arthur Crabtree. (12 Nov. 1955). *The Second Mona Lisa.* D: Arthur Crabtree. (26 Nov. 1955). *The Case of the Misguided Missile.* D: Bernard Knowles. (3 Dec. 1955). *Death in Inner Space.* D: Phil Brown. (10 Dec. 1955). *The Talking Head.* D: Paul Dickson. (17 Dec. 1955). *The Case of the Lively Ghost.* D: Bernard Knowles. (31 Dec. 1955). *The Devil Sells His Soul.* D: Arthur Crabtree. (7 Jan. 1956). *The Silent Vow.* D: Bernard Knowles. (21 Jan. 1956). *Death and the Other Monkey.* D: Bernard Knowles. (28 Jan. 1956). *Stolen Crime.* D: Arthur Crabtree. (11 Feb. 1956). *Error at Daybreak.* D: Phil Brown. (25 Feb. 1956).

Other Works

Crépuscule for harp. *Farewell Companions*: a ballad opera for soli, chorus, and orchestra (1954–5; broadcast BBC Third Programme: 9 Aug. 1955).

1956

The Black Tent. P: William MacQuitty. D: Brian Desmond Hurst. SE: Donald Sharpe. MD: MM (LSO). 93m.

Safari. P: Adrian D. Worker, Irving Allen, Albert R. Broccoli. D: Terence Young. SE: Tony Lower. MD: MM (RPO). Song *We're on Safari*, lyrics by Paddy Roberts. 91m.

Smiley. P, D: Anthony Kimmins. MD: MM (SOL). 97m. Sheet music published by F.D.H. (1957).

Other Works

Symphony no. 3. *The Moor of Venice*: dramatic overture for brass band. Fantasy-Waltzes for piano.

1957

Zarak. P: Phil C. Samuel. D: Terence Young. MD: MM (SOL). Song: Auyar Hosseini, Norman Gimbel (*Climb up the Wall!*). 94m.

Fortune is a Woman (US title: *She Played with Fire*). P, Sc: Frank Launder and Sidney Gilliat. D: Sidney Gilliat. SE: Chris Greenham. MD: MM (RPO). 95m.

The Smallest Show on Earth (US title: *Big Time Operators).* P: Frank Launder, Sidney Gilliat, Michael Relph. D: Basil Dearden. SE: Arthur Cox. MD: MM (SOL). 81m.

Manuela (US title: *Stowaway Girl*). P: Ivan Foxwell. D: Guy Hamilton. SE: John V. Smith. MD: MM (SOL). 95m.

Other Works

Elizabethan Dances (1956–7).

1958

Carve Her Name with Pride. P: Daniel M. Angel. D: Lewis Gilbert. SE: Arthur Ridout, Leslie Wiggins. MD: MM (SOL). 119m.

I Accuse. P: Sam Zimbalist. D: José Ferrer. MD: MM (SOL). 99m.

The Silent Enemy. P: Bertram Ostrer. D: William Fairchild. SE: Chris Greenham. MD: Muir MM. 112m.

A Night to Remember. P: William MacQuitty. D: Roy Baker. SE: Harry Miller. MD: MM (SOL). 123m.

Radio

The Mouth of God: The Tragedy of Girolamo Savonarola. P: Douglas Claverdon. 11 Feb. 1958.

The Seekers (Christmas feature). Arr and P: Laurence Gilliam; Alan Burgess. 25 Dec. 1958.

Other Works

Twelve Preludes for piano.

1959

Shake Hands with the Devil. P, D: Michael Anderson. SE: Rusty Coppleman. MD: MM (SOL). 110m.

The Killers of Kilimanjaro (US title: *Adamson of Africa).* P: John R. Sloan. D: Richard Thorpe. MD: MM (SOL). 91m.

Third Man on the Mountain. P: Bill Anderson. D: Ken Annakin. SE: Chris Greenham. MD: MM (SOL). Songs: Franklyn Marks, By Dunham (*Climb the Mountain*); G. Haenni, Tom Adair (*Good Night Valais*). 103m.
Devil's Bait. D: Peter Graham Scott. MD: MM. 58m.

Other Works

Symphony no. 4. String Trio.

1960

The Professionals. P: Norman Priggen. D: Don Sharp. 61m.

Other Works

Concerto no. 2 for piano and orchestra. Overture: *Derby Day* (1959–60).

1961

The Swiss Family Robinson. P: Bill Anderson. D: Ken Annakin. SE: Leslie Wiggins.
MD: WA (SOL conducted by MM). Songs: Terry Gilkyson (*My Heart Was an
Island*); Buddy Baker (*The Swissapolka*). 126m.
The Empty Sleeve. Episode in television series *Tales of Mystery by Algernon Black-
wood*. Associated Rediffusion Network production. P: Peter Graham Scott. D:
Jonathan Alwyn. Approx 30m. Tx: 26 April 1961.
The Naked Edge. P: Walter Seltzer, George Glass. D: Michael Anderson. SE: Rusty
Coppleman. MD: MM (SOL). 100m.
Drawn from Life. Granada TV Network production. P: Patricia Labone. D: Mike
Wooller. Devised and introduced by John Berger. Approx 30m. Tx: 9 Oct. 1961.

Other Works

Movements for piano solo.

1962

Night of the Eagle (US title: *Burn, Witch, Burn*). P: Albert Fennell. D: Sidney Hayers.
SE: Ted Mason. MD: MM. 87m.
Life for Ruth (US title: *Condemned to Life*; aka: *Walk in the Shadow*). P: Michael
Relph. D: Basil Dearden. SE: Les Wiggins. MD: MM (SOL). 91m.
In Search of the Castaways. P: Hugh Attwooll. D: Robert Stevenson. SE: Peter
Thornton. MD: MM (SOL). Songs (*Casterway, Enjoy It!, Grimpons!* [*Let's Climb*],
Merci Beaucoups): Richard M. Sherman and Robert B. Sherman. 100m.

Other Works

Sonata for clarinet and piano.

1963

The Running Man. P, D: Carol Reed. SE: Peter Thornton. MD: MM (SOL). Title
music: Ron Grainer. 103m.

Other Film Scores

(1937) *Lifeboats.* [Working title?] Strand. No further information.

(1938) *Conquest of the Air.* P: Donald Taylor. D: Alexander Shaw. 3m of music arranged from Monsigny's *La Belle Arsène.* Main score by Arthur Bliss. Monsigny
arrangement not included in extant 1940 rerelease.

(1940) "MoI Five Minuter no. 1" and "MoI Five Minuter no. 2". MSS in WA Archive.
Title music and end titles for both. "Realist films". No further identification.
  Aircraft Recognition. Possibly for film of same title (1940). AKS. Or Royal Air
Force training short.
  "RN Training Film". Possibly *Dartmouth: The Royal Naval College* (1941). Spec-
tator Films. 13m. Or Royal Navy training short.

(1941) *Africans in England.* [Working title?] Unidentified.
  Religious Tolerance. P: Donald Taylor. D: Ralph Keene. Two versions: French
and Arabic. Unreferenced, although advertised by Strand in *Documentary News
Letter,* 2:11 (Nov. 1941): 220. (Score completed Oct. 1941).

(1942) *In Which We Serve.* Music credited to Noel Coward. A piano sketch in Alwyn's
hand for the opening titles, final 20 seconds of the end titles, and other themes
including the main theme, suggests that Alwyn may have orchestrated the music
on behalf of Coward.
  "Sainsbury's Film". Possibly *The Plan and the People* (1946). D: Frank Sainsbury.
19m. No print located

*The following films have, or may have, unattributed pre-recorded library tracks
by WA:*

(1947) *Miranda.* P: Sydney Box. D: Ken Annakin. 80m. Music by Temple Abady.
Title song by Jack Fishman and Peter Hart. WA originally commissioned to write
the underscore and probably precomposed Miranda's song.

(1950) *Morning Departure* (US title: *Operation Disaster*). P: Leslie Parkyn. D: Roy
Baker. 102m. Uncredited library track from WA's *The October Man* reused for titles and scene of submarine putting to sea. Uncredited library track from Gordon
Jacob's score for *The Way We Live* re-used for end titles. There is no other music
in the film.

(1956) *Odongo.* P: Max Varnel. D: John Gilling. Music: George Melachrino. 85m. WA
wrote the song *Safari Blues.*

Unresolved Attributions

(1942) *The Countrywomen.* Seven League in association with Paul Rotha for MoI. D, ph: John Page. 14m. WA is credited by Huntley, *British Film Music*, 191, and Craggs and Poulton, *William Alwyn: A Catalogue of His Music*, 37. Film has short in-vision church choir at start and end, otherwise neither underscore nor composer credit. Perhaps WA advised or his score unused. (Date on credits: 1941).

(1944) *Child Welfare.* A score with this title in the Alwyn Archive, and listed in Craggs and Poulton, *William Alwyn*, 39, 41. Possibly the working title of *Citizens of Tomorrow.*

(1947) *Parents and Children.* Listed only in Craggs and Poulton, *William Alwyn*, 44. Possibly the working title of *Your Children and You* (1945, but incorrectly dated 1947 in Craggs and Poulton).

(1957) **The Abominable Snowman** (US title: *The Abominable Snowman of the Himalayas*). P: Aubrey Baring. D: Val Guest. Music: Humphrey Searle. Randall D. Larson, *Music from the House of Hammer* (Lanham, MD: Scarecrow Press, 1996), 15, claims this film uses uncredited cues by WA "from another source". If this is so, they are well integrated.

(1962) **Miracle of the White Stallions** (US title: *Flight of the White Stallions*). P: Peter V. Herald. D: Arthur Hillier. Music: Paul Smith. *Film Dope*, 39 (March 1988), 7, claims the film includes uncredited library tracks by WA.

(1964) **The Moon Spinners.** P: Bill Anderson. D: James Nielson. Music: Ron Grainer. *Film Dope*, 39 (March 1988), 7, claims the film includes uncredited library tracks by WA. If this is so, they are well integrated.

Select Discography

Film Music

"*The Card* Suite" (reconstructed by Philip Lane): BBC Philharmonic Orchestra (Rumon Gamba, whistler Robert Holliday) on *The Film Music of William Alwyn*, Vol. 2 (Chandos CHAN9959, 2001).

The Crimson Pirate, "Pirate Capers Overture" (reconstructed by Philip Lane): City of Prague PO (Paul Bateman) on *Swashbucklers: Swordsmen of the Silver Screen* (Silva Screen FILMXCD188, 1997); also on *The Great British Film Music Album* (Silva Screen FILMXCD309, 1998).

The Crimson Pirate, "Overture on themes from the film" (reconstructed by Philip Lane): BBC PO (Rumon Gamba) on *The Film Music of William Alwyn*, Vol. 2 (Chandos CHAN9959, 2001).

The Cure for Love, "Theme": LSO (Mathieson, piano Sidney Crook) (HMV B9879, 1949).

Desert Victory, "March": HM Grenadier Guards Band (Lt F. Harris) (Columbia D82140, 1943).

"Suite from *Desert Victory*" (reconstructed by Philip Lane): BBC PO (Rumon Gamba) on *The Film Music of William Alwyn*, Vol. 2 (Chandos CHAN9959, 2001).

"*The Fallen Idol* Suite" (ed. Christopher Palmer): LSO (Richard Hickox) on *The Film Music of William Alwyn*, Vol. 1 (Chandos CHAN9243, 1993).

Green Girdle: BBC PO (Rumon Gamba) on *The Film Music of William Alwyn*, Vol. 2 (Chandos CHAN9959, 2001).

"*The History of Mr Polly* Suite" (arr. Christopher Palmer): LSO (Richard Hickox) on *The Film Music of William Alwyn*, Vol. 1 (Chandos CHAN9243, 1993).

In Search of the Castaways, "Ship's Waltz"; "Rumba": BBC PO (Rumon Gamba) on *The Film Music of William Alwyn*, Vol. 2 (Chandos CHAN9959, 2001).

A Night to Remember, "Main Title"; "Nearer My God to Thee" (J. B. Dykes): City of Prague PO (Nic Raine) on *Disasters* (Silva Screen FILMCD301, 1998).

A Night to Remember, "Main Title": BBC PO (Rumon Gamba) on *The Film Music of William Alwyn*, Vol. 2 (Chandos CHAN9959, 2001).

"*Odd Man Out* Suite" (arr Christopher Palmer): LSO (Richard Hickox) on *The Film Music of William Alwyn*, Vol. 1 (Chandos CHAN9243, 1993).

The Rake's Progress, "Calypso": LSO (Mathieson) on *British Film Music from the 1940s and 1950s* (EMI LC0542, 1994; transcribed from Decca K1544, 1945/6; also on London label).

The Rake's Progress, "Calypso" (arr. Christopher Palmer): LSO (Richard Hickox) on *The Film Music of William Alwyn*, Vol. 1 (Chandos CHAN9243, 1993).

Shake Hands with the Devil, original sound-track recording: SOL (Mathieson) (United Artists UAL4043 (mono), UAS5043 (stereo), 1959).

"*State Secret* Suite" (reconstructed by Philip Lane): BBC PO (Rumon Gamba) on *The Film Music of William Alwyn*, Vol. 2 (Chandos CHAN9959, 2001).

Svengali, "Aria: *Libera me*": Canzonetta Chamber Choir (Jeffrey Wynn Davies, soprano Susan Bullock) on *The Film Music of William Alwyn*, Vol. 2 (Chandos CHAN9959, 2001).

Take My Life, "Aria": BBC PO (Rumon Gamba, soprano Susan Bullock) on *The Film Music of William Alwyn*, Vol. 2 (Chandos CHAN9959, 2001).

"*The Winslow Boy* Suite" (reconstructed by Philip Lane): BBC PO (Rumon Gamba) on *The Film Music of William Alwyn*, Vol. 2 (Chandos CHAN9959, 2001).

In the 1940s and 1950s the J. Arthur Rank Organisation in London issued a series of direct sound-track recordings to television and radio stations in about sixty countries. They are listed, some with comments possibly written by Alwyn himself, in Manvell and Huntley, *The Technique of Film Music*, 1st edn (1957), 229–31:

Captain Boycott, "Opening titles"; "Waltz": PO (Mathieson). FM10, 1947.

The October Man, "Opening Titles and Bus Crash": LSO (Mathieson). FM15, 1947.

Take My Life, "Aria": PO (Mathieson). Victoria Sladen (soprano). FM21, 1947.

The History of Mr Polly, "Punting Scene"; "The Potwell Inn"; "Wedding Scene"; "Cycling": RPO (Mathieson). FM53–4, 1949.

The Rocking Horse Winner, "There Must be More Money"; "Paul's Last Ride": RPO (Mathieson). FM87–8, 1949.

Madeleine, "Waltz"; "Strathspey": RPO (Mathieson). FM100, 1949.

The Magnet, "Prelude": PO (Mathieson). FM101, 1951.

Night Without Stars, "Montage": Unnamed orchestra [RPO] (Mathieson). FM111, 1951.

The Card, "Theme and Variations": Unnamed orchestra [LSO] (Mathieson). FM129, 1952.

The Long Memory, "Prelude": Unnamed orchestra (Mathieson). FM134, 1953.

The Million Pound Note, "Theme": Unnamed orchestra (Mathieson). FM144, 1953.

The Seekers, "Dance of Death": Unnamed choir and orchestra [PO] (Mathieson). FM149, 1954.

The Rainbow Jacket, "Romance; "The Lingfield Race": Unnamed orchestra [PO] (Dock Mathieson). FM150, 1954.

The Black Tent, "Theme": Unnamed orchestra and conductor [LSO (Mathieson)]. FM191, 1956.

An LP record, *The Golden Age of Film Music* (Citadel CT-OFI-1, c1976), with works by several composers, includes "The Punting Sequence" from *The History of Mr Polly*, "Paul's Last Ride" from *The Rocking Horse Winner*, and "Main Titles" from *The Card*. All are conducted by Mathieson and appear to be copies from the Rank Library series. No further information.

The Film Music of William Alwyn, Vol. 3, contains selections from *The Cure for Love*, *Geordie*, *The Magic Box*, *The Million Pound Note*, *Penn of Pennsylvania*, *The Rocking*

Horse Winner, *The Running Man*, *The Swiss Family Robinson*, *The True Glory*, *The Way Ahead*: BBC PO (Rumon Gamba) (Chandos CHAN10349, 2005)

Orchestral Works

Autumn Legend for cor anglais and strings. City of London Sinfonia (Richard Hickox), Nicholas Daniel (cor anglais) (Chandos CHAN9065, 1992).
   LPO (Alwyn), Geoffrey Browne (cor anglais) (Lyrita SRCD230, 1992).
Concerto for oboe, harp, and strings. City of London Sinfonia (Richard Hickox), Nicholas Daniel (oboe) (Chandos CHAN8866, 1992).
Concerto no. 1 for piano and orchestra. LSO (Richard Hickox), Howard Shelley (piano) (Chandos CHAN9155, 1993).
   Bournemouth SO (James Judd), Peter Donohoe (piano) (Naxos, 2005).
Concerto no. 2 for piano and orchestra. LSO (Richard Hickox), Howard Shelley (piano) (Chandos CHAN9196, 1993).
   Bournemouth SO (James Judd), Peter Donohoe (piano) (Naxos, 2005).
Concerto for violin and orchestra. LSO (Richard Hickox), Lydia Mordkovitch (violin) (Chandos CHAN9187, 1993).
Concerto Grosso no. 1 in B-flat major for chamber orchestra. City of London Sinfonia (Richard Hickox) (Chandos CHAN8866, 1992).
Concerto Grosso no. 2 in G major for string orchestra. City of London Sinfonia (Richard Hickox) (Chandos CHAN8866, 1992).
   LPO (Alwyn) (Lyrita SRCD230, 1992).
Concerto Grosso no. 3 in G major for woodwind, brass, and strings. City of London Sinfonia (Richard Hickox) (Chandos CHAN8866, 1992).
Derby Day: Overture. LSO (Richard Hickox) (Chandos CHAN9093, 1992).
   LPO (Alwyn) (Lyrita SRCD229, 1992).
   Bournemouth SO (James Judd), Peter Donohoe (piano) (Naxos, 2005).
Elizabethan Dances, complete. LSO (Richard Hickox) (Chandos CHAN8902, 1992).
   Nos. 1, 2, 5, and 4. LPO (Alwyn) (Lyrita SRCD229, 1992).
Fanfare for a Joyful Occasion for brass and percussion. LSO (Richard Hickox) (Chandos CHAN9093, 1992).
Festival March. LSO (Richard Hickox) (Chandos CHAN8902, 1992).
   LPO (Alwyn) (Lyrita SRCD229, 1992).
Lyra Angelica: Concerto for harp and string orchestra. City of London Sinfonia (Richard Hickox), Rachel Masters (harp) (Chandos CHAN9065, 1992).
   LPO (Alwyn), Osian Ellis (harp) (Lyrita SRCD230, 1992).
   Royal Liverpool PO (David Lloyd Jones), Suzanne Willison (harp) (Naxos, 2005).
The Magic Island: Symphonic Prelude. LSO (Richard Hickox) (Chandos CHAN9093, 1992).
   LPO (Alwyn) (Lyrita SRCD229, 1992).
The Moor of Venice. Williams Fairy Band (Bryan Hurdley) (Chandos CHAN4547, 1997).
Overture to a Masque. LSO (Richard Hickox) (Chandos CHAN9093, 1992).

Pastoral Fantasia for viola and string orchestra. City of London Sinfonia (Richard Hickox), Stephen Tees (viola) (Chandos CHAN9065, 1992).

Sinfonietta for strings. LSO (Richard Hickox) (Chandos CHAN9093, 1993).
> LPO (Alwyn) (Lyrita SRCD229, 1992).
> Royal Liverpool PO (David Lloyd Jones) (Naxos, 2005).

Suite of Scottish Dances for small orchestra. Royal Ballet Sinfonia (Gavin Sutherland) (ASV CDWHL2113, 1999).

Symphony no. 1 in D major. LSO (Richard Hickox) (Chandos CHAN9155/CHAN9429, 1993).
> LPO (Alwyn) (Lyrita SRCD227, 1992).
> Royal Liverpool PO (David Lloyd Jones) (Naxos, 2005).

Symphony no. 2. LSO (Richard Hickox) (Chandos CHAN9093/CHAN9429, 1992).
> LPO (Alwyn) (Lyrita SRCD228, 1992).
> Royal Liverpool PO (David Lloyd Jones) (Naxos, 2005).

Symphony no. 3. LSO (Richard Hickox) (Chandos CHAN9187/CHAN9429, 1993).
> LPO (Alwyn) (Lyrita SRCD228, 1992).
> Royal Liverpool PO (David Lloyd Jones) (Naxos, 2005).

Symphony no. 4. LSO (Richard Hickox) (Chandos CHAN8902/CHAN9429, 1992).
> LPO (Alwyn) (Lyrita SRCD227, 1992).
> Royal Liverpool PO (David Lloyd Jones) (Naxos, 2005).

Symphony no. 5, *Hydriotaphia*. LSO (Richard Hickox) (Chandos CHAN9196/CHAN 9429, 1993).
> LPO (Alwyn) (Lyrita SRCD228, 1992).
> Royal Liverpool PO (David Lloyd Jones) (Naxos, 2005).

Tragic Interlude for two horns, timpani and string orchestra. City of London Sinfonia (Richard Hickox) (Chandos CHAN9065, 1992).

NB: The Lyrita orchestral CDs listed above, digitally remastered from recordings made in the 1970s, are conducted by Alwyn and therefore of especial interest.

Chamber Music

Concerto for Flute and Eight Wind Instruments. Haffner Wind Ensemble of London (Nicholas Daniel, oboe /director). Kate Hill (flute) (Chandos CHAN9152, 1993).

Music for Three Players: Suite for violin, cello, and piano. Leland Chen (violin), Caroline Dearnley (cello), Julius Drake (piano) (Chandos CHAN9152, 1993).

Naiades: Fantasy-Sonata for flute and harp. Kate Hill (flute), Ieuan Jones (harp) (Chandos CHAN9152, 1993).
> Jennifer Stinton (flute), Aline Brewer (harp) (Collins Classics 1297-2, 1992)
> Emily Beynon (flute), Catherine Beynon (harp) (Metier Sound and Vision MSVCD92006, n.d.).
> Anna Noakes (flute), Gillian Tingay (harp) (Guild GMCD7202, 2001)

Rhapsody for piano quartet. Quartet of London. David Willison (piano) (Chandos CHAN8440, 1985).
> Holywell Ensemble. (British Music Label BML010, 1994).

Sonata for clarinet and piano. Joy Farrell (clarinet), Julius Drake (piano) (Chandos CHAN9197, 1994).

Sonata for flute and piano. Kate Hill (flute), Julius Drake (piano) (Chandos CHAN9197, 1994).

Ingrid Culliford (flute), Dominic Saunders (Lorelt LNT107, n.d.).

Sonata for oboe and piano. Nicholas Daniel (oboe), Julius Drake (piano) (Chandos CHAN9197, 1994).

Sonata Impromptu for violin and viola. Leland Chen (violin), Clare McFarlane (viola) (Chandos CHAN9197, 1994).

String Quartet no. 1 in D minor. Quartet of London. (Chandos CHAN9219, 1993).

String Quartet no. 2, *Spring Waters*. Quartet of London. (Chandos CHAN9219, 1993).

String Quartet no. 3. Quartet of London. (Chandos CHAN8440, 1985).

String Trio. Quartet of London. (Chandos CHAN8440, 1985).

Suite for oboe and harp. Nicholas Daniel (oboe), Julius Drake (piano) (Chandos CHAN9152, 1993).

Trio for flute, cello, and piano. Kate Hill (flute), Caroline Dearnley (cello), Julius Drake (piano) (Chandos CHAN9152, 1993).

Instrumental Performances

Crépuscule for solo harp. Ieuan Jones (harp) (Chandos CHAN9197, 1994).

Divertimento for solo flute. Kate Hill (flute) (Chandos CHAN9197, 1994).

Fantasy Waltzes. John Ogdon (piano) (Chandos CHAN8399, 1985).

Julian Milford (piano) (Chandos CHAN9825, 2000).

Green Hills. Julian Milford (piano) (Chandos CHAN9825, 2000).

Movements. Julian Milford (piano) (Chandos CHAN9825, 2000).

Night Thoughts. Julian Milford (piano) (Chandos CHAN9825, 2000).

Twelve Preludes (excerpts). John Ogdon (piano) (Chandos CHAN8399, 1985).

Sonata alla Toccata. Julian Milford (piano) (Chandos CHAN9825, 2000).

Peter Donohoe (piano) (Naxos, 2005)

Vocal, Choral and Operatic Recordings

Invocations: Song cycle for soprano and piano. Jill Gomez (soprano), John Constable (piano) (Chandos CHAN9220, 1993).

A Leave-taking: Song cycle for tenor and piano. Anthony Rolfe Johnson (tenor). Graham Johnson (piano) (Chandos CHAN9220, 1993).

Miss Julie: Opera in two acts. Philharmonia Orchestra (Vilem Tausky). Jill Gomez (soprano), Benjamin Luxon (baritone) (Lyrita SRCD2218, 1992).

Select Bibliography

This bibliography is restricted to a selection from books and articles by, and specifically about, William Alwyn. Some other titles of interest may be found in the notes to each chapter.

Books and Articles by William Alwyn

All Things Incorruptible [novel] (unpublished, 1976).

An Anthology of Twentieth Century French Poetry [compiled and translated] (London: Chatto and Windus, 1969).

"Ariel to Miranda", *Adam International Review*, 316/17/18 (1967), 4–84.

"Art is Meant to be Enjoyed", *William Alwyn Society Newsletter*, no. 6 (Jan. 1999). Adapted from an after-dinner speech to the Northampton Arts Association, 8 Nov. 1971.

"Banned Music", letter to *The Times* (7 June 1975), 13.

"The Composer and the Crown", *Sight and Sound*, 21:4 (April–June 1952), 176–7.

Daphne, or The Pursuit of Beauty [essay on aesthetics in form of a poem] (Southwold: Southwold Press, 1972).

Early Closing: Autobiography of My Childhood (unpublished, 1963).

"Edward Elgar (1857–1934)". Sleeve note written at request of Britten for *The Dream of Gerontius*, LSO conducted by Benjamin Britten. Decca long playing record. (Alwyn's appreciation not reprinted with the CD rerelease).

Film Music: Sound or Silence, lecture to the British Film Association, Edinburgh Film Festival, 31 Aug. 1958, and to the National Film Theatre, Autumn 1958. First part published as "Composing for the Screen", *Films and Filming* (March 1959), 9, 34; repr. in Tony Thomas (ed.), *Film Score: The View from the Podium* (South Brunswick; New York: A. S. Barnes & Co., 1979), 191–5.

"How Not to Write Film Music", *British Film Academy Journal* (Autumn 1954), 7–8.

"Imperfect Reassurance", letter to *The Times* (24 July 1969), 9.

Introduction and notes to Manvell and Huntley, *The Technique of Film Music* (below).

"An Introduction to Film Music", *RAM Magazine*, 154 (Jan. 1953), 32–4.

Letter paying tribute to Walter Leigh, *Documentary News Letter*, 3:7 (July 1942), 105.

Letters to *The Times* on Copyright Bill (16 Nov. 1955), 11; (7 Dec. 1955), 11; (27 March 1956), 11; (2 July 1956), 9; (16 Oct. 1956), 11.

"Loss to Music", letter to *The Times* (16 July 1969), 9.

"Mascagni's *Il Piccolo Marat*", *Opera International Magazine* (Dec. 1977).

"A Memory with a Moral", *William Alwyn Society Newsletter*, no. 3 (Feb. 1997). Believed to have been written for the *Royal Academy of Music Magazine*.
"Mr R. F. J. Howgill", obituary for *The Times* (31 May 1975), 14.
"Music in the Background", 1500-word article in unidentified magazine (*c*.1947),
"The Music of Arnold Bax", *RAM Magazine*, 157 (January 1954), 6–8.
"The Musical Opinions of Dr Crotch", *RAM Magazine*, 206 (Autumn 1974), 7–11; 207 (Spring 1975), 3–8; 208 (Summer 1975), 7–12; 209 (Autumn 1975), 12–16.
"A Musician's Approach to the Documentary Film", *Documentary Film News*, 7:64 (April 1948), 44, 47.
"My Debt to Czech Music", *Czech Music* [Journal of the Dvořák Society], 8:1 (Jan. 1982).
"New Books on Film: *Composing for the Films*. Hans Eisler", review by W. A. (presumed to be William Alwyn), *Documentary Film News*, 7:66 (June 1948), 71.
"*Odd Man Out*", *Film Music Notes*, 7:2 (Nov.–Dec. 1947), repr. by Muir Mathieson in "The Time Factor in Film Music", *Film Industry*, 4:23 (May 1948), 7.
"The Owl and the Nightingale", *Music* 2:3 (Feb. 1953), 15–17.
The Prayers and Elegies of Francis Jammes [trans.] (Hub Publications, 1978).
"The Puccini Homestead", in Gervaise Hughes and Herbert van Thal (eds.), *The Music Lover's Companion* (London: Eyre and Spottiswoode, 1971), 421–3. From *The Golden Girl and the Swallow* (unpublished, 1968).
"Sonata for Clarinet and Piano", *Musical Events*, 17:11(Nov. 1962), 27.
"1066 and All That", *The Composer*, 16 (July 1965), 23–5.
Winged Chariot: An Essay in Autobigoraphy (Southwold: Southwold Press, 1983).
Winter in Copenhagen and *Mirages* [poems] (Southwold: Southwold Press, 1971).
The World in My Mind [essay on philosophy in form of a poem] (Southwold: Southwold Press, 1975).

Broadcast Talks

"William Alwyn on Film Music", BBC Third Programme, 24 Feb. 1957.
"William Alwyn's Opera *Miss Julie*", BBC Radio 3, 16 July 1977; repr. in *Musical Opinion*, 101:1200 (Oct. 1977), 30–31.

Books and Articles about William Alwyn

anonymus, "Twenty Year Old Local Musician", *The Northampton Independent* (4 Sept. 1926), 30.
anonymus, "Hollywood Award for *Desert Victory*", *The Times* (4 March 1944), 3.
anonymus, "William Alwyn" [obituary], *Performing Rights News* (Oct. 1985).
CARMALT, Ian, *William Alwyn, 1905–1985: A Romantic Composer of His Time* (BA diss., Anglia Polytechnic University, 1998).
CRAGGS, Stewart, and POULTON, Alan, *William Alwyn: A Catalogue of His Music* (Hindhead: Bravara Publications, 1985).

CULOT, Hubert, "William Alwyn", *British Music Society Journal*, 7 (1985), 17–29.

DOCHERTY, Jack, "A Tribute to William Alwyn", *The Erich Wolfgang Korngold Society Newsletter*, 13 (Feb. 1986), 1–3.

GREEN, Christopher, "Suffolk Symphonist", *East Anglian Magazine* (June 1982), 358–9.

GREENFIELD, Edward, "A Natural Lyricist" [obituary], *The Guardian* (13 Sept. 1985).

HAYES, Malcolm, untitled CD Review, *Tempo* 183 (Dec. 1992), 46–8.

HESFORD, Brian, "A Critics Choice", *Musical Opinion*, 101:1200 (Oct. 1977), 29.

HOLD, Trevor, "Arnold, Alwyn and Rubbra: Three Northampton Music Men with National Reputations", *The Northampton Chronicle and Echo* (16 Nov. 1970), 2.

——, "The Music of William Alwyn", *The Composer*, 43/44 (Spring 1972), 22–4; (Summer 1972), 15–20.

HUNTLEY, John, "William Alwyn", *Music Parade*, 1:7 (1948), 7–9.

K[ELLER], H[ans], "Bad and Great Work", *Music Review* (May 1950), 145–6; (August 1950), 216–217.

KELLER, Hans, "Film Music: Speech Rhythm", *Musical Times*, 96:1351 (Sept. 1955), 486–7; repr. in Manvell and Huntley, *The Technique of Film Music*, 288–90.

KOWALSKI, Alfons, "William Alwyn", *Pro Musica Sana* [The Miklós Rózsa Society], 8:3 (Summer 1980), 4–11.

LENGNICK & CO., *The Music of William Alwyn* (London: Lengnick & Co., 1958).

LINDGREN, Ernest, "William Alwyn", *Films in 1951: Festival of Britain* (London: BFI Special Publication, 1951), 19–20.

LLEWELLYN, William, "Obituary: William Alwyn, 1905–85", *RAM Magazine*, 219 (Autumn 1985), 24–5.

MANN, W., "Inside a Composer's Mind and Workshop", *The Times* (6 Sept. 1968), 9.

McCABE, John, "Latter-day Romantic", *Records and Recordings*, 22:2 (Oct. 1972), 44.

MANVELL, Roger, and HUNTLEY, John (eds.), *The Technique of Film Music* (London: Focal Press, 1957; rev. edn, 1975). Published under guidance of committee appointed by British Film Academy chaired by Alwyn. Scene-by-scene study of final moments of *Odd Man Out*, 139–49.

OTTAWAY, Hugh, "William Alwyn", in Stanley Sadie (ed.), *The New Grove Dictionary of Music and Musicians*, 1st edn (London: Macmillan, 1980), 300–301.

PALMER, Christopher, "A Master of Many Arts", *The Gramophone*, 72:858 (Nov. 1994), 20–21.

PIRIE, Peter J., "English Backwaters", *Records and Recording*, 27:11 (July 1979), 36.

ROUTH, Francis, "William Alwyn", in *Contemporary British Music: The Twenty-Five Years from 1945–70* (London: Macdonald, 1972), 55–69.

VANSON, Frederic, "William Alwyn: Composer, Artist and Poet", *Northamptonshire and Bedfordshire Life* (Jan. 1975), 37.

——, "Profile no. 13: William Alwyn, FRAM", *RAM Magazine*, 213 (Spring 1977), 3–6.

——, "William Alwyn", *Suffolk Fair* (Feb. 1975), 33.

Related articles are also to be found in the *William Alwyn Society Newsletter*.

Index

Abady, Temple 169

Abbey Theatre, Dublin 166–7, 235

Abercrombie, Sir Patrick 129

Abingdon Park Brass Band 12

Abingdon Park, Nottingham 12

The Abominable Snowman (Guest, 1957) 291

The Abominable Snowman (TV film, 1955)
     291 n. 5

Academy Award ("Oscar") 76, 120, 204, 219,
     243

Accident Service (Dobson, 1944) 111

Ackerman, John 83

Addinsell, Richard 35, 38, 39, 47, 71, 96, 114,
     161, 230 n. 12, 269, 280, 290

Africa Freed (Stewart, 1943) 77–9

Africa Korps 78

Agee, James 149

Aimée, Anouk 222

Air and Variations in E major, "The
     Harmonious Blacksmith" (Handel) 39

Air Outpost (Taylor, 1937) 23, 28, 216, 217

air power; flight music 21–3, 28, 53, 74–5,
     178, 216, 254

Air Raid Precautions (ARP) 29, 41

Air Transport Auxiliary (ATA) 51, 54

El Alamien, Battle of 75

Aldeburgh (Suffolk) Festival 303

Alexander, Donald 25, 28

Alexander, Sir Harold, 1st Earl Alexander of
     Tunis 74

Alexandra Choir 46

"All the King's Horses" (song) 54

"All Things Bright and Beautiful" (hymn) 196

Allen, Lewis 178, 179

Alwyn Archive 55, 169

Alwyn, Jonathan 16, 30

Alwyn, Mary; *see* Carwithen, Doreen Mary

Alwyn, Nicholas 16

Alwyn, Olive (née Pull; wife) 16

Alwyn, Sir Nicholas 11 n. 7

Alwyn, William; *see also titles of individual
     films and works*
personality 3, 8, 10–11, 29, 64, 250, 282
     n. 8, 269, 304–5
early life 11–13
cricket 282 n. 8, 303 n. 4
education 13–15, 304
professor of composition 15, 16, 266, 304
war work 29–30
"blacklisted" 33
friends and acquaintances 8, 12, 18–19, 34,
     145, 200, 217–18, 221, 304
health 15, 199, 266, 302, 303
art and paintings 10, 11, 12, 218 n. 34, 64,
     303, 304
poetry 10–11, 64, 83, 207, 303, 304–5
committees 8, 16, 199, 236
radio composition 46–8, 145, 263
television composition 234, 255, 259–60,
     267, 290
light music 38–9, 181
experiment *passim*
     film as opportunity for musical
         experiment 185
     compositional techniques 6–7
     experiment with persistence of sound
         176
     Humphrey Jennings and Alwyn 64
     speech rhythm as subject for experiment
         197
     The Future's in the Air 19–21
     New Worlds for Old 26
     World of Plenty 56
     critical views of *Our Country* 83
     Your Children and You 127–8
     Black on White 259–60
     The Ship that Died of Shame 263
     Fortune is a Woman 272
pre-planning of scores 4, 140, 152–3, 155,
     164, 170–71, 193–4, 196, 257

Alwyn, William (*cont.*)
  jokes, games, and the comic
    in general 3
    and versatility 7
    Monkey into Man 25
    New Worlds for Old 26
    SOS 36
    They Flew Alone 52
    Welcome to Britain 80, 81
    Atlantic Trawler 92
    On Approval 103, 104, 106–8
    Great Day 115
    The Rake's Progress 135, 137
    I See a Dark Stranger 140–41
    The Fallen Idol 189
    The History of Mr Polly 204, 206–7
    The Cure for Love 239–40
    The Card 242–3
    The Crimson Pirate 250–51
    The Million Pound Note 256–7
    Geordie 264
    The Smallest Show on Earth 276–8
    The Swiss Family Robinson 288
  Hollywood offers 185, 185 n. 11
  Ireland 81–2, 137, 143, 148, 145–58, 165–72,
    235–6, 263, 283–5
  operas 5, 26, 42, 44, 161, 197, 198, 207, 259,
    263–4, 303
  BBC offer of appointment 266
  relationship with musical
    establishment 7–8
  lectures 4, 75, 106, 158, 282–3, 290; *see
    also Film Music: Sound or Silence*
  move to Blythburgh 302
  final years 303–4
  honorary Doctor of Music at University of
    Leicester 303
  awarded CBE 303
Ambler, Eric 96, 173, 174, 237, 242
American Service Film Unit 79
Anderson, Max 57
Anderson, Michael 283, 285
Anderson, Michael, jr 295
Animal Kingdom series (various, 1937–8)
    24–5
Annakin, Ken 169, 257, 258, 287, 288
Anstey, Edgar 17, 25
Anthony and Cleopatra (Shakespeare) 135
Architects of England (Eldridge, 1941) 37

Ardmore Studios 283
Armendáriz, Pedro 278
Armistice Night (1918) 142, 143
Army Film and Photographic Unit
    (AFPU) 72, 77, 110, 119–20
Army Film Center 79, 119
Army Kinematograph Service (AKS) 96,
    124, 172
Arnold, Sir Malcolm 12, 148 n. 7, 230 n. 12,
    234, 288
Arundell, Dennis 43
Asherson, Renée 93, 221
"Asleep in the Deep" (song) 103 n. a
Asquith, Anthony 30, 80, 133, 186, 195
Associated British Picture Corporation
    (ABPC) 30, 302
Atlantic Trawler (Sainsbury, 1944) 92–3
Attenborough, Richard 261
"Au clair de la lune" (song) 232, 233
"Auld Lang Syne" (song) 63
Austen, Jane 291
Autumn Legend (Alwyn) 6, 218
Auxiliary Fire Service (AFS) 64
The Awkward Age (James) 187

Bach, Johann Sebastian 14, 297
Bach Choral Society 239
Baillie, Gwen 128
Baker, Buddy 288
Baker, George 261
Baker, Muriel; *see* Box, Muriel
Baker, Roy Ward 124, 133, 172–3, 282, 282
    n. 8
Balcon, Sir Michael 30, 276, 278
Barbirolli, Sir John 130
Barr, Charles 228, 244, 249
Bartok, Eva 251
The Basement Room (Greene) 186
Bates, Alan 299
Bates, H. E. 93
Bath 24
Battle for Freedom (Orbiston, 1942) 46
The Battle of Russia (Litvak, 1943) 80
Bax, Sir Arnold 7, 8, 302
Baxter, Anne 265
Baxter, John 42
Beatty, Robert 152
Beaumont, Charles 37
Beauplan, Amédée de 225

Beaver, Jack 18

Becker, Henry, III 207–8, 209

Beckwith, Reginald 256

Bedevilled (Leisen, 1955) 265

Beecham, Sir Thomas 270

Beethoven, Ludwig van 27, 40 n. 7

Beldon, Eileen 58

La Belle Arsène (Monsigny) 24

Belsen concentration camp 122

Ben-Hur (Wyler, 1959) 44

Benjamin, Arthur 18, 35

Bennell, Raymond 18

Bennett, Arnold 242

Bennett, Compton 139 n. 6

Bergman, Ingmar 292

Berlioz, Hector 292

Best, Richard ("Dick") 8

The Bible 151 n. 9, 153, 156–7

"A Bicycle Built for Two" (song) 203

Big Ben 54 n. 10, 63, 86, 99, 115, 124

Big City (Bond, 1940) 31–2, 34

"Billy Boy" (song) 31, 40

Birt, Louise 50

Bishop, Terry 219–20

"Black and Tans" (Royal Irish Constabulary Reserve Force) 283, 284

Black on White (Read 1954) 259–60

The Black Pirate (Parker, 1926) 250

The Black Rose (Hathaway, 1950) 230 n. 12

The Black Tent (Hurst, 1956) 6, 266, 268–70

Blair, Janet 292

Bleak House (Dickens) 141

Bliss, Sir Arthur 7, 24, 35, 73, 302

Blitz, London 31, 64, 86

Blitzstein, Marc 120

The Blue Lamp (Dearden, 1950) 296

Blythburgh 302, 303

Board of Health 110

"Bond, James" 301

Bond, Ralph 29, 31

Bondarchuk, Sergei 170 n. 17

The Book of the Dead 22

Boult, Sir Adrian 302

Boulting, John 30, 42, 133, 237

Boulting, Roy 30, 42, 77, 79, 120, 133

Box, Muriel (née Baker) 40, 107

Box, Sydney 40, 99, 107

"Boycott Theme" (from *Captain Boycott*, Alwyn) 170

Boycott, Capt. Charles Cunningham 165, 167, 170, 171

"Boys and Girls Come Out to Play" (song) 40

Boys in Brown (Darnborough, 1949) 302

"The Boys of Wexford" (song, Alwyn) 166, 170–71

Bracken, Brendan 96

Bradley, Scott 206 n. 17

Brand, Christianna 159

Brando, Marlon 299

Bressy Report for London 28

"Bridal Chorus" (from *Tannhäuser*, Wagner) 44

"Bridie's Tune" (from *I See a Dark Stranger*, Alwyn) 137

Bridson, D. G. 46.

Brief Encounter (Lean, 1945) 80 n. 11, 142, 191

Britain to America (BBC feature, 1942) 46

British Filmmakers 242

British Broadcasting Corporation (BBC) 7, 34, 35, 38, 46–8, 125, 157 n. 24, 165 n. 5, 263, 266; *see also* Alwyn, William: radio composition; Alwyn, William: television composition; radio

British Commercial Gas Association 25

British Film Academy 8, 236

British Film Festival (1946) 134 [Pl. 7]

British Film Institute (BFI) 236

British Film of the Year Award 157

British Lion Film Corporation 230

British National Films 42

British Overseas Airways Corporation (BOAC) 216

Britten, Benjamin 17, 19, 47, 234, 263

Brodszky, Nicholas 48 n. 6, 94, 94 n. 15, 95

Bronson, Charles 264 n. 6

Brontë, Charlotte 141

Brook, Clive 99, 106

Brook, Lesley 125

Brooke, Michael, jr 228

Brook-Jones, Elwyn 156

Brown, Royal S. 2

Bryan, Dora 221

Bryant, Gerry 128

Buchan, John 226

Buckingham Palace 53, 54 n. 10

Bugs Bunny series 206

Burgess, Alan 48

Burgh, Eva 252
Burma Victory (Boulting, 1945) 72, 120
Burnford, Paul 25
Butt, Sir Alfred 200
Butterflies and Elephants (Mackrell, 1948) 106 n. 2

Cagney, James 283, 284
Calvert, Phyllis 243
"Calypso" (from *The Rake's Progress*, Alwyn) 38, 92, 133, 134 [Pl. 7], 241, 300
Campbell, Judy 160
Cannes Film Festival 302
Canning, Victor 222
A Canterbury Tale (Powell and Pressburger, 1944) 61
Capra, Frank 79
Captain Boycott (Launder, 1947) 165–72, 175, 305
The Card (Neame, 1952) 235, 242–3
Cardiff, Jack 37
Carey, Joyce 93
Carnival of the Animals (Arnold) 288
Carnival of the Animals (Saint-Saëns) 288
Carrick, Bob 74
Carry On (Rogers, 1958–1978) 222
Carve Her Name With Pride (Gilbert, 1958) 279
Carwithen, Doreen Mary (2nd wife) 9, 261, 302–3
Casablanca (Curtiz, 1942) 224
Casino Theatre, London (London Casino) 224
Cass, Henry 40
"Castaway" (from *In Search of the Cast-aways*, Sherman, Alwyn) 295
Catley, Gwen 165
Cavalcanti, Alberto 17
Central Office of Information (COI) 124, 128
C'era una volta il West (*Once Upon a Time in the West*, Leone, 1968) 264 n. 6
Chagrin, Francis 18
Chamberlain, Cyril 41
Chandos, John 261
Chapman, Edward 173
Chapman, James 254
Charles II 43, 45
"Charleston" (dance) 259–60
Cheltenham Festival 130

"Cherry Ripe" (song) 181–2
Chevalier, Maurice 295
Children's Film Foundation (CFF) 228
Chopin, Frédéric 280
Chorlton, Michael 169
Christmas Features (BBC) 48
Christopher Columbus (Macdonald, 1949) 302
Churchill, Sir Winston 48, 73, 74, 122
Cineguild 161
The Cinema 181
City Set on a Hill 145
A City Speaks (Rotha, 1947) 130–31
Clarissa (Richardson) 141
Clarke, T. E. B. 228, 229, 256
Clemenceau, Georges 281
Clifford, Hubert 38, 47, 84, 89, 90, 90, 186, 195
"Climb the Mountain" (from *Third Man on the Mountain*, Marks, Alwyn) 288
"Clopin Clopart" (from *Latin Quarter*, Coquatrix) 224
Clyde, June 231
Coal Face (Cavalcanti, 1935) 17
Coastal Command (Holmes, 1942) 204
Coates, Eric 181
Cochran, Sir C. B. 200
Cole, Sidney 27
Collard Scholarship (Worshipful Company of Musicians) 16
Collisson, Houston 284
Colonel March of Scotland Yard (TV series, 1955–6) 255
Columbia Pictures 147, 272
Comfort, Lance 42, 71, 114, 115, 117, 172
Comin' thro' the Rye (Hepworth, 1923) 277
Commander of the Order of the British Empire (CBE) 53, 303
commentary; *see* voice-over
Composers' Guild of Great Britain 8, 199, 236
Composing for the Film (Eisler) 185 n. 11
Compton, Fay 149
Concerto for oboe, harp and string orchestra (Alwyn) 130
Concerto Grosso no. 3 (Alwyn) 303
Conquest of the Air (Shaw and others, 1938 / Friend, 1940) 18, 23
Cook, Pam 244, 249

Cooper, Gary 1 n. 7, 289

Cooper, Gladys 200

Cooper, Harold 40

Cooper, Lester 112

Coquatrix, Bruno 224

Coronation of Elizabeth II 48, 302

Cottage to Let (Asquith, 1941) 61

Cottrell, Leonard 48

Country Town, (Wintle, 1945) 114, 115

Covent Garden Opera Company 258

"Covent Garden" (from *London Suite*,
     Coates) 181

Coward, Noel 55, 225

Crabb, Lt Lionel 281–2

Crabtree, Arthur 255

Craig, Michael 281, 296

Cravat, Nick 250, 251

Criminal Investigation Department (CID) 175

The Crimson Pirate (Siodmak, 1952) 250–51,
     251, 256, 277, 288, 295, 305

Cromwell, John 226

Cromwell, Oliver 137, 143

Cross, Joan 168, 170, 172 n. 22

Crown Film Unit 30, 35, 76, 81, 241

Crown of the Year (Keene, 1943) 61, 62
     [Pl. 4], 63, 68 n. 21

Crutchley, Rosalie 161

Culver, Roland 99, 266

The Cure for Love (Donat, Shaw, 1949) 38,
     221–2, 304

Currie, Finlay 200, 205

Curzon, Sir Clifford 15

Cusack, Cyril 284

Cutner, Sidney 180 n. 5

Daffy Duck series 206

Dahl, Arlene 272

Daily Herald 131

Dalrymple, Ian 64, 76

Dangerous Moonlight (Hurst, 1941) 38, 71,
     269, 280

Darnborough, Anthony 255, 302

Darnell, Linda 241

Dartmoor Prison 178

Daughter of Darkness (Comfort, 1948) 172

Davies, Betty Ann 200

Davies, Jack 224 n. 4

Davies, John Howard 207

Davis, Hubert 18

Davis, Sir John 278

Davitt, Michael 171

Daybreak in Udi (Bishop, 1949) 219–20, 257,
     292

D-Day (Allied invasion of Normandy, 6 June
     1944) 91, 96, 119, 123

Dearden, Basil 133, 256, 261, 276, 277, 296

Debussy, Claude-Achille 7, 13, 14, 26, 106

Defensively Equipped Merchant Ships
     (DEMS) 113

Dehn, Paul 157

Del Giudice, Filippo 133, 146, 172

Delius, Frederick 7, 201, 284

The Demi-Paradise (Asquith, 1943) 48 n.
     6, 61

Denham Studios 35, 48, 49, 119, 162 [Pl. 9],
     165, 172, 179, 201, 268, 302

Denham, Maurice 128

Derrybeg Fair (overture, Alwyn) 166

Desert Fury (Allen, 1947) 179

Desert Victory (Macdonald, 1943) 1, 8, 38, 45,
     55, 57, 69, 72–7, 78, 84, 97, 113, 120, 122,
     161, 184, 245, 248, 254, 293

Desny, Ivan 224

Devil's Bait (Scott, 1959) 286–7

Dew, Desmond 172

diegetic music
     possible origin of term 2 n. 4
     as musical contrast 7
     The Future's in the Air 22
     They Flew Alone 53–4
     Fires Were Started 65, 67, 70
     Our Country 88, 89, 90
     On Approval 100, 106
     A Start in Life 111
     Soldier–Sailor 114
     What's the Next Job? 125
     I See a Dark Stranger 138
     Take My Life 162, 164
     Captain Boycott 170–71
     The October Man 174–5
     The Rocking Horse Winner 212
     The Cure for Love 222
     The Golden Salamander 223, 224
     Madeleine 227
     Night Without Stars 231, 232–3
     The Magic Box 239
     Lady Godiva Rides Again 240
     Mandy 247–8

diegetic music (*cont.*)
  The Black Tent 269–70
  The Smallest Show on Earth 277
  The Running Man 300
dialogue and speech rhythms
  stimulus to the imagination 30
  music techniques in melodrama 306
  speech rhythms in Alwyn's operas 319, 320
  dog speech pattern 276
  These Children are Safe 31
  Penn of Pennsylvania 43
  They Flew Alone 54
  The Harvest Shall Come 57–8
  Fires Were Started 65, 67, 70
  Our Country 84
  There's a Future in It 94
  On Approval 100
  Great Day 116, 117
  The True Glory 121
  A City Speaks 131–2
  I See a Dark Stranger 137, 138, 140–41
  voice-overs of *I See a Dark Stranger* and
    The Rake's Progress 42–3
  Odd Man Out 150–51, 153, 155
  The Fallen Idol 189, 190–91
  The Winslow Boy 196–8
  The History of Mr Polly 201
  The Rocking Horse Winner 210–11
  Mandy 247
  The Crimson Pirate 251
  The Long Memory 252
  The Rainbow Jacket 256
  Svengali 259
  The Ship that Died of Shame 263–4
  Fortune is a Woman 272, 276
  Manuela 279
  I Accuse 281
  The Silent Enemy 281
Dickens, Charles; Dickensian 38, 141, 251
Dickinson, Thorold 30, 31 n. 5
Dickson, Paul 255
Dieterle, William 280
Disney, Walt 206, 288, 295
Divertimento for solo flute (Alwyn) 27
Dr Jekyll and Mr Hyde (Mamoulian, 1931) 19
Dr No (Young, 1962) 301
Documentary Movement 17–18, 19–21, 25, 30
Documentary News Letter (*DNL*) 35, 39, 57,
  60, 92

Don Juan (Strauss) 13
Don Quixote (Cervantes) 201
Donat, Robert 48, 170, 221, 237
Dostoyevsky, Fyodor; Dostoyevskian 251
Dragnet (TV series, 1951–9) 289
Drake, Ted 172
Drazin, Charles 157
The Dream of Gerontius (Elgar) 15
dream and psychological music, ethereal,
  hallucinationatory
  The Future's in the Air 23
  Penn of Pennsylvania 45
  Africa Freed 79
  On Approval 107–8
  Penicillin 112
  Great Day 118
  I See a Dark Stranger 137, 138, 139
  The Rake's Progress 142
  Odd Man Out 154–7
  Take My Life 162–3, 164
  "Mermaid's Song (Miranda)" 172
  The October Man 173–6
  So Evil My Love 184
  The Fallen Idol 190
  The Rocking Horse Winner 209–10
  Madeleine 226
  State Secret 227
  The Magnet 229–30
  The Magic Box 238
  Saturday Island 241
  Mandy 246
  Svengali 259
  The Million Pound Note 256
  The Ship that Died of Shame 262–3
  Fortune is a Woman 273–5
  Carve Her Name With Pride 280
  The Silent Enemy 281–2
  Devil's Bait 287
Dresdel, Sonia 186
Dreyfus, Alfred; Dreyfus Affair 280, 281
"drumroll" technique 5, 98, 119, 160, 213,
  220, 290
du Maurier, Daphne 141
du Maurier, George 258, 259
du Maurier, Sir Gerald 177
Dunne, Irene 230
Dunne, Philip 177
Dvorak, Ann 71, 93, 94, 280
Dvořák, Antonín 265

Each for All (Tully, 1946) 131
Ealing Studios 15, 24 n. 15, 114, 228, 243, 245, 256, 276
Easdale, Brian 17
Easter Rising 263
Edinburgh Festival 158, 282
Edmonds, Fella 256
Edwards, Meredith 228
"Eileen Oge" (song) 284
Ein feste Burg ist unser Gott (A Mighty Fortress is Our God, Cantata 80, Bach) 297
Eisenhower, Dwight David 119, 120
Eisler, Hanns 185 n. 11
Eldridge, John 36, 82, 83, 87 [Pl. 5], 215, 216, 276
Electrical and Musical Industries (EMI) 15
Elgar, Sir Edward; Elgarian 7, 15, 26, 52, 73, 123, 195, 236, 249
Elizabeth is Queen (Thomas, 1953) 302
Elizabeth II 48
Ellitt, Jack 85
Elstree Studios 18, 268
Elton, Arthur 17, 25
Elton, S. Raymond 40
Elvey, Maurice 115
Emmet, Robert 263
Emmett, E. V. H. 100
Empire Air Mail Programme 18
The English Inn (Baker, 1941) 40
Enigma Variations (Elgar) 249
Enough to Eat? (Anstey, 1936) 17
Equity (actors' union) 95
Escape (Mankiewicz, 1948) 177–8
Escape to Danger (Comfort, 1943) 71
Evans, Clifford 43
Eve of Battle (Macdonald, 1944) 119–20
"Everyone Sang" (Sassoon) 116

The Faerie Queen (Spenser) 11
Fairbanks, Douglas 250
Fairbanks, Douglas, jr 226
Fairchild, William 281
The Fairy Fiddler (Alwyn) 12
The Fallen Idol (Reed, 1948) 1, 3, 127, 158, 186–95, 210, 234, 246, 255, 273, 305
The Farewell Companions (radio opera, Alwyn) 263
Farrar, David 231

Faust (Gounod) 215
Faustus; Faustian 215
Fay, W. G. 146
Fellini, Federico 222 n. 2, 279
Fennell, Arthur 221
Fenton, Leslie 93
Ferrer, José 280
Festival in London (Leacock, 1951) 236
Festival March (Alwyn) 236, 267
Festival of Britain 129, 234, 236, 239, 276
Field, Capt. D. P. 121
Film Centre 25, 35
Film Music (radio programme) 165 n. 5
Film Music Notes 204
Film Music: Sound or Silence (Alwyn)
    reference 2 n. 2
    composer to be versatile 7
    composer to have individuality 7
    must give of one's best 8
    composer's fee for documentaries 27
    how film music should be experienced 282–3
    value of silence 4–5
    "drum-roll" technique 160
    speech rhythm 196–7
    heightening of atmosphere by cumulative musical sounds 191–2
    film music not descriptive 3, 106
    music can work on different plane from visuals (e.g. *The October Man*) 175–6
    sound film's origin in stage 3
    music portrays actor's emotions 175
    film music must be subtle 290
    art of film lies in craft co-operation 36
    film music best pre-planned 4
    pre-planning *Odd Man Out* 148
    pre-planning in *The Fallen Idol* 193–4
    sound effects to be used with imagination and discretion 138–9
    working with sound editor on *Odd Man Out* 153
    Henry Moore's opinion of Alwyn score 234
    often prefers small orchestra 234–5
    art demands experiment 21
    experimental score for *Black on White* 259–60
    rough cuts inspirational 4
    sequencing, as in *Desert Victory* 75

film music techniques in general 1–7, 19,
    51–2, 94, 203–4; *see also Film Music:
    Sound or Silence* (Alwyn)
The Film till Now (Rotha) 18
Films and Filming 64
Films of Fact 110, 123; *see also* Paul Rotha
    Productions; Rotha, Paul
The Finest Years (Drazin) 157
Fingal's Cave (*The Hebrides*,
    Mendelssohn) 106
Fingers and Thumbs (Spice, 1938) 106 n. 3
Fires were Started (Jennings, 1943) 1, 3, 29,
    37, 39, 40, 63–71, 72, 81, 97, 128, 229, 305
"The First Noel" (Christmas carol) 63
First String Quartet (Carwithen) 302
Firth, Anne 40, 41
Fisher, Terence 255
Fishman, Jack 169
Fitzgerald, Geraldine 183
Five Preludes for Orchestra (Alwyn) 15
"Five-Minute Films" 29, 49
Flaherty, Robert 30, 216
Fletcher, Paul 215
Flowers of the Field (Johns) 11
Flynn, Errol 251
Fonda, Henry 264 n. 6
Foot, Geoffrey 225
Footsteps in the Night; *see Night Watch*
"For Johnny" (Pudney) 95
Forbes, Bryan 269
Forrest, Steve 265
Forshaw, J. H. 129
Forth Bridge 91
Fortune is a Woman (Launder, 1957) 272–6
49th Parallel (Powell, 1941) 42
Fox, William 228
Fox Talbot, William 239
François Villon Society 14
Frankel, Benjamin 24
Freeman, H. W. 57
French Resistance 279
French Town: September 1944 (Shaw, 1945)
    112–13
French, Percy 284
Frend, Charles 24, 133, 228
Friese-Greene, William 237–9
Furse, Roger 156 n. 21
The Future's in the Air (Shaw, 1937) 18–23,
    28, 31, 178, 216, 217

Gaillard, Marius François 17
Gainsborough Pictures 169
Galsworthy, John 177, 178
Gardens in the Rain; *see Jardins sous le pluie*
Gate Theatre, Dublin 235
Gaumont British Instructional Films
    (GBI) 18, 111
Gaumont British News 100
Gaumont British Studios, Lime Grove 18
The Gen (RAF, 1944–5) 110
General Post Office (GPO) Film Unit 17, 18, 19
Geordie (Launder, 1955) 264–5
George VI 78, 236
Gershwin, George 127
Gershwin, Ira 127
G. E. Turner Films 30
Gilbert, Lewis 217–18, 279
Gilels, Emil 218
Gilkyson, Gerry 288
Gilliam, Laurence 47, 48
Gilliat, Sidney 133, 135, 136, 139 n. 7, 141, 143,
    159, 226, 227, 239, 240, 264, 272, 276
"The Girl I Left Behind Me" (song) 170
Giro-Tiller 41
Globe Theatre, London 2
Glyn-Jones, John 47 [Pl. 3]
Goehr, Walter 47–8
"Going Home" (from Symphony no. 9,
    Dvořák) 265
Gold, Harry 172 n. 22
The Golden Salamander (Neame, 1950) 219,
    221, 222–4, 229
Goring, Marius 161
Gorsen, Norah 264
Gough, Michael 235
Gounod, Charles 215
Grainer, Ron 301
Grainger, Percy 88
Granger, Stewart 165
Gravett, George 66
Gray, Donald 241
Gray, Nadia 231
Great Day (Comfort, 1945) 45, 61, 114–19,
    145, 229, 267, 305
Great Expectations (Lean, 1946) 200, 205
The Great Mr Handel (Walker, 1942) 42
Greater London Plan 129
Green, F. L. 151 n. 9
Green, Guy 225

Green, Philip 255
Green Belt; see *Green Girdle*
Green for Danger (Gilliat, 1947) 159–61, 227
Green Girdle (Keene, 1941) 6, 39, 61, 116
Greene, Graham 3, 18, 32, 186, 187, 194
Greenpark Productions 30, 61, 129, 172
Greenwood, Joan 173
Greenwood, John 35, 48
Greenwood, Walter 221
Grenfell, Joyce 114
Grieg, Edvard 7, 218
Grierson, John; Griersonite 17, 18, 25, 30, 32, 83, 234
Grierson, Ruby 25
Griffin, Eleanor 287
Griffith, Jane 256
Griffiths, Fred 66
Groves, Reg 32, 131
Grunwald, Anatole de 42, 195
The Guardian (Manchester) 289
Guinness, Alec 235, 242, 244, 254
Guthridge, John 296
Gynt, Greta 161

Habberfield, Mary 24
Hallat, Henry 124
Hallé Orchestra 130, 131
Hamer, Robert 133, 251, 253–4
Hamilton, Guy 34, 278
Hamlet (Shakespeare) 2
Hammer Films 273, 290
Hampstead Garden Suburb 16, 29
Hamshere, Keith 295
Hanau, John 48
Handel, George Frideric 39
Hardwicke, Sir Cedric 112, 197
Harmon, Jympson 224 n. 4
Harrison, Kathleen 117
Harrison, Rex, 133, 177
Hart, Peter 169
Hartley, James 165 n. 5
Hartnell, William 97, 177
The Harvest Shall Come (Anderson, 1942) 3, 57–61, 236
Harvey, Laurence 281, 299
Haslemere, Surrey 15
Hassell, Christopher 218
Hathaway, Henry 230 n. 12
Havelock-Allan, Anthony, 161

Havergal, Francis R. 297
Hawes, Stanley 25
Hawkins, Jack 243, 257, 272
Hawks, Howard 203
Hayers, Sidney 291
"The Heights of Alma" (song) 170
Heisler, Stuart 241
Heller, Otto 278, 296
Hely-Hutchinson, Victor 48
Hendricks, Gordon 208
Henrey, Bobby 186, 188, 194
Henry Moore: Sculptor (Read, 1951) 234, 259
Henry V (Olivier, Walton, 1944) 135, 151
Hereford Cathedral 15
"Here We Go Round the Mulberry Bush" (song) 160
Herrmann, Bernard 65
"Highland Laddie" (song) 75
Hill, Dr Charles, MP (Lord Hill of Luton) 125
Hillier, Erwin 117, 289
His Master's Voice (HMV) 15
The History of Mr Polly (1949) 2, 91, 200–207, 229, 231, 264, 305
Hitchcock, Alfred; Hitchcockian 19, 23, 65–6, 136, 140, 141, 161, 165, 226, 291
Hitler, Adolf 33, 78
HMS Minelayer (Cass, 1941) 40
HMS *Torrin* 55
Hobson, Valerie 207, 214, 242
Hodson, J. L. 73, 76, 77, 78
Hogarth, William 134
Hold, Trevor 7, 304
Hollingsworth, John 172 n. 22
Holloway, London 15–16
Holloway, Stanley 96
Holst, Gustav 7, 22, 81, 292, 293
Home and School (Bryant, 1947) 111, 128–9
Home Guard 60, 115
"Home Sweet Home" (song) 81
Hondo (trawler) 93
Honegger, Arthur 19
Hope, Bob 80
Hope, Philip 226
Hopkins, Anthony 94 n. 15, 216, 217, 302
Horn, Charles Edward 181
Houghton, Johnny 66
Houses of Parliament 129, 157
Housing Problems (Anstey/Elton, 1935) 17
Howard, Leslie 47 [Pl. 3]

Howard, Trevor 97, 136, 222, 278
Huckvale, David 291
Hugo, Victor 235
Hunt, Martita 52
Hunter, Tab 241
Huntley, John 4, 165 n. 5, 230, 231, 262, 266, 304
Huntley, Raymond 136, 183
Hurst, Brian Desmond 81, 254, 269
Huxley, Julian 24
Hyde-White, Wilfred 224, 295
Hylton, Jane 286

I Accuse (Ferrer, 1958) 280–81
"I Do Like to be Beside the Seaside" (song) 67
"I Got Plenty o' Nuttin'" (song) 127
"I Know where I'm Going" (song) 169
"I'm Going to See You Today" (song) 114
The Informer (Ford, 1935) 204
I See a Dark Stranger (Launder, 1946) 40, 45, 107, 118, 136–42, 143–4, 163, 164–5, 193, 205, 272, 305
I Was a Fireman 64 n. 12; *see also Fires Were Started*
"I've Got a Lovely Bunch of Coconuts" (song) 92
"I've Got Sixpence" (song) 95 n. 17
Illing, Peter 281
Imperial Airways 18, 22, 24, 28, 215
Imperial Chemical Industries (ICI) 57, 60
In Autumn (Grieg) 218
In Search of the Castaways (Stevenson, 1962) 295, 296
"In the Atlantic or the Med" (song) 281
In Which We Serve (Coward/Lean, 1942) 55
Independent Producers 133, 241
Individual Pictures 133, 135, 226, 239
Industrial Revolution 64
International Fair of Contemporary Music, New York 27
"Internationale" (anthem) 48, 49
Irish music 7, 45, 81, 136, 137, 140, 143 n. 9, 165–72, 235–6, 263, 284, 285; *see also* keen
Irish National Land League 171, 172
Irish Republican Army (IRA) 3, 118, 136, 138, 146, 152, 154 n. 18, 157, 283–5
Irish Traditional Music Archive 167

Irving, Ernest 15
Isaiah, Book of 297 n. 5
It Comes from Coal (Fletcher, 1940) 37
Iwerks, Ub 206

Jackman, Bob 288
Jacob, Gordon 48
Jago, Jo 83, 87 [Pl. 5]
Jamaica Inn (Hitchcock, 1939) 136
James, Henry; Jamesian 187, 191, 193
Jane Brown Changes Her Job (Cooper, 1941) 40, 51
Jane Eyre (Brontë) 141
Jardins sous le pluie (*Gardens in the Rain*, Debussy) 106
Jaubert, Maurice 17
Jeakins, A. E. 112
Jenkins, Megs 200
Jennings, Humphrey 30, 64, 66, 67, 68
"Jerusalem" (song) 115, 119
Jesus Christ, 44, 148 n. 7, 156
"Jingle Bells" (song) 80
Joan of Arc 112
"John Brown's Body" (song) 38
John, Rosamund 93
Johns, Rev. C. A. 11
Johnson, Amy 51–5, 178
Johnson, Anthony Rolfe 303
Johnson, Katie 140
Johnson, Nunnally 230
Johnston, Denis 48
Johnston, Margaret 136, 237, 293
Johnston, Peter 286
Joyce, Eileen 40
Juan, or The Libertine (Alwyn) 5, 303
The Jungle Book (Korda, 1942) 288
"Jupiter" (from *The Planets*, Holst) 22, 81

Kanin, Garson 120
Karas, Anton 195, 216
Karlin, Fred 204
Karloff, Boris 255
Katscher, Robert 53
Keen, Geoffrey 286
Keene, Ralph 23, 39, 61, 129, 169, 215
keen (*caoineadh*) 82, 167–9
Keighley, William 251
Keller, Hans 208, 212, 214, 221, 222, 223, 262, 263, 276

"Kelly, the Boy from Killane" (song) 137
Kelly, Dermot 286
Kemp, Philip 244, 245, 249
Kern, Jerome 148 n 7
Kerr, Deborah 43, 136, 289
Kimmins, Anthony 270
Kinematograph Weekly 114, 115, 117
King Arthur and the Knights of the Round
    Table (*Le Morte d'Arthur*, Malory) 201,
    202
King of the Mists (ballet, Alwyn) 166
King, Harold 85
Knight, Eric 56
Knowles, Bernard 255
Koestler, Arthur 49
Korda, Alexander 19, 23, 34, 35, 42, 133, 186,
    195, 200, 221, 226, 230, 264
Korda, Vincent 187
Korda, Zoltan 288
Korngold, Erich Wolfgang 250
Krasker, Robert 146, 299
Kuhn, Annette 72, 73, 74, 77

Labour Party 111, 125; *see also* Socialism
Lady Godiva Rides Again (Launder, 1951)
    239–40, 241
The Lady Vanishes (Hitchcock, 1936) 136
Lambert, Constant 16
Lancashire Land Clubs 63
Lancaster, Burt 250, 251
Land of Promise (Rotha, 1946) 123–4
Landry, Gerard 231
Langley, Noel 258
Lant, Antonia 94
The Lark Ascending (Vaughan Williams) 117,
    302
"The Last Post" (bugle call) 70, 112
Latin Quarter (Nesbitt) 224
Launder and Gilliat Productions 239
Launder, Frank 113, 133, 135, 139 n. 6, 141,
    143, 165, 172, 226, 239, 240, 264, 272, 276
Laura (Preminger, 1944) 176
Laurie, John 97, 241
Lawrence, D. H. 207, 208, 214
Lawrence, Shirley 287
Lawson, Alan 234
Leacock, Philip 236
Lean, David 55, 80, 80 n. 11, 133, 142, 145, 161,
    191, 205, 224, 225, 226, 302

"A Leave-Taking" (song, Alwyn) 303
Legg, Stuart 17, 25, 28
Leigh, Janet 65, 266
Leigh, Walter 17, 18, 19, 21
Leisen, Mitchell 265
Lejeune, C. A. 95, 98, 200
Leone, Sergio 264 n. 6
"Let Him Go, Let Him Tarry" (song) 95: fn17
A Letter From Ulster (Hurst, 1943) 81–2, 269
Letter to the Corinthians (St Paul) 156–7
Lewis, John 38
Life Begins Again (Rotha, 1942) 50
Life for Ruth (Dearden, 1962) 3, 6, 296–9, 304
The Life of Emile Zola (Dieterle, 1937) 280
Lift Your Head, Comrade (Hankinson, 1942)
    49
Lillie, Beatrice 80, 99
Lilliput 100
Lipstone, Louis 180
Liszt, Franz 7, 14, 26, 292
Living With Strangers (Sainsbury, 1941) 39, 92
Lohr, Marie 197
Lom, Herbert 139 n. 6
Lomas, Herbert 124
London County Council (LCC) 129, 130
London Film Productions 34, 186, 264
London Suite (Coates) 181
London Symphony Orchestra (LSO) 15, 19,
    37, 39, 46, 47 [Pl. 3], 48, 61, 157 n. 24, 167,
    172, 236
"Londonderry Air" (song) 81
London Zoological Society of London) 24
Long Live the Queen (radio, Alwyn) 48
The Long Memory (Hamer, 1953) 251–4
Lonsdale, Frederick 99
"Lord, Speak to Me that I May Speak"
    (hymn) 297, 299
Lord, Walter 282
The Lord's Prayer 283
Lorentz, Pare 97
Loughborough College 219
Louisiana Story (Flaherty, 1948) 216
"Love in a Cottage" (from *The Harvest Shall
    Come*, Alwyn) 59–60, 236
"Love Me Tonight" (song) 180
Lucas, Leighton 48
Lucifer; *see* Mephistopheles
Lyra Angelica (Alwyn) 237
Lyric Pieces (Grieg) 218

McAllister, Stewart 66, 68, 72

MacArthur, James 288

McCall, P. J. 137

McCallum, John 252

McCarthy, Joseph; McCarthyite 199

McCormick, F. J. 146

Macdonald, David 72, 74, 119, 120, 302

McFarlane, Brian 115, 296, 297–8

McGonigle, Dr 128 n. 4

McGoohan, Patrick 297

Mach's mit mir Gott nach deiner Güt (Schein) 297

McKechnie, James 157 n. 24

Mackendrick, Alexander 133, 243–9

McKenna, Siobhan 172

McKenna, Virginia 261, 276, 279–80

Mackenzie, Sir Alexander 13, 14

MacNeice, Louis 47, 145

McQuitty, William 282

Madeleine (Lean, 1949) 221, 222, 224–6

The Magic Bow (Knowles, 1946) 255

The Magic Box (Boulting, 1951) 8, 237–9

The Magic Island (Alwyn) 6, 130

The Magnet (Frend, 1950) 203, 228–30, 261

Malleson, Miles 53, 124, 207

Malory, Sir Thomas 201

The Malta Story (Hurst, 1953) 254–5, 269

Mamoulian, Rouben 19

The Man in the White Suit (Mackendrick, 1951) 24, 243

"The Man who Broke the Bank at Monte Carlo" (song) 25

The Man who Knew Too Much (Hitchcock, 1934) 290

Manchester (suite, Alwyn) 130, n. 8

Mancini, Henry 180

Mander, Kay 111

Mandy (Mackendrick, 1952) 3, 243–9, 250, 251, 305

Mankiewicz, Joseph L 177, 178

Manuela (Hamilton, 1957) 3, 278–9

Manvell, Roger 75, 122, 262, 266; *see also* RM

"March" (from *Desert Victory*, Alwyn) 38, 78, 80, 113, 120, 122

Marks, Franklyn 288

The Marriage of Heaven and Hell (oratorio, Alwyn) 16, 18

"Mars" (from *The Planets*, Holst) 292, 293

"La Marselleise" (anthem) 80, 280

Martin, Edie 205

Martinelli, Elsa 278

Marx, Harpo 250

Mason, James 139 n. 6, 146, 147 [Pl. 8], 169

Mass Observation (MO) 71

Massy, Jane 127

The Master of Ballantrae (Keighley, 1953) 251

Mathieson, James Muir

  background 34–5

  emotional 4

  games and jokes 3

  inspired commissioning 7

  film music training scheme 302

  arranges Alwyn's first feature contract? 42

  BBC music director 46, 47 [Pl. 3]

  records *Squadron Leader X* 48

  In Which We Serve 55

  score markings on *On Approval* 108

  records *The True Glory* 121 [Pl. 6]

  conducts at the British Film Festival 134 [Pl. 7]

  starts music on censor's certificate 147, 148

  conducts at Denham Studios 162 [Pl. 9]

  explores potential of folk music 165

  conducts *Take My Life* radio version 165 n. 5

  records *The October Man* 172

  conductor of *So Evil My Love* 179

  interview in *The Cinema* 181

  Alwyn works without him 186

  disappointment over *The Third Man* 195

  plays role of Sir Arthur Sullivan 239

  associations with Darnborough 255

  music director on *Bedevilled* 265

  records *Safari* 268

  jokes about *The Black Tent* 269

  mistimes *Fortune is a Woman* 275

  shuns underscore in *A Night to Remember* 282, 296

  orchestrates Alwyn's Disney films 287 n. 5

  appears in *The Naked Edge* 290

  fails to notice 12-tone series 297

  orchestrates *The Running Man* 300

Mature, Victor 266

Maugham, Robin 269

Measor, Beryl 149

Medal for the General (Elvey, 1944) 61, 115

Méliès, Georges 154

Men of the Lightship (Macdonald, 1940) 72

Mendelssohn Bartholdy, Felix 106

Mephistopheles 213, 215

Mercer, David 128

Meredith, Burgess 80–81, 85

"Mermaid's Song (Miranda)" (Alwyn) 169

Merton Park Studios 30, 39, 107, 127, 219

Meyer, Ernst 17

mickey-mousing
  Penn of Pennsylvania 43
  They Flew Alone 51–2
  World of Plenty 56
  Summer on the Farm 63
  A Start in Life 110–11
  Home and School 129
  Green for Danger 159
  The Fallen Idol 189, 192
  The History of Mr Polly 203–7
  The Rocking Horse Winner 209, 210, 212, 214
  The Mudlark 230
  Night Without Stars 233
  The Magic Box 238
  The Card 242
  The Crimson Pirate 250
  The Master of Ballantrae 251
  The Million Pound Note 257
  Fortune is a Woman: 273

Miles, Bernard 75, 276

Milhaud, Darius 17

Milland, Ray 179

Millar, Daniel 64

Miller, Harry 96, 153, 203, 243

Miller, Mandy 243

The Million Pound Note (Neame, 1954) 256–7, 295

Millions Like Us (Launder and Gilliat, 1943) 84, 133

Mills, Hayley 295

Mills, John 93, 123, 124, 173, 199–200, 205, 207, 251–2

Mills and Boon (publishers) 43

Ministry of Agriculture 57, 61

Ministry of Education 128

Ministry of Information (MoI) 30, 35, 57, 63, 80, 82, 93, 96, 110, 124, 129

Mirages (songs, Alwyn) 303

Miranda (Annakin, 1948) 169

Les Miserables (Hugo) 235

Miss Julie (opera, Alwyn) 5, 263, 303

"Miss McLeod's Reel" 170, 226

Mites and Monsters (Alexander, 1938) 25

A Modern Miracle (Dickinson, 1942) 286

Moeran, E. J. 181

Mollison, Jim 51–4

Monkey into Man (Hawes, 1938) 25

Monsigny, Pierre Alexandre 24

Montgomery, Bernard Law, 1st Viscount Montgomery of Alamein 74

Monthly Film Bulletin (*MFB*) 123, 129, 231

Montreal 34

Moore, Eileen 287

Moore, Henry 234

"Moorland Theme" (from *Britain to America*, Alwyn) 46

Morgan, Michèle 186, 187

Morgan, Terence 243, 259

"Morning" (*Peer Gynt* Suite no. 1, Grieg) 218

Morning Departure (Baker, 1950) 173, 282

Morriconi, Ennio 264 n. 6

Morse, Barry 93

Mortimer, John 299, 301

Mousehole, Cornwall 36

Moviola 64, 286

Mozart, Wolfgang Amadeus 5, 37

The Mudlark (Negulesco, 1950) 230–31

Munch, Edvard 156

Munden, Max 128 n. 4

Munro, Janet 296

Murray, Don 283

Murray, Stephen 84

"Music for Lovers" (from *Britain to America*, Alwyn) 46

The Musical Opinions of Dr Crotch (Alwyn) 14

Musical Times 262

musique concrète (Schaefer and others) 19

Musk, Cecil 37, 39

Mutiny on the Bounty (Milestone, 1962) 299

"My Foolish Heart" (song) 180

"My Heart was an Island" (from *The Swiss Family Robinson*, Gilkyson, Alwyn) 288

"My Old School" (song) 31

The Naked Edge (Anderson, 1961) 2, 289–91

national anthem ("God Save the King/ Queen") 34, 138, 280

National Broadcasting Company (NBC) 46

National Film Finance Corporation (NFFC) 186

National Film School 244

National Film Theatre (NFT) 9, 73, 147, 158, 282

National Fire Service (NFS) 64, 110

National Health Service (NHS) 125

Nazis; Nazism 133, 136, 140, 143

Neagle, Anna 51

Neame, Ronald 55, 133, 161, 222, 235, 237, 242, 256

"Nearer My God to Thee" (hymn) 282, 283

Neff, Hildegarde 258, 259

Negulesco, Jean 133, 230

Nesbitt, Robert 224

The New Britain (Keene, 1940) 31, 32–4, 147

The New Lot (Reed, 1943) 96

New Music Society 16, 199

New Worlds for Old (Rotha, 1938) 19, 25–6, 92, 123

Newton, Robert 51, 156, 156 n. 21

Niall, Ian 235

Night Mail (Wright, 1936) 17, 19

Night of the Eagle (Hayers, 1962) 291–4, 295

A Night to Remember (Baker, 1958) 282–3

Night Watch (Taylor, 1941) 41

Night Without Stars (Pélissier, 1951) 231–3, 288

"Nimrod" (from *Enigma Variations*, Elgar) 249

Niven, David 96

No Resting Place (Rotha, 1951) 235–6

Noble, Denis 47 [Pl. 3]

Noble, George 18

"Nocturne" (from *They Flew Alone*, Alwyn) 280

Northampton Grammar School 12

Northampton; Northamptonshire 7, 11, 12

Northanger Abbey (Austen) 291

Northumberland, Dukes of 11

Le notti di Cabiria (*Cabiria*, Fellini, 1956) 222 n. 2

"O Tannenbaum" (Christmas carol) 288

O'Dea, Denis 156

O'Malley's pub, Cornamona 165, 167

O'Neill, Norman 15

The Observer 200

"O Come All Ye Faithful" (Christmas carol) 128 n. 4

The October Man (Baker, 1953) 3, 32, 172–6

Odd Man Out (Green) 148 n. 7

Odd Man Out (Reed, 1947)
  background and analysis 145–58
  "man on the run" scenario 161
  serious pretentions of 304
  pre-recording 169
  John Huntley worked on 304
  hallucinatory effects 142
  unstable mental state of Johnny 173, 174
  romanticism in 191
  Kathleen's parting from Johnny 305
  "Unfinished" Symphony as humour 3
  cinema release 159
  quarrels between Reed and Rank 186
  "classic" 1
  satisfaction of composer with 261
  referred to in Symphony no. 3 270
  composer stoops to second-rate 255
  orchestrations compared with *The Way Ahead* 79
  comparison with *Great Day* 118
  comparison with *I See a Dark Stranger* 137, 138, 144
  beginning of *Captain Boycott* compares with main theme 167
  comparison with *Escape* 177
  comparison with *So Evil My Love* 182
  comparison with *The History of Mr Polly* 203
  comparison with *Shake Hands With the Devil*, 283, 285
  musical interpretation of *Life for Ruth* as rewarding as 304

Odeon, Leicester Square, London 157

ODTAA Overture (Carwithen) 302

Of All the Gay Places (Pollard, 1937) 24, 37

"Old Man River" (song) 148 n 7

Oliver Twist (Lean, 1948) 8, 302

Olivier, Laurence 135

Olympic Games 264

On Approval (Brook, 1944) 7, 92, 99–108, 115, 182, 189, 205

"Once in Royal David's City" (Christmas carol) 125

Once Upon a Time in the West; see C'era una volta il West

"One Man Went to Mow" (song) 68, 70

One Man's Story (Munden/Shand, 1948) 128 n. 4

"Onward Christian Soldiers" (hymn) 257

"Oranges and Lemons" (song) 40

Oscar; *see* Academy Award

Ottaway, Hugh 304

Our Country (Eldridge, 1945) 82, 83–91, 92, 95, 113, 215, 216, 217, 267, 305

Our Film (French, 1942), 48–9, 218

Our Town; *see Country Town*

Our Town (Wood, 1940) 114 n. 10

"Over There" (song) 81

Overtones and Undertones: Reading Film Music (Brown) 2 n. 4

Owen, Bill 256

Paganini, Nicolo 255

Pakeman, Kenneth 172

Palmer, Christopher 188

Palmer, Lilli 133, 136

Paramor, Norrie 160

Paramount Pictures Corporation 179–80

Paramount Symphony Orchestra 179

"La Parjure" (song) 225

Parker, Cecil 165

Parker, Clifton 172

Parnell, Charles Stewart 170–71, 171

Parry, C. Hubert H. 115, 119

Passacaglia for string quartet, bass clarinet, and vibraphone (from *Henry Moore, Sculptor*, Alwyn) 234

Pather Panchali (Ray, 1955) 217

Les Patineurs (The Skaters, Waldteufel) 38, 39

"The Paul Jones" (dance) 160

Paul Pry (Poole) 181

Paul Rotha Productions 30, 49, 50, 56, 110, 123; *see also* Films of Fact; Rotha, Paul

Paul, Saint 156

Peace Thanksgiving (Walker, 1945) 119

Pears, Sir Peter 303

Peck, Gregory 256

Peer Gynt Suite no. 1 (Grieg) 218

Pélissier, Anthony 133, 200, 201, 205, 207, 211, 214, 231, 233, 255

Penicillin (Shaw/Mander, 1945) 111–12

Penn of Pennsylvania (Baxter, 1941) 42–5, 118, 230

Penn, William 42–5, 230

Performing Right Society 8, 199

Périnal, Georges 187

Perry, George 228

Personal Affair (Pélissier, 1953) 255–6

Peter and the Wolf (Prokofiev) 288

Petre, Henry W. 103 n. *a*

Philharmonia Orchestra 172, 179

Piano Concerto (Alwyn, 1930) 16

Piano Concerto in A minor (Grieg) 218

Piano Concerto in E-flat major, Op. 73, "The Emperor" (Beethoven) 40

Piano Concerto no. 2 in C minor (Rachmaninoff) 80

Piccadilly Theatre, London 19

Pierrot lunaire (Schoenberg) 263

Pinewood Studios 9, 49, 72, 77, 172, 224, 258

Pioneer Corps 49

The Plan and the People (Sainsbury, 1945) 129

The Planets (Holst) 22, 81, 292, 293

Playtime (Elton, 1941) 12, 40, 50, 61, 188

Pleasance, Donald 279

"Please Don't Talk About Me When I've Gone" (song) 69

Le Poème de l'extase (Scriabin) 13

Pollard, W. B. 24

Pomp and Circumstance (Elgar) 236

Poole, John 181

"Pop Goes the Weasel" (song) 111

Portman, Eric 71, 115, 289

Post 23 (1941) 29

Potato Blight (Hunter, 1944) 60 n. 6

Powell, Michael 42

"A Prayer for Nicholas" (song?) 167

Prélude à l'après-midi d'un faune (Debussy) 13

Prelude no. 15 in D-flat major ("Raindrop") (Chopin) 280

"Prelude" (from *The Fallen Idol Suite*, Alwyn) 188

Preminger, Otto 176

Pre-Raphaelites 302

Prévert, Jacques 251

Price, Dennis 240, 272

Price, Nancy 247

The Prime Minister, (Dickinson, 1941) 42

The Prisoner of Zenda (Hope) 226

The Prisoner of Zenda (1937, Cromwell) 226

The Private Life of Henry VIII (Korda, 1933) 34

Prokofiev, Sergei 288, 292

Promenade Concerts 15, 130

Prométhée, Le Poème du feu (Scriabin) 13

propaganda
  propaganda of the late 1930s 27–8
  musical value in wartime 2
  wartime propaganda, film companies 30–31
  Mathieson as music director 35
  The New Britain 32–3
  Queen Cotton's reminder of war effort 38
  Our Film 48–9
  short propaganda films 39–42, 49–51,
    54–5, 56–7, 80–82, 92–3, 110–13
  covert propaganda 109–10
  radio 46–7
  Penn of Pennsylvania 42, 45
  In Which We Serve 55
  The Harvest Shall Come 56–64
  Fires Were Started 66–70
  battle films 72
  Desert Victory 72–6
  Africa Freed 77–8
  Tunisian Victory 79–80
  propagandist purpose of *Our Country* 83,
    90, 91
  There's a Future in It 93–5
  The New Lot and *The Way Ahead* 95–8
  Prologue to *On Approval* 100
  Soldier–Sailor 113–14
  The True Glory 119–22
  post-war reconstruction 123–8
  national anthem and ordinary people in
    I See a Dark Stranger 138

The Proud City (Keene, 1945) 129, 286

Psycho (Hitchcock, 1960) 65, 289

Puccini, Giacomo 14, 26, 161

Pudney, John 95

The Pupil (James) 187

Purcell, Noel 235

Quai des brumes (Prévert, 1938) 251

Queen Cotton (Musk, 1941) 37, 38, 39, 130, 220

Queen's Hall, London 14

Quilter, Roger 181

Rachmaninoff, Sergei 80, 180, 191, 290, 292

radio 47–8, 61, 63, 125, 145, 200, 217, 231–2,
    235, 240; *see also* British Broadcasting
    Corporation

Radio Doctor; *see* Hill, Dr Charles, MP

Radio Éireann 235, 263

The Rainbow Jacket (Dearden, 1954) 256, 261

"A Rake's Progress" (Hogarth) 133

The Rake's Progress (Gilliat, 1946) 38, 92,
    133–6, 141–3, 145, 165 n. 5, 241, 300

Raki, Laya 258

Raksin, David 176

Randal, Terry 84

Rank, J. Arthur; Rank Organization 35, 133,
    146, 147, 177, 186, 208, 221, 222, 226, 241,
    242, 244, 278

The Rape of Lucretia (Britten) 234

Rat Destruction (Rotha, 1942) 49–50, 286

Rattigan, Terence 93, 195

Rawsthorne, Alan 17, 47, 120, 121 [Pl.6], 124

Ray, Andrew 230

Ray, Satyajit 217

Raybould, Clarence 18

Raylton Pictures 40

Read, John 234, 259

Realist Film Unit 25, 27, 30, 39, 57, 110, 111,
    112, 125, 130

Rebecca (du Maurier) 141

Rebecca (Hitchcock, 1940) 141

Red River (Hawks, 1948) 203

Redman, Joyce 157 n. 24

Redmond, Liam 143

Reed, Sir Carol 3, 72, 96, 98, 118, 120, 133,
    137, 145, 146, 147 [Pl.8], 148, 152, 153, 154,
    155, 156, 157, 158, 186, 187, 188, 189, 190
    n. 9, 191, 193, 194, 195, 187 n. 5, 246, 285,
    299, 300, 301

Reisz, Karel 152, 153

Relph, Michael 261, 276, 296

Remick, Lee 299

Rhapsody for piano quartet (Alwyn) 27

Rhodes, Christopher 285

Rhodes, Marjorie 115

Richards, Jeffrey 61

Richardson, Ralph 186

Richardson, Samuel 141

"The Ride of the Valkyries" (from *Der Ring
    des Nibelungen*, Wagner) 96, 131, 205,
    256, 264

Rilla, Walter 224, 226

Rimsky-Korsakov, Nikolay 23

The River (Lorentz, 1937) 98

RKO-Radio Pictures 48, 241

RM (Roger Manvell?) 123
Roadrunner series 206
Roads Across Britain (Cole, 1939) 27–8
Roberts, Paddy 267
Robeson, Paul 258
Robson, Flora 117
The Rocking Horse Winner (Pélissier, 1949) 2,
    3, 142, 207–15, 223, 224, 229, 231, 244,
    261, 263, 273, 305
Rodgers W. R. 145
Rogers, Jimmy 37
"Roll Out the Barrel" (song) 80
"Romance" (from *The Magic Bow*, Green) 255
Rommel, Erwin 76
Roosevelt, Eleanor 115, 119
Rose, William 276, 277
Ross Scholarship, RAM 14
Rossetti, Dante Gabriel 218 n. 34
Rota, Nino 222, 279
Rotha, Margot 134 [Pl. 7]
Rotha, Paul 18, 19, 23, 25–6, 27, 30, 49, 50,
    56–7, 110, 123, 124, 130, 131, 134 [Pl. 7]
    160, 172, 234, 235, 320; *see also* Films of
    Fact, Paul Rotha Productions
Rothwell, Evelyn 130
Routh, Francis 6
Royal Academy of Music (RAM) 13–16, 26,
    186, 221, 266, 302, 303
Royal Academy of Music Club 16
Royal Academy of Music Orchestra 14
Royal Air Force (RAF), 28, 40, 93, 110, 241
Royal Broadcasts on Christmas Day 48
Royal College of Music (RCM) 34, 35
Royal Festival Hall (RFH), London 130, 236,
    270
Royal Mile, Edinburgh (Bishop, 1943) 127
Royal Navy (RN) 55
Royal Philharmonic Orchestra (RPO) 266
Royal Philharmonic Society 14
Royal River (Smith, 1951) 6, 129, 236–7
Royal Ulster Constabulary (RUC) 156, 285
Rózsa, Miklós 24, 34, 35, 44, 179–80, 241,
    288
Rubbra, Edmund 12, 16
"Rule Britannia" (song) 240
The Running Man (Reed, 1963) 300–301, 301
rural myth 49, 61–3, 87–8, 114–15, 119
Russell, Evelyn 70
Rutherford, Margaret 276

Ryan, Kathleen 146, 147 [Pl. 8], 156 n. 21, 165
Ryder, Winston 164
Rylance, Mark 2

Sabbon, Jean 169
Sadler's Wells Opera Company 161, 168
Safari (Young, 1956) 6, 266–8
Sainsbury, Frank 25, 39, 92, 129
St John's Gospel 151 n. 9
St Paul's Cathedral 70, 86, 87 [Pl. 5], 129
Saint-Saëns, Camille 288, 292
Salute to Farmers (Tully, 1941) 40–41, 61
Sandri, Anna Maria 269
Sansom, William 64
Sapphire (Dearden, 1959) 296
Sargent, Sir Malcolm 236
Sassoon, Siegried 116
Satan; *see* Mephistopheles
Saturday Island (Heisler, 1952) 241, 246, 304
Saturday Night and Sunday Morning (Reisz,
    1960) 296
Saury, Alain 279
Savile Club 8, 200
Scala Theatre, London 121 [Pl. 6]
Scarlatti, Domenico 43
Schein, Johann Hermann 297
Schell, Maria 238
Schoenberg, Arnold 13, 14, 263, 269
Schroeder, Kurt 34
Schubert, Franz Peter 3
Schwarzkopf, Elisabeth 259
Schweitzer, Albert 230
Scott of the Antarctic (Frend, 1948) 168, 204
Scott, Peter Graham 8, 286, 287
Scriabin, Alexander 13, 26
The Sea Hawk (Curtiz, 1940) 250
Second String Quartet (Alwyn) 303
The Seekers (Annakin, 1954) 257–8
Sellars, Elizabeth 252
Sellers, Peter 276
Sennett, Mack 206
sequencing (musical) 66, 75–6, 78, 97, 111,
    160–61, 182, 233, 248, 286, 291, 292, 293
Seven League Productions 30
The Seventh Seal; *see Det sjunde inseglet*
The Seventh Veil (Bennett, 1945) 139 n. 6
Shake Hands with the Devil (Anderson,
    1959) 283–5, 289
Shakespeare, William 5, 7, 11, 135

The Shakspere Stores 11, 12–13

Shand, Dennis 128 n. 4

Shaw, Alexander 18, 19, 23, 24, 30, 31, 111,
    112, 113, 125, 128, 133, 221

Shaw, George Bernard 5

Sheherezade (Rimsky-Korsakov) 23

"Shenandoah" (song) 39

Shepperton Studios (Sound City) 186, 230

Sherriff, R. C. 148 n. 7

Sherman, Richard M. and Robert B. 295

The Ship that Died of Shame (Dearden, 1955)
    2, 261–4, 276, 296, 305

Showboat (Kern) 148 n. 7

Shuken, Leo 180 n. 5

Sidney, Basil 239

Sieber, Matyas 18

Sight and Sound 64, 70

silence, in contrast with sound effects or
    music
  principle explained 4–5
  as contrast 7
  The Future's in the Air 22
  These Children are Safe 31
  The New Britain 33
  It Comes from Coal 37
  Penn of Pennsylvania 45
  They Flew Alone 54
  World of Plenty 57
  Fires Were Started 65
  Desert Victory 75
  The Way to the Stars 94
  The Way Ahead 96, 98
  On Approval 102
  Great Day 117, 118, 119
  The True Glory 122
  Your Children's Sleep 128
  The Rake's Progress 142
  Odd Man Out 150, 151–2, 155
  Green for Danger 160
  Take My Life 163–4
  So Evil My Love 179
  The Fallen Idol 192–3, 194
  The Rocking Horse Winner 213, 214
  Daybreak in Udi 220
  The Golden Salamander 224
  The Magic Box 238–9
  The Card 243
  Mandy 247–8
  The Long Memory 252, 253

The Malta Story 255

The Ship that Died of Shame 262, 263

Manuela 278

The Silent Enemy 281–2

A Night to Remember 283

Shake Hands with the Devil 285

Devil's Bait 287

The Night of the Eagle 293

Life for Ruth 298, 300

"Silent Night" (Christmas carol) 210

Sim, Alastair 159, 172, 241

Sim, Sheila 116

Sime, David 83, 113

Simmons, Jean 95 n. 17

Sinclair, Hugh 207

Sinfonia of London 270, 297

Sinfonietta for strings (Alwyn) 303

Siodmak, Robert 250

Sir Michael Costa Scholarship, RAM 14

"Sir Roger de Coverly" (song) 88

Six-Thirty Collection (Anstey, 1934) 19

Det sjunde inseglet (*The Seventh Seal*,
    Bergman, 1957) 292

Slade School of Art 11, 18, 303

Slade, Jack 164

Sladen, Victoria 161

Slater, John 9, 57, 131, 132, 252

Slobodskaya, Oda 239

The Smallest Show on Earth (Dearden, 1957)
    3, 240, 276–8, 296

Smiley (Kimmins, 1956) 270

Smith, Ada (mother) 11, 12, 16

Smith, Brian 110, 125, 127, 217–8, 229, 236

Smith, Jim (brother) 11

Smith, Madeleine 224–6

Smith, Shelley, 299

Smith, T. P. 66

Smith, Una (sister) 11

Smith, Vida (sister) 11

Smith, William Alwyn; *see* Alwyn, William

Smith, William James (father) 11, 15

Snape Maltings Proms, Aldeburgh 303

So Evil My Love (Allen, 1948) 7, 178–85

Socialism 123, 124, 129, 131–2; *see also*
    Labour Party

Society for the Promotion of New Music 8,
    199

Society of Authors 199

Soldier–Sailor (Shaw, 1945) 113–14, 133, 216

Song of Ceylon (Wright, 1935) 21
SOS (Eldridge, 1941) 36, 147
Sotheby's 302
sound-effects
  close integration with music 9
  The Future's in the Air 22
  Air Outpost 23
  Big City 32
  The New Britain 33
  SOS 36
  Salute to Farmers 41
  Penn of Pennsylvania 45
  Battle for Freedom 46
  WVS 51
  World of Plenty 56
  Fires Were Started 65
  Desert Victory 74
  Africa Freed 77, 79
  Welcome to Britain 80
  Wales: Green Mountain, Black Mountain
    82
  Our Country 84, 85, 86, 87–8, 89–91
  The Way to the Stars 94
  There's a Future in It 95
  The Way Ahead 96–8
  On Approval 101, 105
  Eve of Battle 119
  The True Glory 120–21, 122
  Total War in Britain 123
  A City Speaks 130, 131
  I See a Dark Stranger 138–41, 144
  The Rake's Progress 142
  Odd Man Out 153, 154, 155
  Green for Danger 160–61
  Take My Life 164–5
  The October Man 174–5
  Brief Encounter 191
  The Winslow Boy 195
  The History of Mr Polly 200, 203, 205
  The Rocking Horse Winner 210, 213
  State Secret 227
  The Magnet 229
  The Magic Box 237–9
  The Card 242, 243, 244
  Mandy 244–5, 247
  The Long Memory 252–3
  The Malta Story 254–5
  The Seekers 258
  Black on White 259–60

  The Ship that Died of Shame 262–3
  Fortune is a Woman 273
  Manuela 278–9
  A Night to Remember 282, 283
  Shake Hands with the Devil 284
  Devil's Bait 286–7
South Bank Exhibition and Festival Pleasure
    Gardens, Festival of Britain 236–7
Sovfilm 48
"Spanish Dance" (from *Christopher
    Columbus*, Carwithen) 303
Sparkling Cascades (Alwyn) 12
Spectator Short Films 30
Spellbound (Hitchcock, 1945) 241
Spenser, Edmund 11
Spice, Evelyn 25
The Spiral Staircase (Siodmak, 1945) 241
Spitfire (aeroplane) 40, 254–5
Spolianski, Mischa 35
Spring on the Farm (Keene, 1943) 61, 62
    [Pl. 4], 63
Springett, Gulielma ("Guli") 43, 45
Squadron Leader X (Comfort, 1942) 48
Squire, Ronald 207
Stalin, Joseph 122
Stalling, Carl 206, 240
Staniland, Molly 83
A Start in Life (Smith, 1944) 110–11
State Secret (Gilliat, 1950) 226–8, 250
Steel Goes to Sea (Lewis, 1941) 39
Steel, Anthony 269
Stefano, Joseph 289
Steiner, Max 204, 280
Stevens, Bernard 8
Stevens, George 119
Stewart, Hugh St Clair 77, 79, 80, 157 n. 24,
    231
Stinson, Bill 180
Stirling Boys Orchestra 34
Stockton on Tees 128 n. 4
Storm, Lesley 255
La strada (Fellini, 1954) 222 n. 2
Strand Film Company 18, 24, 28, 30, 31, 32,
    34, 35, 37, 41, 46, 80, 82, 83, 93
Strand Zoological Productions 24–5
The Stranger Left No Card (Toye, 1953) 302
Stratton, George 167
Stratton, John 221
Strauss, Marion 129

Strauss, Richard 13, 14
Stravinsky, Igor 26
Strick, Philip 64
Strindberg, Johan August 263
Stroud, Pauline 239
subtexts 1, 2, 3, 32, 51, 61, 66, 84, 85, 152, 208,
    244, 245, 248–9, 253, 256, 261, 276–8,
    299–300
Sullivan, Francis L. 161
Sullivan, Sir Arthur 239, 257
Summer on the Farm (Keene, 1943) 61, 62
    [Pl. 4], 63
Surfling, Anne 9 n. 3
Surrealism 38, 64, 66, 87
Suschitzky, Wolfgang 19, 235
Svengali (Langley, 1954) 258–9, 263, 264
"Sweet Sue" (song) 180
The Swiss Family Robinson (Annakin,
    1961) 288
"The Swissapolka" (from *The Swiss Family
    Robinson*, Jackman, Alwyn) 288
Sydney, Basil 239
Symphony no. 1 in D major (Alwyn) 130, 137,
    158, 199
Symphony no. 2 (Alwyn) 6, 130
Symphony no. 3 (Alwyn) 6, 267, 269, 270–71
Symphony no. 5 (*Hydriotaphia*, Alwyn) 6,
    303
Symphony no. 9 in E minor (*From the New
    World*, Dvořák) 265
Symphony no. 8 in B minor ("Unfinished",
    Schubert) 3
Symphony no. 3 (*A Pastoral Symphony*,
    Vaughan Williams) 81, 169
Symphony no. 7 (*Sinfonia Antartica*,
    Vaughan Williams) 168
Szabo, Violette 279–80
Szymanowsky, Karol 13

Take it From Here (radio programme) 240
Take My Life (Neame, 1947) 2, 148, 161–5,
    259
"Take My Life" (aria from *Take My Life*,
    Alwyn) 161, 162
Tanitch, John 205
Tannhauser (Wagner) 44
"Ta-ra-ra-boom-de-ay" (song) 25
A Taste of Honey (Richardson, 1961) 296
Tawney Pippet (Miles, 1944) 61

Taylor, Donald 18, 23, 24, 35, 37, 41, 83
Taylor, John 17, 23, 125
Tchaikovsky, Pyotr Ilyich 14
teamwork, craft co-operation
    Alwyn states the principle 1–2
    Alwyn's belief 36
    early involvement of composer 4
    The Future's in the Air 19
    It Comes from Coal 37
    Fires Were Started 65
    Desert Victory 74
    Our Country 83, 84
    The Way Ahead 96, 98
    On Approval 100
    What's the Next Job? 124
    *Your Children and You, Your Children's
        Sleep* 125–8
    The Rake's Progress 135–6
    I See a Dark Stranger 137, 140, 141
    Odd Man Out 146, 153, 155, 156–7
    The History of Mr Polly 200, 204
    The Rocking Horse Winner 210–12
    The Magnet 230
    Personal Affair 255
    The Long Memory 252
    The Million Pound Note 257
    Life for Ruth 296, 298
    The Running Man 299
Te Wiata, Inia 258
Tearle, Godfrey 115
Technicolor 37, 236
The Technique of Film Editing (Reisz) 152, 153
The Technique of Film Music (Manvell and
    Huntley) 275, 266
Telekinema 236
Teynac, Maurice 231
"Theme" (from *The Cure for Love*, Alwyn) 38
There's a Future in It (Fenton, 1944) 93–5,
    280
These Children Are Safe (Shaw, 1940) 31, 40,
    50, 61
They Flew Alone (Wilcox, 1942) 51–5, 94 n.
    16, 178, 280
Things to Come (Menzies, 1936) 35
The Third Man (Reed, 1949) 158, 187 n. 5, 195,
    216, 224, 300
Third Man on the Mountain (Annakin,
    1959) 287–8
Third String Quartet (Alwyn) 303

The Thirty-Nine Steps (Buchan) 226
The Thirty-Nine Steps (Hitchcock, 1935) 226
This England (Macdonald, 1941) 61
This Happy Breed (Lean, 1944) 55
Thomas, Dylan 46, 47, 82, 83, 84, 85, 86, 87,
    87 [Pl. 5], 89, 91
Thompson, Flora 302
Thorpe, Frances, and Pronay, Nicholas 109, 111
Three Choirs Festival (Hereford) 15
Three Dawns to Sydney (Eldridge, 1949) 215–
    17, 218
Thunder Rock (Boulting, 1942) 42
Tiger Moth (aeroplane) 53
Time 289
The Times 170
Tiomkin, Dmitri 72, 79, 80, 203
"Tipperary" (song) 238
Titanic 282–3
Todd, Ann 139 n. 6, 179, 224, 225
Topolski, Feliks 134
Toronto, Canada 34
Total War in Britain (Rotha, 1946) 123, 160
"Touch Her Soft Lips and Part" (from *Henry v*,
    Walton) 151
Toye, Geoffrey 35
Toye, Wendy 302
Trades Union Congress (TUC) 131, 132
Travel and Industrial Development
    Association (TIDA) 24, 30
Travers, Bill 264, 276
Trilby (du Maurier) 258
The True Glory (Reed, 1945) 72, 74, 119–22,
    145, 254
Tufnell Park, London 16
Tully, Montgomery 41, 131
Tunisian Victory (Boulting/Capra, 1942) 72,
    79–80, 119, 120, 254
The Turn of the Screw (Britten) 234, 263
The Turn of the Screw (James) 187
Turnbull, John 93
Turner Films; *see* G. E. Turner Films
Twain, Mark 256
twelve-tone serialism 7, 269, 297
20th Century-Fox Film Corporation 177,
    186, 230
Two Cities Films 93, 146, 186, 208

Ullman, James Ramsey 287
Ulster (Keene, 1940) 169

Under Milk Wood (Thomas) 91
Under One Roof (Gilbert, 1949) 7, 217–19
"Unfinished" Symphony; *see* Symphony no. 8
    in B minor ("Unfinished", Schubert)
United Nations Film Board 217
University College Hospital, London 199
University of California 56
University of Leicester 303
Ustinov, Peter 96

V1 Bomb 159
Valentine, Val 272
Valentino, Rudolph 240
Vaughan Williams, Ralph 1, 7, 8, 80, 117,
    168–9, 191, 204, 302
Vaughan, Dai 151
V-E Day 95, 114, 124
Venice Film Festival 234
Verity Films 30, 40, 99, 131
Verne, Jules 295
Vernon, Richard 42
Vetchinsky, Alex 296
Via Dolorosa 148
Victim (Dearden, 1961) 296
Victoria, Queen 230
Villon (Wallace) 14
Vinten camera 120
voice-over
    These Children are Safe 31
    Big City 32
    The New Britain 32–3
    Salute to Farmers 41
    World of Plenty 56
    Desert Victory 72–3, 74
    Wales: Green Mountain, Black Mountain 82
    Our Country 85, 89
    There's a Future in It 93, 95
    On Approval 100, 101–5
    The True Glory 121, 122
    Land of Promise 124
    A City Speaks 130, 131–2
    The Rake's Progress 136
    I See a Dark Stranger 138, 140
    comparison between *The Rake's Progress*
        and *I See a Dark Stranger* 141–4
    Take My Life 161, 163–4, 165
    Captain Boycott 170
    So Evil My Love 182
    Brief Encounter 191

voice-over (*cont.*)
  The Winslow Boy 196
  Three Dawns to Sydney 217
  Mandy 247
  The Seekers 258
  The Smallest Show on Earth 277
  Carve her Name with Pride 280

Wagner, Richard; Wagnerian 1, 7, 26, 42, 44,
    96, 131, 183
Wales: Green Mountain, Black Mountain
    (Eldridge, 1943) 82, 84
Walker, Dr 15
Walker, Norman 119
Wallace, Dr William 14
Wallis, Hal 179–80
Walsh, Kay 173
Walton, Sir William 5, 7, 73, 135, 151
"Waltzing Matilda" (song) 22
Wapshott, Nicholas 299
Warner Brothers Pictures 206, 250, 251
Warrack, Guy 48
"Warsaw Concerto" (from *Dangerous
    Moonlight*, Addinsell) 38, 71, 230 n. 12,
    269, 290
Waterloo (Bondarchuk, 1970) 170 n. 17
Watford Grammar School 11
Watkins, A. W. 35
Watson, Diana K. 286
Watt, Harry 17
The Way Ahead (Reed, 1944) 1, 49, 61, 78,
    95–8, 99, 145, 254, 258, 283
The Way to the Stars (Asquith, 1945) 61,
    93–4, 94 n. 15, 95 n. 17
"We're on Safari" (from *Safari*, Alwyn) 267
Weatherby, W. J. 157–8
Webb, Roy 241
Welcome to Britain (Asquith, 1943) 80–81
Wells, H. G. 200, 201, 207
Wells, Paul 276, 277
Welwyn Garden City 29, 30
Welwyn Studios 29
Went the Day Well? (Cavalcanti, 1942) 61
Westminster Players 167
Westwood Ho! (Dickinson, 1940) 31 n. 5
Wexford Rising (1798) 137
What Maisie Knew (James) 187
"What Shall We Do with the Drunken Sailor"
    (shanty) 251

What's the Next Job? (Baker, 1945) 124–5, 172
"When Day is Done" (song) 53, 54
"When Johnny Comes Marching Home"
    (song) 25
Whisky Galore (Mackendrick, 1949) 243
Wilcox, Herbert 36, 51
Wilde, Oscar; Wildean 99
Wilhelm, Wolfgang 136
Williams, Charles 48, 94
Williams, Hugh 161
Wilson, Clive 46
Wings over Empire (Legg, 1939) 28
Winnington, Richard 200
The Winslow Boy (Asquith, 1948) 186, 195–8,
    263
Winter on the Farm (Keene, 1942) 61, 62
    [Pl. 4], 63
Withers, Googie 99, 240
Wolfit, Donald 258
Women's Land Army 40
Women's Institute (WI) 115, 119
Women's Royal Naval Service (WRNS) 125
Women's Voluntary Service (WVS) 50–51
Wood, Sir Henry 14, 15
Woods, William 278
Wooland, Norman 224
Worker and Warfront (Rotha, 1942–5) 110,
    123
World Film News 32
world, folk, and traditional music; *see also*
    Irish music, keen
  Alwyn versatile in national and folk music 7
  nursery and traditional tunes in short
    films 31, 39–40, 111
  nostalgia feeds rural myth 63
  The Future's in the Air (Arabic) 22–3
  Monkey into Man (primitive) 25
  Desert Victory (Scottish piper) 75
  Our Country (English) 87–8
  Atlantic Trawler (calypso) 92
  On Approval (Scottish) 106
  Soldier–Sailor (Arabic) 113
  The Rake's Progress ("Calypso") 133
  Take My Life (Dutch) 161
  The Fallen Idol (East-European) 189–90
  Three Dawns to Sydney (various) 216–20
  Madeleine (Scottish) 226
  Night Without Stars (Latin-American,
    French) 231–3

Lady Godiva Rides Again (mock-Arabic)
  240
The Crimson Pirate (pirate, circus, Gypsy)
  250, 251
The Long Memory (English folk) 253
The Seekers (Maori) 257–8
Geordie (Scottish) 264
Safari (African) 267
The Black Tent (Arabic) 268–70
Manuela (continental, "Italian") 279
The Swiss Family Robinson (German
  Swiss) 288
The Running Man (various European)
  300
The World is Rich (Rotha, 1947) 172
World of Plenty (Rotha, 1943) 56–7, 123
Worshipful Company of Musicians 16
Wright, Basil 17, 47, 234

WVS (Birt, 1942) 50–51
Wyngarde, Peter 292
Wynter, Dana 285
Wyss, Johann 288

"Yankee Doodle" (song) 80, 256, 257
The Young Mister Pitt (Reed, 1942) 42
Young, Paul 264
Young, Terence 99, 266
Young, Victor 179–81
Your Children and You (Smith, 1946) 125–7,
  229, 305
Your Children's Ears (Pearl, 1945) 125
Your Children's Eyes (Strasser, 1945) 125
Your Children's Sleep (Massy, 1948) 125,
  127–8, 129, 229, 273
Your Children's Teeth (Massy, 1945) 125
Yule, Lady Annie 42, 80